The Kremlin and the Prague Spring

INTERNATIONAL CRISIS BEHAVIOR SERIES

Edited by Michael Brecher

The
Kremlin
and the
Prague Spring

KAREN DAWISHA

UNIVERSITY OF CALIFORNIA PRESS
BERKELEY   LOS ANGELES   LONDON

University of California Press
Berkeley and Los Angeles, California

University of California Press, Ltd.
London, England

Library of Congress Cataloging in Publication Data
Dawisha, Karen.
The Kremlin and the Prague spring.
(International crisis behavior series; v. 4)
Bibliography: p.
Includes index.
1. Czechoslovakia—History—Intervention, 1968–
2. Czechoslovakia—Foreign relations—Soviet Union.
3. Soviet Union—Foreign relations—Czechoslovakia.
I. Title. II. Series.
DB2232.D38 1984   327.470437   83-21351
ISBN 0-520-04971-3

Printed in the United States of America

1 2 3 4 5 6 7 8 9

To Adeed
whose impatience forced me on
but whose good humor kept me going

Contents

Foreword

To dissect Soviet decision making and behavior in foreign policy crises requires diverse skills: a knowledge of the language, the history, and the political system and ideology of the USSR, as well as insight into the personality traits and interpersonal relations of Soviet leaders; an ability to apply psychological findings on the dynamics of small group behavior to the pivotal group at the apex of the Soviet power pyramid, the Politburo; a familiarity with the methods of modern social science and a disposition to combine rigorous, systematic inquiry with foreign area specialization; a mastery of the available source materials, written and oral, which are indispensable for an in-depth case study; a capacity to assemble the evidence from a myriad of sources, much of it open to conflicting interpretation, and to relate such data to basic questions about the decision-making process; and, finally, a talent for clarifying the often blurred features of Soviet behavior. All of these skills are displayed in abundance in the pages that follow.

Karen Dawisha makes no claim to definitiveness in her fascinating study of the Kremlin and the Prague Spring. Indeed, at the outset, she presents the reader with an intriguing analogy between a parishioner at a Russian Orthodox church service and a researcher investigating Soviet politics. Both priest and politician disappear behind screens, and the most important parts of the communion (or Politburo deliberations and decisions) are conducted in a sanctuary obscured from view; much is a matter of the judgment, discernment, and prior convictions of the parishioner (or of the analyst). Notwithstanding the author's modesty, however, this volume is an outstanding contribution to our understanding of Soviet politics, especially Soviet foreign policy, crisis behavior, and contemporary international relations, with particular focus on decision making and action within the Communist bloc.

The author's objectives are twofold: first, to uncover the extent to which the quality of Soviet decision making was affected by the escalation and deescalation of tensions during various periods of the crisis that attended the Prague Spring; and second, to contribute to the literature on decision making in international crises. The first objective is attained by an illuminating account of Soviet perceptions, decisions, and actions. The second is accomplished by a rigorous and imaginative use of the International Crisis Behavior (ICB) framework to generate comparative findings for theory building on crisis. And both are enhanced by a lucid presentation of the drama and significance of the Prague Spring and its denouement in 1968–1969.

Dawisha's analysis of Soviet perceptions is subtle and revealing. At first, each of the principal decision makers filtered the information about the Prague Spring through a different perceptual lens: Brezhnev was primarily concerned with domestic dissent; Suslov focused on the menace from Peking; Kosygin, who alone had a complex, differentiated, and nonstereotyped image of the international environment, was worried about the effects on economic reform and arms limitation; and Grechko emphasized the direct threat of U.S. military activity. As the crisis intensified, however, all concurred that events in Prague constituted the major challenge to Soviet power in Eastern Europe.

The theoretically oriented findings about Soviet behavior are instructive. First, with respect to the psychological environment, the Soviet leaders did not manifest conceptual rigidity in coping with the complexities and ambiguities of the situation in Prague as the crisis escalated, in contrast to the expectation derived from psychological research. They did rely, in part, on past experience to guide their behavior, notably the grave threat to Soviet security that had arisen from the Second World War and the danger to bloc cohesion that had been posed by the Yugoslav withdrawal in 1948, the Polish events in 1956, and the Hungarian uprising the same year. And unlike European decision makers in the 1914 crisis, Soviet leaders did not lose sight of long-term objectives as the crisis escalated.

Both the perceived need and the consequent quest for information about the unfolding of events in Prague were intensive from the outset of the crisis, since traditional patterns and sources had been disrupted with the ouster of Novotný and other hard-line party leaders. Direct contacts with the leadership of Soviet bloc states increased noticeably. And, as expected, the involvement of senior decision makers in the information process grew with stress—in high-level negotiations and fact-finding missions and in written and telephone communication with Czechoslovak leaders.

Dawisha's findings about the decisional forum are striking. Although the Politburo remained the institutional focus for all formal and major decisions, an inner core acted both formally in the negotiations with the Czechoslovak party leaders and informally as a self-appointed crisis management group. The membership of the two groups overlapped and included Brezhnev, Kosygin, Podgorny, Suslov, and Shelest. This decisional core was not fully cohesive at any stage of the crisis: Kosygin and Suslov were persistent advocates of caution, Shelest of intervention; Brezhnev aligned with the majority at all times but did not provide leadership; and Kosygin was frequently excluded from decisions by the inner core within the Politburo. Throughout the crisis, however, the number of persons and groups consulted by Soviet decision makers did not change markedly.

As in other foreign policy crises, increasing Soviet stress during the Prague Spring reduced the number of alternatives under consideration and narrowed the range of perceived Soviet options from ten during the pre-crisis period to four during most of the crisis period and, finally, in August 1968, to two: political pressure on Dubček to prevent the further growth of anti-Soviet elements, and a full-scale invasion to support an alternative Czech Communist leadership. Ironically, Moscow's mixture of the strategies of coercion and compromise may have inadvertently made an invasion more likely.

In a concluding chapter Dawisha provides an insightful analysis of the costs and consequences of the invasion. Within the Soviet Union, the primary effect was to set rigid and narrow limits for reform and revision in the political, economic, and cultural spheres. Throughout Eastern Europe, the invasion cast a shadow over all debate on political reform. Yugoslavia, convinced that an invasion would have been deterred by a higher risk of East-West confrontation, sought and obtained a U.S. security guarantee. Among the bloc leaders, only Hungary's Kádár and Bulgaria's Zhivkov survived the political fallout from the invasion. Albania decided to withdraw from the Warsaw Pact, turning to Peking instead.

Karen Dawisha's ultimate explanation of the Kremlin decision to suppress the Prague Spring by force provides valuable guidance about the USSR's probable future foreign policy behavior: when the Soviet objective was to maintain the Soviet position in Eastern Europe "for eternity," the transient alienation of one or two generations of significant segments of the population and elites within the bloc mattered very little.

Michael Brecher

Acknowledgments

This book could not have been written without assistance from many individuals and organizations. My first debt of gratitude goes to Michael Brecher, who invited me to participate in the International Crisis Behavior Project in 1977 and then patiently and meticulously read and commented on the drafts of this manuscript. The Canada Council, which supported the project and generously funded my own research, also deserves a special mention. So too does the University of Southampton, which financed my trips to the USSR and Eastern Europe and gave me a study leave to undertake parts of my research.

For a book such as this, many libraries and archives must be consulted. The unparalleled archives of the Press Library at the Royal Institute of International Affairs, together with the unending assistance of its staff, made the research both more enjoyable and more profitable. For this project, I obtained many previously classified U.S. documents from the White House, National Security Council, State Department, and the Central Intelligence Agency. They were declassified under the U.S. Freedom of Information Act, and I would like to thank the staff at the State Department and the Lyndon Baines Johnson Library staff in Austin, Texas, for their assistance. I would finally like to thank the staff of the libraries at the London School of Economics, London University's School of Slavonic and East European Studies, the Lenin Library in Moscow, and the Social Science Library of the Soviet Academy of Sciences.

I also interviewed and corresponded with many people who held official positions in 1968. They included, among the Czech officials, Edward Goldstücker and Zdeněk Mlynář; among the American officials, John Baker (U.S. Embassy, Prague), Bob Baraz (U.S.

State Department), Jacob Beam (U.S. ambassador, Prague), Paul Cook (U.S. Embassy, Moscow), Paul Costolanski (U.S. State Department), Raymond Garthoff (U.S. State Department), Helmut Sonnenfeldt (U.S. State Department), and Walt W. Rostow (National Security Advisor to the president). Among the British officials I would like to thank Joe Banks (British Embassy, Prague), Malcolm Mackintosh (Foreign and Commonwealth Office), Christopher Mallaby (Foreign and Commonwealth Office), David Mervyn-Jones (Foreign and Commonwealth Office), and Sir Cecil Parrott (former British ambassador, Prague).

While writing and rewriting the manuscript, I had the chance to benefit from discussions with many scholars, individually and at various seminars, and my appreciation goes to the London School of Economics; St. Antony's College, Oxford; the Brookings Institution and the Kennan Institute, both in Washington, D.C.; and Columbia University's Harriman Institute. Also a special note of thanks goes to Galia Golan at the Hebrew University, Jerusalem, for painstaking comments on the entire manuscript.

My visits to the Soviet Union and East Europe allowed me an opportunity to discuss the subject of my book as well as general themes related to Soviet policy in Eastern Europe and Soviet behavior in crisis conditions. Of course, not everyone I talked with can be thanked personally, but I would like to acknowledge Artur Starewicz, a secretary of the Polish United Workers Party (PUWP) in 1968 and a participant in the Bratislava negotiations. Also the staff of the Polish Institute for International Affairs was most helpful in arranging discussions at the institute and with officials and journalists outside it. Among those who helped me in Moscow, I would like to thank the staff of the Institute of World Economy and International Relations and the Institute for the Study of the USA and Canada for their insights into East–West relations and the centrality of Eastern Europe in Soviet concerns.

In the preparation of the manuscript, thanks go to many including Hilary Parker for her expert typing and Janet Hurst and Robert Houdek for their skillful drawing of the map of Czechoslovakia. A belated thanks also goes to Emma Kinner for persevering all those years ago when she first taught me Russian. And finally, my appreciation goes to Marilyn Schwartz, Alice Rosenthal, and the staff of the University of California Press for maintaining such high standards of technical quality in their publications.

PART ONE

Introduction

CZECHOSLOVAKIA

SCALE IN KILOMETERS
0   50   100   150

N

GERMAN DEMOCRATIC REPUBLIC

FEDERAL REPUBLIC OF GERMANY

POLAND

SOVIET UNION

BYELORUSSIAN S.S.R.

UKRAINIAN S.S.R.

ROMANIA

HUNGARY

AUSTRIA

NORTHERN BOHEMIA
CENTRAL BOHEMIA
WESTERN BOHEMIA
EASTERN BOHEMIA
SOUTHERN BOHEMIA
NORTHERN MORAVIA
SOUTHERN MORAVIA
WESTERN SLOVAKIA
CENTRAL SLOVAKIA
EASTERN SLOVAKIA

West Berlin
EAST BERLIN
Dresden
Karl-Marx-Stadt
Nuremberg
Munich
Salzburg
Linz
VIENNA

Karlovy Vary
Plzeň
PRAGUE
Ústí nad Labem
Hradec Králové
Pardubice
České Budějovice
Olomouc
Ostrava
Gottwaldov
Brno
Bratislava
Komárno
Banská Bystrica
Košice
Čierna nad Tisou
Uzhgorod

BUDAPEST

Legnica
Wrocław
WARSAW
Łódź
Częstochowa
Katowice
Cieszyn
Kraków
Radom
Lublin
Lvov

R.J.H

CHAPTER ONE

Soviet Foreign Policy Analysis and Crisis Behavior

This is not the first book to be written about what has come to be known as the Prague Spring of 1968.[1] Nor is it the first attempt to analyze and explain the motivations behind the Soviet intervention in Czechoslovakia.[2] Nevertheless, it seeks to make a substantive contribution to the literature on Soviet decision making during the months leading up to the entry of Warsaw Pact troops on the night of August 20, 1968. The focus of the study, therefore, is not the Prague Spring per se, but the way the Soviet leadership reacted to changes in Czechoslovakia and the extent to which the quality of decision making was affected by the escalation and deescalation of tensions that characterized the various periods of the crisis.

This is the major aim of the study, and the reader will find that the book emphasizes a detailed and rigorous account of Soviet responses and reactions to events in Prague as they developed from January 1968 onward. My source material includes interviews and previously classified U.S. government telegrams and memoranda released to me under the Freedom of Information Act. These documents, in addition to research trips to the USSR, Poland, the United States, and various West European countries, have un-

[1] The best analyses of the Prague Spring remain Galia Golan, *The Czechoslovak Reform Movement*; Galia Golan, *Reform Rule in Czechoslovakia*; and H. Gordon Skilling, *Czechoslovakia's Interrupted Revolution*. A very thorough bibliography has been prepared by Vladimir V. Kusin and Z. Hejzlar, eds., *Czechoslovakia, 1968–69*.

[2] The two main accounts have been written by Jiri Valenta, *Soviet Intervention in Czechoslovakia, 1968*; and Fred H. Eidlin, *The Logic of "Normalization."* Valenta's account covers the period from July onward and utilizes a revised version of Graham Allison's bureaucratic politics model. Eidlin concentrates on the week following the invasion.

earthed much previously unknown information about Soviet decision making.

In spite of this information, the progress of my research has been slow and impeded by methodological difficulties. Any scholar seeking to clarify the motivations and images of decision makers in a system such as the Soviet Union is faced first with the almost insurmountable problem of evidence. Without access to Politburo minutes, political memoirs, and records of open debates or interviews with officials, it is almost impossible to draw concrete conclusions about the values, images, and motivations of individual Soviet leaders. It is equally difficult to assess the relative importance of various factors or to isolate and measure the specific impact of any single variable.

In research on Soviet politics, and on decision making in particular, one is struck by the analogy between the researcher and the parishioner at a Russian Orthodox church service. The priest chants, and the choirs, divided into sections, issue forth with gloriously ritualistic and hypnotic replies. The smell of incense, the lighting of candles in front of icons spread throughout the congregation, and the parading of the cross around the outside of the church produce a feeling that one has participated in and derived intimate knowledge of the proceedings. Only on reflection does one realize that the priest has often disappeared behind a screen and that the most important parts of the communion itself have been conducted in the sanctuary, obscured from view. One assumes that the priest spends his time there offering prayers, but one has no way of knowing for sure that he does not also count the number of kopeks received in the last collection. The babushka will "know" that he offers prayers; the cynical urban agnostic may conjure up visions of a latter-day Father Gapon, using his time behind the iconostasis to draw up a list of parishioners for police records; the unknowing Western tourist may be so bedazzled by the form, spectacle, and outward trappings of the service that the priest's absence goes unnoticed. Much is left to the judgment, discernment, and prior convictions of the onlooker.

So too with Soviet politics. The Soviet leadership is very much in control of the image it presents to the public—an image of solidarity, conviction, purpose, and collective leadership, an image of goals achieved "ever higher, ever faster, and ever better." The assessment of what goes on behind the iconostasis of Soviet politics is also a matter of the judgment, discernment, and prior convictions of the analyst. Thus more than twenty years after Daniel Bell's "Ten Theories in Search of Soviet Reality,"[3] Soviet specialists are still debating whether the Kremlinological or totalitarian approaches should be replaced by models that take more cognizance of bureaucratic politics and interest groups. It is an important debate, and one in which this author has been involved,[4] but it is unlikely to be resolved once and for all because of the difficulty of verifying any particular hypothesis.

Advances in the methodology of the social sciences have offered the prospect that new models and more sophisticated methods would at last solve some of the mysteries of Soviet politics. One of the major contributions of these new approaches has been to turn out Soviet specialists with broader training and an inclination to study previously ignored aspects of the Soviet political system such as local government elections and interest groups. But few would deny that the central focus of authority, particularly in the realm of foreign policy, remains within the highest echelons of the party and state hierarchy and that therefore analysts interested in understanding the actions taken by the Soviet Union will still end up trying to glimpse behind the proverbial screen.

Few new tools have been developed to aid the analyst in this effort. Content analysis is one such tool. It can take one of three forms, depending on the availability of data:

1. *Intensity of crisis perceptions*, derived from any statement expressing an awareness of threat, time constraint, and/or probability of war.

2. *Analysis of attitudes*, based on statements of friendship and hostility, expressions of satisfaction with the status quo, and demands for change in the status quo. It is measured by the "pair comparison" scaling method developed by D. A. Zinnes.[5]

3. *Advocacy analysis*, measured along a nine-point advocacy statement scale the analyst constructs from expert knowledge of the individual case, using prototype sentences and designed to code all goals enunciated by the decision makers in the course of the crisis.[6]

---

[3] Daniel Bell, "Ten Theories in Search of Soviet Reality," in Alex Inkeles, ed., *Soviet Society* (London: Constable, 1961).

[4] Karen Dawisha, "The Limits of the Bureaucratic Politics Model." The article includes comments by Graham Allison, Jiri Valenta, and Fred Eidlin, and a rejoinder by the author.

[5] D. A. Zinnes, "'Pair Comparison' Scaling in International Relations," in R. C. North et al., *Content Analysis* chap. 5.

[6] For an illustration see Michael Brecher, *Decisions in Israel's Foreign Policy*, chaps. 6–8.

The value of these various forms of content analysis in the assessment of Soviet politics lies in two main areas. First, if used to form a general picture of Soviet elite views over a long time span or to develop attitudinal profiles of individual leaders over the entire length of their careers, content analysis has proved useful particularly in revealing interesting nuances of difference between occupational or generational groups.[7] Second, in specific case studies such as this one, content analysis has served to supplement or confirm detailed research, particularly by measuring the changes in the intensity of crisis perception by the leadership as a whole.

At the same time, the limits on the value of content analysis are great in the Soviet case because of the absolute paucity of data and the nature of the data being analyzed. Thus for a single case study such as this one, where the focus is on the activities and speeches of only two or three dozen top political and military leaders over a short period, the results are not always commensurate with the massive effort required, primarily because public utterances by leaders bear a remarkable outward semblance of unity. This unity is fully reflected in the results of the content analysis and discernible to any reader at a glance. One of the major criticisms leveled by Soviet General Secretary Leonid Brezhnev against Czechoslovakia's party leader Alexander Dubček in the course of the postinvasion negotiations in Moscow was that Dubček had failed to submit his major policy speeches to the Soviet leadership for prior approval. Here in Moscow, he told Dubček, "even I give my speeches to all the members of the Politburo in advance for their comments. . . . We have a collective leadership here . . . and that means you have to submit your opinions to the approval of others."[8] This devotion to collective leadership in public does not vitiate the possibility of important private splits over policy. Nor does it rule out important differences among speeches. But these differences lie more in the realm of esoteric communication and therefore frequently elude quantification. The outside observer of Soviet politics must be equally sensitive to both what is said and what is not said. In analyzing a short series of speeches, all of which may have been written according to some preagreed formula, the number of times a set phrase is repeated takes on much less significance

[7] See, for example, Jan F. Triska and David O. Finley, *Soviet Foreign Policy*; and the articles by Charles Gati, Dan C. Heldman, Michael P. Gehlen, and Michael McBridge in Roger E. Kanet, ed., *The Behavioral Revolution and Communist Studies*.

[8] Quoted in Zdeněk Mlynář, *Night Frost in Prague*, p. 239.

than even a single word of dissent; yet quantitative content analysis would classify that single word of dissent as insignificant.

This study also reveals that drawing inferences about the positions of top leaders from views expressed in the editorial columns of certain newspapers is extremely difficult. Such inferences have been drawn in previous studies to verify the existence of differences among elite groups or bureaucracies over issues such as participatory attitudes, the Middle East, or even Czechoslovakia.[9] Although great differences have sometimes been gleaned by the comparison of individual articles or a study of the overall trend of editorials over time, the assumption that unsigned editorials in any newspaper represent the previously unknown views of a specific leader or faction is questionable. First, all newspapers are published by the party committee within the ministry or public body concerned. *Krasnaya zvezda*, for example, is formally the newspaper of the party committee within the Ministry of Defense, not a paper in which the military can express independent views. And this is the case with every newspaper, whether it be a central publication such as *Izvestia* or a regional publication such as *Pravda Ukrainy*: all are under party control. Second, top leaders have access to a number of newspaper outlets. In 1968 military leaders often published in *Pravda* or *Izvestia*. Kosygin had several articles published in *Pravda* rather than *Izvestia*, and there often appeared to be differences of opinion among commentators working for the same newspaper. And newspaper staffs are frequently posted to new positions in other publications, further reinforcing party control and limiting the ability of any newspaper to develop a distinct line. To take but one case, Konstantin Zarodov, who in 1968 was chief editor of the *World Marxist Review*, a theoretical and information journal for Communist and allied parties that is sold in about 150 countries, had previously been first deputy editor of *Pravda* and chief editor of *Sovetskaya Rossiya*, as well as a candidate member of the Central Committee. While not denying that he may have had his own views on Czechoslovakia or any other issue, it was his loyalty to the party line, rather than to the newspaper, which gained him promotion. The only real opportunity for offering differing assessments of crucial issues comes when the

[9] See, in particular, Milton C. Lodge, *Soviet Elite Attitudes Since Stalin*; David W. Paul, "Soviet Foreign Policy and the Invasion of Czechoslovakia;" and Ilana Kass, *Soviet Involvement in the Middle East: Policy Formulation, 1966–1973* (Boulder, Colo.: Westview Press, 1978).

party line is not yet firmly established or is under challenge from within the party. In such circumstances, persistently divergent opinions among published commentaries are usually a fair indication of splits at the top. But even here, it is difficult, because of the mobility of journalists and leaders' use of various newspapers to air their views, to connect any one faction with a single publication. Thus, although *Literaturnaya gazeta* and *Sovetskaya Rossiya* were often the most outspoken in their condemnation of events in Prague and the appearance of critical articles led to the escalation of tensions between the Soviet Union and Czechoslovakia, there is still insufficient evidence to justify concluding that a specific leader was advocating a particular course of action such as military intervention.

Despite these limitations, the importance of analyzing Soviet decision making is undiminished. The data base available on Soviet behavior in the 1968 Czechoslovak crisis is better than that for many other Soviet crises, mainly because a wealth of information from Czechoslovak sources exists and the Soviet press and leadership were involved in an open and lengthy dialogue with their counterparts in Prague in the months preceding and following the crisis. Whereas difficulties of the type outlined above remain, therefore, it is possible to present a fuller picture of Soviet perceptions and actions than might otherwise be possible.

A second purpose of this book is to contribute to the literature on decision making in crisis conditions. *Crisis* is a term with many meanings, primarily because it is considered self-explanatory. The term has frequently been "used without explanation and with the tacit assumption that its general meaning will somehow be understood. Unfortunately, the assumption does not appear to be a safe one, and the result is a great deal of confusion about the precise meaning of the concept."[10] In order to overcome the confusion arising from the "heavy popular usage of the word in ordinary discourse,"[11] a number of scholars have endeavored in the past decade or so to define *crisis* rigorously. One of the first political scientists

[10] Oran R. Young, *The Intermediaries: Third Parties in International Crises* (Princeton: Princeton University Press, 1967), p. 9, quoted in Philip Williams, *Crisis Management*, p. 20.

[11] Charles McClelland, "Crisis and Threat in the International Setting: Some Relational Concepts" (typescript), quoted in Michael Brecher, "Towards a Theory of International Crisis Behavior," p. 40.

to do so was Oran Young, who identified the characteristics of an international crisis as "a sharp break from the ordinary flow of politics; shortness of duration; a rise in the perceived prospect that violence will break out; and significant implications for the stability of some system (or pattern of relationships) in international politics."[12]

Although this definition is appropriate for describing and explaining the effect of stress on the relations among states, the emphasis in this specific study is on the crisis facing the decision makers of one particular state, the Soviet Union. In other words, our concern is *foreign policy crisis* rather than *international crisis*.[13] Within this perspective the most widely accepted definition of crisis is the one forwarded by Charles Hermann:

> A crisis is a situation that (1) threatens high priority goals of the decision-making unit, (2) restricts the amount of time available for response before the decision is transformed, and (3) surprises the members of the decision-making unit by its occurrence. . . . Underlying the proposed definition is the hypothesis that if all three traits are present then the decision process will be substantially different than if only one or two of the characteristics appear.[14]

Michael Brecher and a number of associates in the International Crisis Behavior (ICB) Project have endeavored to refine the Hermann definition by modifying some of its conceptual elements. In the first place, they found the term *basic values* more pertinent than *high-priority goals* as the focus of threat. Basic values include "core" values, which rarely vary and are few in number, and "high-priority values," which derive from ideological and/or material interests as defined by the relevant decision makers. The second point of departure from Hermann's definition relates to time. In the ICB's terms of reference, it is not so much the shortness of time that influences the crisis behavior of decision makers, but rather the awareness of finite time for their response to the value threat. In other words, an element of crisis perception is the realization

---

[12] Oran R. Young, *The Politics of Force: Bargaining during International Crisis* (Princeton: Princeton University Press, 1968), p. 15, quoted in Williams, *Crisis Management*, p. 25.

[13] The distinction is drawn by Williams, *Crisis Management*, pp. 21–27. This distinction corresponds to the analytical difference between the decision making and systemic approaches, as elaborated in Charles F. Hermann, ed., *International Crises*, pp. 6–17.

[14] Charles F. Hermann, "International Crisis as a Situational Variable," p. 414, quoted in Brecher, "Towards a Theory," p. 42.

that although a decision could be delayed, it could not be delayed indefinitely. The third point of contention is with Hermann's assumption that surprise is a necessary condition for a crisis situation. Brecher argues that some situations perceived by decision makers to involve threat, the likelihood of military hostilities, and finite time may be clearly foreseen. This belief is reinforced by the skepticism of other scholars about the "surprise" dimension.[15] L. P. Brody has found that Hermann's typology is "not as successful as . . . predicted,"[16] and D. M. McCormick has concluded that surprise is "not measurable from content analysis."[17] Thus, in its ICB usage, surprise is not a necessary or universally present condition of crisis, but when it exists, it may heighten the impact of time pressure.

Finally, a most crucial addition to the Hermann definition is ICB's inclusion of "perceived high probability of war" as a necessary condition. Indeed, whereas the likelihood of military involvement presupposes a perceived value threat, "the reverse does not obtain. Thus, probability of war is the pivotal condition of crisis, with threat and time closely related. . . ."[18] The perception that war is likely is also closely related to the notion of uncertainty. Indeed, uncertainty about war, reinforced by value threat and time salience, necessitates "crisis-type" decision making.

Given these refinements of the Hermann definition of crisis, Brecher offered the following more elaborate definition:

> A crisis is a situation with three necessary and sufficient conditions, deriving from a change in its external or internal environment. All three conditions are perceptions held by the highest level decisionmakers:

[15] Hermann himself later acknowledged this. See Charles F. Hermann, "Threat, Time and Surprise: A Simulation in International Crises," in Charles F. Hermann, ed., *International Crises*, p. 208.

[16] L. P. Brody, "Threat, Decision Time and Awareness: The Impact of Situational Variables on Foreign Policy Behavior" (Ph.D. diss., Ohio State University, 1974), p. 258, quoted in Brecher, "Towards a Theory, " p. 42.

[17] D. M. McCormick, *Decisions, Events and Perceptions in International Crises*, vol. 1, *Measuring Perceptions to Predict International Conflict* (Ann Arbor, Mich.: First Ann Arbor Corporation, 1975), p. 16, quoted in Brecher, *Decisions in Israel's Foreign Policy*, p. 42.

[18] Michael Brecher, *Decisions in Crisis: Israel, 1967 and 1973*, p. 6. Glen Snyder too considers the perceived probability of war as a necessary condition of crisis. See Glen H. Snyder and Paul Diesing, *Conflict Among Nations*, pp. 6–7. There are, of course, other types of crises; but for ICB purposes, a crisis refers solely to military or security issues. For a purely economic crisis, see Michael Brecher, "India's Devaluation of 1966: Linkage Politics and Crisis Decision-Making," *British Journal of International Studies* 3 (1977): 1–25.

1. *a threat to basic values*, with a simultaneous or subsequent
2. *high probability of involvement in military hostilities* and the awareness of
3. *finite time for response to the external value threat.*[19]

This definition of crisis refers to the perceptions and behavior of a single relevant state in a crisis situation. The behavior of other states and institutions in the international system is conceptualized primarily as inputs influencing "the behavior of the crisis actor by shaping its definition of the situation and then its response. . . . [Thus] the state actor remains the central object of investigation— how its decision-makers perceive environmental change and how they choose, in the context of escalating or de-escalating perceptions of threat, time pressure, and probability of war."[20] In keeping with this definition, this study analyzes *Soviet* perceptions and behavior during the Czechoslovak crisis.

This crisis-behavior model is a refinement of the ICB formulation published in 1977,[21] which posited an interactive process between an independent variable defined as perception of crisis (consisting of threat, time pressure, and high probability of military involvement) and a dependent variable defined as choice or decision.[22] R. S. Lazarus has defined threat as "the anticipation of harm of some kind, an anticipation that is created by the presence of certain stimulus cues signifying to the individual (or group) that there is to be an experience of harm."[23] Time pressure refers to the variance between the deadline for choice and available time. The crucial indicator is not the shortness of time but its finite nature. Time pressure is closely related to uncertainty, as is high probability of war. Although the three independent variables are logically separable, interrelations occur among them; the three crisis components are mutually interactive.

The composite independent variable perception of crisis induces "stress" among the decision makers. Holsti and George offer this definition of stress:

[19] Brecher, *Decisions in Crisis*, p. 1.
[20] Ibid., p. 2.
[21] Brecher, "Towards a Theory," pp. 52–54.
[22] This section draws on Brecher's elaboration of the model in *Decisions in Crisis*, chap. 1.
[23] R. S. Lazarus in *International Encyclopaedia of the Social Sciences*, vol. 15 (1968), p. 340.

The anxiety or fear an individual experiences in a situation which he perceives as posing a severe threat to one or more values. . . . Psychological stress requires an interpretation by the subject of the significance of the stimulus situation. Psychological stress occurs either when the subject experiences damage to his values or anticipates that the stimulus situation may lead to it. "Threat," therefore, is not simply an attribute of the stimulus; it depends on the subject's appraisal of the implications of the situation. Thus, the perception of threat is regarded as the central intervening variable in psychological stress.[24]

The ICB conception of stress differs slightly. To Holsti and George, stress is caused by a perception of threat; in ICB terms, stress is induced by the composite independent variable crisis perception, which is composed of threat, time pressure, and the probability of war. Thus, the terms "stress" or "crisis-induced stress" will represent the perception of threat and/or time salience and/or war likelihood.

The model postulates that the initial response of decision makers to a perception of threat (coping) is to seek information about the threatening act. The model assumes that stress induces a greater need, and broader quest, for information. Following this initial step, decision makers embark on consultative and decisional processes that may vary in size, structure, and frequency. They will search for and evaluate all possible alternatives in order to make a specific choice. "Search" and "evaluation" have been defined as follows:

> *Search* refers to the processes of obtaining and sharing relevant information, and of identifying and inventing alternative options; [and] *analysis* (or evaluation) refers to the processes of examining and evaluating the relative appropriateness of alternative options with reference to stated or alternative objectives and values.[25]

[24] Ole R. Holsti and Alexander L. George, "The Effects of Stress on the Performance of Foreign Policy-Makers," *Political Science Annual* 6 (1975): 257. The connection between "threat" and "stress" is also emphasized by Jarvis and Mann, who maintain that stress "is used as a genuine term to designate unpleasant emotional states evoked by threatening environmental events or stimuli," Irving L. Jarvis and Leon Mann, *Decision Making: A Psychological Analysis of Conflict*, p. 50.

[25] This definition, by Simon, March and Cyert, is quoted in Holsti and George, "The Effects of Stress," p. 271 n. 10. However, Brecher notes that "several processes identified by Holsti and George with the search stage of decision-making, have been separated in the ICB model: 'obtaining' information is in our 'information processing'; 'sharing' information is in all our four coping mechanisms; and 'identifying and inventing alternative options' is in our 'search for alternatives.' Information sought about the threatening event, act and/or change, at the outset, is made available to the consultative circle and decisional forum and is revised during the consideration of alternatives." See Brecher, *Decisions in Crisis*, p. 22 n. 25.

Clearly the intensity of stress, particularly in terms of time availability, will affect the search for and evaluation of alternatives. Thus, here too, a causal link is established between the perception of crisis and the process of arriving at a decision.

During the crisis, several choices are apt to be made, and many of these will be made in varying conditions of escalating and deescalating stress. To specify the changes that take place within the entire time span of the crisis, a three-period model was devised: the inception of the crisis (the pre-crisis period), its peak (the crisis period), and its decline (the post-crisis period). In more detail,

> The *pre-crisis period* is marked off from a preceding noncrisis period by a conspicuous increase in perceived threat on the part of decision-makers of the state under inquiry. It begins with the event (or cluster of events) which triggers a rise in threat perception.
>
> The *crisis period* is characterized by the presence of all three necessary conditions of crisis—a sharp rise in perceived threat to basic values, an awareness of time constraints on decisions, and an image of the probability of involvement in military hostilities (war likelihood) at some point before the issue is resolved. It, too, begins with a triggering event (or cluster of events). If war occurs at the outset of the crisis period or within its time frame, the third condition takes the form of a perceived decline in military capability vis-à-vis the enemy (or adverse change in the military balance), i.e., increasing threat.
>
> The *post-crisis period* begins with an observable decline in intensity of one or more of the three perceptual conditions—threat, time pressure, and war probability. If the onset of this period is synonymous with the outbreak of war, the third condition is replaced by an image of greater military capability vis-à-vis the enemy (or favorable changes in the military balance), i.e., declining threat.[26]

Finally, the application of the model is meant to produce comparative findings for theory building. Thus, the basis of the ICB project is one fundamental inquiry, from which several other questions derive: what is the impact of changing stress (manifested in changes in perceptions of threat, time salience, and the probability of war) on the decision makers' coping mechanisms and choices? The individual case studies thus attempt to answer nine specific questions. What are the effects of escalating and deescalating crisis-induced stress

on information: 1. cognitive performance
             2. the perceived need and consequent quest
               for information

[26] Brecher, *Decisions in Crisis*, pp. 23–25.

3. the receptivity and size of the information-
   processing group

on consultation: 4. the type and size of consultative units
                      5. group participation in the consultative
                         process

on decisional forums: 6. the size and structure of decisional forums
                        7. authority patterns within decisional units

on alternatives: 8. the search for and evaluation of alternatives
                      9. the perceived range of available
                         alternatives[27]

These questions constitute the focus for comparative analysis. The findings of this particular study will be used to assess the validity of major hypotheses on crisis behavior.

If the entry of Warsaw Pact troops into Czechoslovak territory during the night of August 20–21, 1968, precipitated a major crisis within the Prague leadership, the invasion also marked the culmination of a long crisis period for Soviet decision makers. Indeed Brecher's definition of crisis is particularly suited to the Soviet case. Not only were all four necessary and sufficient conditions present—a change in the environment, perceptions of a threat to basic values, a high probability of involvement in military hostilities, and a finite time for response—but Brecher's alteration of conventional definitions of crisis facilitates in the Soviet case a much closer conceptual fit. Specifically, his omission of the element of surprise as a necessary condition of crisis enables the examination of a case in which the decision-making unit reacts over a long period of time in a calculated and varied way to a dynamic situation for which it may not be wholly responsible but to which it has certainly contributed. The omission of surprise, with its connotation of purely responsive and defensive behavior, and the replacement of a short response time by a finite time enhance the application of Brecher's definition of crisis to Soviet behavior toward Czechoslovakia in 1968 and make it possible to test the model's hypotheses about decision making under crisis conditions.

[27] Ibid., p. 27; see also Michael Brecher, ed., *Studies in Crisis Behavior*.

CHAPTER TWO

Prelude to the Crisis

It is difficult to pinpoint the date or specific event in Prague that produced perceptions of threat within the Soviet leadership sufficient to trigger the pre-crisis period. The complex international situation and the growing disunity within the bloc naturally affected Soviet responses to changes in Czechoslovakia. Increased dissent in Poland, in the Ukraine, and among intellectual circles within the USSR met with a hard-line response from Soviet leaders, and heightened their sensitivity to similar unrest in Czechoslovakia. Within the Kremlin itself, three years after the ousting of Khrushchev, a clear foreign policy line had yet to emerge. Thus the "Prague Spring" unfolded against a backdrop of dispute and uncertainty on vital policy issues. The Soviet response to Czechoslovak reforms would be the benchmark for the future development of Soviet domestic and foreign policy.

Given this situation, it is rather surprising that the crisis took as long to develop as it did. As early as the summer of 1967, leading intellectuals and officials in Prague were debating highly sensitive issues. At the Fourth Writers' Congress in June, speeches attacked the party's domestic and foreign policy. Official censorship was condemned by many speakers, and a letter on this subject by Alexander Solzhenitsyn and addressed to the Soviet Union of Writers was read. This letter had been suppressed in the USSR, thereby creating a rather novel and, from the Soviet standpoint, alarming precedent whereby Soviet dissidents might find an official outlet in a friendly socialist country for material censored in Moscow.[1]

[1] Professor Edward Goldstücker, interviewed on October 24, 1977, confirmed that at his instigation the letter was omitted from the official conference proceedings out of consideration for "the grave repercussions such an act would have in Moscow." Also see H. Gordon Skilling, *Czechoslovakia's Interrupted Revolution*, pp. 69–70.

At the Central Committee plenum in Prague in October 1967, the practice of duplicating top party and state posts was criticized, and the resignation of First Secretary Antonín Novotný was demanded. Novotný appealed to the Soviets for assistance in maintaining his position, but, all sources agree, Moscow did not interfere to prevent a diminution in Novotný's power. Czechoslovakia had been one of the few bloc states to escape de-Stalinization, and it was generally believed that the heavy concentration of authority in Novotný's hands and the overcentralized and bureaucratized power structure were responsible for the economic stagnation that had characterized the system since the early 1960s. Moreover, Novotný's personal objection to the ouster of Khrushchev had not endeared him to the new Soviet leaders.[2] When Brezhnev made an unscheduled visit to Prague at Novotný's request in December 1967, he refused to intervene decisively on Novotný's behalf, telling the latter "Eto vashe dyelo!" (This is your affair!)[3] Once reassured that the changeover would not bring any reprisals or upheavals, the Soviet leadership supported, or at least did not prevent, Novotný's demotion.[4]

Although Alexander Dubček was not well known in Moscow (his earlier career had been as a provincial party *apparatchik*), he was acceptable to the Soviets as a new first secretary. As one who had grown up in the Soviet Union and who had contributed solidly to establishment of Communist influence in Czechoslovakia, Dubček was considered in Moscow to be a good Communist, loyal to the USSR and likely to act as a moderating force.[5] Dubček is said to

[2] According to the following sources: E. Goldstücker, interview, October 24, 1977; Jiří Hájek, *Dix ans après—Prague, 1968–1978*, p. 76; a high-ranking Dubček aide writing under a pseudonym (see Moravus [pseud.]), "Shawcross's Dubček—A Different Dubček," p. 208. Also a CPCz Praesidium statement expressed "surprise and emotion" at Khrushchev's ouster and appreciation of his "struggle to accomplish peaceful coexistence and the disclosure of the erroneous methods in the period of the cult of personality," *New York Times*, August 21, 1968. For background to this period, see Galia Golan, *The Czechoslovak Reform Movement*.

[3] Josef Smrkovský, *An Unfinished Conversation*, p. 7; Skilling, *Czechoslovakia's Interrupted Revolution*, p. 169; and Michel Tatu, *Le Monde*, January 14, 1968. Also a Polish newspaper published an article by a Prague correspondent deploring the spread of anti-Sovietism in Czechoslovakia, made even "more perfidious since it is generally known what position was taken by Brezhnev during his visit to Prague in the critical days" when it became apparent "that the Soviet Union did not intend to interfere in Czechoslovakia's internal affairs" (*Zycie Warszawy*, May 4, 1968).

[4] The Soviet decision not to save Novotný had been a victory for Kosygin's liberal group in the Politburo, according to well-informed Yugoslav sources quoted by Lajos Lederer, *The Observer* (London), March 24, 1968.

[5] Hájek, *Dix ans après*, p. 76.

have reassured Brezhnev by telephone on January 6 that no further personnel changes would be needed now that Novotný had been removed.[6] Not surprisingly, therefore, the election of Alexander Dubček as first secretary of the Communist Party of Czechoslovakia (CPCz) on January 5, 1968, was regarded in Moscow as a possible solution to long-standing problems in Czechoslovakia, not as the beginning of a crisis.

Throughout January and February, relations remained openly cordial. Dubček's visit to Moscow at the end of January, as described in the official communiqué, took place in an atmosphere of "cordial friendship, sincere and friendly understanding," with "complete agreement" on all issues discussed.[7] The celebrations of the twentieth anniversary of the February 1948 Communist takeover in Czechoslovakia occasioned visits by Soviet and bloc leaders to Prague. Brezhnev praised the "outstanding part" played by the CPCz "in strengthening and developing the socialist community" and supported "the creative approach of your party to the solution of problems arising at all stages of the struggle for the victory of socialism."[8] Although the Soviet newspapers carried almost no in-depth analysis of the leadership changes, the few reports that did appear were, on the whole, favorable.[9]

This public facade of unity and support did not always conceal indications to the contrary, however. The Moscow meeting between Dubček and the Soviet leaders on January 29–30 was perhaps the first occasion at which some doubts were openly expressed. The authoritative Soviet explanation of the reasons for the invasion, issued by *Pravda* on August 22, 1968, clearly stated that there had been cause for worry as early as January:

> Our party took an understanding attitude toward the decision of the January 1968 plenary session of the CPCz Central Committee. Nevertheless, it was already evident at that time that the developing situation could lead to a weakening of the Czechoslovak Communist Party and to the growth of sentiments dangerous to socialism among certain circles of Czechoslovak society that were under the influence of bourgeois views and imperialist propaganda.

[6] William Shawcross, *Dubček*, p. 153.

[7] *Izvestia*, February 1, 1968.

[8] *Izvestia*, February 23, 1968.

[9] *Pravda*, January 6, 1968, published Brezhnev's telegram of congratulation to Dubček with a lengthy and positive biographical sketch of the new first secretary. Also see *Pravda*, January 19, 22, 23, 31, and February 8, 9, and 17; and *Izvestia*, January 21 and February 6, 1968.

In the talks between CPSU leaders and Czechoslovak leaders held in Moscow in January and in Prague in February, these apprehensions were voiced openly, in a party spirit. At the same time it was stated in no uncertain terms that the choice of paths of building socialism and the choice of forms and methods of party guidance of social processes were within the full and exclusive competence of the CPCz Central Committee.[10]

During the January meeting in Moscow, Brezhnev is said to have supported Dubček against the conservatives and to have offered to replace them. Zdeněk Mlynář, a CPCz secretary who was present at the postinvasion Moscow negotiations, recalls that during those August negotiations Brezhnev reminded Dubček of this support:

> From the very beginning, I was prepared to help you against Novotný, . . . and I asked you as early as January: You are threatened by his men, aren't you? Do you want to change them? Do you want to have another Minister of Internal Affairs? You said at that time that this would not be necessary, because they were good comrades. And only subsequently did I hear that you had changed the Minister of Internal Affairs, the Minister of Defense, other Ministers and Secretaries of the Central Committee.[11]

The February meeting in Prague, despite its ceremonial purpose, was also an occasion of some tension. Soviet leaders objected to portions of Dubček's public address in which he spoke of Czechoslovakia's interests in Europe, "in the center of which our country is located." He openly advocated the establishment of normal relations between all the countries of Europe, regardless of the differences in their social systems. This statement was interpreted as expressing Prague's interest in establishing links with West Germany. As such, it alarmed not only the USSR, but also the East Germans, who feverishly were seeking continued adherence to the 1967 Karlovy Vary agreement that no other member of the Warsaw Pact would establish diplomatic relations with the Federal Republic until the German Democratic Republic was itself recognized by the West. In his speech Dubček also called for "our own specific path" in which the "directive" methods of the past would be displaced by "a new type of democracy."[12] According to Mlynář, Brezhnev, in his ad hoc lecture during the postinvasion August negotiations,

[10] *Pravda*, August 22, 1968.
[11] Zdeněk Mlynář, *Nachtfrost*, p. 298.
[12] *Rudé právo*, February 23, 1968. The speech was also carried in *Izvestia*, February 23, 1968.

reprimanded Dubček: "[in February] I told you of my objection to your speech and called to your attention some formulations which were not correct. But you didn't change them. Here when I prepare a speech, even I myself must give the text to the other members of the Politburo, in order that they should give their judgement. . . . We have a collective leadership and that means that one has to subordinate one's views to others."[13] This February incident was confirmed after the invasion by Vasil Biľak, head of the Slovak Communist party and one of Dubček's opponents throughout 1968. He reported that on February 27, Brezhnev, having received an advance copy of Dubček's speech, telephoned Dubček. According to Biľak: "Comrade Brezhnev, afraid, tried to explain a long time on the telephone, what kind of scandal would occur if such a speech were presented at . . . the Central Committee. They would probably react to it and leave." Although some changes in the speech were in fact made, Biľak claims, they still fell far short of Soviet demands.[14]

Yet the January and February incidents were not sufficiently serious to trigger a major crisis. Gustáv Husák, Dubček's successor, subsequently stated that Brezhnev and other East European leaders who had gathered in Prague for the February meeting "expressed quite frankly their support for the new leadership and its generally advocated aims. In other words, they backed the leadership, its aims of supporting socialism, doing away with mistakes, and providing greater scope."[15]

LEADERSHIP CHANGES CONCERN MOSCOW

In the month following the February celebrations, however, Soviet apprehensions grew to such a level that a crisis seemed unavoidable. Of central importance in precipitating the crisis were leadership changes that threatened the structure of party, police, and army channels through which the Soviets had traditionally exercised considerable informal influence over Czechoslovak affairs.

[13] Mlynář, *Nachtfrost*, p. 298–99. Brezhnev's objection to parts of Dubček's speech was also confirmed in Ladoslav Bittman, *The Deception Game*, p. 184.

[14] *Rudé právo*, September 3, 1969, quoted in Jiri Valenta, *Soviet Foreign Policy Decision-Making and Bureaucratic Politics*, pp. 168–69.

[15] Speech by Husák at Prague, August 19, 1969, to the all-state *aktiv* of chairmen of primary party units in industry, construction, and transport. British Broadcasting Corporation, *Summary of World Broadcasts* [hereafter *SWB*], East Europe, EE/3157/C/13.

Cadre changes began when General Václav Prchlík, then head of the Main Political Administration (MPA) of the Czechoslovak Ministry of National Defense, replaced Miroslav Mamula as chief of the crucial eighth department of the party Secretariat, the department responsible for supervision of the army and the security services.[16] Prchlík's old job in the MPA was then filled by another Dubček supporter, General Egyd Pepich. The reasons for the changes became clear a week later when, on February 25, General Jan Šejna, head of the important party committee within the Ministry of National Defense, defected to the United States amid reports that he and Mamula had been at the center of attempts to use the military to prevent Novotný's downfall the previous December. Despite numerous rumors, the precise role of the Soviet military in these clandestine activities was never made public.[17] Soviet concern over the leadership changes and the defense ramifications of the possibility that Šejna had taken top military secrets with him[18] were sufficient for the Soviets to place mobile air and light armored units in the Carpathian military district on alert.[19] Then, on February 28, Marshal I. I. Yakubovsky, the supreme commander of the Warsaw Pact forces, arrived in Prague in the first of many attempts to assess the effect of changes inside Czechoslovakia on Soviet strategic concerns. Yakubovsky held talks with Dubček, President Novotný, Party Secretary Jozef Lenárt, and Defense Minister Bohumír Lomský; and sources indicate that the discus-

[16] The extensive powers of the eighth department were subsequently revealed by Col. Dr. Oskar Bizik, Prchlík's deputy, who in an interview on Bratislava television on March 27, 1968, maintained that "it ran the work of the Ministry of National Defense, the Ministry of the Interior, the Prosecutor's Office, the courts of law, and the militias" (*SWB*, EE/2739/C1/6).

[17] Michael Stepanek-Stammer, at that time personal press officer to the minister of defense and later to President Svoboda, maintains that Šejna received support from Soviet military advisors in Prague who were "unofficially active" in supporting Novotný. He also supports Šejna's subsequent statement that General Janko had been told by Soviet officers "that a military attack by the Soviet army would be inevitable if the revisionists in Prague continued with their work of destruction." See Michael Stepanek-Stammer, *Die Tschechoslowakische Armee*, pp. 22–24. The newspaper of the Czechoslovak People's party, *Lidová demokracie*, on June 5, 1968, also reprinted a *New York Times* article alleging that Šejna had been able to leave the country because he was in possession of a diplomatic passport issued by a Soviet general. This allegation was never confirmed officially and was the subject of vehement Soviet diplomatic denials and articles in the Soviet press, e.g., *Pravda*, June 11, 1968.

[18] Victor Zorza in *The Guardian*, July 12, 1968, and August 21, 1968; and John Erickson in *The Sunday Times*, September 1, 1968.

[19] *Aviation Week and Space Technology*, March 25, 1968.

sions centered on the Šejna affair, leadership changes in the *apparat*, and the spring Warsaw Pact maneuvers long scheduled to take place in Czechoslovakia.[20]

Whatever reassurances Yakubovsky may have received in private, public calls in Prague for the resignation of conservative leaders implicated in the attempts to prevent Novotný's fall did not cease following his visit. On the contrary, Šejna's defection and the de facto lifting of censorship at the beginning of March helped launch a full-scale campaign against Novotný's supporters. On March 5 Jiří Hendrych lost the key post of head of the party's Ideological Commission to Josef Špaček, who the previous June had roundly criticized the monopolistic way the party was exercising its leading role.[21] Pressure on the conservative faction was maintained throughout March, with three trade union leaders resigning on March 12. On March 14, it was announced that Deputy Defense Minister General Janko had committed suicide, following revelations that he had been involved with Šejna and Mamula in the attempted putsch. On the same day, Politburo member Michal Chudík, who had opposed Dubček the previous December, resigned as chairman of the Slovak National Council; and Čestmír Císař, a well-known liberal, was brought back from "exile" as ambassador to Rumania and put in charge of the Central Committee's important department for education, science, and culture. Also on March 14, the Praesidium of the National Assembly passed a vote of no confidence against the prosecutor general, Jan Bartuška, and the minister of the interior, Josef Kudrna. Not only were two more conservatives to lose their jobs, but they had been removed by a body whose constitutional right to take such action had not previously been exercised. The control of cadres had always been the exclusive concern of the party *apparat*; and the specter of a shift in these powers to the National Assembly contributed to Soviet fears that the CPCz was surrendering its leading role. Furthermore, since these two posts were crucial to the maintenance of Soviet influence over Czechoslovakia, the Soviets had always tried to insure that those appointed were sympathetic to Moscow's interests. As Brezhnev subsequently stated, in the passage cited above,[22] the

---

[20] *The Christian Science Monitor*, April 4, 1968; and David Floyd, "The Czechoslovak Crisis of 1968," pp. 35–38.

[21] *Nová mysl*, no. 13 (June 27, 1967): 3–6, as quoted in Skilling, *Czechoslovakia's Interrupted Revolution*, p. 158.

[22] Zdeněk Mlynář, *Nachtfrost*, p. 298.

Soviets had been willing to replace Kudrna as minister of the interior in order to strengthen Dubček's hand. What they could not countenance was Moscow's exclusion from the selection process altogether.

A tide of newspaper articles demanded change, and far from stemming this outcry, many CPCz officials, including Dubček himself, were speaking out in favor of progressive policies. At a municipal party conference in Brno, Dubček stated that "the Party is seeking out ways adequately to express the needs of the nations, of society, of social groups, and of the individual. The search is a complicated process. But without such a search it is not possible to lead society." [23] The Praesidium of the party had endorsed these views broadly at its March 14 meeting, in which it resolved to submit to the April Central Committee plenum proposals for cadre changes and a wide-ranging "action program" that would serve as a blueprint for the reform movement. A key issue was censorship, which had been effectively abolished at the beginning of March when the Praesidium decided to remove the Central Publications Board from the jurisdiction of the Ministry of the Interior. A campaign legally to ban preliminary censorship altogether was supported not only by journalists and writers but by the minister of culture and information. There was, however, far from universal support for such an unprecedented step in a Communist country. Significantly, a Praesidium communiqué outlining the results of its March 14 meeting admitted that recent developments had awakened fears among some party members. Nevertheless, the communiqué stressed, "these fears are the result of old habits, former ways of thinking and methods of social practices. . . . Criticism . . . must become a permanent feature of our life. . . . The Praesidium considers it right to declare that this is a definite settling of accounts with the deformations which have in the past endangered the development of society." [24]

SOVIET PREOCCUPATION ELSEWHERE

The response of the Soviet press to these developments was cautious in the extreme. There was a virtual blackout on any detailed analysis of Czechoslovak affairs. The few articles that did appear

[23] *Rudé právo*, March 17, 1968.
[24] Prague home service, March 15, 1968, *SWB*, EE/2723/C/4–5.

were neutral reports of selected events such as the regional party conferences or the Czechoslovak stand at the Sofia meeting of the Warsaw Pact's Political Consultative Committee.[25] Certainly the press gave no indication during the first three weeks of March of imminent crisis. Editorials reflected concern with other issues, domestic and foreign; and indeed the leadership's preoccupation with more pressing, if related, problems explains the lull before the storm.

On the domestic front the Soviet leadership had two major problems associated with the growth of dissent. First, the January trial of four intellectuals, including Alexander Ginzburg, had elicited unexpected protests and petitions from leading figures in the artistic and cultural world.[26] In Leningrad, the party committee was officially reprimanded for its slackness in ideological education;[27] and a major editorial in Pravda on March 14 calling for greater vigilance against the subversive influence of bourgeois propaganda and other foreign ideologies marked the beginning of a major crackdown against intellectual dissent. The second problem concerned the Ukraine, where dissent traditionally had been tinged with nationalist and separatist sentiments. Efforts to deal with the problem in a moderate fashion, as had seemed possible in January,[28] were hampered by the rivalry between the Ukrainian party's first secretary, Piotr Shelest, and the Ukrainian prime minister, V. V. Shcherbitsky. Both were in the CPSU Politburo, but Shelest was a

[25] See Izvestia, March 5, 8, and 15, 1968; and Pravda, March 2, 7, and 10, 1968. The March 10 Pravda editorial "Under the Banner of Proletarian Internationalism" was very moderate in tone: "Communist parties today operate in the most varied conditions. This is why there can be no question of organizing a leading center of the Communist movement. There is no need for such a center. Present-day forms of unity and coordinated action among the fraternal parties are sufficiently mobile and flexible."

[26] For details of these protests, see The Daily Telegraph, January 4, 1968; The Morning Star, January 8, 1968; The Times, January 10, 1968, and February 8, 1968; The Sunday Telegraph, February 11, 1968; and New York Times, February 16, 1968.

[27] Pravda, January 19, 1968, quoted the resolution of the latest Leningrad City Party Conference: "In ideological work, the disproportion between intentions and plans on the one hand and concrete results on the other is great. The sharpest and frankest discussion of the conference was on this theme." The conference expressed the need to "raise the level of the ideological and political upbringing of the working people, especially young people, to that of present-day requirements."

[28] In January 1968, Ivan Dzyuba was reinstated as head of the department of literary criticism for the journal of the Ukrainian Writers' Union. He had been dismissed in 1965 after writing the dissident tract Internationalism or Russification? A Study in the Soviet Nationalities Problem. Also in January the controversial novel Sobor by the Ukrainian writer Oles' Honchar received favorable reviews. See Michael Browne, ed., Ferment in the Ukraine.

full member, whereas Shcherbitsky was a nonvoting candidate member.[29] The two men previously had cooperated in molding a more independent cultural policy in the Ukraine, but the growing intolerance of the central leadership in Moscow for any form of dissent made such a policy impossible. Shelest, in particular, became a vociferous opponent of political reform. Many observers felt that his opposition was increased by concern for the security of his own position, which was further undermined by Shcherbitsky's reported close affiliation with Brezhnev. Shelest's keynote speech in Kiev on February 17, which, notably, was not published even in condensed form outside the Ukraine, was a sustained criticism of the party's failure to combat subversion and nationalist elements and represents an attempt to distance himself from policies for which he had been more than partly responsible.[30] The plenum of the Ukrainian party Central Committee, which met at the end of March, called for improvement in the activities of the party in the realm of information and led to the demotion of the secretary in charge of that department.[31] Thus in domestic affairs prior to the Dresden meeting, which marked the beginning of the pre-crisis period, there emerged a more unyielding ideological policy. This hard line would be endorsed officially at the April Central Committee meeting and would substantively affect Moscow's approach to dissent in Czechoslovakia.

In foreign affairs, too, the Soviet leadership was far too preoccupied with events in Rumania, Poland, and the GDR to focus exclusive attention on Prague. At the Budapest meeting of Communist leaders, called at the beginning of March to prepare an agenda for the forthcoming International Communist Conference, Soviet diplomats had concentrated on preventing the walkout by the Rumanian delegation. As confirmed by Zenon Kliszko, a member of the Polish delegation, the walkout occurred because the Syrian delegate criticized Rumania's refusal to break relations with Israel following the June 1967 war.[32] Vladimír Koucký, the Czechoslovak representative, expressed disagreement with the Rumanian stand

[29] See Grey Hodnett and Peter J. Potichnyj, "The Ukraine and the Czechoslovak Crisis," pp. 22–23.

[30] *Pravda Ukrainy*, February 17, 1968.

[31] Radio Free Europe [hereafter RFE], *Research, Communist Area, USSR*, April 4 and 8, 1968.

[32] Television interview of March 3, 1968, as reported by RFE, *Polish Press Survey*, no. 2129, April 17, 1968. Also see *New York Times*, March 9, 1968.

and supported the Soviet call for an early convocation of the international conference. Koucký, however, also supported efforts encouraging Moscow to reverse the anti-Yugoslav line adopted by the 1957 and 1960 meetings. Even in early March the Soviets showed their concern over growing sympathies between Belgrade and Prague by lodging an official complaint with the Yugoslav Ministry of Foreign Affairs over the pro-Czechoslovak line adopted by the Yugoslav press.[33] Nevertheless, at this time the dominant view in Moscow was that "revisionism" (in this case pro-Yugoslav views) might have to be tolerated if they were to construct an effective front against the Chinese.

The March 6 meeting in Sofia of the Warsaw Pact's Political Consultative Committee also failed to bring Rumania back into the fold. Among the issues discussed, according to Kliszko, were "certain problems connected with the work of the headquarters of the Warsaw Pact."[34] Some of the East Europeans, not untypically perhaps, were resisting Soviet efforts to further centralize and integrate the military command structure and were putting forward alternative proposals, among these a rotation of leading posts between member states that would thereby effectively reduce Soviet control.[35] Rumania's President Nicolae Ceauşescu later confirmed that participants at the meeting had agreed to refer reform plans back to their ministers of defense and to submit fresh proposals within a six-month period.[36] But Rumania was excluded from subsequent discussions about Pact reform as a result of its efforts to check Soviet influence.

Also on the agenda at the Sofia meeting was the Nuclear Nonproliferation Treaty, on which the USSR had expended considerable effort over the previous months. Soviet leaders were especially worried that West Germany would refuse to adhere to the treaty; and they may have calculated that unanimous expression of

[33] *New York Times*, March 29, 1968.

[34] Kliszko's March 9 television interview, in RFE, *Research, East Europe, Czechoslovakia*, May 21, 1968.

[35] Reports also suggest President Ceauşescu, of Rumania, was opposed to importing any arms from the USSR that could be produced in Rumania. East European resistance to further increases in defense spending was also an issue at the time, particularly the budget for military aid to the Arab states, Vietnam, and Cuba. See *New York Times*, March 9 and 10, 1968; *The Guardian*, March 7, 1968; *The Observer Foreign News Service*, Report no. 24919, March 11, 1968; *Soviet News*, March 12 and 19, 1968; and *Neues Deutschland*, March 9, 1968.

[36] Agerpress, April 4, 1968, as quoted in RFE, *Research, East Europe, Czechoslovakia*, May 21, 1968.

support for the treaty within the Pact might spur the Americans to put similar pressure on their own allies in Paris and Bonn. It was therefore a grave setback when Rumania refused to sign a joint statement affirming the intention of all Warsaw Pact members to adhere to the treaty. Ceauşescu subsequently gave his reasons for refusing to sign the declaration:

> Rumania has been and is in favor of a non-proliferation treaty. We think, however, that further efforts must be made to obtain improvements to this treaty, particularly the pledge to take measures regarding nuclear disarmament and the giving of guarantees to countries renouncing nuclear weapons that those weapons would not be used against them and that they would not be subjected to blackmail with these weapons, and insuring for all states the possibility of unlimited utilization of nuclear energy for peaceful purposes.[37]

Czechoslovakia's position was more moderate, but Dubček did state that although Rumania's refusal to sign the declaration was not "realistic," there were in fact other Pact members who felt the need to link the treaty with further efforts toward nuclear disarmament.[38]

UNREST IN POLAND

If the Rumanian revolt of early March deflected much Soviet attention from Czechoslovakia, so too did the large-scale riots that broke out in Poland after March 8. Demonstrating students and intellectuals protested the government's increasingly repressive policies, particularly in the cultural field; and many of the participants' placards expressed support for the Czechoslovak reforms and demanded a "Polish Dubček." Although the riots were quickly controlled, they had lasting repercussions. The media launched a campaign

[37] Speech by Nicolae Ceauşescu to the Bucharest Party *Aktiv*, April 26, 1968, from Robin Alison Remington, ed., *Winter in Prague*, p. 59.

[38] Radio Bratislava of March 8, 1968, as quoted in RFE, *Research, East Europe, Czechoslovakia*, March 11, 1968, p. 3. Not all of the Czechoslovak press was as cautious as Dubček in support of Rumania. The following excerpt is reminiscent of the dialogue between the West Germans and Americans at the time:

> The clause on guarantees that non-nuclear states will have no access to nuclear weapons of the forces of a great power which are on their territory, also concerns the other member countries of the Warsaw Treaty. . . . If the creators of the Soviet strategic concept today no longer regard it necessary to reply to an attack on one of the socialist countries with a nuclear strike . . . the member countries of the Warsaw Treaty may ask questions similar to those which, some time ago, led de Gaulle to quit NATO. (From Prague Radio Home Service, March 6, 1968, in *SWB*, EE/2715/C3/2)

blaming the disorders on Zionists, intellectuals, and neo-Stalinists. Further, any demands for reform, it was claimed, would weaken Poland's capability to withstand the subversive intentions of West German revanchism, whose aim was to revise the postwar boundaries of Europe. These allegations presaged a fairly comprehensive purge of liberal intellectuals and officials, many of them Jewish.

The purges were the result not only of the riots but also of a major challenge to Gomułka's leadership that had taken place "under cover" of the demonstrations.[39] The challenge came from the right-wing and ultranationalist "Partisan" faction headed by Mieczysław Moczar, minister of the interior and head of the secret police. Gomułka was also attacked by Edward Gierek, who previously had been identified as a moderate and technocratically minded reformer in the leadership.[40] Gomułka responded to this dual onslaught in a major speech to the Warsaw Party *aktiv* on March 19. In an effort to strengthen his position, he attempted to find common ground between the factions. Favoring a right-wing turn in domestic politics to please his detractors, he simultaneously emphasized the need for strengthened relations with the Soviet Union, a move designed to convince Moscow that he was the best guarantor of Soviet interests in Warsaw. Gomułka openly admitted that the party was hopelessly split, with the leadership "still not in a condition to formulate, much less unravel, all the problems" that face the country.[41] As a result, Gomułka was in no position to support or even ignore the Prague reform movement, even if, as has been suggested, he had sympathies to the contrary.[42] He emerged from the March crisis much weaker domestically and more dependent on

[39] An editorial in *Prawo i Życie*, March 24, 1968, by Kazimierz Kakol blamed the riots on attempts by a clique in the party to overthrow Gomułka. "We have long known that, taking advantage of a certain degree of disintegration in the international communist movement, it was decided to make 1968 a year of 'political earthquakes' . . . to 'ease out' certain persons in our party leadership. . . . We have had to deal with attempts to strike at the leadership . . . with attempts at a coup d'état" (quoted from RFE, *Polish Press Survey*, no. 2124, April 1, 1968). For other analyses of this phase, see M. K. Dziewanowski, *The Communist Party of Poland*, p. 300; Thomas W. Wolfe, *Soviet Power and Europe*, pp. 366–69; and A. Ross Johnson, "The PUWP Leadership Crisis: The Central Leadership," RFE, *Research, East Europe, Poland*, May 7, 1968.

[40] Gierek blames "revisionists" for hampering Poland's economic development and called for a purge of remaining liberal elements: "The dirty scum which floated on the vortex of the October events eleven years ago has not completely been removed on the tide of our life" (see A. Ross Johnson, "The PUWP Leadership Crisis," p. 2).

[41] *Pravda*, March 22, 1968.

[42] Zdeněk Hejzlar, head of Czechoslovak radio in 1968, subsequently stated that until the Dresden meeting "the Czechoslovak leadership could count . . . on the relatively benevo-

the Soviet Union. It was not clear whether he could survive any further unrest in Poland such as might spill over from Czechoslovakia. Thus Gomułka was one of the first bloc leaders to imply that events in Czechoslovakia were having a negative effect on the bloc as a whole. In his March 19 speech, he maintained that "imperialist reaction and the enemies of socialism have come forth under various flags. Active in our country, *and active in the countries neighboring on Poland*, they are attempting to weaken the ties binding the Warsaw Treaty states."[43]

It was a full three days before the Soviets made up their minds to support Gomułka against the Moczar-Gierek factions. Moscow's indecision was evident in the complete absence of any mention in the Soviet press of the events in Poland. Then, on March 22, *Pravda* published Gomułka's speech in full with an article the following day attesting to the popular support in Warsaw for the Polish leader. On March 25, *Pravda* firmly maintained that "the authors of the excesses have not succeeded in creating a split" but had only succeeded in splitting themselves from the Polish people.[44] The Soviet decision to back Gomułka must have taken into account the Polish leader's own admission that his position was weak and that events in Czechoslovakia could not be allowed to undermine that position any further. This would serve as a powerful constraint on any Soviet inclination to support the Prague Spring in the months to come.

ALARM IN EAST GERMANY

The East German regime was equally threatened by the events in Poland and Czechoslovakia, knowing that disaffection in these two states could easily spread across the borders into the GDR itself.

---

lent attitude of Gomułka. . . . He hoped that if Czechoslovakia succeeded in achieving a certain liberalization, he could profit from this by getting some more independence for his policy towards Moscow. This changed subsequently" (from Vladimir V. Kusin, ed., *The Czechoslovak Reform Movement 1968*, p. 60).

[43] *Pravda*, March 22, 1968 (emphasis mine).

[44] The Soviet ambassador to Poland, Averki Aristov, referred explicitly to these events during a speech marking the twenty-third anniversary of the signing of the Soviet-Polish Friendship Treaty: "We were glad when the Polish United Workers' Party, with the favourite son of the Polish nation, Władysław Gomułka, at its head was safeguarded against all black forces of reaction," which had attempted "to sow distrust between us, to drag some of our citizens through the quagmire of nationalism and chauvinism" (quoted in the *New York Times*, April 21, 1968).

Even if it did not, the regime feared that any major leadership or policy change in either Warsaw or Prague might further isolate the GDR and undermine Ulbricht's efforts to maintain East Germany's key role in determining bloc policy on the German question. Diplomatically, the leadership of the ruling Socialist Unity Party (SED) was in a most precarious situation. Following Rumania's unilateral recognition of the Federal Republic at the beginning of 1967, the Karlovy Vary conference of bloc leaders in April of that year had agreed on a common platform that subordinated member states' specific interests in improving relations with Western Europe to a policy designed to strengthen East Germany's position. They agreed that the FRG would have to recognize the inviolability of the Oder-Neisse border, the boundary between the two Germanies, and the existence of two sovereign and equal German states as preconditions for the establishment of diplomatic relations between the FRG and any East European state. In this way the GDR was placed at the center of the Soviet bloc's European policy, and because of this centrality, Ulbricht's own position as a self-appointed coordinator and watchdog of that policy was enhanced.[45] It soon became apparent, however, that Ulbricht's control over the bloc's German policy was limited. The Soviets were reported by the *New York Times* to have submitted to West German Foreign Minister Willy Brandt in January 1968 proposals offering to restore the four-power status of Berlin in return for reduction in the Federal Republic's presence in that city.[46] Any Soviet connivance to decrease the GDR's claim to sovereignty over Berlin was anathema to the East German leadership, particularly since the Soviets publicly maintained their absolute support for the East German claim.[47] The number of high-level meetings between Soviet and East German leaders in the early months of 1968 indicates the sensitivity of the issue. The East Germans feared that the Soviets, despite their

[45] See N. Edwina Moreton, "The Impact of Détente on Relations Between the Member States of the Warsaw Pact," chap. 3.

[46] *New York Times*, January 17, 1968, as cited in ibid., p. 197.

[47] For example, in a major review of issues facing Soviet foreign policy, the German question was listed as one of the eight top-priority areas where it had been decided to go on the "counter-attack" (*Pravda*, November 25, 1967). In December, an official Soviet note attacked West Germany for condoning the rise of neo-Fascist organizations and alleged that the West Germans were secretly developing nuclear weapons (*Pravda*, December 9, 1967, cited in Moreton, "The Impact of Détente," p. 145). Another Soviet note to the West Germans condemning their "New Eastern policy" was similarly designed to allay East German fears (see *Pravda*, March 5, 1968).

public protestations, might subordinate previous commitments to the GDR to an agreement with West Germany over Berlin. Perhaps hoping to forestall any such agreement, in February they published ahead of schedule a new draft GDR Constitution that claimed all of Berlin as the capital of the GDR.[48] In March they also began to disrupt the transit routes to Berlin, clearly implying that no agreement on that city would work without their approval.

If the East Germans were worried that Moscow might serve its own interests by a more flexible interpretation of the Karlovy Vary agreements, their fears were not assuaged by the developments in Poland and Czechoslovakia. Brandt's announcement on March 18, in the midst of the Polish crisis, that the FRG would respect the Oder-Neisse line as the western boundary of Poland until the signing of a peace treaty[49] was seen throughout Eastern Europe as an effort to tempt the Poles away from their commitments and to further isolate the GDR.[50] Gomułka maintained his position and rejected the West German offer, and for the time being, the East Germans seemed reassured that the Poles, at least, were not likely to respond positively to West German initiatives.

Such was not the case in Czechoslovakia, however. Dubček's February speech asserting Czechoslovakia's intention to establish normal relations with all European states irrespective of their social system was interpreted as a direct reference to West Germany. Under Novotný, the West Germans had succeeded in establishing a trade mission in Prague, and after Dubček's accession to power, this mission's functions began to increase. Moreover, Czechoslovak efforts to obtain a massive hard currency loan for the restructuring of the economy met with initial support in Bonn.[51] This created a dual fear in East Germany. Not only would such a loan inevitably lead to improved economic and political relations between Czechoslovakia and the FRG, without forcing concessions from Bonn, but also the GDR's own vital trade links with Czechoslovakia might be

---

[48] See Ulbricht's rather interesting article on the new constitution in *Pravda*, February 14, 1968.

[49] DPA, March 18, 1968, in RFE, *Research, Communist Area, USSR*, March 22, 1968.

[50] See, for example, the colorful editorial in the Albanian party newspaper *Zeri i Popullit*, entitled "The Working Class in Revisionist Countries Must Come Down to the Battlefield and Restore the Dictatorship of the Proletariat," which forecast that events in Poland and Czechoslovakia would further isolate the GDR and eventually "smash the Warsaw Treaty and the CMEA" (released by ATA, March 24, 1968, *SWB*, EE/2736/A2/1–6 and EE/2737/A2/1–9).

[51] *New York Times*, March 26, 1968.

affected. The East Germans felt that they had more to lose than any other bloc state, including the USSR, by an improvement in Czechoslovakia's relations with the Federal Republic. On March 19, in a speech marking the first anniversary of the Czechoslovak–East German Treaty of Friendship, Cooperation, and Mutual Assistance, Ulbricht referred to treaty commitments binding Prague to a united front against West German militarism. He stated that on this occasion "the state leaderships declared that they would strictly uphold that treaty." Yet in fact the Czechoslovak anniversary telegram to Ulbricht did not contain any such explicit declaration.[52] A major speech delivered by GDR Politburo member Kurt Hager at the end of March openly condemned Czechoslovakia and made it clear that any links with the FRG would only serve Bonn's aim of "subverting the socialist countries from within, of dividing them, and especially of isolating the GDR."[53]

The East Germans were also greatly worried about the effects of the Prague Spring on domestic stability within their own country. As early as March, they were reported to have ceased issuing tourist visas for travel to Czechoslovakia.[54] Prague students returning from visits to East Berlin also reported they had been prevented from participating in prescheduled public debates.[55] Czechoslovak journalists complained that two issues of a German-language weekly published in Prague had been banned in the GDR. They also alleged that Soviet newspaper articles republished in the East German party daily *Neues Deutschland* were being censored, with all positive references to events in Czechoslovakia removed.[56] This fear of "spillover," together with the links between Prague and Bonn, put the East Germans at the forefront of those bloc leaders encouraging the Soviets to halt the reform movement.

THE BREAKING POINT IN MOSCOW

The events in Poland and East Germany coincided with a sharp rise in the Soviet perception of threat emanating from Czechoslovakia after March 21. On March 19, Prime Minister Černík had

---

[52] *New York Times*, March 24, 1968.

[53] *Neues Deutschland*, March 27, 1968, as cited in RFE, *Research, Communist Areas, USSR and East Europe*, March 27, 1968.

[54] *New York Times* and *Sunday Telegraph*, March 24, 1968.

[55] Ibid.

[56] *New York Times*, March 30, 1968.

flown to Moscow for talks with Prime Minister Aleksei Kosygin and
Gosplan chief Nikolai Baibakov on coordination of the 1971–75 plans
and a possible large-scale loan to Czechoslovakia for economic revitalization.[57] This was the first meeting in which the top leaders of
the two countries discussed Czechoslovakia's planned economic reforms—reforms which if implemented would reorient that country's external trading links away from the socialist bloc and toward
the West. Major General Egyd Pepich, the new head of the Czechoslovak army's Main Political Administration, was also in Moscow
conferring with the minister of defense, Marshal A. A. Grechko,
and the head of the Soviet Main Political Administration, General
A. A. Yepishev. A Soviet communiqué suggests the existence of
tensions by noting that the meeting had taken place in a "friendly
and working atmosphere" in which Pepich had "replied to a series
of questions concerning the development of the process of democratization in Czechoslovakia."[58] In an interview with *Obrana lidu*,
the Czechoslovak military newspaper, on his return, Pepich maintained that he had initiated the visit and that the Soviets had
expressed their belief that the present policy in Prague would
strengthen socialism. He did concede, however, that although
there was not "one specific question" on internal developments
and cadre changes in the military, the Soviets were interested in
the effects of the Šejna case, a concern Pepich regarded as "understandable and logical."[59]

Certainly events in Prague had been monitored closely in Moscow since January, when Dubček replaced Novotný as first secretary. The Šejna case, cadre changes, and statements by the new
leaders had elicited further concern in Moscow. But the Soviets'
preoccupation with other, more pressing issues and their initial
willingness to allow Dubček some time to settle in appear to have
diminished Soviet alarm over the developments in Czechoslovakia. By the end of the third week of March, however, indications
are that the Soviet leadership felt it could no longer sanction the
events taking place in Prague. The maverick policy of Rumania,
the riots in Poland, strong East German hostility toward Prague
reforms, and even Hungarian warnings that matters must not be
allowed to get out of hand in Czechoslovakia as they had in Hun-

---

[57] *New York Times*, March 20, 1968; RFE, *Research, East Europe, Czechoslovakia*,
March 20, 1968.

[58] ČTK (the Czechoslovak News Agency) in English, March 21, 1968, *SWB*, EE/2728/
C/1–2.

[59] Interview released by ČTK, *SWB*, EE/2735/C/2.

gary in 1956[60] all further motivated the Soviet leaders, who were already taking stricter action against dissent at home, to call the Czechoslovak leadership to order.

The breaking point occurred on March 21 when, under immense pressure of public opinion in Czechoslovakia, Antonín Novotný resigned as president. Clearly, had the Soviets been attached to Novotný they would have prevented his ouster from the post of first secretary the previous January. Rather, the core of the issue was that the Czechoslovak Praesidium had in no way consulted Moscow in the determination of Novotný's successor. Instead it had launched a nomination campaign in which public organizations were asked to put forward their preferred candidates. The names proposed included not only Ludvík Svoboda, the eventual victor, but also Edward Goldstücker, Čestmír Císař, and Josef Smrkovský, three of the most liberal architects of the reform movement. As seen from Moscow (and also from Berlin and Warsaw), if the Czechoslovaks were allowed to choose a new president without Soviet consent, a dangerous precedent would be set. Not only might Polish opponents to Gomułka conclude that Moscow would no longer intervene to influence leadership selection, but also if the Kremlin could not influence the selection of a new president, the position of the remaining conservatives within the CPCz would be hopelessly weakened; and they would have no chance of surviving the forthcoming April CPCz Central Committee plenum.

Novotný's resignation focused bloc attention squarely on Czechoslovakia. The prospect of a complete and imminent collapse of conservative and pro-Soviet influence in Prague made it imperative to act before a successor could be named, and Moscow made the crucial decision to convene an emergency meeting of bloc leaders in Dresden. Thus Novotný's resignation produced both a conspicuous increase in the perceived level of threat and an important element of time salience, thereby triggering escalation to the pre-crisis period.

[60]János Gosztonyi's editorial in the Hungarian party newspaper *Népszabadság* on March 21, 1968, compared certain "disturbing" phenomena he had recently observed in Czechoslovakia with those prevailing in Hungary prior to 1956. Although he described the Prague Spring as a "renaissance, full of political hopes and socialist in its content," he also cautioned that "for us, the renaissance . . . cost a high sum. . . . The counterrevolution did not start in our country by killing Communists and other honest men. This was done only later. First they only repeated that it is necessary to correct the mistakes of socialism. . . . Total freedom of criticism was gradually turned to complete negation [leading to] the transfer of the criticism of certain mistakes and leaders to an attack against the whole system" (the Hungarian News Agency [MTI], March 21, 1968, *SWB*, EE/2730/C1/4).

PART TWO

The
Pre-Crisis
Period

CHAPTER THREE

Phase One:
March 22–April 10

THE DRESDEN MEETING

There is universal agreement among both Soviets and Czechoslovaks that the decision to call the Dresden meeting marked the real beginning of the crisis. There had been alarm within sections of the Soviet political and military hierarchy for some weeks, but only with this decision did the leadership as a whole acknowledge the need for action lest events in Czechoslovakia get out of hand. Dresden also forced on CPCz leaders an awareness that their bloc allies did not consider the changes taking place in Prague to be purely an internal affair. Of the Czechoslovak leaders, Gustáv Husák, Drahomír Kolder, Jiří Hájek, Vasil Biľak, Zdeněk Mlynář, and Zdeněk Hejzlar all subsequently and independently stated that Dresden was indeed the turning point.[1] The draft "Analysis of the Party's Record and of the Development of Society since the Thirteenth

---

[1] Husák, in a speech to the CPCz Central Committee plenum on September 25, 1969, stated: "It is already a known fact that the fraternal parties publicly welcomed the changes which occurred in Czechoslovakia after January 1968. They declared this stand publicly in fraternal meetings on the occasion of the 20th anniversary of February 1948. However, developments in this country took the course we have briefly outlined. Out of concern for this development in Czechoslovakia, and of concern for the danger for the whole socialist camp, a conference of six Communist Parties was convened in Dresden on 23 March 1968" (ČTK, September 28, 1969, *SWB*, EE/3190/C/17). Biľak, in a subsequent interview, noted: "Looking back, it seems to me, *that Dresden was an important turning point* [italics in original]" (*Rudé právo*, September 3, 1969, reproduced in *Pravda pobezhdaet*, p. 133). See similar statement by Kolder, ibid., p. 156; a major *Rudé právo* editorial, "Why was Alexander Dubček expelled from the CPCz?" July 16, 1970, in ibid., p. 360; Jiří Hájek, *Die Zeit*, August 22, 1975; Hejzlar, in Vladimir V. Kusin, ed., *The Czechoslovak Reform Movement 1968*, p. 60; Vasil Biľak, "The Truth Versus Lies," *New Times*, no. 33 (August 1978), p. 20; and Zdeněk Mlynář in an interview with the author, June 1, 1979.

Congress," which was to have been presented at the planned Fourteenth CPCz Congress, also apparently perceived Dresden as a
landmark; it contained a section tracing Czechoslovak attempts
"from the Dresden meeting up to the present Congress" to allay
foreign "fears" about "the process of rebirth in Czechoslovakia."[2]
On the Soviet side, both the July 15 "Warsaw letter," addressed to
the Czechoslovaks by the five bloc parties,[3] and the authoritative
August 22, 1968, *Pravda* editorial singled out the importance of
Dresden. According to the August 22 article:

> Events showed that an atmosphere of disorder, vacillations and un-
> certainty was beginning to take shape within the CPCz itself. Reac-
> tionary, antisocialist forces supported by world imperialism were
> rearing their heads.
>   All this alarmed not only our party. The fraternal parties of Bul-
> garia, Hungary, the GDR and Poland were as seriously disturbed as
> we were by the course of events in Czechoslovakia. It became neces-
> sary to hold a collective meeting and exchange opinions with the
> leaders of the CPCz and the ČSSR. By mutual consent, this meeting
> was held on March 23 in Dresden.

Evidence suggests that the Soviet decision (*number 1*) to call a
bloc meeting was made on March 22 under heavy pressure from
the Poles and East Germans. The Czechoslovak ambassador to Moscow, Oldřich Pavlovský, was summoned to the Kremlin on March
21 for a two-hour meeting, during which Brezhnev is reported to
have angrily discussed events in Czechoslovakia and above all
press criticisms of twenty years of Communist rule. Pavlovský was
not informed, however, of the decision to convene a bloc summit;
and it was only after the meeting had begun on the morning of
March 23 that the Czechoslovak media announced that Dubček
had left for Dresden.[4] Well-placed Czech sources maintained that
the meeting had been called at the insistence of Poland and East
Germany.[5] Radio Belgrade, commenting on the Dresden meeting,

[2] Contained in Jiří Pelikán, ed., *The Secret Vysočany Congress*, p. 249.

[3] The Warsaw Letter, which appeared in *Pravda* on July 18, 1968, under the heading "To
the Czechoslovak Communist Party Central Committee" stated: "We expressed these fears
at a meeting in Dresden." In discussing the origins of bloc concern, Dresden was the first
meeting mentioned.

[4] *The Observer*, March 24, 1968; and the *Christian Science Monitor* (London Edition),
March 25, 1968.

[5] *New York Times*, March 24, 1968. Although both Kádár and Gomułka had held bilateral
meetings with Dubček in February, Ulbricht reportedly had turned down two offers to confer with Dubček in Czechoslovakia, preferring a multilateral meeting instead, presumably
because greater pressure could be brought to bear on the recalcitrant Czechoslovaks.

agreed that "it is not a secret that changes in Czechoslovakia were not welcomed in the GDR and to a certain degree in Poland."[6] West Germany's foreign minister Willy Brandt attributed the primary initiative for calling the meeting to Ulbricht.[7] Zdeněk Mlynář, who became a CPCz secretary soon after Dresden, also confirmed that Poland and East Germany, and the latter especially, were important forces behind the convocation of the meeting, and that the Soviets and Brezhnev himself did not appear to be at the forefront of efforts to control Czechoslovak affairs.[8] Soviet insistence on a collective meeting because the other fraternal parties "were as worried as we were"[9] was corroborated by Dubček, who confirmed that the initiative for the meeting had come from "several parties."[10] That the meeting was held in the GDR certainly suggests that the East Germans were keen to convene the summit.

Present at the conference were delegations from the USSR, the GDR, Poland, Hungary, Bulgaria, and of course Czechoslovakia. Rumania, however, had not been invited. The Soviets were represented by Brezhnev, Kosygin, A. P. Kirilenko, a Politburo member and secretary of the CPSU Central Committee; P. Ye. Shelest, the first secretary of the Ukraine Communist party; N. K. Baibakov, chairman of the USSR State Planning Committee (Gosplan); and K. V. Rusakov, listed as a member of the CPSU Central Inspection Commission,[11] but who was soon to be named head of the Central Committee's Department for Liaison with Ruling Communist and Workers' Parties, having been first deputy head of that department since 1965. Notable were the absence of Suslov and the presence of Shelest. Suslov, reported by some to be ill,[12] was replaced by Kirilenko. Shelest, who as a regional party secretary had no formal

[6] Radio Belgrade, March 25, 1968, quoted in RFE, *Communist Area, USSR and East Europe*, March 27, 1968.

[7] Willy Brandt, *People and Politics*, p. 210.

[8] Interview with author, June 1, 1979.

[9] *Pravda*, August 22, 1968.

[10] Dubček interview with ČTK, published in *Pravda*, March 28, 1968.

[11] *Pravda*, March 25, 1968.

[12] *The Observer*, March 31, 1968, and the *New York Times* of March 31 and April 13, 1968, which reported that Suslov had not been present at the funeral of Cosmonaut Yuri Gagarin and had only reappeared in public on April 12. Also see RFE, *Communist Area, USSR*, April 4, 1968. Not only was Suslov absent from the Gagarin funeral, he was not present at the Moscow City Party Conference (*Pravda*, March 29, 1968). Other leaders absent from both the Gagarin funeral and the conference were Pel'she, Shelest, Kunaev, Masherov, Mzhavanadze, Rashidov, and Shcherbitsky. All, with the exception of Pel'she, were involved in Union Republic activities at that time.

competence in the foreign policy field, was included, as head of the Soviet republic closest to Czechoslovakia, because any spillover from the Prague Spring might be expected to affect the Ukraine first.

On the agenda were a number of issues: economic relations, Warsaw Pact operations, the international situation, particularly in Central Europe, and, of course, the events in Czechoslovakia. The economic matters explain the presence of Baibakov and his counterparts from the other bloc states. The official communiqué issued after the Dresden talks noted:

> The participants in the meeting expressed their views on prospects for further growth of the socialist economy on the basis of the utilization of economic ties within the framework of the Council for Mutual Economic Assistance and on a bilateral basis. . . . They unanimously reaffirmed their determination in the near future to effect concrete measures . . . for cooperation in achieving a further upswing in the economies of the socialist commonwealth. For the purpose of considering common economic problems, the parties agreed to hold an economic conference on the highest level in the near future.[13]

Subsequent reports suggest that at issue were efforts to dissuade Prague from seeking a hard currency loan from the West and the growing demands of Czechoslovaks to restructure their trade relations to better suit their own needs.[14] According to "Communist sources in East Berlin," the USSR and the GDR agreed to consider the possibility of extending substantial soft-currency credits to Prague to prevent her turning to the West.[15] Within this context Dubček's remarks about the economic aspects of the Dresden meeting might best be understood. According to Dubček, Kosygin "spoke at great length about the prospects for the growth of the

[13] *Pravda*, March 25, 1968.

[14] In a March 4 Prague radio discussion entitled "Problems and Difficulties in the CMEA," the panelists maintained that because Czechoslovakia was more advanced than its other bloc partners, trade was less advantageous to Prague, for she did not require most of the materials produced elsewhere in the bloc. Czechoslovakia had built up a very favorable trade balance, especially with the USSR and Poland. Moreover, the planned economic reforms giving enterprises the right to engage directly in external trade were meaningless unless the other bloc states instituted similar reforms or unless Prague reorientated its trade more toward the West (*SWB*, EE/2714/C2/14–18). A *Pravda* article on March 14, with the curiously similar title "Problems of Economic Cooperation in the Socialist Countries," saw further integration as the only solution to any problems.

[15] *New York Times*, March 26, 1968; also John Erickson, "International and Strategic Implications of the Czechoslovak Reform Movement," in Kusin, ed., *Czechoslovak Reform Movement 1968*, p. 41.

economies of the socialist countries. He spoke about the many possibilities for strengthening economic cooperation and said that in the framework of the CMEA too there are many unused resources. Responsible bodies in individual countries should prepare proposals for the coming talks on the highest level in order to find new and real ways for the development of the economic system."[16] Apparently, the Soviets hoped to forestall any Czechoslovak approach to the West by assurances that the bloc was capable of solving its own economic problems. The decision to examine the matter in greater depth as a prelude to an economic summit conference clearly was intended to assure Prague of everyone's good intentions without actually committing anyone to a specific course. The promise of substantial credits would be used to extract political concessions from the Czechoslovaks.

In the area of military security the participants, according to the communiqué, "reaffirmed the coincidence of their views on the question discussed and the unity of their positions as set forth at the Sofia conference of the Political Consultative Committee of Warsaw Pact states. . . . They unanimously reaffirmed their determination in the near future to effect concrete measures for strengthening the Warsaw Treaty Organization and its armed forces. . . ."[17] The discussion of Pact reform was clearly meant to isolate Rumania and to kill before its inception any support that Rumanian proposals might find among other bloc states such as Czechoslovakia. The "concrete measures" referred to Moscow's continuing efforts to strengthen its position in both the joint military command and the Political Consultative Committee. Dubček later admitted that the Soviets had no intention of waiting the six months agreed to at Sofia for bloc members to suggest reforms; instead the participants had agreed to "a speedy elaboration of proposals to perfect the way in which the joint command acts."[18]

President Nicolae Ceauşescu of Rumania was furious that discussions had been held about CMEA and WTO affairs without Rumanian participation. In a speech on the Dresden meeting, he declared: "We are astonished that the military command of the Warsaw Pact member states was discussed, because it was decided in Sofia by all delegations that the ministers of the armed forces

[16] Dubček interview, Bratislava radio, March 26, 1968, *SWB*, EE/2732/C/4.
[17] *Pravda*, March 25, 1968.
[18] Dubček interview, Bratislava radio, March 26, 1968, *SWB*, EE/2732/C/4.

should draw up within six months proposals for improving the activity of this command. . . . Our country is determined to make its direct contribution to the activity of the Political Consultative Committee of the Warsaw Pact, including the activity of the military high command of the states participating in this pact."[19] However determined Ceaușescu may have been to participate in reform of Warsaw Pact structures, the Soviets were equally determined to block such reforms. At Dresden it first became clear that the Soviets were willing to forego Rumanian support in return for a more cohesive inner grouping of bloc states, which of geographical necessity would have to include Czechoslovakia.

On the subject of Czechoslovakia the discussions were most heated and the communiqué least specific; indeed it was restricted to a broad statement: The Czechoslovak delegation had "provided information on progress in the realization of the January plenary session. Confidence was expressed that the working class and all the working people of the ČSSR, under the leadership of the Czechoslovak Communist Party, will ensure the further development of socialist construction in the country."[20] Yet cadre changes, the successor to Novotný, the April Central Committee plenum agenda, and evidence of "anti-socialist acts" were among those items known to have been discussed.

Dubček initially denied that cadre changes had been proposed at Dresden either "officially or unofficially,"[21] but later he explained this denial: "I was not in favor of revealing the fact that in Dresden there had been talk about the change of President in Czechoslovakia."[22] The bloc parties apparently considered Svoboda an acceptable candidate and wanted to prevent any of the more outspoken reformers from obtaining the post. In particular the dismissal of Smrkovský, one of the presidential candidates, was sought by Brezhnev, who supported Dubček but said that he was "becoming a prisoner of reactionary and anti-Communist elements."[23] Vasil Bil'ak, a leading conservative, provided the fullest account of the

[19] Ceaușescu's speech to the Bucharest Party *Aktiv*, April 26, 1968, in *Scinteia*, April 28, 1968.

[20] *Pravda*, March 25, 1968.

[21] Dubček to the April CPCz Central Committee plenum, quoted in H. Gordon Skilling, *Czechoslovakia's Interrupted Revolution*, p. 208.

[22] Dubček's speech on September 26, 1969, to the CPCz Central Committee plenum, in William Shawcross, *Dubček*, p. 285.

[23] According to Pavel Tigrid, *Why Dubček Fell*, p. 57, and the author's interview with E. Goldstücker, October 24, 1977.

Dresden meeting; he maintained that apart from the issue of who should succeed Novotný, the bloc leaders were concerned that "by permitting the recall of the President without any preliminary discussion of such a serious step by the Central Committee," the Czechoslovak leaders had "violated . . . the basic principles of cadre policy."[24]

Firm control by the party of appointments to all leading posts in the state and government hierarchy (known as the *nomenklatura* system) is a fundamental feature of Soviet-style socialism. Czechoslovak violation of this principle in allowing the selection of a new president without party interference threatened to undermine the party's hegemonial position within Czechoslovak society. Furthermore, because the USSR exercised its own control of East European developments by maintaining the closest ties with the ruling Communist parties, any diffusion of power away from the party also weakened the ability of the Soviet Union to supervise and control events. For these reasons, rather than out of loyalty to Novotný, the incident became a key factor in the Soviet decision to convene the Dresden meeting.

Soviet and bloc leaders also sought information at Dresden about "antisocialist tendencies," particularly in the mass media. As the Soviets subsequently stated:

> At the Dresden meeting the Czechoslovak comrades did not deny that some negative processes were developing in the country, that the radio, television and press had broken away from party control and were in fact in the hands of antisocialist elements and that rightwing forces were consolidating themselves. At the same time the Czechoslovak representatives stated that on the whole the party was in control of the situation and that there was no cause for serious alarm.
>   The Soviet representatives and all the delegations of the fraternal parties noted with complete candor that they saw the picture in a different light. They pointed out the real danger of the situation that had taken shape.[25]

Czechoslovak participants concur that the Soviets insisted on urgent measures to reestablish control of the press, to end attacks on

---

[24] Bil'ak interview, September 3, 1969, in *Pravda pobezhdaet*, p. 134. Zdeněk Mlynář, interviewed by the author on June 1, 1979, maintained that Bil'ak's version of the Dresden meeting represented a fair summary of the minutes, which were distributed in the 1969 Central Committee plenum.

[25] *Pravda*, August 22, 1968.

the party and its history, and to prevent the reactivation of mass associations and non-Communist political parties.[26] Brezhnev, according to Bil'ak, stated that whereas certain antisocialist tendencies previously had been regarded purely as "transitional phenomenon," there was now a growing discrepancy between "words and deeds." He is said to have pleaded with the Czechoslovaks to "mobilize the party and the working class in time" to prevent "chaos."[27]

The Soviets' conclusion that "there was evidence of developments that could lead to a counterrevolutionary coup"[28] found support from other delegations. The Czechoslovaks were specifically warned by the Soviets, the Poles, and also by Kádár himself that they must take measures to prevent a repetition of the 1956 Hungarian counterrevolution.[29] According to Bil'ak,

> They [the Soviets] warned us that counterrevolution does not always begin with murders, but often with demogogy, pseudosocialist slogans and appeals to freedom, harmful to the party, the state and societal apparat, with the weakening and demoralization of the instruments of power—the army, the security organs, the courts and the procuracy. . . . And such symptoms were said to be gaining strength in the ČSSR.[30]

Ulbricht, too, expressed concern about developments in Czechoslovakia and was particularly worried about spillover effects. Bil'ak cites Ulbricht as saying that "any weakening of the CPCz will lead

[26] Dubček conceded that "it is not surprising that certain concern was shown . . . that antisocialist elements should not take advantage of the process of democratization." Bratislava radio, March 26, 1968, *SWB*, EE/2732/C/4. Husák, speaking after the invasion, was more outspoken: "All five parties very urgently pointed to the dangerous developments in Czechoslovakia, to the activity of antisocialist forces, to the operations of rightist forces, to the work of the mass communications media, to the various KAN and 231 clubs, to the wrecking of the state apparatus, etc. They very urgently demanded of and begged our leadership to institute order in these things because this was a dangerous road . . . for socialism in Czechoslovakia, because this would weaken the entire socialist camp" (speech to a CPCz *aktiv* August 19, 1969, *SWB*, EE/3157/C/13). Husák made a similar statement to the CPCz Central Committee plenum on September 25, 1969, in *SWB*, EE/3190/C/17, as did Oldřich Švestka in his *Rudé právo* article of August 21, 1969, in *SWB*, EE/3158/C/7. Zdeněk Hejzlar stated that the Soviets specifically had sought the modification of the April CPCz Central Committee plenum agenda (in Kusin, ed., *Czechoslovak Reform Movement 1968*, p. 60), whereas Kamil Winter later quoted Brezhnev as expressing disbelief that it was beyond Dubček's power to control the press (BBC television documentary marking the 10th Anniversary of the invasion, on August 21, 1978).

[27] Bil'ak, *Pravda pobezhdaet*, pp. 135–36.

[28] *Pravda*, August 22, 1968.

[29] Prague Radio, March 24, 1968, *SWB*, EE/2730/i; and Bil'ak, *Pravda pobezhdaet*, pp. 135–37.

[30] Ibid., p. 136.

to a weakening of socialism in the ČSSR, a weakening of the alliance with the socialist countries and the foundations of socialism in general."[31] Other sources maintain Ulbricht was rather more blunt in his analysis of the dangers of the Prague Spring. One report, which rings true if only because it attributes to Ulbricht that unique directness of approach he had shown on numerous other occasions, quotes him as follows: "If the January line is continued in Czechoslovakia, all of us here will be running into great danger. We may all find ourselves kicked out."[32] Although the bloc's policy toward West Germany was far from being the central issue, East German concern that the common approach to the Federal Republic might be disintegrating appears to have been responsible for the communiqué's condemnation of the "latest steps of the Kiesinger-Brandt government, which are directed against the interests of the German Democratic Republic and the other socialist countries."[33]

Although the Dresden conference lasted only for the one day of March 23, both the decision to hold the conference and the decisions reached and conclusions drawn from that meeting had an important impact on future events. From the Soviet perspective, the following decisions were made:

Decision 1: to hold the March 23 conference.

Decision 2: to hold a high-level economic conference in the near future to consider, among other things, Czechoslovakia's request for a loan to restructure her economy.

Decision 3: to continue with plans for the integration of the military high command of the Warsaw Pact and to widen the scope of activity of its Political Consultative Committee.

Decision 4: not to intervene further in Czechoslovak internal affairs provided that the assurances and promises received from the Czechoslovak delegation were acted upon.

The language of the communiqué is moderate: "Confidence was expressed that [the CPCz leadership] will ensure the further development of socialist construction in the country."[34] But Bil'ak maintains that an earlier version of the communiqué had referred

[31] Ibid., p. 137.
[32] David Floyd, "The Czechoslovak Crisis of 1968," p. 39.
[33] *Pravda*, March 25, 1968.
[34] Ibid.

to promises to deliver a "decisive rebuff to enemy forces."[35] Bil'ak later stated that "at that meeting we promised to restore order and to take the guidance of the state firmly into our hands within two months."[36] Husák, too, refers to the fact that "there were notifications and promises that we would institute order and would take action on these matters."[37] The Soviets expressed confidence that the CPCz leadership would heed bloc advice without further sanctions or warnings, but they gave no indication that they had yet developed a clear policy on how they would respond if their confidence in the Czechoslovaks were disappointed. They gained some political leverage in promising to consider Prague's request for a loan, but beyond this, other specific policy options did not emerge at Dresden.

REACTION TO DRESDEN

It is customary for *Pravda* to announce that the outcome of a delegation's foreign negotiations had received the approval of the Politburo, and sometimes the approval of the Council of Ministers and/or the Central Committee. This was in fact done for the Sofia and Budapest meetings held only weeks before,[38] yet no such announcement appeared for Dresden. It is possible that Brezhnev's inclusion in the delegation gave it sufficient authority to act independently without requiring subsequent Politburo approval. Yet Brezhnev's trips to Sofia earlier in March, to Warsaw in July, and to Czechoslovakia in July and August at the head of similar delegations were indeed the subject of subsequent meetings.[39] That the Dresden results were to be confirmed by the forthcoming Central Committee plenum might also have vitiated the necessity of specific approval by the entire Politburo. Nevertheless, it is a rather curious anomaly, and it appears that either approval was not sought or could not be obtained. The possibility of a split in the Politburo at this stage exists, although the evidence is not at all clear-cut.

Soviet press reports following the meeting reaffirmed the importance of bloc unity, of ties with Czechoslovakia, and the belief, or at least the hope, that the CPCz leadership was both willing and able

---

[35] Bil'ak, *Pravda pobezhdaet*, p. 139.
[36] Bil'ak, "The Truth Versus Lies," p. 20.
[37] Husák's August 19, 1969, speech, *SWB*, EE/3157/C/13.
[38] *Pravda*, March 12, 1968 (Budapest), and *Pravda*, March 13, 1968 (Sofia).
[39] *Pravda*, March 13, July 20, and August 7, 1968.

to bring the domestic situation firmly under control, as the Polish party was doing.[40] The stand adopted by the Politburo after Dresden (or by a dominant faction within it) was signaled in an authoritative article in *Pravda* on March 28 by I. Alexandrov, a pseudonym used for editorials expressing top level party policy.[41] The decision to refrain from any kind of public polemic with Prague or overt interference in Czechoslovak domestic politics was restated when Alexandrov condemned as "imperialist scribblers" all those who were "striving to sow distrust among the Communist parties" by raising allegations of Soviet pressure on Czechoslovakia's new leadership. It described events there positively: "Now the CPCz is carrying out great [bol'shyyu] work in the activation of the Communist party organization and the state administrative apparatus." While reaffirming the deep bonds uniting the two countries and parties, the editorial also contained the most explicit statement yet to appear in the Soviet press of the Soviet leadership's unconditional determination to maintain Czechoslovakia's position as a foremost member of the socialist community:

> The peoples of the Soviet Union and Czechoslovakia and our Communist parties are linked by indissoluble ties of fraternal friendship. This friendship has deep historical roots. It has been sealed with the blood of the best sons of the Soviet and Czechoslovak peoples, shed together in the struggle against the common enemy, fascism, the struggle in which the unshakeable alliance between the USSR and Czechoslovakia emerged. The Communist parties of the Soviet Union and Czechoslovakia, united by fidelity to the principles of Marxism-Leninism and proletarian internationalism, inspire and direct our friendship. . . . No one and nothing, under any conditions, can shake our fraternal friendship, which serves the vital interests of the Soviet Union and Czechoslovakia.[42]

Brezhnev did not elaborate on this stand in the published version of his speech to the Moscow City Party Conference on March 29. Although, according to *Pravda*, he did "inform" the delegates of

[40] See, for example, the front-page *Pravda* editorial on March 27, 1968, entitled "Brotherly Unity," reaffirming that the CPCz was fully capable of managing its own affairs and of participating in efforts to strengthen the solidarity of the bloc.

[41] In July, during a press conference in Sweden, Kosygin conceded that the Alexandrov editorials reflected Politburo opinion. Kosygin, referring to Alexandrov's July 11 *Pravda* article "Attack on the Socialist Foundations in Czechoslovakia," advised the journalists to read it saying "it reflects our assessment of the events now taking place in Czechoslovakia." The Kosygin interview is in *Pravda*, July 15, 1968.

[42] I. Alexandrov, *Pravda*, March 28, 1968.

the results of both the Sofia and Dresden meetings, he chose to deal almost exclusively with domestic political and ideological matters. The conference was devoted primarily to the social responsibilities of scientists, writers, and the intelligentsia and the need for them to display greater "political maturity." Brezhnev's speech was a hard-line call for increased party discipline particularly in the realm of ideological work, which he labeled "the fiercest front of the class struggle." Indeed an editorial in *Sovetskaya Rossiya* that appeared two weeks later on April 13 quoted Brezhnev as warning conference delegates that those "renegades" holding bourgeois views "cannot count on impunity." In an apparent reference to Czechoslovakia, he maintained that "imperialism is trying to weaken the ideological and political unity of the working people of the socialist countries. In doing so, it is chiefly gambling on nationalist and revisionist elements."[43] Although the bulk of Brezhnev's speech dealt with the domestic situation, his reference to processes in socialist countries in general indicates that he considered his analysis applicable throughout the bloc and that he was well aware of the influence that events in Poland and Czechoslovakia were having on that section of the Soviet intelligentsia the party was seeking to bring under control. The president of the USSR Academy of Sciences, Mstislav Keldysh, was more explicit. Speaking of the appeals against the imprisonment of Ginzburg and others, he condemned as "politically immature" anyone who could support "political slanderers and double dealers . . . criminals who had nothing to do with literature." He asserted that those who failed to comprehend the serious implications of any dissent for the political stability of Communist rule should examine the recent events in Poland, where fortunately the "party and the working class have exposed in a timely way the secret mechanisms of provocative and antipopular subversive activities directed against the gains of Socialist People's Poland."[44]

The failure of Brezhnev, Keldysh, and the other speakers specifically to mention Czechoslovakia might reflect avoidance of a polemic that would exacerbate the efforts of the CPCz leaders to control their own internal situation. This restraint is somewhat surprising since other East European regimes were showing no hesitation in offering detailed and public analyses of the Czechoslovak

[43] *Pravda*, March 30, 1968.
[44] *Pravda*, April 1, 1968.

situation. At a philosophy congress on March 26, Kurt Hager, the leading ideologist in East Germany's ruling Socialist Unity party (SED), launched a blistering and personal attack on Josef Smrkovský, who was at that time still a candidate for the Czechoslovak presidency. Hager maintained that Smrkovský and others like him were giving West German politicians reason to "place their hopes in 'evolution,' 'liberalization' and 'Sturm und Drang' days in Prague."[45]

The negative impression of the Hager speech was balanced somewhat by a more circumspect appraisal from Zoltan Komócsin, the Hungarian party secretary in charge of interparty and foreign affairs. In an interview reflecting official opinion, Komócsin made the following statement on the Czechoslovak reform movement:

> Its basic characteristic feature and main trend is to strengthen the Communist party, to develop and render more independent the work of the socialist government organs, and social organizations and, with the active participation of the working masses, one by one to eliminate the faults committed. For our part we approve of the fundamental aspirations of the fraternal Czechoslovak party. . . . Bearing in mind the experience of Hungary in 1956, in my opinion, for the sake of the realization of the objectives decided upon, in Czechoslovakia it has become necessary for the Communists and the forces of socialism to go into battle on two fronts: against the retarding conservative forces and against the nationalist forces.[46]

The entreaty to "go into battle on two fronts" was based on Kádár's strategy for reform in Hungary and formed the foundation of the cautious yet sympathetic Hungarian approach to the developments in Prague.

East European opinion, especially from Poland and East Germany, clearly influenced the Soviet evaluation of events in Prague. So too did the domestic Soviet campaign against dissident intellectuals and insufficient party discipline. Both factors enhanced the growing conviction among some Soviet leaders that "dogmatism"—the threat from the right particularly from Maoist ideas—was no longer the most immediate danger either to the internal stability of party rule or to the external unity of the Communist bloc. Indeed, the Soviet leadership increasingly viewed revisionism in the form

[45] *Neues Deutschland*, March 27, 1968. "Sturm und Drang" or "Storm and Stress" is a reference to a play by Friedrich von Klinger which stimulated a heady political discussion led by Goethe in the late eighteenth century.

[46] MTI, March 26, 1968, *SWB*, EE/2733/A2/1–5. Komócsin's interview was not reprinted in the Soviet press.

of attacks from the left and from the intelligentsia as an even more serious danger to basic values. In Poland, the Soviet Union, and now in Czechoslovakia, the major ideological challenges in recent months had come from the left, not from the right. As a result, the theses governing party work since the Twenty-Third CPSU Congress, which had stressed the necessity for closing ranks against the "splitting tactics" of Maoism, were no longer appropriate to the current domestic and intrabloc situation and would require rethinking.

THE APRIL PLENUM OF THE CPCz

The greatest spur to this reevaluation was the April plenum of the CPCz Central Committee, with its wholesale leadership changes and adoption of the Action Program. It had appeared at first that the plenum would not substantially weaken conservative influence within party and state organs. The statement following the CPCz Praesidium's March 25 meeting, for example, had asserted that "the Praesidium has further dealt with the preparations for the election of the president of the Republic. It took note of the information by Alexander Dubček about the discussion of our delegation at . . . Dresden."[47] As a result of that meeting, General Ludvík Svoboda became the party's presidential nominee, and the positive appraisals in the Soviet press of Svoboda's background and his unswerving support for "the indestructible alliance with the peoples of the USSR" indicate that his candidacy was entirely acceptable to Moscow.[48]

If the Soviets hoped that Svoboda's selection augured well for the maintenance of conservative influence in the leadership, the plenum proved them wrong. In the course of the session, Oldřich Černík was endorsed as the party's candidate for prime minister, Josef Smrkovský as chairman of the National Assembly, and František Kriegel, another strong advocate of reform, as chairman of the National Front. Dubček, Drahomír Kolder, and Černík were the only persons from the pre-January Praesidium who were reelected to that body as full members. Similarly, in the party Secretariat, Dubček, Štefan Sádovský, and Kolder were the only remaining pre-January members. Certainly, conservatives such

[47] Prague radio, March 26, 1968, *SWB*, EE/2732/C/2.
[48] *Pravda*, March 24, 1968. Also see *Pravda*, March 26, 1968; *Izvestia*, March 27, 1968; and *Pravda*, March 31 and April 1, 1968, for favorable interviews with Svoboda and reports of his speeches.

as Bilʼak, Oldřich Švestka, Jozef Lenárt, Alois Indra, and Štefan Sádovský managed to keep their positions. Yet the elevation of Zdeněk Mlynář, Čestmír Císař, and Václav Slavík to important Secretariat posts and the simultaneous demotion of Novotný and almost all of his closest associates helped swing the balance of forces within both the party and state *apparats* away from the conservatives.

The plenary session also adopted the Action Program to guide party policy until the next (the fourteenth) party congress. The program reaffirmed the party's leading role but criticized the "insufficient development of socialist democracy within the party." It also upheld the right of non-Communists to form social organizations that would work with the party in a rejuvenated National Front. Adding to the Soviet perception of threat were proposals calling for a new constitution, further guarantees for the freedoms of assembly and association, a law lifting censorship, a law governing the procedure for political rehabilitation, changes in the electoral system, and the reorganization of the security apparatus and the public prosecutor's office. The Action Program also called for the formulation of a "more active European policy," although it reaffirmed the basic orientation of Czechoslovak foreign policy toward "alliance and cooperation with the Soviet Union."[49]

Whatever reassurance the promise of fidelity may have provided, Soviet hopes that the plenary session would be used to consolidate the leadership's hold on the reform movement and put an end to all the uncontrolled demands for change were not realized. The Soviets later charged that the promises made at Dresden had not been fulfilled, thereby "confirming the fraternal parties' conclusions about the strength of antisocialist feeling inside not only the country but also the Party itself."[50] The Soviet leadership concluded that the plenum had shown itself "unable to stabilize the situation." Indeed Moscow subsequently maintained that "a number of propositions in the CPCz Action Program adopted at that plenary session were in fact used by rightists as a sort of legal platform for further attacks on the Communist Party, the foundations of socialism, and the friendship of the Czechoslovak and Soviet peoples."[51] The official Czechoslovak post-Dubček account of that

---

[49] The text of the Action Program can be found in Robin Alison Remington, ed., *Winter in Prague*, pp. 88–137.

[50] *Pravda*, August 22, 1968.

[51] Ibid.

plenum, an account heavily influenced by Soviet orthodoxy, placed an equally negative interpretation on the influence of the Action Program in encouraging antisocialist elements.[52]

SECURITY ISSUES

In addition to Moscow's worries about the political and ideological implications of decisions reached at the CPCz plenum, there was at the same time a rather sharp increase in the perception of threat concerning the Action Program's stand on internal security. The program had condemned the "violations of law and . . . the privileged position of the security force in the political system" and had made proposals for the reform of the entire structure. The monopoly of police power enjoyed by the minister of the interior was to be ended and a new state security service given jurisdiction solely for "defending the state from the activities of enemy centers abroad." The Action Program guaranteed that the political convictions of Czechoslovak citizens, previously the prime concern of the security organs, "cannot be the object of attention of the bodies of the State Security services. The Party declares clearly that this apparatus *should not be directed toward or used to solve internal political questions* and controversies in socialist society."[53] Clearly, the curtailment of the powers of the secret police and the severing of the minister of the interior's influence over all the steps in the judicial process from arrest, investigation, and prosecution to judgment and imprisonment were necessary prerequisites for the liberalization of public life in Czechoslovakia. At the same time the termination of the party's control over the Ministry of the Interior would dismantle in a single blow the Soviet-style police system set up by Moscow in the postwar period.[54] It would also disrupt the substantial network of agents used by the Soviets to monitor and influence developments in Czechoslovakia. Zdeněk Mlynář has claimed that when he was elected to the party's Secretariat in

[52] "The Lessons of the Crisis Development in the Communist Party of Czechoslovakia and in Society after the 13th Congress of the CPCz," document adopted at the plenum of the Central Committee of the CPCz in December 1970, in *Pravda pobezhdaet*, p. 29.

[53] From the Action Program, in Remington, ed., *Winter in Prague*, p. 111 (emphasis in original).

[54] These proposals were endorsed by the Ministry of Interior on March 26. On March 29 the National Assembly established a committee for military and security questions that would inherit the party eighth department's functions of overseeing the military and security forces.

April, the information then available suggested that of the 10,000 full-time employees in the Ministry of the Interior's Prague offices, 30% (roughly 3,300) were also working for the Soviets. Although the system of Soviet liaison officers largely had been disbanded under Khrushchev, nevertheless, Mlynář maintained, most of the assistant heads of departments worked for Moscow, thereby giving the Soviet security services substantial control over the Prague Ministry of the Interior.[55] The breakup of the ministry and the purge of the conservative elements within it would dislocate, if not destroy, that control.

At the same time demands for the rehabilitation of political figures imprisoned in the 1940s and 1950s continued to surface and achieve official sanction. The Action Program's admission that the security forces had violated the law in the past gave impetus to calls for investigations into various activities, including the circumstances surrounding the death in 1948 of Jan Masaryk, a leading Social Democrat and son of the first president of inter-war Czechoslovakia, whose presence as foreign minister in the post-February 1948 cabinet had served as a focus for non-Communist sentiments in Czechoslovakia. On April 3, the Prague journal *Student* published a letter sent in March from Ivan Sviták to the prosecutor general demanding that investigations into the death of Masaryk be reopened. Sviták alleged that Masaryk had been murdered, possibly by Major Franz Schramm, whom he described as a liaison officer between the Czechoslovak State Security and the Soviet NKVD (the forerunner of the KGB).[56] The whole Masaryk investigation was to cause a lot of friction between Czechoslovakia and the Soviet Union in the weeks to come, and the announcement on April 3 that the Czechoslovak Public Prosecutor's Office was to reopen the case must certainly have caused alarm among informed circles in Moscow.

A final security issue certain to have concerned Moscow was the report from the Bavarian Ministry of the Interior that Czechoslovak border guards had taken down a series of barbed wire and electrical fences on the frontier with West Germany.[57] Clearly, the So-

[55] Mlynář, interviewed by the author, June 1, 1979, claimed that the Ministry of Interior had 147,000 agents and informers on its books, with a total *apparat* of 20,000 throughout Czechoslovakia, 10,000 of these based in Prague alone.

[56] *Student*, April 3, 1968, in Skilling, *Czechoslovakia's Interrupted Revolution*, p. 381; also *Le Monde*, April 5, 1968.

[57] Prague radio on April 3, quoting the report, commented: "If the report is true it must be welcomed. But one cannot welcome the fact that it comes to us from Munich and not

viets had good reason to worry about such a measure. Not only could foreign agents more easily infiltrate into Czechoslovakia but Czechoslovaks and, more important, Soviets and East Europeans would have illegal egress from the bloc via this route. Surely, the Soviets and East Germans did not withstand all the international ignominy surrounding the construction of the Berlin Wall in 1961 in order to see another uncontrolled exit route created.

DEBATES IN MOSCOW

The lack of firm reassurance from the Czechoslovak Central Committee plenum combined with certain negative indications about Prague's internal security policy formed the backdrop for the debates beginning within the Soviet leadership. The first indicator of a possible debate was a rather interesting difference of emphasis between two major articles that appeared in the Soviet press. On April 3 *Pravda* published a lengthy TASS despatch quoting from Dubček's report to the CPCz Central Committee plenum. The article, not surprisingly, emphasized those aspects of his speech most favorable to the Soviet position, but it was the longest and fullest account of the situation in Prague yet to appear in the Soviet press. Dubček's promise that the CPCz "will always be the decisive, organized progressive force of our society" was reported, as was his assurance that "anyone who tries to place in doubt the indestructible Czechoslovak-Soviet friendship will suffer defeat." On the other hand, *Pravda* also included Dubček's statement that reform had to go beyond mere replacement of personnel, although the pace of reform needed to proceed more slowly. His criticism of some aspects of party work was included, as was his avowal of the need to pursue a more active European policy.[58]

On the very next day, *Sovetskaya Rossiya* carried an article by a Soviet ideologue, V. Kozlov, who denounced in general terms, without mentioning Czechoslovakia, the notion of a "specific path to socialism" or "a national form of Marxism." He maintained such views were un-Marxist insofar as they gave undue emphasis to a state's national circumstances. Kozlov echoed the denunciation de-

---

from Czechoslovak authorities" (*SWB*, EE/2739/ii). Also *Le Monde*, April 5, 1968, and *Daily Telegraph*, June 5, 1968.

[58] *Pravda*, April 3, 1968 (also in *Izvestia*, April 4, 1968).

livered by Hager only days earlier when he declared that the search for national forms was a violation of internationalism, a supreme principle that must be protected, for not to do so would undermine bloc unity and ultimately socialism itself.[59] The strength of the *Sovetskaya Rossiya* denuncation was all the more apparent in its being the only editorial of its kind to appear in the period preceding the Soviet Central Committee plenum, normally a time reserved for enunciating the formal party line. It is also unusual for a major editorial propounding, or at least proposing, official party policy on international Communist affairs to appear in newspapers other than *Pravda*. Its appearance in a republic party newspaper supports (but does not in itself prove) the contention that a hardline lobby was emerging within the leadership with views not yet acceptable to the majority.

Kosygin's decision to cut short his visit to Iran and return home a day early, on April 7, encouraged speculation about leadership splits. Kosygin had left Moscow on April 1, arriving in Tehran on April 2, following an overnight stay in Erevan.[60] This was the first visit by a Soviet prime minister to Iran since Stalin met there with Churchill and Roosevelt in 1943. The visit was of the utmost economic and political importance to the USSR, and the papers reported Kosygin's progress daily. It was therefore all the more surprising that he should return a day early to Moscow, leaving Iran without even allowing Prime Minister Hoveida enough time to see him off from Shiraz airport, the provincial capital Kosygin happened to be touring when he decided to return.[61] Before beginning his visit, Kosygin would have heard Lyndon Johnson's March 31 announcement not to stand for another term as U.S. president, so it seems unlikely that this was responsible for the early flight back to Moscow. Reports at the time suggested that Kosygin returned to attend the Central Committee meeting.[62] An official visit to Tur-

[59] *Sovetskaya Rossiya*, April 4, 1968. This attack produced an immediate response from the Czechoslovaks. See Evžen Löbl, "The Right to a Specific Path," *Pravda* (Bratislava), April 12; and Ivan Synek, "On the Specific Path to Socialism," *Rudé právo*, April 19, 1968.

[60] *Soviet News*, March 12, 1968, announced that Kosygin was to visit Iran from April 2 to 8. *Pravda*, April 2, reported that Kosygin was seen off on April 1 by Voronov, Kirilenko, Mazurov, Polyansky, Andropov, Kapitanov, and Kulakov. On April 3, *Pravda* carried a long article about his arrival on the previous day.

[61] *Pravda*, April 8, 1968. He was met by Kirilenko, Pel'she, Polyansky, Andropov, Kapitanov, and Kulakov.

[62] *The Times*, April 10, 1968.

key by Georgian party leader and Politburo candidate member Mzhavanadze was also canceled at the last minute,[63] which would further indicate that the decision (*number 5*) to hold an immediate Central Committee plenum was taken at the end of the first week of April. A number of Politburo members were not in Moscow at this time,[64] and considering Kosygin's own abrupt change of schedule, it would certainly appear that this decision was taken without first consulting all Politburo members. Irrespective of any efforts to isolate Kosygin or any of the other leaders not in Moscow at the time, this Central Committee plenum did prove to be the most hard-line party meeting called for years.

CPSU APRIL PLENUM

The plenum convened in Moscow on April 9 and 10 and, according to official press reports, was devoted exclusively to the discussion of Soviet foreign policy. It began with a report by Brezhnev significantly titled "On the Actual Problems of the International Situation and the Struggle of the CPSU for the Cohesion of the World Communist Movement." The speakers who participated in the debate represented a curious cross section of those with functional responsibilities for foreign and military policy (A. A. Gromyko, the foreign minister, and A. A. Grechko, the defense minister) and those in charge of the major cities and republics with a history of dissident problems (V. V. Grishin, Moscow; V. S. Tolstikov, Leningrad; P. Ye. Shelest, Ukraine; V. P. Mzhavanadze, Georgia; P. M. Masherov, Belorussia; Sh. R. Rashidov, Uzbekistan; I. G. Kebin, Estonia; and I. I. Bodyul, Moldavia). Also involved were key cultural and ideological figures, including the director of the Central Committee's Institute of Marxism-Leninism, P. N. Fedoseev; the secretary of the board of the Soviet Writers' Union, G. M.

[63] U.S. Department of State, Director of Intelligence and Research, *Research Memorandum RSE-127*, August 16, 1968 (declassified).

[64] Of the full and candidate members of the Politburo, a surprising number appear to have been preoccupied elsewhere during the first week of April, including Mazurov (in Finland), Voronov (meeting Tito in Novosibirsk), Pel'she (in GDR), and Suslov (reported ill). Marshal Grechko was in the Middle East from March 20 to April 4. Other party leaders were absent from the funeral of Yuri Gagarin on March 31, including most of the regional party secretaries (Shelest, Kunaev, Masherov, Mzhavanadze, Rashidov, and Shcherbitsky), but it is not known whether they were in Moscow during the first week of April. Shelepin was preoccupied with a World Federation of Trade Unions (WFTU) congress on Vietnam, which opened in Moscow on April 8.

Markov; the head of the Young Communist League (Komsomol), S. P. Pavlov; the minister of culture, Madame E. A. Furtseva; and the editor of *Pravda* (who previously had also been the ambassador to Prague), M. V. Zimyanin.[65] The only leaders responsible for foreign policy and bloc affairs who did not participate were Prime Minister Kosygin, Party Secretary Suslov, and KGB chief Yuri Andropov. The interesting mixture of participants in itself indicates the strong interconnection made within the Soviet leadership between threats to the cohesion of the bloc and problems of internal dissent. The silence of Kosygin and Suslov might be explained by the former's exclusion from preliminary preparations and the latter's reported illness. It is more difficult to determine the reason for Andropov's silence. As a member of the Central Committee with long experience in bloc affairs (he was ambassador to Hungary in 1956 before being promoted to party secretary in charge of relations with ruling Communist parties) and current responsibility as head of the KGB for both the internal and external security of the USSR, one might have expected Andropov to participate, particularly if he shared the concern about revisionism and subversion reflected in the final resolutions. But then Andropov's last speech had been in December 1967, and as he made no speeches at all during 1968, it is possible that his silence was attributable to his style of leadership rather than to his views.

One other person who did give a speech was Konstantin F. Katushev, who prior to the plenum had been party secretary in Gorky. He was promoted at this plenum to Central Committee secretary in charge of liaison with ruling Communist and workers parties, thus filling the post left vacant since May 1967 by Andropov's promotion to head of the KGB. Katushev had no previous experience in this field. Konstantin V. Rusakov also moved up from first deputy head to head of the Department for Liaison with Ruling Communist and Workers Parties, but because of Katushev's higher position in the secretariat, Rusakov was effectively subordinated to him. Some analyses state that Katushev actually replaced Rusakov as secretary because Rusakov was not considered "hard enough." According to this view, Katushev was maneuvered into place by a coalition in favor of military intervention in Czechoslovakia.[66] But

---

[65] *Pravda*, April 10 and 11, 1968.

[66] Jiri Valenta, *Soviet Intervention in Czechoslovakia, 1968*, pp. 30–31. Jerry F. Hough and Merle Fainsod, in *How the Soviet Union is Governed*, p. 464, also state incorrectly that Katushev was promoted to party secretary at the July rather than the April Central Commit-

Rusakov had never held the position of secretary, and he was himself promoted. Moreover, he continued to take an active part in the formulation of bloc policy. Nevertheless, as Katushev's own command of his job grew, Rusakov increasingly was excluded from bloc enclaves that discussed the Czechoslovak crisis.[67]

The full proceedings of the April plenum (like those of all other plenums) were never published. Yet both the press editorials appearing during the session and the resolutions and reports issued at its close underlined the movement within the party to reassert the necessity for party control over the intelligentsia. In a leading editorial that appeared the first day of the plenum, the director of the Institute of the International Workers' Movement, T. Timofeyev, made it clear that the party's vanguard role was being challenged not only in the Soviet Union but in other countries as well. He rejected the Maoist formulation that the historic mission of the proletariat could be fulfilled by the peasantry or the army. Equally, he asserted, those who maintain that the proletariat should follow the intelligentsia or its vanguard were also "undermining the scientific principles of revolutionary Marxism." Timofeyev continued: "It is no accident that their endeavor to belittle the role of the working class is combined with attempts at denying the Communist parties' vanguard role. Such conceptions, regardless of their origin, in fact reflect the influence of petit bourgeois ideology."[68]

The resolution issued following the session reiterated these themes. Although it did not refer specifically to developments in Czechoslovakia, the formulations used and the reports later circulated indicate that Czechoslovakia was indeed discussed and that the plenum consensus did not entirely favor a sympathetic interpretation of the Prague Spring.[69] The resolution, in placing special emphasis on the importance of the Dresden meeting, reaffirmed

---

tee plenum. The Soviet announcement of Katushev's promotion is contained in *Pravda*, April 11, 1968, and *Spravochnik Partiinovo rabotnika*, p. 14. Also see the *International Herald Tribune*, May 7, 1968, for details of Katushev's and Rusakov's backgrounds and B. Lewytzkyj and J. Stroynowski, *Who's Who in the Socialist Countries*, pp. 272 and 524.

[67] Rusakov was present, for example, along with Katushev at the Moscow talks with Yugoslavia's President Tito at the end of April, with the Dubček leadership in early May, and with East German leaders at the end of that month. From then on, however, Rusakov was not listed as present at any of the negotiations at which Czechoslovakia was discussed.

[68] *Izvestia*, April 9, 1968.

[69] *Mladá fronta*, April 25, 1968, reported that events in both Czechoslovakia and Poland had been discussed.

the decisions reached there "to do everything necessary for the steady political, economic and defensive consolidation of the socialist commonwealth." In the interest of "exposing revanchism and militarism in West Germany," the resolution emphasized the need to "increase the solidarity of the socialist countries . . . against West German imperialism." However, the present period was characterized not as one of open conflict between East and West but as one in which the greatest dangers stemmed from imperialist subversion. "The entire massive apparatus of anticommunist propaganda is now directed at weakening the unity of the socialist countries and the international Communist movement . . . and attempting to undermine socialist society from within." The policy directives that emerged from the plenum were clear: Domestically, all efforts must now be directed at "an offensive struggle against bourgeois ideology" (*decision 6*), involving an extensive information and propaganda campaign within the party, public organizations, and the press, to emphasize the need for greater discipline and vigilance against "foreign ideological subversion." Externally, the party endorsed the decisions reached at Dresden stressing the need for greater bloc unity (*decision 7*).[70] Neither the plenum resolution nor any subsequent reports suggest that at this time a decision was made to invade Czechoslovakia or to interfere in any direct form in its affairs.[71] On the contrary, the Soviets are said to have told the CPCz leaders that Czechoslovakia was actually discussed in "temperate terms," and it appears that the specific decisions reached at Dresden were not altered by the April plenum.[72]

The April plenum did, however, contribute significantly to the debate over Czechoslovakia by clearly biasing the parameters of that debate in favor of hard-line opinion. This was done, first, by resolving that in dealing with dissent at home, bourgeois ideological influence had to be combated, whatever its source. It therefore was possible to argue that if the Prague reform movement were to have a negative effect inside the USSR, the Prague Spring could no longer be considered a purely internal Czechoslovak affair, and So-

[70]The resolution appeared in *Pravda*, April 11, 1968.

[71]Some confusion has arisen about Brezhnev's speech to this meeting. See note 12 of chapter 4 for an explanation.

[72]According to Bil'ak's account of discussions with Soviet leaders at the May 4 Moscow meeting, given in his CPCz Central Committee plenum speech in May 1968, in Skilling, *Czechoslovakia's Interrupted Revolution*, p. 664 n. 12.

viet leaders then would have the right to involve themselves. This aspect of the resolution attached conditions to the principle of non-interference and undermined the argument that the Soviet leadership did not have the authority to demand changes in Prague.

The plenum's second contribution to a hard line was to attribute domestic dissent and bloc disunity to the same factor: imperialism's efforts to subvert socialism from within. This made it difficult to support the Prague Spring without appearing insufficiently cautious about the West's intentions in the area. The campaign against West Germany's policy of bridge-building was inevitably bolstered by the April plenum, as was Soviet sensitivity to rumors of rapprochement between Prague and Bonn. At the same time, by emphasizing that imperialism's major thrust was now subversion, the plenum, in effect, supported the argument that Soviet security—and indeed the security of the entire bloc—was threatened by events in Czechoslovakia. As a result, a new orientation began to emerge: a decreasing concern with direct external military threats and greater concern with issues such as the morale of the bloc armies. Political assessments of the reform movement became bound up with broader considerations relating to Soviet strategic interests and bloc security. If Czechoslovakia became the "weak link" in the Warsaw Pact, East Europeans and, more importantly, the Soviet defense establishment could legitimately enter the political debate over the reform movement.

The interdependence of political and strategic considerations emerged at the April plenum also with the campaign against bourgeois ideology at home and within the bloc. By laying the ideological foundations first, hard-liners within the leadership would have the authority of the Central Committee behind them should Czechoslovak leaders fail to bring antisocialist elements under control. The slow process of consensus building that characterized Soviet decision making in the months prior to the invasion of Czechoslovakia had begun in earnest. The conditional right to interfere in Czechoslovak affairs that emerged from the plenum was the initial step in the formulation of what was to become the Brezhnev Doctrine, with its fundamental premise that the USSR had not only the right but also the duty to interfere with whatever means necessary if socialism were threatened in Czechoslovakia or elsewhere in the bloc.

With the April Central Committee plenum, the first phase in the pre-crisis period ended. It had begun with the decision (*num-*

ber 1) to call the Dresden meeting—a decision motivated by the sharp increase in the perception of threat and the consequent quest for information. The affirmation of the Dresden decisions (*numbers 2, 3, and 4*) by the Central Committee plenum (*decision number 7*) underlined the desire to expand the size of the consultative unit primarily for the purposes of consensus building. The lack of any mention of Politburo or Council of Ministers confirmation of the results of the Dresden meeting may have indicated a split within the top Soviet leadership, thereby necessitating a wider debate at the Central Committee plenum. Brezhnev's speech at the Moscow City Party Conference, the tone of editorial reports up to and during the plenum, the composition of the debate participants, and the published resolutions indicated, with few exceptions, the increasing authority of hard-line opinion. The plenum imposed a party line against ideological diversity, thereby allowing the search for alternatives to begin in earnest. This search was spurred by time salience, which introduced a further element of stress and the beginning of the second phase of the pre-crisis period.

CHAPTER FOUR

Phase Two:
April 10–May 4

EVENTS IN PRAGUE

The continuing deterioration of the situation in Prague heightened the perception of threat in Moscow. On April 8, Oldřich Černík's new government was sworn in. Among the new ministers were some of the chief advocates of reform, including Ota Šik and Gustáv Husák as deputy prime ministers and Jiří Hájek, General Martin Dzúr, and Josef Pavel as ministers of foreign affairs, defense, and interior, respectively. There was the beginning of a revival in both the National Assembly, under Josef Smrkovský's new leadership, and the National Front, with František Kriegel as chairman. Smrkovský advocated a National Assembly that would be not only "a passionate and aggressive tribunal for the exchange of opinions" but also a true legislature that could "lead to the rejection, or to the approval, or to the improvement of draft proposals."[1] Non-Communist parties and organizations were also rejuvenated in April, with a number of groups previously banned reappearing.

The CPCz held a series of regional party conferences in April that Moscow viewed with particular concern. Secret ballot elections for regional party secretaries almost completely removed the conservative incumbents. This produced an anomolous situation, for these conservatives, although deprived of their regional power bases, were still able to exert influence through their continued membership in the Central Committee. And they could only be voted off the Central Committee by the next full party congress,

---

[1] *Rudé právo*, April 19, 1968.

which was not scheduled to meet before 1970. Knowledge that the most radical reforms would be blocked so long as these conservatives maintained their seats in the Central Committee led to an increasing number of calls to convene an early extraordinary congress to remove them. Dubček was willing to move the congress forward to the spring of 1969, but some of the most important regional organizations, including South Moravia, West and South Bohemia, and Prague municipal, passed resolutions urging a congress by the end of 1968 at the latest, in order to avoid, in the words of the Prague resolution, the "loss of confidence in the party and the real danger . . . that people would seek a solution of problems outside or against the party."[2] Growing pressure for an early plenum to institutionalize the reform movement and change the composition of the Central Committee meant that the Soviet leadership might have a shorter period of time than expected to agree on what could be done to prevent events in Prague from getting out of hand.

The sense of urgency produced by calls for an early congress was exacerbated by further indications from the Ministry of the Interior that the conservatives there were also losing their positions. Minister Josef Pavel's April 12 article in *Práce*, entitled "What Next in the Security Field?" set out his reform plans for the ministry. His intention to move quickly to reform the security apparatus became apparent toward the end of April when he announced that three or four of his deputies would soon be replaced, along with other top officials. Moreover, he stated that the ministry was now under government, and not party, control.[3]

A series óf radical articles in the Czech press elaborating the fundamental features of the reform movement presented little prospect that the Czechoslovak leadership seriously intended to bring the media under control.[4] Articles directly implicating Soviet agents in the death of Jan Masaryk and the purge of Rudolf Slánský (the party's general secretary until the anti-Semitic purges of the early 1950s) appeared in mid-April amid calls for the official rehabilitation of those two Czechoslovak leaders.[5]

[2] *Rudé právo*, April 27, 1968.

[3] *The Guardian* and *The Daily Telegraph*, May 1, 1968.

[4] See, for example, K. Kosík, "Our Present Crisis," *Literární listy*, April 11, 1968; R. Selucký, "The Program of a Democratic Revival of Socialist Czechoslovakia," *Práce*, April 11, 1968; and P. Pithart, "National Front or Parliament," *Literární listy*, April 18, 1968.

[5] See *Rudé právo*, April 12, 14, and 16, 1968.

REACTION IN MOSCOW

The CPCz regional party conferences, calls for an early congress, demotions in the Ministry of the Interior, and revelations in the press about past Soviet wrongdoings were interpreted in Moscow in the context of the new harder line adopted at the April plenum. A *Pravda* editorial of April 12, commenting on the CPCz Central Committee meeting, did not adopt an overtly hostile tone; but it nevertheless stressed that the Czechoslovaks had delivered "a decisive rebuff to all alien, demagogic, un-Marxist and antisocialist views."[6] *Sovetskaya Rossiya* on the following day refrained from direct mention of Czechoslovakia, but it carried a sweeping condemnation of Western efforts to subvert socialism from within. Maintaining that the Western policy of "building bridges" was the major manifestation of these efforts, the editorial warned:

> Communists cannot ignore instances of ideological immaturity and vacillation in some representatives of the intelligentsia. . . . It is the Party organizations' obligation . . . to deal a resolute rebuff to those who hold bourgeois views, to various renegades and to their defenders and yes-men. "Renegades cannot count on impunity," Comrade L. I. Brezhnev . . . said at the Moscow City Party Conference [on March 29]. . . .[7]

On April 17, *Pravda* published excerpts of the Czechoslovak Action Program for the first time, thereby giving the Soviet public its first glimpse of this major reform platform. The paper indicated Soviet disquiet about the program by also carrying an editorial on the party's role as the leading force in all socialist societies. The author, F. Petrenko, stressed that the current situation was particularly dangerous because "the target of the most fierce attacks by imperialist reaction is the vanguard of the working class—the Communist parties of the socialist countries."[8]

The growing strength of negative opinion on Czechoslovakia and the campaign against revisionism generally combined with the increased salience of time to spur the search for alternative ways of dealing with the situation in Prague. Part of this search involved increased links between Soviet officials and leading conservatives in Czechoslovakia. Continuing purges within this group were grad-

---

[6] *Pravda*, April 12, 1968.
[7] "The Sharpest Front of the Class Struggle," *Sovetskaya Rossiya*, April 13, 1968.
[8] *Pravda*, April 17, 1968.

ually depriving the Soviets of "reliable" sources of information about events within the highest levels of leadership. Thus it was reported during April that Soviet Ambassador Chervonenko had held secret talks with leading conservatives, including Novotný. Dubček is said to have stated his objections about these contacts to Chervonenko personally, on April 23, but this was later officially denied by a government spokesman in Prague, although Dubček never added his own denial.[9]

MILITARY CONTINGENCY CONSIDERED

At this time the first public indications appeared that the CPSU hierarchy was seriously considering the military option. At the end of April, there was a series of regional party meetings throughout the Soviet Union designed to familiarize party cadres with the results of the Central Committee plenum. On April 18 a meeting of over 6,000 party workers from the Moscow City and Regional Party Organizations was opened by V. V. Grishin, the first secretary of the Moscow City Party Committee (gorkom) and addressed by Brezhnev and other party workers including General A. A. Yepishev, the director of the Main Political Administration of the Soviet Army and Navy. Mazurov, Suslov, Kapitanov, and Ponomarev also were present. The resolution noted that the results of the Dresden meeting had "particular significance" and spoke of the "acute exacerbation of the ideological struggle between capitalism and socialism," maintaining that "all ideological means must be concentrated on developing communist convictions, patriotism, proletariat internationalism, ideological firmness [and] the ability to resist all forms of bourgeois influence."[10] This was the basic theme of all the other conferences held throughout the country and attended by various other Politburo members.[11] Kosygin was the only Politburo member not to give a speech at any

[9] *International Herald Tribune, Daily Telegraph*, April 24, 1968; RFE, *Research, East Europe, Czechoslovakia*, January 22, 1969, p. 5.

[10] *Leninskoye znamya*, April 19, 1968.

[11] *Pravda*, April 19, 1968, provided the following schedule of leadership movements: Brezhnev (Moscow), Podgorny (Leningrad), Shelest (Kiev), Kirilenko (Baku), Suslov (Sverdlovsk), Voronov (Kalinin), Andropov (Riga), Demichev (Ryazin), Kunaev (Alma-Ata), Katushev (Gorky), Solomentsev (Kazan). *Pravda*, April 20, 1968, completed the list of speaking engagements: Pel'she (Voronezh), Polyansky (Ashkhabad), Masherov (Minsk), Ustinov (Bashkiria), Shcherbitsky (Crimea), Kulakov (Krasnodar), Ponomarev (Tula), Sirov (Dagestan), Shelepin (Lithuania), Grechko (Ministry of Defense) and Mzhavanadze (Georgia).

of the regional conferences, as he was on a state visit to Pakistan and India from April 16 to 21.

The speeches by Brezhnev and Yepishev were not published. A report of the proceedings, however, was leaked via Prague to Michel Tatu of *Le Monde*. Brezhnev is said to have spoken in very pessimistic terms about the situation in Prague. Without doubting the loyalty of Dubček, whom he praised, Brezhnev reportedly stated that Dubček was becoming a prisoner of reactionary and anti-Communist elements. And there was now a real possibility, according to Brezhnev, that the events in Prague were endangering "the conquests of socialism" not only in Czechoslovakia, but in other East European countries as well. Brezhnev apparently did not make any concrete proposals for action, however. This was done, according to Tatu, by Yepishev, who stated that one could not exclude the possibility that a group of "loyal Communists" from Czechoslovakia might address an appeal to the Soviet Union and other socialist states for help in safeguarding socialism in their country. Under such conditions, Yepishev continued, "the Soviet army is ready to do its duty."[12]

Only days later, leading hard-liners found an opportunity to make yet another attack on ideological laxness at home and abroad. On April 22 Grishin delivered a speech at a meeting marking the ninety-eighth anniversary of Lenin's birth. The meeting was attended by Politburo members, including Brezhnev, Kosygin, and Podgorny. Well over half the speech dealt with international issues, and primarily with efforts to combat imperialist subversion.

---

[12] *Le Monde*, May 5–6, 1968. Tatu states incorrectly that this meeting took place on April 23. There has been much confusion in secondary sources about the Yepishev and Brezhnev remarks. H. Gordon Skilling, *Czechoslovakia's Interrupted Revolution*, p. 662, maintains that Brezhnev and Yepishev delivered speeches condemning Czechoslovakia at the Central Committee plenum held on April 9–10. The sources cited by Skilling are ČTK, May 7, 1968, and Heinz Brahm, *Der Kreml und die ČSSR*, p. 24. Both of these sources, however, claimed to rely on Michel Tatu's report in *Le Monde* of May 5 (sometimes cited as May 5–6, since it was the weekend edition). Jiri Valenta, *Soviet Intervention in Czechoslovakia*, p. 22, also quotes the *Le Monde* article as the source for his statement that Yepishev spoke at the April Central Committee plenum. Yet Tatu does not mention the plenum, and Yepishev is not included in any other official or unofficial Soviet or Western source as having been a speaker at the April 9–10 meeting. However, *Leninskoye znamya*, the official daily newspaper of the Moscow Party *oblast'*, states on April 19, 1968, that both Brezhnev and Yepishev spoke at the meeting of the Moscow Party *aktiv* on April 18. It seems likely that Tatu is referring to this meeting and not to either the previous Central Committee plenum or the subsequent (April 23) meeting of the Moscow obkom. The list of speakers and participants for this latter meeting was printed in *Leninskoye znamya* on April 24, 1968, and neither Brezhnev nor Yepishev were even reported as present.

Grishin's speech was notable both for its hawkishness and its authority. He went beyond the standard formulations, stating that imperialism is seeking not the mere weakening of socialism but the actual restoration of capitalism in the socialist countries. A large part of the speech elaborated the principles on which the CPSU Central Committee based its relations with fraternal states—"proletarian internationalism, brotherly mutual aid, equality of rights and sovereignty." He went on to qualify this: "Our party" considers that "now as never before, the unity of the countries of the socialist commonwealth and the harmonization of the national interests of each fraternal country with the general interest of the world socialist system and the international communist movement is paramount." Completely missing from Grishin's list of principles was the standard reference to noninterference. In its place, there appeared "brotherly mutual aid" and the idea that the individual interests of member states could no longer take primacy over the general interests of the bloc. Needless to say, these general interests were to be defined by Moscow in such way as to best serve Soviet interests.

The introduction by Grishin of "brotherly mutual aid" was a qualitative step forward in the development of the ideological raison d'être for the invasion. All that was required was agreement that all forms of aid, including military means, could be extended to safeguard socialism. And Grishin provided this as well. After reaffirming the results of the Dresden meeting, without, however, mentioning Czechoslovakia, Grishin announced that "the Soviet Union will extend to those people whose freedom and independence is threatened by imperialism all-round political, economic, and—if necessary—also military aid."[13]

That such a major policy statement was made by a relatively junior Politburo member (Grishin had only become the Moscow party boss in 1967), outside proper party organs (the change was not signaled previously at the Central Committee plenum, the meeting of the Moscow party *aktiv*, or at one of the regional party conferences), and published in *Izvestia* rather than *Pravda* suggests that the escalation of the crisis was not universally approved within party ranks.

The deputy chief editor of *Pravda*, Vadim Nekrasov, was quoted on April 21 as presenting an entirely contrary view of develop-

[13] *Izvestia*, April 23, 1968.

ments in Prague. During a Moscow radio forum, he stated that both the March–April CPCz plenum and the Action Program had pointed out the existence of antisocialist trends and had resolved both to "strengthen the ideological unity of the CPCz and to increase its leading role in society." Nekrasov was forthright in his support for the Prague Spring: "In my opinion, if one sums up very briefly what is now happening in Czechoslovakia, it is not events in Czechoslovakia which are of an unhealthy nature, but the interest displayed in them by imperialist propaganda."[14] Along the same lines, *Pravda* published a major article from its Prague correspondent on April 30 that positively described the Action Program and the regional party conferences, stressing the efforts to improve party work and suppress antisocialist elements.

It is possible that these two divergent views represented equal yet conflicting trends within the Politburo. Nekrasov's impromptu remarks, however, cannot be compared with the report presented by Grishin. The presence of the Soviet triumvirate and the many indications in Grishin's speech that his formulations had the authority of the party behind them would certainly make any thesis suggesting factional activity questionable. Furthermore, speeches delivered on such anniversaries tend to be set piece affairs, reflecting the general line; it would not be typical for statements to be made that did not meet with Politburo approval. Yet the absence from Moscow of Kosygin and many other Politburo members would certainly have made it possible for the speech to have been passed by a Politburo minority. And since there is no indication that these major policy changes were communicated to the party during the series of regional party meetings on April 18–19, it seems likely that the decision (*number* 8) to include "brotherly mutual aid" as a principle governing relations and military assistance as a possible modality was made either while the majority of the Politburo was dispersed in the regions (April 18–19) or after only some of them had returned to Moscow (April 20 or 21). In either case, Kosygin could not have been present. On April 21 he left Pakistan (a day later than previously scheduled) and instead of returning to Moscow as originally planned, he made a detour to New Delhi for a brief conversation with Mrs. Gandhi. He could not therefore have been in Moscow before the early hours of April 22.[15] Grishin's speech

[14] Moscow radio, April 21, 1968, *SWB*, SU/2751/A2/i.

[15] On April 5, 1968, *Pravda* announced that Kosygin was to visit Pakistan between April 17 and 20. He left Moscow on April 16, arriving in Rawalpindi on the 17th, leaving Pakistan

and the previous remarks by Brezhnev and Yepishev, therefore, seem to indicate that contingency plans for an invasion were seriously being contemplated at this time.

The Soviet military appears to have been highly involved in this process, and coinciding with Yepishev's remarks at the Moscow meeting, Czechoslovak sources reported that Warsaw Pact headquarters decided between April 18 and 20 to send Marshal Yakubovsky to Prague for negotiations on Warsaw Pact maneuvers (*decision 9*). Negotiations for holding these maneuvers in Czechoslovakia had begun in 1967; and although the new Czechoslovak leadership had succeeded in postponing them and reducing their scope, pressure from Warsaw Pact headquarters became more intense at this time.[16] Marshal Yakubovsky visited Prague on April 24–25 as part of a tour including Poland, the GDR, Hungary, and Bulgaria for discussions on "questions concerning a further increase in the defense preparedness of the Warsaw Treaty member states."[17] Yakubovsky held talks with Svoboda, Dubček, Černík, and the defense minister, Martin Dzúr; and it was Dzúr who subsequently confirmed that the talks had indeed centered on military exercises. He denied reports that he had entirely rejected Pact maneuver plans. Yet at the same time, he made it clear that the exercises were not to be on a massive scale:

> The extent of the exercises—which are indeed to take place this year on our territory—will have to be . . . precisely defined in the same way as has always been done. Moreover, there are to be staff maneuvers and not exercises of such a size as the Vltava maneuvers of 1966.[18]

Dzúr's chief of general staff, General Karol Rusov, was more explicit about the results of Yakubovsky's visit. The exercises, he

---

for New Delhi on April 21. He held a brief conversation with Mrs. Gandhi before flying back to Moscow. The flying times would have made it impossible for Kosygin to be back in Moscow before midnight on the 21st. For reports of his visit, see *Pravda*, April 22, 1968; *SWB*, SU/2746/i; *Keesings Contemporary Archives*, July 6–13, 1968, p. 22795.

[16] In a televised interview on May 21, 1968, Martin Dzúr, the Czechoslovak minister of national defense, stated that because of the situation in the army between January and April and the fear in December 1967 that the army would misuse its power, earlier plans to hold large-scale maneuvers in Czechoslovakia "had been cut" (*SWB*, EE/2777/C/1). This appeared to confirm reports circulating at the end of March that the Warsaw Pact Headquarters had advised Prague it was scheduling spring maneuvers in Czechoslovakia but that Prague had requested the maneuvers to be held elsewhere (*New York Times*, March 24, 1968).

[17] GDR and Bulgarian press agencies, April 21, 1968, in *SWB*, EE/2751/i; Prague radio, April 24, 1968, *SWB*, EE/2753/i; and MTI, April 27, 1968, *SWB*, EE/2756/i.

[18] Prague radio, May 3, 1968. *SWB*, EE/2764/C2/2.

stated, were planned for late summer or fall. Czechoslovak forces would first carry out staff maneuvers, and only then, "if the plan were fulfilled," would exercises of allied staffs be arranged.[19] Clearly, the Czechoslovak leaders were still resisting pressure to hold full-scale troop exercises, and the more they resisted, the more the Soviet military and political leadership grew concerned about Prague's reliability as a member of the Warsaw Pact. Yakubovsky's failure to obtain anything more than the vague assurance that maneuvers of some type would be held before the end of the year subject to further negotiations contributed significantly to the escalation of the crisis and was to precipitate a series of high-level Soviet military visits to Prague in May.

The last week of April also saw the publication of important articles in *Pravda* by leading party officials, including V. V. Zagladin, deputy head of the International Department of the Central Committee and P. N. Fedoseev, director of the Institute of Marxism–Leninism, who had been one of the speakers at the April Central Committee plenum.[20] On April 25, *Pravda* published an article on "Marxism and the Contemporary Ideological Struggle" by S. Kovalev, the party official whose September 26 *Pravda* article justifying the invasion was to become known as the "Brezhnev Doctrine."[21] In an attack on the democratic ideals of the Prague Spring, Kovalev made the following statement:

> Only those to whom the interests of the working people are alien could call for "absolute" freedom, right down to freedom of antisocialist activity in the countries of socialism. In socialist society there is not and cannot be freedom for those who make attempts on the gains of the working people. . . . There is no freedom for criminals, for propagandists of war and racism, for counterrevolutionaries. . . . Socialist democracy . . . is inconceivable without the guidance of society by the Communist Party. To oppose the guiding role of the Communist Party in socialist society is to make an attempt on the very foundations of this society, on the fundamental vital interests of the working masses.[22]

[19] Czechoslovak television, May 7, 1968, in RFE, *Czechoslovakia*, May 21, 1968.
[20] P. N. Fedoseev, "Leninism—the Marxism of the Twentieth Century," *Pravda*, April 22, 1968; and V. V. Zagladin, "The 150th Anniversary of Marx's Birth: On the True Revolutionary Path," *Pravda*, April 29, 1968.
[21] S. Kovalev, "Sovereignty and the Internationalist Obligations of Socialist Countries," *Pravda*, September 26, 1968.
[22] *Pravda*, April 25, 1968.

This linking of calls for freedom with counterrevolution and attacks on the very foundations of socialism clearly did not augur well for the Czechoslovak reformers. Nevertheless, Kovalev made no mention of the "brotherly mutual aid" formula. Indeed his statement that "life exposes both right-wing and 'left' revisionism, particularly Maoism" seems to indicate that he still regarded the ideological threat from China as more dangerous.

The Czechoslovak press reacted immediately to the increased activity of the Soviet leadership and press. *Práce* on April 25 accused Grishin of making unfair generalizations and demanded an explanation of Soviet intentions. *Mladá fronta* on the same day complained that the Soviet press was presenting a distorted picture of events in Czechoslovakia. It criticized the Soviet Union for seeking to impose ideological control over the bloc and attributed Soviet apprehensions to the fear of spillover. Perhaps even more damaging to Soviet–Czechoslovak relations were the relevations by Karol Bacílek, the former Czechoslovak minister of public security, that the arrest and trial of Rudolf Slánský had been ordered personally by Stalin, supervised by Anastas Mikoyan, and carried out by Soviet "advisers" working in the Czechoslovak ministry at the time.[23] Following these revelations, there were two more suicides in the Ministry of the Interior, bringing to twenty-six the reported number of suicides in that ministry during April.[24]

The ecstatic and jubilant atmosphere that characterized the May Day demonstration in Prague was in sharp contrast to the usual, more orderly and sombre parades in the other bloc capitals. Television viewers were able to watch Dubček being greeted by Czechoslovak-style hippies carrying homemade placards and even an American flag.[25] Later that evening, a group of students protested against the conditions of their Polish counterparts; and on May 2 in Stare Mesto square, thousands gathered to hear speeches by reform leaders in what *Pravda* described as a "provocative assembly."[26]

Soviet leaders, by this time, were drawing very negative conclusions from almost all the events in Czechoslovakia. By the beginning of May they had decided that the March–April CPCz Central

[23] *Smena*, April 28, 1968; *International Herald Tribune*, April 29, 1968.

[24] *New York Times*, April 30, 1968.

[25] As shown in the BBC television documentary by Keith Kyle, marking the tenth anniversary of the invasion.

[26] *Pravda*, August 22, 1968.

Committee plenum had been "unable to stabilize the situation." *Pravda* released the official account of Soviet reaction to the May crisis on August 22, 1968:

> [Soviet] anxiety increased still further when . . . a wide-scale campaign was launched in the country to discredit all the previous activity of the CPCz; when a process of mass replacement of party and state personnel developed on a wide scale . . . ; when a clearly instigated wave of anti-Soviet propaganda rose in the press, radio and television; and when all sorts of organizations opposed to the Communist Party began to emerge. . . . This was why the CPSU Central Committee . . . again proposed that a bilateral meeting be held.

On May 3, the decision (*number 10*) was taken to summon the Czechoslovak leadership to Moscow for immediate talks.

SUMMONS TO MOSCOW

Insofar as the Czechs had expressed their desire to discuss economic matters, they could claim with some justification that the Moscow meeting convened on May 4 had been called at their initiative. Yet this seems to have been more a face-saving device to ameliorate the effect of having to leave for Moscow without any prior notice. Dubček, Smrkovský, Černík, and Bil'ak arrived there at 2:00 A.M., and talks began immediately.[27] The Soviet delegation consisted of Brezhnev, Kosygin, Podgorny, Katushev, and Rusakov. The communiqué published in *Pravda* on May 6 reported that the talks took place in an "open and comradely spirit," but mentioned nothing about total agreement, thus indicating that the meeting did not stop the serious deterioration in relations between the two sides.

Economic matters were indeed on the agenda, with the Czechoslovak loan application under consideration. Perhaps in response to increasing reports that Czechoslovakia was seeking a loan from various Western sources, including the World Bank and the International Monetary Fund,[28] it had been made known in Prague that

---

[27] Michel Tatu, *Le Monde*, May 5–6, 1968; *Le Figaro*, May 6, 1968.

[28] A White House Memorandum for the Record, dated April 26, 1968, of a National Security Council meeting on Eastern Europe held in Washington on April 24, 1968, confirmed that Czechoslovakia had indeed put out "feelers" about possible membership in the World Bank and the International Monetary Fund. It also revealed that Hungary was similarly exploring such possibilities. The meeting was attended by President Johnson, Secretaries Rusk, Clifford, and Fowler, CIA Director Helms, Deputy Under Secretary Bohlen, and others. The memorandum was declassified and released to the author under the Freedom of

the Soviets might be favorably disposed to extending the loan themselves.[29] At the meeting, however, the Soviets sought further clarification on Czechoslovakia's investment plans. As Smrkovský makes clear, Kosygin in particular appeared to be concerned lest the Czechoslovaks reorient their economic development toward the West:

> Černík . . . explained our need to modernize our manufacturing industry. . . . We needed about 400 to 500 million rubles. We wanted to have the loan from the Soviet Union and we said that if the Soviet comrades couldn't manage to lend us that much, we would apply to the international bank or some other source. We underlined that in the event of our borrowing from the West, the deal on our side would be treated on a strictly commercial basis without political strings.
>
> The reply to that—from Kosygin—was casual, that they would examine our request. But Kosygin didn't forget to remark—for whom did we actually want to manufacture consumer goods? For export? He said that the West didn't need our consumer goods and wouldn't want them in future. So then we'd be wanting to get our goods on the markets of the socialist countries, especially of the Soviet Union, with the help of investment capital from the western countries. But the socialist market didn't want our consumer goods either, it needed our investment goods.[30]

Judging from the composition of the two negotiating teams and the reports that circulated later, other important items were also on the agenda. As in the Dresden meeting, the Soviets wanted an explanation from the Prague leadership for the increase in anti-

Information Act. For other accounts of reports in Prague of efforts to seek Western loans to reorient its economy, see Galia Golan, *Reform Rule in Czechoslovakia*, p. 39, and Skilling, *Czechoslovakia's Interrupted Revolution*, p. 696.

[29] According to Zdeněk Mlynář, quoted by the *New York Times*, May 1, 1968. Michel Tatu (*Le Monde*, May 4, 1968) also quotes "good sources" in Prague to the effect that the USSR was favorably disposed to studying the possibility of extending a $400 million loan in gold or convertible currency to Prague. In connection with these reports, it was rumored that Kosygin was due to visit Prague, possibly for the VE Day celebrations on May 9. For a detailed analysis of the background to Czechoslovakia's loan application, including the paradoxical fact that the GDR, Poland, and the USSR owed Czechoslovakia 11,200 million foreign exchange crowns (almost $1.56 billion), see RFE, *Research, East Europe, Czechoslovakia*, May 28, 1968. Mlynář also maintained that the Soviet Union had withheld its quarterly supply of wheat to Czechoslovakia. This provoked an immediate official denial, with ČTK announcing that 125,000 tons of wheat had been delivered between April 1–25, with shipments during the last nine days higher than usual. *New York Times*, May 2, 1968.

[30] Josef Smrkovský, *An Unfinished Conversation*, p. 12. That the loan application had been discussed at the Moscow meeting was also confirmed by Smrkovský in his testimony to the National Assembly Foreign Affairs Committee, *ČTK*, May 15, 1968; by Dubček in his *Rudé právo* interview on May 6, 1968; and by Jiří Hájek, *Dix ans après*, p. 80.

socialist activity. Brezhnev spent much of the time reading aloud excerpts from newspapers or reports of meetings, many of which were previously unknown to the Czechoslovak leaders themselves. The following account by Smrkovský provides an excellent indication of the tone of the meeting:

> On the whole, we spent the day listening to a long list of the things which . . . the Soviet representatives disliked about developments in our country. In effect, it was a reading of the *White Book* from a working draft. . . .
>
> During the talk, secretaries kept coming, bringing Comrade Brezhnev more and more information about what this or that newspaper or magazine was writing about us, what this person or that had said.
>
> It's a fact that none of us had any idea about many of the things they read out to us, especially Brezhnev. What was in some district newspaper, that there was such and such an article, a meeting someplace, where somebody spoke and what he said. How could we have known it all?
>
> They gathered the information—and here [in Prague] Ambassador Chervonenko did it—from the people who were later called the conservatives. Those people collected all kinds of gossip and handed them to the Soviet embassy—and from there the stuff went to Brezhnev. . . .
>
> We countered, especially Dubček and others, with facts and information of much greater weight. . . . We were disconcerted to find that they showed no interest whatsoever in May Day, where the participation had been so impressive. . . . That didn't interest them. They were interested in meetings of KAN and K 231, attended by fifty or a hundred people, sometimes less. We were sickened by the whole business, because we realized they weren't interested in the facts, in our overall situation, but were looking for pretexts for opposing us.[31]

Following the meeting, in his testimony to the National Assembly's Foreign Affairs Committee, Smrkovský stated that the Soviets had been trying to discern whether the Prague leadership had control of the situation in their own country. Although he reiterated Dubček's assurance[32] that the Soviets had received Czechoslovak explanations with some understanding, Smrkovský's defiant promise that "no force, whether international or domestic" would deflect Czechoslovakia from establishing a "humanist, democratic

[31] Smrkovský, *An Unfinished Conversation*, p. 11. In his testimony to the National Assembly Foreign Affairs Committee, Smrkovský admitted that the Czechoslovak delegation had been confronted with "a number of specific facts" about nonsocialist forces.

[32] *Rudé právo*, May 6, 1968.

and socialist society"[33] clearly implies that the talks had not ended in agreement. Indeed, this is confirmed by the statement in his memoirs: "We came back from Moscow so disillusioned that we couldn't, in all conscience, say anything to our public at home, since it was impossible to speak about the actual content of the talks."[34] Dubček, too, made it clear that disagreements had been voiced, and in an interview with *Rudé právo*, which, interestingly enough, was reprinted in *Pravda*, Dubček made only the most transparent effort to present the negotiations as normal and trouble-free:

> It is proper among good friends . . . not to hide behind diplomatic politeness but to speak out openly, as an equal with equals. In this spirit, the Soviet comrades expressed concern lest the process of democratization in our country be used against socialism.[35]

Bil'ak, the most conservative member of the Czechoslovak delegation, and one who, according to Smrkovský and Hájek, agreed with the Soviet assessment of the situation in Prague,[36] also subsequently provided a full account of the May meeting. In the Soviets' judgment, Bil'ak maintains, the CPCz leadership had not carried out the promises made at Dresden and, on the contrary, the situation had deteriorated since then. According to Bil'ak:

> They literally begged us to recognize the danger which threatens the CPCz and ČSSR arising out of the growth of counterrevolutionary forces. In that situation no aid of any kind could in effect improve the position of the republic and the standard of living of its people, when the leadership of the party and government were not taking matters into their own hands. . . . They implored us to realize that disorder and chaos would inevitably spread from the political sphere to the national economy which could lead to a catastrophe.

The Soviets, he said, "begged us not to forget that the Western boundaries of the ČSSR were at the same time the boundaries of the socialist camp." They emphasized the sacrifices that Soviet leaders had made in establishing socialism in Czechoslovakia and declared that "under no circumstances would it be permitted for

[33] ČTK, May 15, 1968, quoted in RFE, *Research, East Europe, Czechoslovakia*, May 16, 1968. Also *Rudé právo*, May 16, 1968, and an interview with Smrkovský by Prague radio, May 10, 1968, *SWB*, EE/2768/C/4.

[34] Smrkovský, *An Unfinished Conversation*, p. 12.

[35] *Pravda*, May 8, 1968.

[36] Smrkovský, *An Unfinished Conversation*, p. 11; and J. Hájek, *Dix ans après*, p. 80.

events to develop in such a way that sooner or later socialism would
be liquidated in Czechoslovakia. This had become the concern not
only of Czechoslovakia, but of international socialism as a whole."[37]
In his speech to the September 1969 CPCz Central Committee
plenum, Bil'ak paraphrased the Soviet position as follows: "To permit Czechoslovakia to fall out of the socialist camp would mean the
betrayal of socialism and the annulling of the results of the second
world war . . . and this *they could not permit even at the cost of a
third world war.*"[38]

Husák and Mlynář were not at the May meeting but were certainly in a position to know what happened, and they have supported the negative assessment of the meeting provided by the
participants on the Czechoslovak side. Husák contends that "after
prolonged discussions, there was again the conclusion that order
would be brought about in our country, that actions would be taken
in our country against all this, and that the wrecking of the socialist
society would not be permitted."[39] Mlynář confirmed Bil'ak's account of the meeting as essentially correct, adding that Brezhnev is
said to have "assured" his Czechoslovak counterparts that "we will
never give you up!"[40]

Finally, the Soviets themselves in their account of the development of events portray the May meeting as called at the initiative
of the Soviet leadership, "to reemphasize its fears for the fate of
socialism in Czechoslovakia." The Soviets maintained that the
Prague leaders themselves had spoken of "the seriousness of the
situation in the country," and quoted them as saying in the course
of the meeting that the negative aspects of the Prague Spring "ex-
ceed the bounds of purely internal affairs of ours and affect the fraternal countries, for example, the Soviet Union and Poland." According to the Soviet side, "it was impossible to disagree with
this." The Soviet account confirms the Czechoslovak description of
the meeting as essentially negative in tone and outcome. The Soviets were by now demanding firm and specific administrative measures to prevent the growth of antisocialist groups. According to
the Soviet account, the Prague delegation "admitted . . . that in-

[37] *Rudé právo*, September 3, 1969, reprinted in *Pravda pobezhdaet*, pp. 140–42. These
points were reiterated in the major *Rudé právo* article of July 16, 1970, also in *Pravda
pobezhdaet*, p. 360.
[38] *Svědectví* 10, no. 38 (1970): 284–85.
[39] Speech by Husák, August 19, 1969, in *SWB*, EE/3157/C/14.
[40] Author's interview with Mlynář, June 1, 1979.

creased demands were being made for creating a legal political opposition to the CPCz that by nature could only be an antisocialist opposition. . . . They said they knew the specific people responsible for this and asserted that an end would be put to it."[41]

The results of the May 4 meeting were a setback for Czechoslovak negotiators. Although their application for an economic loan was to be considered further, it was clear that the Soviets would not allow its use for any fundamental reorienting of Czechoslovakia's trading links or industrial development. Further, it would appear that Moscow firmly tied the question of a loan to the success of the CPCz leaders in carrying out political measures to put an end to antisocialist activities. The Soviets called for the suppression of KAN (the Club of Nonparty Activists), K 231 (a human rights club open to anyone imprisoned under 1948 Law No. 231 for the defense of the republic) and similar groups, and the reintroduction of censorship. Dubček conceded that military maneuvers had also been discussed. While he agreed that "joint military exercises held in individual Warsaw Pact countries constitute a . . . necessary precondition of high combat readiness,"[42] the absence from the communiqué and from Dubček's remarks of any confirmation of the date or venue for the maneuvers points to continued disagreement on this point as well.

The major purpose of the meeting had been to warn Prague that events in Czechoslovakia were not, and could no longer be, the internal affair of the Prague leadership alone. The Soviets argued that they had made sacrifices in the past and would do so in the future to guarantee Czechoslovakia's place in the socialist camp. The failure of this meeting fundamentally to reassure Moscow of the ability of the CPCz to keep control of the situation in Prague forced the Soviets to consider the use of military means for the maintenance of Soviet-style socialism in Prague. As a result, the probability of involvement in military hostilities was considerably increased, thus bringing the escalation from the pre-crisis to the crisis period.

[41] *Pravda*, August 22, 1968.
[42] *Pravda*, May 8, 1968.

CHAPTER FIVE

Findings

DECISIONS

There were ten decisions taken in the two phases of the pre-crisis period:

Decision Number	Date	Content
		PHASE ONE: MARCH 22–APRIL 10
1	March 22	Under heavy pressure from Poland and East Germany, Soviet leaders decide to convene a bloc summit in Dresden to discuss, among other issues, the situation in Czechoslovakia.
2	March 23	The Soviet delegation to the Dresden meeting agrees to hold a high-level bloc economic conference in the near future to consider, among other things, Czechoslovakia's request for a loan to restructure her economy.
3	March 23	The Soviet delegation to the Dresden meeting agrees to continue with plans for the further integration of the military high command of the Warsaw Pact and to widen the scope of activity of its Political Consultative Committee.
4	March 23	The Soviet delegation to the Dresden meeting agrees not to intervene further in Czechoslovak internal affairs provided that the Czechoslovak delegation acts on the assurances and promises it has given.

Decision Number	Date	Content
5	April 6–7	The decision is taken, possibly by an ad hoc group within either the Politburo or the Secretariat, to alter the last-minute arrangements for the CPSU Central Committee plenum.
6	April 10	The party's Central Committee plenum confirms that a campaign must be waged to tighten ideological discipline within the CPSU and the country as a whole.
7	April 10	The Central Committee endorses the need for greater bloc unity as called for at the Dresden meeting.

PHASE TWO: APRIL 10–MAY 4

Decision Number	Date	Content
8	Between April 18 and 21	A group within the Politburo decides to include "mutual brotherly aid" as a principle governing relations between communist states and "military assistance" as a possible modality.
9	Between April 18 and 20	Warsaw Pact headquarters decides to send Marshal Yakubovsky to Prague for negotiations on Pact maneuvers.
10	May 3	The Politburo decides to summon the Czechoslovak leadership to Moscow for immediate bilateral talks.

THE PSYCHOLOGICAL ENVIRONMENT

The pre-crisis period began with the decision to call the Dresden meeting on March 22 and ended with the bilateral meeting between Soviet and Czechoslovak leaders in Moscow on May 4. There were seven speeches or articles by the political and military leadership published in full during this period,[1] only two of which were directly relevant to the situation in Czechoslovakia. These were the speeches by Brezhnev to the Moscow City Party Conference on March 29 and Grishin at the meeting marking the ninety-eighth anniversary of Lenin's birth on April 22. Czechoslo-

---

[1] Descriptions of these speeches and excerpts quoted are from the following sources: Brezhnev, *Pravda*, March 30, 1968; Kosygin, *Literaturnaya gazeta*, April 3, 1968; Shtemenko, *Krasnaya zvezda*, April 7, 1968; Shelepin, *Trud*, April 9, 1968; Grishin, *Izvestia*, April 23, 1968; Grechko, *Pravda*, May 2, 1968; Pel'she *Neues Deutschland*, May 3, 1968.

vakia was also the subject of debate at the April CPSU Central Committee plenum and the meeting of the Moscow party *aktiv* addressed by Brezhnev and Yepishev, but neither the proceedings nor the speeches were published. Other speeches, however, particularly those by Shelepin, Grechko, and Pel'she on various international themes, reinforce the results of the analysis of the Brezhnev and Grishin speeches.

All the speeches maintained that the increased aggressiveness of U.S. imperialism was the major source of tension in international affairs. Probably the most severe denunciation of the United States came from Shelepin. This is not too surprising as the occasion of his speech was the Day of Solidarity with the Vietnamese people. He might have taken this opportunity to attack U.S. policies in general in areas other than Vietnam, such as the Middle East or Central Europe. But this he did not do, and even in his mention of the results of the Warsaw Treaty Organization (WTO) meeting in Sofia, he confined himself to that section of the Sofia resolution on Vietnam.

Grechko's speech, at the May Day parade in Red Square, was very much a set-piece affair. Socialism, he declared, continued to enjoy new successes, but he warned that imperialism was embarking on a more aggressive policy. The sources of this increased threat were, in the order listed by Grechko, open military ventures such as Vietnam, "ideological subversion against socialist states, blatantly interfering in the domestic affairs of other countries," and "the increased activity of the militarist and revanchist forces in West Germany." For dealing with these challenges he proposed raising combat preparedness, improving unity between socialist countries, and implementing "specific measures" for strengthening the Warsaw Pact. Grechko reminded the audience that the Central Committee plenum recently had reaffirmed its readiness "to do everything necessary" for the further consolidation of the socialist commonwealth. His speech, therefore, while paying lip service to the subversive dangers of U.S. imperialism revealed him as concerned primarily with meeting direct military challenges, such as those presented in Vietnam and Central Europe.

Pel'she's orientation was somewhat different. His speech, marking the 150th anniversary of Karl Marx's birth, was delivered in the GDR. The subject matter and the venue lent themselves to an orthodox and hard-line oration, and Pel'she certainly did not disappoint anyone. Apart from speaking about Marx, he praised the new

GDR constitution as an exemplar of socialist legality and democracy and condemned the rise of neo-Fascism and militarism in the Federal Republic, which he described as a serious threat to European security. The situation in Europe filled the Soviet leadership and other progressive forces with anxiety, according to Pel'she, and one action to meet this danger was the forthcoming November meeting of Communist and Workers parties, which would help unify the Communist movement and all revolutionary forces. Revealing himself as a staunch, orthodox Marxist, unlikely to greet Brandt's policy of "building bridges" with any enthusiasm, Pel'she nevertheless did not dwell on subversion as a particular threat to socialism and did not advocate any drastic or specific course of action.

This was, of course, in some marked contrast to the speech by Grishin, already analyzed in depth in chapter 4. Grishin was the only political or military leader to advocate the specific use of military means to defend the freedom and independence of peoples threatened by imperialism, wherever and however they might be threatened, and to link that advocacy closely to the results of the Dresden meeting. He must be classified, therefore, as the major spokesman for hard-line opinion in the leadership during the pre-crisis period, and the fact that his speech was made at an important party occasion in the presence of the "triumvirate" indicates that such opinion was not, even at this stage, insubstantial.

Brezhnev's speech to the Moscow City Party Conference of March 29 concentrated primarily on domestic ideological issues and revealed his strong concern about revisionism, nationalism, and intellectual dissent. Unlike some of his colleagues, Brezhnev did not consider Vietnam or Central Europe the front line in the struggle between East and West. Indeed the major threat was not a direct external attack at all: "To put it briefly, the ideological struggle is today the fiercest front of the class struggle." Whereas Shelepin and Grechko felt that imperialism was more than capable of launching a direct military attack, Brezhnev feared a more indirect approach: "Not daring to engage in a frontal attack on the world of socialism, imperialism is trying to weaken the ideological and political unity of the working people of the socialist countries." Brezhnev's attack on revisionism and the absence of any mention of dogmatism must also distance him from Pel'she, who supported the convening of the November International Communist Conference, aimed at closing ranks with such revisionists as the Yugoslavs, the Rumanians, and the Euro-communists against the "splitting tactics" of the Chinese dogmatists.

Based on the actual speeches made during the pre-crisis period from March 22 to May 4, 1968, one may conclude that as yet Czechoslovakia was not the universal and overriding concern for the Soviet leadership. Brezhnev, because of his concern for ideological subversion, might naturally have shared the views of Shelest and even the Polish and East German leaderships about events in Prague, but all indications are that Brezhnev still had confidence in Dubček's ability to control the situation. By the end of the pre-crisis period, however, when the Czechoslovak leadership was summoned to Moscow, there was growing evidence that Brezhnev was losing patience with Prague and becoming more assertive within the Soviet leadership. Nevertheless, he still was a great adherent of consensus politics, and thus to the extent that his stance on Czechoslovakia hardened toward the end of the pre-crisis period, it was probably his response to a general shift in the leadership's view of the Prague Spring.[2]

Brezhnev's opinions on the dangers of revisionism, nationalism, and imperialist subversion put him roughly on the same side of the ideological spectrum as Shelest, Grishin, and Yepishev; whereas Shelepin and Grechko were much more concerned with imperialism's overt activities in places such as Vietnam rather than with the threat of subversion. Shelepin, Pel'she, Suslov, and Ponomarev were all anxious to isolate the Maoists and prevent them from exercising their "splitting tactics" on the rest of the international Communist movement. Suslov in particular had worked steadily ever since Khrushchev's overthrow to form a broad united front to combat Chinese "dogmatism." This front was to encompass as many ruling and nonruling Communist parties as possible: all the East European parties, the Yugoslavs, the Euro-Communists, and the Japanese Communist party, plus Socialist parties and national liberation movements.[3] The culmination of Suslov's efforts was to be a meeting of the international Communist movement in November whose overriding purpose was to isolate the Chinese. The success of Suslov's united front tactics depended entirely on preserving dogmatism as the main danger and preventing the CPSU from con-

[2] This view of Brezhnev is supported by A. Avtorkhanov, *Sily i bessiliye Brezhneva*.

[3] Suslov's views are further discussed in Jiri Valenta, "Soviet Foreign Policy Decision-Making and Bureaucratic Politics," pp. 38–67.

demning revisionism, for such a condemnation would alienate the vast majority of parties upon whom the success of the conference depended.

Suslov also hoped that the Socialist party in West Germany (the SPD), headed by Willy Brandt and currently part of the ruling coalition, would be represented; and Shelepin, for his part, had established contacts with the non-Communist trade unions in the Federal Republic. References in Soviet speeches about the need to recognize the existence of "realistic elements" in West Germany must be seen against the backdrop of efforts by a number of Soviet leaders to establish links with West Germany, in itself a very contentious issue within the CPSU. Thus, for example, while Pel'she publicly backed the convocation of the November conference, in the same speech he delivered a blistering attack on neo-Nazism in West Germany. This set him apart from Suslov and Shelepin on this issue and established him as one who shared East German paranoia about links between Prague and Bonn—paranoia that was fueled by East Germany's almost certain knowledge that their Soviet allies were *de sous* establishing similar links.

Kosygin, who made no major public speeches during this period, appears to have been frequently outmaneuvered, finding himself abroad or outside of Moscow when key decisions were taken. In Iran only days before the convening of the April CPSU Central Committee, which he cut short his visit to attend, Kosygin upheld the Soviet Union's "strict observance of equality, national independence, and noninterference in the internal affairs of other states and people."[4] Absent was any reference to "mutual support," "proletarian internationalism," or any of the similar formulations that were gaining currency at that time. Of course, speaking in Iran, Kosygin could hardly have echoed Grishin's call for "military aid," since the Tehran government would almost certainly have thought it applied to them rather than the recalcitrant Czechs.

Kosygin's main concern at this time was domestic economic management and reform, which naturally also gave him an interest in the Council for Mutual Economic Assistance (CMEA) and the economic performance of East European states. Although the continued poor performance of the Czechoslovak economy threatened to further burden the Soviet Union, the economic reorientation of

[4] *Pravda*, April 3, 1968.

Czechoslovakia toward the West might deprive Soviet markets of needed capital goods; also excessive or uncontrolled reform might jeopardize the survival of Kosygin's own, more limited, efforts to reform the Soviet economy.

Kosygin had another interest during these months, namely, the beginning of disarmament and arms control negotiations with the West. Negotiation of the Nuclear Nonproliferation Treaty was to pass its first hurdle in early summer when the United States, the Soviet Union, and Great Britain were to be its first signatories. The real object of the exercise for the Soviet Union, however, was to pressure the United States into obtaining West German adherence to the treaty; and in order to achieve this, all the Soviet Union's own allies would have to show willingness to sign. Soviet problems began when Rumania announced that it would not support any treaty that legitimized the superpower monopoly of nuclear weapons. When sympathy for this view was expressed in Prague, it began to appear that this major diplomatic initiative would amount to very little. Thus Prime Minister Kosygin, who with Foreign Minister Gromyko had personally guided the negotiations, might have had little reason to feel sympathy for Prague's independent stand on this issue.

At the same time, initial contacts between the United States and the Soviet Union began on strategic arms limitation. Kosygin was entrusted with maintaining and developing these contacts which were the precursors to the SALT negotiations. Both he and Gromyko developed a keen personal interest in the negotiations, despite grave misgivings and mistrust by other members of the leadership.[5] Although not so apparent at this point, the issue of whether to negotiate with the United States at the same time that the Russians were engaging "U.S. imperialism" directly in Vietnam and indirectly in Czechoslovakia became intricately intertwined with the Soviet handling of the Prague Spring and also very possibly with continued attempts within the Politburo to discredit Kosygin and his policies. George Breslauer has cogently detailed the rivalry between Brezhnev and Kosygin over domestic policy, which was particularly acute during 1968.[6] This domestic rivalry was certainly paralleled in foreign policy, but in the latter area there had not yet emerged within the leadership a clear split be-

[5] See John Newhouse, *Cold Dawn, The Story of SALT.*
[6] George W. Breslauer, *Khrushchev and Brezhnev as Leaders.*

tween hard-liners and soft-liners, or hawks and doves. There were crosscurrents and cleavages but few, if any, cohesive or dominant factions, although the marked isolation of Kosygin was so acute as to serve almost as a public signal of his political decline. Even at this stage, Kosygin had very few allies.

Yuri Andropov, the head of the KGB, although probably not a major figure in the inner decision-making circle, may have shared some of Kosygin's views. He made no speeches during the pre-crisis period; his last had marked the occasion of the fiftieth anniversary of the founding of Soviet intelligence services at the end of December 1967.[7] His comments at that time, however, were not without significance for the debate taking place during the pre-crisis period. He maintained that imperialism, rather than becoming more aggressive, had lost its "previous position of dominance." He emphasized neither the military threat nor the threat of imperialist subversion; the international situation was "complex," he said, and Soviet success demanded a "persistent struggle on all fronts—economic, political, and ideological." He did point out that Mao's "splitting tactics" worked to the advantage of imperialism, but he did not go so far as to back Suslov's call for an international Communist conference. Two statements, however, revealed him as particularly sensitive to changes in Eastern Europe. First, he referred to the importance of strong ties between the KGB and fraternal intelligence services, who together could deliver a "rebuff to enemy intrigues." Second, he made the peculiarly geopolitical observation that the Soviet Union's own border security was immeasurably enhanced by the contiguity of the other socialist states— essentially a restatement of the notion that Eastern Europe serves as a buffer zone for the USSR. It would be very difficult on this basis to conclude that Andropov had a particular view on Czechoslovakia, but his rather mild formulations on the international system would not have put him among those who feared either an increase in American aggressiveness or a revival of neo-Fascism in West Germany. If anything, Andropov's reference to the need for struggle on the economic front—a rather unusual statement for the head of the KGB—might have placed him as a liberal, although his emphasis on security links with Eastern Europe would have inclined him to be cautious about the negative political repercus-

[7] *Pravda*, December 21, 1967.

sions of any economic reform. One should remember that although Andropov was currently head of the KGB, he had from 1962 to 1967 served on the Central Committee as secretary in charge of the Department for Liaison with Ruling Workers' and Communist Parties. In that position, he had been considered a progressive counterweight to Suslov and was thought to have reported favorably on the initial calls for reform in both Czechoslovakia and Hungary. As the former ambassador to Budapest, he had a special interest in the Hungarian reforms introduced in January 1968 and apparently appreciated Kádár's "neither right nor left" approach to political management (see chapter 14 for a further assessment).

These differences of opinion between the leaders are subtle, but they gained significance as the crisis escalated. In the light of these differences, one can appreciate the extent to which the resolutions passed by the April Central Committee plenum really did represent at best a conglomerate and at worst an uneasy compromise between these varying images of the external environment. Attacks were made at the plenum on both dogmatism and revisionism, on both Western subversion and its high level of military preparation, on both U.S. imperialism and West German revanchism. The leadership had concluded that there was heightened threat from the external environment, but certainly there was not yet complete agreement that Czechoslovak "revisionism" and "imperialist subversion" were the primary sources.

CRISIS COMPONENTS

As was noted in Chapter 1, the pre-crisis period is distinguished from the preceding non-crisis period by a conspicuous increase in perceived threat on the part of decision makers triggered by an event or cluster of events. Events surrounding the dismissal of Novotný from his post of first secretary and the first tentative attempts at reform by the new Dubček leadership in January and February may be considered the prelude to crisis. But it was not until the worrying information from Prague accumulated sufficiently to require convening of the multilateral Dresden conference that the pre-crisis period really began.

The threat to values was diffuse, yet specific events did represent a particular threat. The prospect of cadre selection proceeding in Prague without Moscow's direct approval represented a clear-cut challenge to Soviet control. Details of the CPCz Action Program and criticisms in the Czechoslovak press of the past twenty years of Communist rule in the ČSSR threatened the legitimacy of all Soviet-style systems. And Prague's procrastination on the issue of Warsaw Pact maneuvers presented the worrying prospect of another Rumanian-style defection, this time from the very heart of the pact's central front and thus constituting a conspicuous threat to the unity of the socialist camp and to the security of the Soviet Union itself. Except for Grishin's comments about "military aid," there is no real indication that the Soviet leadership had as yet decided that the Czechoslovak reform movement must be stopped, even if by military means. Indeed as late as the beginning of May, the Soviet leaders subsequently claimed, there was still "understanding both for the objective complexity of the situation and for the complexity of the position of the CPCz leadership itself" which prompted them "to abstain from making any public appraisals and statements" about Czechoslovakia that might exacerbate relations between Moscow and Prague even further.[8]

COPING MECHANISMS

Our model of crisis behavior seeks to examine the extent to which a crisis situation affects the way decisions are made. It examines the impact of the crisis on the various functions performed in the course of arriving at decisions: information processing, the pattern of consultation, the structure of decisional forums, and the consideration of alternatives.

Looking first at information processing, it is certainly possible that the perceived complexity of the international situation and the diffuseness of threat perception affected the cognitive performance of Soviet decision makers by leading them to process and interpret information about Czechoslovakia in different ways. But on the whole, natural differences in outlook and functional responsibilities within the leadership would predispose individual leaders to process information diversely, and at this stage of the crisis, there is no clear-cut indication that crisis-induced stress was affecting cognitive performance.

As for the effect of crisis on the perceived need and consequent quest for information, certainly the communiqué of the Dresden meeting admitted that one main purpose of the conference was to

---

[8] *Pravda*, August 22, 1968.

obtain information about Czechoslovakia.[9] The growing number of purges of conservatives from within the Czechoslovak security services and party *apparat* was depriving Moscow of its usual information sources about the highest levels of the leadership. This led the Soviets to increased use of alternative sources, especially the Soviet embassy in Prague, whose ambassador opened up informal communication channels with leading conservatives, many of whose political careers were being threatened.

It is difficult to determine how a crisis affects the receptivity and size of the information-processing group because little is known about who receives and processes information on Czechoslovakia during non-crisis periods. Yet it is interesting that only at the end of the pre-crisis period, at the bilateral Moscow meeting of Soviet and Czechoslovak leaders, is any mention made of Brezhnev reciting excerpts from the Czechoslovak press verbatim from press clippings. This was to be a feature of several later meetings as well and suggests that by the beginning of May crisis escalation had the effect of increasing the amount of raw data reaching the top leadership.

In terms of the second coping mechanism, the pattern of consultation, two groups seem to have been especially important from an early stage. The first was the Central Committee. It is important to note that pressure for convening the Central Committee plenum at the beginning of April came from within the *apparat* itself, particularly from party ideologues anxious to achieve a firmer policy primarily toward dissent at home but also toward revisionism abroad. This group was supported by the second major consultative group, the East European leaders. The East German and Polish leaderships, more fearful of the effects of the spillover from the Prague Spring than the Soviets were at the outset, did not wait to be consulted; by all accounts they imposed their views on Moscow and advocated a harder line toward Czechoslovakia from March onward. Neither the Central Committee nor the East European leaders could be classified as part of the decisional forum in the pre-crisis period, but their functions nevertheless extended well beyond mere passive consultation. From the beginning they acted as policy advocates, constituted pressure groups, and served as allies in the slow process of consensus-building that began in the pre-crisis period, but really only gained momentum later on. Neither the Central Committee *apparat* nor the East European lead-

[9] *Pravda*, March 25, 1968.

ers represented a unified group; there were crosscurrents of opinion in both groups. It is interesting, however, that in both cases hard-line opinion was apparently ascendant from the beginning, even before the Prague Spring became the overriding preoccupation of the Soviet leadership.

As to decisional forums, information here is very scant but several conclusions can be drawn:

1. Authority for all strategic or policy decisions rested with the Politburo. During the pre-crisis period, only two other formal organizations were involved in decision making, and both made only tactical or implementing decisions. The Central Committee formally took decisions 6 and 7 at their plenum, but the strategic decision to call the plenum at all was made at a higher level. Also, the choice of speakers and the tone of the resolutions would have been decided at the top. Similarly, military pressure to hold maneuvers as represented in decision 9 was a continuation of past policy, not a new departure.

2. The Politburo did delegate full authority to a subgroup, its negotiating team at Dresden. The Soviet team did, after all, consist of Brezhnev, Kosygin, Kirilenko, Shelest, Baibakov, and Rusakov; and evidence suggests that negotiations were far from pro forma. Furthermore, the subgroup did not seek, or at least did not obtain, post hoc approval of the results of the Dresden meeting from the full Politburo, although this was eventually forthcoming from the Central Committee plenum.

3. A subgroup of the Politburo did appear to act either in the name of the Politburo or as a purely ad hoc group. Because it is not known what constitutes a quorum for a Politburo meeting, it is impossible to determine whether those decisions (numbers 5 and 8) taken while important Politburo members were absent from Moscow were taken in the name of the Politburo or on a purely informal basis. What does seem clear is that even at this stage, the decisional unit was not particularly cohesive. Indeed, the pressure to call a Central Committee plenum and to revise the set of principles governing inter-Communist relations appears to have come not from a united Politburo but from an ad hoc group acting in league with influential elements in the party Secretariat and Central Committee *apparat*.

The final point of inquiry is the effect of escalating stress in the search for and range of alternatives. The behavior of the Soviet leaders at the various negotiations with their Czechoslovak counterparts indicates that Moscow considered the range of alternatives available to be great, including dialogue and persuasion, economic assistance, minatory sanctions, and diplomacy. By the end of the pre-crisis period, at least some of the Soviet leaders also felt that "military aid" was a possible alternative for dealing with the threats imposed by the Prague Spring, but this argument was not resolved until the crisis period.

PART THREE

The Crisis
Period

CHAPTER SIX

Phase One:
May 5–June 6

MOSCOW CONSIDERS THE MILITARY OPTION

In Brecher's definition, the crisis period is differentiated from the pre-crisis period by several key factors.[1] First, there must be a measurably sharp rise in the salience of time. Of equal importance, the increased perception of threat is such that the decision makers widen their search for alternatives. And for the first time the possibility of involvement in military hostilities becomes a high probability by active consideration of this option.

In Czechoslovakia, calls for the early convocation of an Extraordinary Fourteenth Party Congress to institutionalize the reform movement and carry out cadre changes increased throughout May, making it clear in Moscow that the time available for bringing the negative aspects of the Prague Spring under control was clearly limited.[2] The CPCz leadership's decision at the end of May to convoke the congress on September 9 established a finite time for Soviet response. Also, in accord with Brecher's definition, there is good evidence to suggest that during May four separate but related military decisions were made that increased the probability of involvement in military hostilities. Details will be presented later in the chapter, but to summarize briefly, Soviet leaders decided

a. to hold extensive and prolonged Warsaw Pact maneuvers in Czechoslovakia beginning in June;

[1] Michael Brecher, "Towards a Theory of International Crisis Behavior," pp. 55–58.
[2] *Pravda*, April 30, 1968, published a lengthy article on the party conferences in Czechoslovakia noting that "at some conferences demands were heard for the convention this year of an extraordinary congress."

   b. to press as an urgent matter for the permanent stationing of Soviet troops on Czechoslovakia's western frontier;

   c. to use military maneuvers and the presence of Soviet troops as minatory diplomacy to deter anti-Soviet behavior and to support conservative elements in their attempts to stage a comeback;

   d. to prepare for an invasion should all other means fail.

According to a variety of persuasive sources, military options were first considered a viable alternative in May. Brezhnev is credited with saying, during the postinvasion Moscow negotiations, that in May the Politburo first decided that military intervention might become necessary.[3] Officials at the U.S. Departments of State and Defense and in the British and West German Foreign Ministries all concluded independently that military preparations for the ultimate invasion began in May, and indeed even in early May.[4] There also were several reports that party cadres throughout Poland, East Germany, and Bulgaria had been informed in May that, in the words of the Polish brief, "real" Communists in Prague "may need our help."[5] A leaked East German memorandum was

---

   [3] Zdeněk Mlynář, *Nachtfrost*, p. 206.

   [4] According to Eugene V. Rostow, under secretary of state in the Johnson administration, because the Central Asian troops used in the invasion required four months for complete mobilization, the plans for invasion must have been initiated by early May at the latest (see G. R. Urban, "The Invasion of Czechoslovakia, 1968," p. 110). The U.S. Department of Defense also considered the likelihood of Soviet invasion to have increased in May. Alain C. Enthoven, the assistant secretary of defense for systems analysis, prepared an 11-page memorandum in May which concluded that a Soviet invasion of Czechoslovakia would not upset the balance of power in Central Europe: Enthoven concluded that "Soviet forces are being maintained in a state of increased alert and they have deployed several additional divisions in Eastern Europe. On the other hand, the fact that the Czech forces are less reliable and that the Warsaw Pact must neutralize these forces as well as the Czech population reduces the threat" to NATO of an invasion. The memo was subsequently published in the NATO newsheet, *Atlantic News*, No. 83 (October 31, 1968), and referred to in the next two issues. In Germany, the intelligence service chief, General Gerhard Wessel, angrily claimed after the invasion that he had warned Bonn government leaders during May that "non-Czech Warsaw Pact troops were being trained and earmarked for the invasion" (see *The Sunday Times*, August 25, 1968). Sir William Hayter, British ambassador to Moscow, also stated that Soviet contingency planning and military preparations began in May (see Sir William Hayter, *Russia and the World*, p. 37.

   [5] *New York Times*, May 12, 1968, and *Frankfurter Allgemeine Zeitung*, May 13, 1968. Moreover, three Polish papers—the mass circulation *Życie Warszawy*, the army newspaper, *Żolnierz Wolności*, and a Communist youth paper, *Szlander Mlodych*—carried articles on May 4, 1968, by the Prague correspondent of PAP (The Polish Workers' Agency press service) criticizing the emergence of "neutralist and anti-Soviet tendencies" in Czechoslovakia. The articles spoke of attempts "to introduce a 'dictatorship of the intelligentsia' and to minimize the influence of the working class" in Czechoslovakia and asserted that some members

even more explicit: the Dubček leadership, it claimed, "is guilty of treason against its allies," and as such "the provisions of the Warsaw Pact make possible an intervention which would be in keeping with the interests of the socialist countries." Warning its party workers that such an intervention would also involve the use of East German troops, the memo stated: "However, in the event of an intervention, which might include military intervention, collective measures will have to be taken."[6] A similar circular was reported on May 5–6 to have been read at party meetings in Bulgaria.[7]

It is not known whether similar information bulletins were distributed to party cadres in the USSR, although a secret U.S. Department of State telegram to its embassies in Europe revealed that Soviet diplomats at the UN and elsewhere were circulating stories that the Soviet Union had the moral and legal right to intervene militarily in Czechoslovakia if an antisocialist or bourgeois government were to be established there.[8] All these reports strongly support the argument that the decision to begin invasion preparations was taken in early May as part of a more active bloc strategy to explore the widest number of alternatives to bring Czechoslovakia into line.

It may be impossible to isolate the precise day on which this decision was taken, and there is not much direct evidence pointing to a particular day. Indeed, the transition from the pre-crisis to the crisis period may not be a result of a specific event or events bringing on a sudden increase in threat perception. For a decision viewed by the analyst as marking a qualitative jump in the escalation of the crisis sufficient to distinguish between a pre-crisis and a crisis period may not be perceived by the decision makers in the same light. What the analyst considers a qualitative escalation, the

---

of the Central Committee of the Czechoslovak Communist party were apprehensive that recent developments might "push Czechoslovakia off the path of socialist development." In reply, three Czechoslovak writers commented in *Práce* on May 8, 1968, that the Polish leaders should ask themselves "whether the demonstrations of Polish university students are not rooted in dissatisfaction with the state of society, as was the case in Czechoslovakia."

[6] *Literární listy*, May 30, 1968; and Francois Fejtö, "Moscow and its Allies," p. 36. At a press conference on May 30, the Czechoslovak foreign minister denied any reports that the GDR leadership was preparing its cadres for invasion (*Financial Times*, June 1, 1968). No supporting denial was issued, however, in East Germany.

[7] Michel Tatu, *Le Monde*, May 5–6, 1968.

[8] U.S. Department of State, *Telegram No. 164394*, May 15, 1968. Also see *The Sunday Times*, May 12, 1968.

decision maker may consider an incremental escalation. And this possibility is enhanced if the management of the crisis is inherently cautious, with escalation achieved only gradually and against considerable opposition. In such circumstances, the chances of a major decision being blurred are considerably enhanced.

Such was the Soviet case, and it is likely that the various splits and debates in the Politburo decreased the clarity of decisions and simultaneously increased the scope of interpretation for any particular decision. Although it is probable, therefore, that the decisions marking the beginning of the crisis period and facilitating the invasion were taken in early May, it is possible that the decision makers may not have seen it in those terms.

THE SUMMIT FAILURE ESCALATES THE CRISIS

Despite the gradual buildup of hard-line and even interventionist opinion, marked by the April Central Committee plenum and the speeches by Grishin, Brezhnev, and Yepishev at the end of April, it was the essential failure of the May 4 summit to resolve the dispute between the two sides that produced a clear shift in Soviet behavior. This was marked by a renewal of press polemics, increased bilateral and multilateral bloc negotiations, and a notable increase in the use of military displays of force against Czechoslovakia, as part of a general campaign of minatory diplomacy. This shift became noticeable immediately following the May 4 summit and signaled an important decision (*number 11*) made directly after the departure of the Czechoslovak delegation on May 5. U.S. State Department officials, after consultations with Jacob Beam, their ambassador in Prague, also concluded that on May 5 the Soviets had decided to pursue a policy of "decisive half-measures" and "a war of nerves" toward Czechoslovakia.[9] This decision apparently encompassed a renewal of press polemics, including an increase in Moscow radio Czech-language broadcasts, the use of military maneuvers near the Czechoslovak border, increased contacts with Czechoslovak and bloc leaders to gauge opinion and gather information, and finally the approval of contingency plans for a possible invasion.

The evidence strongly suggests the decision to prepare for in-

---

[9] *New York Times*, May 12, 1968, and May 27, 1968. Also the author's interview with former U.S. ambassador to Czechoslovakia, Jacob Beam, on November 16, 1979.

vasion was indeed taken in early May. Yet because of the tenuous balance of forces within the Politburo, the decision was probably couched in terms of both increasing the number of alternatives available for dealing with the crisis and ensuring that the Soviet Union was prepared for any eventuality, including a Hungarian-style uprising or a military move by NATO states to take advantage of events in Prague. It was the very uncertainty and complexity of the situation that may have convinced the more recalcitrant Soviet leaders that the development of military contingencies would not in itself escalate the crisis but rather enable the Soviets to respond to any eventuality more effectively.

The Czechoslovak foreign minister, Jiří Hájek, flew to Moscow for urgent consultations with Gromyko and Kosygin on May 6, only one day after the departure of Dubček's delegation from the Soviet capital. In his report to the National Assembly's Foreign Affairs Committee, Hájek stated that measures to increase direct contacts between the two ministries had been discussed and that Gromyko also had considered it necessary "to warn me about some disturbing manifestations in the Czechoslovak press and to explain how the Soviet government understood this."[10] Sources claimed the Soviets sought Prague's renewed commitment not to establish diplomatic relations with either West Germany or Israel.[11] Soviet reportage of Hájek's talks with Kosygin omitted any reference to the visit having taken place in a "cordial atmosphere."[12]

Also on May 6, the new Czechoslovak ambassador to Moscow, the former CPCz Central Committee secretary Vladimír Koucký, presented his credentials at the Kremlin. In the course of the "welcoming" ceremony, Nikolai Podgorny, in his capacity as head of state (formally the chairman of the Praesidium of the Supreme Soviet), took the unusual step of wishing Czechoslovakia success "in the struggle against the intrigues of circles hostile to the course of progress and socialism." He reassured the new ambassador that "our people's socialist gains are reliably guaranteed against the encroachments of imperialism by the power of the indestructible

[10] Prague Radio, May 16, 1968, EE/2773/C1/1. Prague Radio, May 6, 1968, EE/2763/i, in announcing the "short friendship visit" stated that Hájek had gone to Moscow for "a wide exchange of opinion." Despite the statement that the invitation had been extended shortly after the new government had been formed in April, the announcement of his trip was not made until he was already in Moscow.

[11] *International Herald Tribune*, May 7, 1968.

[12] RFE, *East Europe, Polish Situation Report*, May 9, 1968.

military alliance among the fraternal socialist countries joined by the Warsaw Pact."[13]

This unmistakably hard-line rhetoric was accompanied by an end to Soviet silence over Czechoslovak claims of Russian complicity in the 1948 death of Jan Masaryk. On May 7 TASS denounced these claims as "lies from start to finish."[14] On the same day, *Literaturnaya gazeta* published an attack on Jan Procházka, one of the leaders of the Czechoslovak Writers' Union, calling him a "bourgeois nationalist."[15]

In the midst of this period of increased tension, speeches were being delivered by Soviet and bloc leaders marking the 150th anniversary of Marx's death. Pel'she's speech, discussed previously, was delivered at the beginning of May; it was a rather unoriginal defense of Marxist orthodoxy. Suslov's speech, examined in greater detail in Chapter 11, was almost entirely devoted to an attack on Chinese dogmatism and Mao's "splitting tactics." Nowhere did he mention Czechoslovakia or even revisionism, much less attack it. His whole speech was directed entirely against the Chinese and showed Suslov's own continuing predisposition to concentrate on forming a united front to isolate Peking.

If there were still Soviet leaders who failed to be convinced that the Prague Spring was "heretical," the speech on the same occasion by Čestmír Císař, a secretary of the CPCz, did much to change that. On the one anniversary most associated with pro forma declarations of ideological orthodoxy, Císař proclaimed that "every Marxist-Leninist party must have its own policy, which takes into account national conditions." Unity of Communist parties must be achieved "not on the basis of any monopoly in the interpretation of Marxism in contemporary conditions, or on the basis of the subordination of a part of the movement to another part of the movement, but only on the basis of the recognition of the right of every party to an autonomous policy and on the basis of equality of rights and fraternal cooperation of all countries."[16] That a leading figure of the CPCz should make this statement on such an occasion added to the immediate impact of Císař's article and ensured the Soviets' regarding it as "a repudiation of Leninism, a

[13] *Pravda*, May 7, 1968.
[14] *Pravda*, May 8, 1968.
[15] *Literaturnaya gazeta*, No. 19, May 18, 1968.
[16] *Rudé právo*, May 7, 1968.

negation of its international significance and a denial of the premise that Leninism is a guide to action in present day conditions."[17]

THE MOSCOW MEETING OF FIVE

A further impact of the Císař article was to contribute to the Soviet
decision (*number 12*), probably taken on May 7, to convene a summit of the "five" to consolidate positions and consider further measures. The last-minute timing of the decision is suggested by the
fact that the first announcement of the summit was on the actual
day of the meeting, May 8. Ordinary multilateral meetings, such
as those surrounding the planned International Communist Conference, were typically publicized in advance. The Czechs themselves learned of the meeting only at the last minute; and since the
East Germans and Poles had been pressing for an immediate summit, once the Soviets themselves had decided to hold one, Ulbricht
and Gomułka apparently supported immediate convocation.

On May 8, the Soviets convened a meeting in Moscow with
party leaders from Poland, Hungary, Bulgaria, and East Germany.
This was to be the only multilateral meeting throughout the entire
crisis to which neither Czechoslovakia nor Rumania was invited
(the Prague leadership was invited to the July Warsaw meeting but
declined to attend it). When Foreign Minister Hájek inquired why
the number of participants at this meeting was limited to five, he
was officially told that the recent visit of the Czechoslovak delegation to Moscow "had rendered superfluous their participation in
these multilateral consultations."[18] Although only Gomułka, Kádár, Zhivkov, and Ulbricht represented their countries, the Soviet
delegation was larger, consisting of Brezhnev, Kosygin, Podgorny,
and Katushev.

The terse communiqué issued after the meeting spoke of an
"exchange of opinions on topical problems of the international situation and the world Communist and workers' movement."[19] A
Pravda editorial two days later substituted the term "urgent" for

[17] *Pravda*, August 22, 1968. Also the article by Konstantinov in *Pravda* on June 14, 1968,
directly answered Císař's speech. The piece by V. Stepanov in *Izvestia* on May 11, 1968,
while not referring to Císař by name, openly refuted the notion that on the question of the
basic principles of party rule, there could be multiple interpretations based on national
conditions.
[18] Jiří Hájek, *Dix ans après*, p. 81.
[19] *Pravda*, May 9, 1968.

"topical" and described the meeting as "a continuation of development of a number of important joint measures . . . to solve tasks of further unity in the international Communist movement and of the steady political, economic, and defense consolidation of the socialist commonwealth."[20] Czechoslovakia's very absence appeared to confirm the numerous reports that the Prague Spring was the major subject of discussion.[21] The failure of the communiqué to mention a "unanimity of views," referring instead to a mere "exchange of opinions," points to a substantive inability to reach agreement.

The Polish and East German leaderships are said to have strongly pressed the Soviets to convene the summit, whereas Kádár was said to have attended only with "strong reservations."[22] Ulbricht was reported by Czechoslovak sources to have repeated the demand that Soviet troops be stationed permanently in Czechoslovakia.[23] These measures and other sanctions, including according to some reports military intervention, were debated by the five in Moscow, apparently without conclusion.[24] Economic sanctions were discussed, but it was evidently felt that such measures would only serve to further increase Czechoslovakia's links with the West. Indeed, sources in Prague reported that the chances of securing a loan from the bloc actually may have increased after the summit, although clearly no loan would be proffered without political strings.[25]

Kádár undoubtedly played a pivotal role in supporting the re-

[20] *Pravda*, May 11, 1968.

[21] UPI, AFP, Reuters, Radio Zagreb, and Radio Bratislava, May 9, 1968; and Radio Prague, May 10, 1968.

[22] According to Hájek, *Dix ans après*, p. 82; and *Borba*, May 11, 1968.

[23] The first report that Ulbricht had demanded the stationing of troops in Czechoslovakia originated in Prague and appeared in the *International Herald Tribune*, May 7, 1968. The story that he also pressed for stationing at the summit and was supported by Gomułka was reported in the *New York Times*, May 19, 1968, by Tad Szulc quoting informed Czechoslovak sources and in Hanswilhelm Haefs, ed., *Die Ereignisse in der Tschechoslowakei*, pp. 109–110.

[24] Mlynář (*Nachtfrost*, p. 206) maintains that military intervention was discussed, with Gomułka and Ulbricht as its primary adherents. Adolf Müller (*Die Tschechoslowakei auf der Suche nach Sicherheit*, p. 265) similarly states that the summit marked the "beginning of honest preparation for the eventual armed intervention of Czechoslovakia, which in this meeting was apparently demanded by Ulbricht." Other reports reaching Washington suggested that the Soviets were under pressure to do something positive in Czechoslovakia because of their perceived weakness in responding fully to the American bombing of North Vietnam (*Christian Science Monitor*, May 11, 1968).

[25] *Práce*, May 13, 1968, in an article by Ervin Jiříček, their Moscow correspondent, quoting unofficial Soviet sources.

form movement. He was reliably reported to have opposed the imposition of any sanctions on Czechoslovakia, and indeed he apparently defended the basic trends of the Prague Spring and offered to act as a mediator to settle the growing dispute.[26] Clearly Hungary's own experiences in 1956 and Kádár's hope to enact his own New Economic Model served as the bases for his moderate attitude. Kádár is also said to have presented a report on the preparations for the International Communist Conference scheduled to begin on November 25, 1968, in Budapest. The importance of the conference running smoothly may also have contributed to Kádár's desire for moderation on the Czechoslovak issue.[27] Some reports also credit Bulgarian party leader Todor Zhivkov with having adopted a wait-and-see attitude on the question of military intervention.[28]

While most reports of the summit agree that there was no unity of views on the measures that should be taken, none of the sources report any open disagreement among the members of the Soviet delegation. That there were divisions within the leadership is suggested, however, by several factors. First, Podgorny's unusual outburst against Czechoslovakia two days before the meeting when receiving the credentials of the new Czechoslovak ambassador to Moscow singles him out as an activist favoring an escalation of tensions. Second, the disproportionately large size of the Soviet delegation compared with the single-leader representation of the other

[26] As reported in U.S. Department of State, *Telegram No. 164394*, May 15, 1968. Also reported by Yugoslav sources on Radio Zagreb, May 10, 1968, quoted in RFE, *Research, East Europe, Hungary*, May 15, 1968; and Tanyug, May 21, 1968, EE/2777/C/7. Hungarian sources released a similar report to the *Christian Science Monitor*, May 15, 1968, indicating that Kádár "resisted pressure tending toward a common anti-Czechoslovak platform or any kind of intimidation of Prague." This was confirmed by "an authoritative source close to the Foreign Ministry" in Budapest and leaked to the *New York Times*, May 26, 1968, and openly declared in the HSWP Central Committee statement reported in *Le Figaro* of June 22–23, 1968. Also, Czechoslovak television stated on June 13, 1968—the very day Dubček arrived in Budapest to begin a state visit—there had been more than "a grain of truth" in reports that Kádár had supported Czechoslovakia against the criticisms of Soviet, Polish, and East German leaders at the May 8 meeting (see RFE, *Hungarian Situation Report*, June 14, 1968). In an interview in November 1968, Kádár confirmed that at all the conferences Hungarian representatives had consistently supported the adoption of a "political solution" to the crisis and had "urged that the problems of Czechoslovakia's Communist Party could and should be solved by it, and that the problems of Czechoslovakian society could and should be solved by the society" (quoted in C. L. Sulzberger, *An Age of Mediocrity*, p. 477).

[27] *Rudé právo*, May 12, 1968, and Tanyug, April 22, 1968, both quoted in Valenta, "Soviet Foreign Policy Decision-Making and Bureaucratic Politics," p. 324.

[28] Zagreb Radio, quoting a dispatch from its Moscow correspondent, May 12, 1968, EE/2768/C1/1–2.

states suggests that no one Soviet leader could adequately represent the views of the entire Politburo. Third, the freedom with which East European leaders apparently expressed widely divergent policy proposals is itself a solid indication that the Soviets did not convene the summit to communicate a set of decisions on how the bloc would handle the crisis. Rather, it appears that the enclave was called for genuine consultation with bloc leaders in an effort not only to reassure Gomułka and Ulbricht that the Soviets were taking the crisis seriously, but also to establish the parameters within which the crisis would be handled, and possibly also to resolve the differences within the Soviet leadership itself.

From the reports of the meeting, the subsequent divergencies in the Soviet and bloc press, and the contradictory actions that marked Soviet behavior during May, it would seem that although both extremes—accepting the reform movement and mounting an immediate invasion—were ruled out, no single interpretation or united strategy emerged from the conference. As told by unofficial Soviet sources to Czechoslovak reporters in Moscow, "there was no unity of views on the developments in Czechoslovakia" at the May 8 meeting.[29] In an attempt to narrow the differences between the parties, Kádár and Ulbricht stayed on in Moscow for additional consultations after Gomułka and Zhivkov returned home. Kádár left for Budapest one day later, but Ulbricht remained in the USSR until the end of May. The TASS statement that he was staying there "on holiday as a guest of the CPSU Central Committee"[30] implied that some top party officials were not averse to seeing him remain in Moscow where his influence as the Warsaw Pact's most long-serving leader would be greatest.

In assessing the results of the summit, therefore, it appears that out of the disunity and indecision emerged a greater freedom of maneuver for contending views and approaches. This meant that continuing patient negotiation and accommodation with the Prague leaders would now be accompanied by the simultaneous use of press polemics, military maneuvers, political pressures, and minatory diplomacy aimed at supporting conservative elements in Prague. By introducing the possibility of military intervention at some later stage and by sanctioning low-level military pressures in the interim, the summit represented a continuation of the May 5

[29] *Práce*, May 13, 1968.
[30] *Pravda* and *Izvestia*, May 11, 1968.

decision (*number 11*) for measured escalation. Yet one important outcome of the summit was the decision (*number 13*) to welcome a greater role by the East European leaders in crisis management. The acceptance of Kádár's offer of mediation and the increased links between Polish and East German leaders on the one hand and Czechoslovak conservatives on the other represented a considerable increase in the size of decisional and consultative forums. The management of the crisis also became commensurately more difficult, since now each faction within the Politburo was supported not only by domestic constituencies but also by different East European allies. The Politburo no doubt considered these leaders to be fulfilling a consultative and implementing role, but some of those leaders—notably Ulbricht and Gomułka—were by all accounts playing their own games and were expecting to be considered equal members of the inner decisional forum in Moscow.

MILITARY PARTICIPATION

At the same time that East European leaders were making their views known in Moscow, a high-level Soviet military delegation arrived in Prague on a fact-finding tour. This visit initiated a period of very high military participation in crisis management. The delegation, ostensibly in the country to participate in the twenty-third anniversary celebrations of the liberation of Prague, was led by Marshal Konev and included Marshal Moskalenko and General Zhadov. They remained in Czechoslovakia until May 14, and in addition to delivering hard-line speeches at the celebration ceremonies, they visited military units, factories, and agricultural cooperatives in fifteen cities.[31] They also held talks on "problems of defense" with their Czechoslovak counterparts.[32] Konev's speech on May 9 was unswervingly hawkish, denouncing West German revanchism and promising that the USSR and its allies will "always firmly and reliably defend our socialist gains as well as our [sic] frontiers of the socialist camp." Having emphasized the readiness of the Soviet armed forces to protect not only the security of the bloc but also its socialist nature, he made his point even more explicit: "Vigilance is particularly necessary by the ČSSR, which is

---

[31] *Pravda*, May 15, 1968; ČTK in English, May 11 and 12, 1968, EE/2769/C1/6–7.

[32] Budapest Radio, May 11, 1968, in RFE, *Research, East Europe, Hungary*, May 15, 1968.

the bridgehead situated right next to the capitalist world." He concluded with a warning: "I can say outright that events cannot catch us unawares. The Soviet forces are always in complete combat readiness."[33] For anyone who failed to understand Konev's message, he repeated it in a speech to workers in Kladno, where he encouraged them to further strengthen their militant proletarian traditions and promised that "we shall permit no one to break the fraternal ties binding our people."[34]

The military delegation's fact-finding tour was intended primarily to assess the strength of popular support for the reform movement and to judge the likelihood of a conservative comeback. Visits to factories, militia units, and military barracks—the traditional bastions of conservatism—were designed both to gauge the response of working class elements to what the Soviets considered primarily an intelligentsia-based phenomenon and to encourage these elements to continue, in Konev's words, their militant proletarian traditions.

Yet Konev's voice was not the only one heard among the Soviet military. Marshal Moskalenko was reported by Prague radio and television on May 13 to have stated that the USSR would "not interfere in the internal affairs of Czechoslovakia." He was said to have spoken "very positively" about events in Czechoslovakia and to have denounced "various slanders" that were "trying to drive a wedge between the friendship of the Czechoslovak and Soviet nations." The USSR, he said, was ready to "do its utmost in strengthening friendship" and to provide "help in all that is needed." Significantly, the report was not carried by the Soviet media, and Moskalenko's speeches received none of the coverage that Konev's enjoyed.[35]

While the military delegation was in Prague, Soviet troops in Poland, East Germany, and the Ukraine began to move toward the Czechoslovak border. Western diplomats and tourists were prevented from traveling inside Poland,[36] and although the Czechoslovak news agency later stated that Prague officials had been

[33] Prague Radio, May 9, 1968, EE/2767/C/3.

[34] Moscow Radio, May 13, 1968, SU/2769/A2/1.

[35] U.S. Department of State, *Telegram No. 163375*, May 14, 1968; U.S. Department of State, *Telegram No. 164394*, May 15, 1968; and William F. Robinson, "Czechoslovakia and its Allies," p. 164.

[36] *International Herald Tribune, New York Times, Daily Telegraph,* and *The Guardian,* May 10, 1968; also Alan Levy, *Rowboat to Prague,* p. 205.

informed of these maneuvers,[37] it was in fact clear that the troop movements were part of the escalation of pressure on Prague. Western intelligence sources concluded that "the Czechs undoubtedly were not aware of the movement of large numbers of Soviet troops toward their border" and that the Soviets had stage-managed the maneuvers, leaking information about them deliberately, in order to put pressure on the Dubček government.[38] Prague Radio did in fact respond rather anxiously to the maneuvers, with one broadcaster pleading, "For God's sake, let us not have a . . . repetition of . . . 1956."[39] According to estimates, several thousand men at most were involved, mainly in headquarters units. In addition, in East Germany an estimated twelve tank and mechanized divisions of the Red Army and two East German divisions moved southeast toward the Czechoslovak border, taking up positions in the Erz Gebirge, an area that had never before been used for military maneuvers.[40] Once the troops were in position, they remained there even after the completion of the exercises, thus marking the end of the first stage of military preparations for the invasion.[41]

SOVIET DEBATES

The maneuvers and the activities of the military delegations were accompanied by an upsurge of polemics between forces for and against the Prague Spring. The Soviet press did not abound with articles praising the Prague Spring for its positive contribution to the creative development of Marxism-Leninism. The time for this had clearly passed, and articles that could be construed as supportive of Czechoslovakia were those that did not openly attack the reform movement or that expressed confidence in the ability of the CPCz leadership to solve its own problems. Similarly, articles that

[37] *New York Times*, May 11, 1968.

[38] U.S. Department of State, Director of Intelligence and Research, *Intelligence Note 591*, July 26, 1968; U.S. Department of State, *Telegram No. 164394*, May 15, 1968; U.S. Department of State, *Telegram No. 162651*, May 11, 1968; and Tad Szulc, *Czechoslovakia Since World War II*, p. 318.

[39] Radio Prague, May 9, 1968, EE/2767/C/4.

[40] According to General James H. Polk, at that time commander of NATO's Central Army Group, in "Reflections on the Czechoslovakian Invasion, 1968," p. 31; and *International Herald Tribune*, May 21, 1968.

[41] U.S. Department of State, *Telegram No. 166761*, May 18, 1968, and U.S. Department of State, Director of Intelligence and Research, *Intelligence Note 591*, July 26, 1968, confirmed that troops remained in place after the end of the maneuvers.

deflected criticism of Prague's "rightist revisionism" by centering attention instead on the equal or greater danger of Chinese "leftist dogmatism" could also be classified as indirectly supportive of the Prague Spring, insofar as it was considered by some to be the lesser of two evils.

Using these criteria, one can find a whole series of articles and statements favorably disposed or at least neutral toward the trend of events in Czechoslovakia. The Brezhnev-Kosygin-Podgorny triumvirate sent a very supportive telegram to the ČSSR government on the anniversary of Prague's liberation, expressing their "firm conviction that relations between the Soviet Union and socialist Czechoslovakia will be developed and strengthened for the welfare of the Soviet and Czechoslovak peoples and in the interests of socialism and communism."[42] In addition, articles by both Svoboda and Černík expounding views on the nature of the new course were printed in the Soviet press on May 9.[43] Also during May there was a fair amount of noneditorial reportage of events in Czechoslovakia, such as the party conferences and various delegation visits.[44] At the same time a number of articles reflected the line adopted by Suslov in his May speech attacking only leftist dogmatism.[45] Others, such as one by T. Kolesnichenko, proposed a strategy of "struggle against all deviations from Marxism-Leninism, and against nationalistic, dogmatist and revisionist distortions of its revolutionary principles."[46] And in *Kommunist*, the *World Marxist Review*, and *New Times*, articles appeared attacking Maoism as the greatest danger confronting the unity of the bloc, or singling out certain aspects of Šik's economic reform or the Action Program for serious analysis and support. These articles suggest that there was a considerable body of opinion in top party circles that did not regard the Prague events as totally negative and threatening.[47] This was

[42] *Pravda*, May 9, 1968.

[43] Černík, *Izvestia*, May 9, 1968; and Svoboda, *Pravda*, May 9, 1968.

[44] *Pravda*, May 8, May 15, May 25, 1968.

[45] Suslov, *Pravda*, May 6, 1968.

[46] *Pravda*, May 12, 1968.

[47] "O politicheskom kurse Mao Tsze-duna na mezhdunarodnoi arene," *Kommunist*, no. 8 (May 1968), pp. 104–06, complained that the strict application of Marxism-Leninism, ensuring proletarian hegemony, has been rejected in the Maoist model where the peasantry plays a decisive role. "This phenomenon complicates the development of the revolutionary process because the nonproletarian strata bring to it their own ideas. . . . Such ideas can, under certain conditions, deform proletarian ideology." The article warned that the Chinese case shows that proletarian internationalism must be upheld against nationalist sentiments or national particularism which now "represent the most serious danger for the Communist and

particularly true in intellectual circles. In May, a delegation of distinguished, and hardly dissident, Soviet writers visited Prague. In the course of discussions, K. Simonov described the reform movement as "a great contribution for world socialism," and Boris Polevoy, another member, added, "what is good for you is good for us."[48] Significantly, however, whereas these views were openly published in the Czechoslovak and Hungarian press, they were not reprinted in the Soviet Union.

This rather unusual state of affairs also applied to Foreign Minister Gromyko's interview with *L'Unità* and Prime Minister Kosygin's interview with *Magyar Hirlap*, neither of which received any coverage in the Soviet mass media.[49] In Kosygin's interview, which was actually given during a visit to Czechoslovakia, he issued a harsh denunciation of West German neo-Nazism, whose reactivation, he said, had come about with the connivance and encouragement of the government of the Federal Republic. At the same time, Kosygin made a specific reference to "positive tendencies in Europe" and also made the intriguing statement that the stand of the Soviet Union and the Hungarian People's Republic was uniform in the evaluation of every fundamental problem of international life. In light of Hungary's divergent evaluation of the Prague Spring at the May 8 Moscow summit, this statement aptly reflects Kosygin's own identification with the Hungarian position. Compared with the Kosygin interview, Gromyko's press conference with *L'Unità* displayed some interesting similarities and differences. He also condemned manifestations of neo-Nazism in West Germany, which he claimed were "a serious obstacle to the consolidation of peace and security in Europe." He focused his attention, however, very much on the National Democratic party as the embodiment of neo-

entire revolutionary movement." D. Volsky ("Where the Past Meets the Present," *New Times*, no. 12 [May 14, 1968]) publicly supported the views of Prague Professor Šnejdárek, who claimed that there were "realistic" forces in West Germany that should be supported. The *World Marxist Review* (vol. 2, no. 5 [May 1968]: pp. 84–90) also gave favorable coverage to the Czechoslovak Action Program.

[48] *Reportér*, May 8–15, 1968; and MTI, May 29, EE/2784/C/10, quoting *Magyar Hirlap*. The positive evaluation of Simonov and many other writers was confirmed in the author's interview with E. Goldstücker, October 24, 1977.

[49] Gromyko, *L'Unità*, May 12, 1968; Kosygin, *Magyar Hirlap*, May 19, 1968, EE/2775/A2/1. *Neues Deutschland* of May 20, 1968 and *Soviet News* (London) of May 21, 1968, published a shortened and distorted version of the interview, deleting all references to "positive tendencies in Europe" and the phrase that "the stand of the Soviet Union and the Hungarian Peoples Republic is uniform in the evaluation of every fundamental problem of international life."

Nazism. Although appearing to dismiss the possibility of a positive Soviet response to the new Eastern policy of the Kiesinger-Brandt government, Gromyko did in fact admit that a number of positive ideas had been put forward in Western Europe that would strengthen peace and security. He also laid down rather moderate conditions for the improvement of West German relations with the socialist bloc, including acceptance of European frontiers, renunciation of access to atomic weapons, the cessation of attacks from West Berlin, and recognition of the validity of the Monaco agreement. He did not demand for example, as even the Czechs had done, that West Germany renounce, *ab initio*, any territorial claims on lands now governed by socialist regimes. And, interestingly, neither Gromyko nor Kosygin made any reference to any of the recurrent themes that might have signaled their concern over events in Czechoslovakia—threats to the unity of the socialist bloc, the aggressive intentions of NATO, the subversive plans of imperialist circles, or Western responsibility for the resurgence of revisionist and nationalist tendencies within the socialist community.

Finally, the speech by V. V. Kuznetsov, first deputy foreign minister, to the United Nations on May 20, announcing his government's readiness "to reach an agreement on practical steps for the limitation and consequent reduction of the strategic means for delivering nuclear weaponry" did not receive the publicity in the Soviet press that this major breakthrough on SALT warranted.[50] All in all, therefore, the events in Czechoslovakia were increasingly being linked to the issue of greater East-West cooperation with the emerging hard-line consensus in the Politburo affecting both areas adversely.

In contrast to the constraints operating on those wishing to voice support of Czechoslovakia, no such problems were encountered in the publication of openly hostile, even provocative, attacks on the reform movement in general or on individual Czechoslovak leaders. The most outspoken of these was an article in *Sovetskaya Rossiya*, now increasingly identified as the bastion of hard-line sentiments. On May 14, it claimed that Czechoslovakia's first presi-

---

[50] John Newhouse, *Cold Dawn, The Story of SALT*, p. 103. In a May 21 address, undersecretary of state Eugene Rostow conveyed the administration's receptivity to Soviet overtures, indicating that the key to U.S. relations with the Communist world lay in the president's desire to "search for every possible agreement that might conceivably enlarge, no matter how slightly, or how slowly, the prospect for cooperation between the United States and the Soviet Union" (U.S. Department of State, *Bulletin*, June 10, 1968, pp. 741–49).

dent, Tomáš Masaryk, was an "imperialist hireling bent on destroy-
ing Bolshevik power" who had financed émigrés involved in a plot
to assassinate Lenin. The article concluded: "We would not be discussing this now if voices were not being raised in fraternal Czechoslovakia by those who deliberately or mistakenly advanced the
slogan 'Back to Masaryk!'"[51] It is interesting that Brezhnev subsequently apologized to a visiting ČSSR parliamentary delegation led
by Josef Smrkovský for this article and for other "extreme tendencies" that characterized Soviet behavior toward Prague during
May. Brezhnev claimed rather meekly that he "had never given instructions for anything to be done one way or the other."[52] Smrkovský added that the Soviet leaders "were not very pleased with the
article by Shiryamov on Tomáš Masaryk . . . [and] that certain consequences have been drawn so as to prevent any possible repetition of this kind of occurrence."[53] It is incredible that at the very
time the Soviets were complaining about the lack of press "discipline" in Prague, they were also claiming to be experiencing similar difficulties in keeping their own journalists in order. Such articles, however, could not have appeared in the Soviet press without
sponsorship at the highest levels,[54] and indeed despite Brezhnev's
statement that measures were taken to prevent a repetition, dia-
tribes against individual leaders continued to appear, particularly
in *Komsomolskaya pravda*, *Trud*, and *Literaturnaya gazeta*.[55]

A parallel series of articles was published in the Soviet press at
this time. These did not openly address events in Czechoslovakia

[51] *Sovetskaya Rossiya*, May 14, 1968.

[52] Report of the ČSSR parliamentary delegation visit, headed by Smrkovský, to the
USSR in June, written by Josef Zednik, deputy speaker of the National Assembly and released to the *New York Times*, June 18, 1968.

[53] ČTK, July 3, 1968, EE/2813/C/1–2.

[54] The claims against Masaryk that Brezhnev reportedly found so objectionable in May
were in fact repeated verbatim in the major unsigned *Pravda* editorial that appeared on
August 22, 1968, justifying the invasion: "After all, it is a fact that there has been a recent
revival of the cult of Masaryk, who was always a sworn enemy of the Communist movement
and was an instigator of the intervention against Soviet Russia. It is a strange development
when even some Communists in Czechoslovakia laud a bourgeois figure at whose instructions the Czechoslovak Communist Party was persecuted."

[55] *Komsomolskaya pravda*, May 11, 1968, attacked *Student* for promoting a students'
union independent of party control and printing articles "implacable in their obscurantism,"
including those of Ivan Sviták who "attacks Marxism, the Communist party and the dictatorship of the proletariat with almost maniacal bitterness." *Trud*, May 15, 1968, criticized
L. Sochor for his interpretation of Marxism and promotion of a pluralist society. *Literaturnaya gazeta*, no. 19 (May 8, 1968) and no. 20 (May 18, 1968), assailed Jan Procházka and
V. Havel for their antisocialist orientations.

but attempted to provide an ideological restatement of the fundamental principles of socialist construction and proletarian internationalism. A major *Pravda* editorial emphasized the "struggle on two fronts" as "one of the most important tasks of Marxist-Leninist parties." Relinquishing the leading role of the party could "jeopardize the gains of socialism," and this was claimed to be "the most important political lesson" of events not in Czechoslovakia, but in China. The Prague Spring was not named specifically in the article, but the following excerpt, with clear applicability to events there, shows a certain moderation as well as a much more well-defined ideological stance than had previously been evident:

> Discussion of the problems of the development of socialist democracy, criticism of its shortcomings and quests for the best ways of improving its effectiveness are profoundly positive phenomena. But all this is so only under the absolutely necessary condition that these quests are based on the principles of socialist democracy and do not encroach upon its fundamental principle—the leadership of the Communist party. He who forgets this necessarily takes a position of revisionism, breaks with Marxism and acts in the interests of the bourgeoisie against socialism.[56]

Accompanying these articles was an unusually large number of pieces on foreign policy and strategic themes, many of them written by military leaders. The basic trend represented was a hardening in the attitude toward the West and an almost universal condemnation of Bonn's policy of building bridges as, in the words of an *Izvestia* article, a "reactionary policy of the ruling groups of finance capital, a policy calculated to achieve the strategic aims of imperialism—the restoration of capitalism everywhere."[57] In general, therefore, the ideological tone of the polemic was still moderate, but the content of articles on Czechoslovakia was undoubtedly more hostile, with views favorable to Prague infrequent and muffled. Moreover, the Soviet press, and in particular the military press, reacted sharply to allegations that Moscow had been in touch

[56] *Pravda*, May 19, 1968. Also see *Pravda*, May 12, May 25, 1968; and *Izvestia*, May 11 and May 27, 1968, on the intelligentsia in society, imperialism's attempts to subvert socialism, and the essential role of the party as the vanguard of the proletariat.

[57] *Izvestia*, May 16, 1968. Also see *Pravda*, May 9, 1968, for Grechko; May 14, 1968, for Yakubovsky on the Warsaw Pact; May 18, 1968, denying Soviet-American collusion over Czechoslovakia; May 29, 1968, for condemnation of W. German emergency laws. *Krasnaya zvezda*, May 9, 1968, for Shtemenko; May 25, 1968, on the loyalty of the armed forces to Marxism-Leninism; and May 30, 1968, on social progress and the ideological struggle. *Trud*, May 9, 1968, also published an article by Marshal Moskalenko.

with high officials in Washington to ascertain American attitudes to the crisis.[58] Judging from the nature of the press campaign, Brezhnev's subsequent disavowal of its more extreme tendencies, and the inability of moderate leaders and intellectuals to get their views into print, it would appear that the hard-liners were on the offensive and had quite considerable support, particularly in the Central Committee departments responsible for information and propaganda.

EAST EUROPEAN ECHOES

The conservatives also had growing support in East Germany and Poland, where anti-Czechoslovak activity increased after the May 8 meeting. The East Germans printed an article on May 9, the day the maneuvers began, alleging the presence of American tanks and troops on Czechoslovak territory.[59] Prague responded that since it was well known that these tanks were in the country to make a film, this allegation was a clear provocation and required an apology. None was forthcoming, and indeed East German ambassador Florin protested against Czechoslovakia's anti-GDR press reporting.[60]

In Poland, an unsigned editorial appeared in *Trybuna ludu* on May 9 calling on Czechoslovak "comrades" to "forcibly silence" and "paralyze" antisocialist voices.[61] Two days later, Prime Minister

[58] *Krasnaya zvezda*, May 24, 1968. Also *Pravda*, May 18, 1968, alleged that the report of Soviet-American contacts on Czechoslovakia carried in *La Stampa* "belongs to the series of fabrications to which Western propaganda has resorted of late in the expectation of sowing distrust in the relations between the USSR and Czechoslovakia."

[59] *Berliner Zeitung*, May 9, 1968. The charge was repeated the following day in *Junge Welt*, *Neue Zeit*, and *National-Zeitung*. *Neues Deutschland* on May 9, 1968, reprinted *Literaturnaya gazeta*'s attack on Jan Procházka. On May 11, 1968, it criticized two Czech academics who had participated in a round-table discussion on West German radio. The next day it carried an article denouncing recent trends in Czechoslovak literature, and on May 24 its assistant editor wrote a major piece implicating West Germany as the instigator of the Prague Spring. Moreover, the East Germans at this time began to jam German language broadcasts from Prague (Melvin Croan, "Czechoslovakia, Ulbricht, and the German Problem," p. 3).

[60] *Berliner Zeitung*, May 11, 1968. They were particularly sensitive about allegations made in *Rudé právo* on May 3 that the GDR was deliberately provoking crises in Berlin to heighten tension in the region and make it more difficult for Czechoslovakia to pursue a reform program.

[61] Early in May, before the May 8 summit, Prague liberals had specifically criticized repression and anti-Semitism in Poland, and in a highly controversial gesture, Charles University offered teaching posts to two Polish intellectuals recently dismissed from Warsaw Uni-

Cyrankiewicz delivered a speech that left no doubt about Warsaw's view of events in Prague. He stated that "there exists in the socialist camp the superior raison d'être in the shape of common interests of all socialist countries. These interests demand the ability to harmonize the policy of every country and of every party with the interests of socialism as a whole." Cyrankiewicz made it crystal clear that his interest in preventing Prague from pursuing an independent policy was motivated not only out of devotion to abstract notions of proletarian internationalism: "It is also a dictate of the instinct of self-preservation, in order that we may not be grabbed by the throat one by one, in order that the weakest links shall not be picked out from our camp, and so that those links shall not be thrown at others."[62]

In a speech on May 16, during a signing of a new Polish-Hungarian Friendship Treaty, Gomułka too was indirectly critical of the Prague Spring. Claiming that ideological subversion and the weakening of socialist systems from within was now the "primary weapon" being used by imperialism, he maintained in a clear reference to Czechoslovakia that imperialism "frequently camouflages its subversive activity with the mask of 'improving' socialism." He labeled as counterrevolutionary those activities aimed at "the undermining and questioning of the leading role of the party, the reshaping of socialist democracy on the pattern of bourgeois democracy." Apart from calling for "increased vigilance" and the "heightening of the unity of the socialist states," Gomułka made no other policy prescriptions in public.[63]

In contrast, Kádár's speech on the same occasion, while also call-

---

versity. Polish officials naturally reacted strongly to these events, lodging an official protest and denying visas to Czech students wishing to visit Poland.

[62] Warsaw Radio, May 11, 1968, EE/2769/C2/7. On the same day, Polish television carried an interview with the deputy editor-in-chief of *Trybuna ludu*, Josef Barecky, who was willing to concede that Czechoslovakia had never undergone de-Stalinization, thereby "slowing down socialist construction and causing difficulties in human relations." Yet he unreservedly condemned certain specific aspects of the Prague spring, including the creation of a "bourgeois-like opposition party," the activities of "semilegal, antisocialist groups," and attacks on the leading role of the party, on party cadres, and on the state apparatus. Also efforts to reorient Czechoslovak foreign policy toward West Germany and Israel were singled out as "contrary to the unified solidarity of policy of the socialist countries" (RFE, *East, Europe, Polish Press Survey,* May 22, 1968).

[63] PAP, May 16, 1968, EE/2774/A2/1. Edward Goldstücker, in an interview with the author on October 24, 1977, claimed that during this visit, Gomułka had unsuccessfully tried to convince Kádár of the necessity of intervention. Goldstücker maintained that he had been told this by an assistant to Kádár.

ing for "vigilance, cohesion and an active stand of the forces of progress," made no specific reference to the situation in any Communist state and indicated neither active support nor denigration of the reform movement.[64] This air of neutrality was also shown by the Hungarian press. It is interesting, for example, that the official party paper, *Népszabadság*, did not even report Kádár's departure for the Moscow summit. Neither did it publish the text of the communiqué nor any of the major Soviet, Polish, or East German denunciations of Prague. As the Czechoslovak paper *Práce* correctly observed on May 14, "the Hungarian press does not publish any problematic articles which might provoke an undesirable atmosphere." Nor did they follow the lead of their Yugoslav, Rumanian, and Euro-Communist counterparts who were by now openly supporting the Prague Spring and the principle of noninterference.[65]

DELEGATIONS TO PRAGUE

The ten days following the May 8 summit, therefore, were marked by a high degree of tension surrounding the maneuvers near the Czechoslovak border, the activities of the Soviet military delegation, and the press polemics between supporters and detractors of the Prague Spring. The situation was not immediately improved by the simultaneous arrival in Czechoslovakia on May 17 of two

[64] MTI, May 16, 1968, EE/2774/A2/1.

[65] At the end of the official visit to Prague, on May 15, 1968, Marko Nikezic, the Yugoslav foreign minister, declared: "We are convinced that the Czech and Slovak peoples, their present government and the communist party leadership are able to look after their own problems and to find effective solutions to them" (ČTK, May 15, 1968, EE/2772/A2/1). In Rumania, at a reception for French president de Gaulle, Ceauşescu stated: "We firmly declare ourselves for the inalienable right of each people to decide its own fate, for every nation's free development, unhampered by any outside interference" (Agerpress, May 14, 1968, EE/2771/A1/1). Following Ceauşescu's visit to Yugoslavia at the end of May the two countries issued a communiqué openly supportive of the events in Prague: "the two sides attach particular importance to the consistent application of the principle of independent and equal rights, proletarian internationalism, observance of national particularities, and the creative development of socialist theory and practice. . . . The two sides resolutely support all the efforts aimed at the continuous democratic development of socialist society and underscore the exclusive right of each party to independently fashion its policy in building socialism in its own country" (Agerpress, June 1, 1968, EE/2786/A2/4). Luigi Longo, leader of the Italian Communists, declared at a press conference in Prague: "What is happening in Czechoslovakia today is an experiment which will also help certain socialist countries, and in particular the Communist parties of the capitalist countries, in the struggle to create a new society—young, open and modern" (*L'Unità*, May 8, 1968).

separate delegations: one, an assemblage of top military officers[66] led by Grechko, which arrived in Prague to full honors; the other, a "delegation" of one, consisting solely of Prime Minister Kosygin, whose visit, it was announced, was for the purpose of taking the waters at Karlovy Vary.

It had been rumored since the beginning of May that Kosygin might take up the invitation of the ČSSR government to visit Prague,[67] and as late as May 14 Černík stated that the invitation was still open but that "no exact date has been set." He assumed that the visit would "not take place in the foreseeable future."[68] On May 15, Czechoslovak leaders were informed that Kosygin would in fact be taking up their invitation and would be arriving in under forty-eight hours.[69] Similarly the announcement of Grechko's visit was made only after his plane had actually landed.

The unannounced, unexpected, and sudden nature of both visits points to yet another last-minute decision in Moscow. Indeed certain evidence suggests that another Politburo compromise decision (*number 14*) was made following Konev's return on May 14 and prior to informing Prague of Kosygin's imminent visit on May 15. The core of the decision was to demand military maneuvers in Czechoslovakia and to increase contacts with conservative forces in Prague, making it clear that once troops were in place, they would be free to help "stabilize" the situation. A Western report quoting "Czechoslovak official sources" revealed on May 18 that "as late as last week Moscow still seriously considered military intervention on the assumption that conservative pro-Soviet Communists would succeed in forming a meaningful leadership group and request Soviet assistance."[70] A U.S. Department of State intelligence report in August concluded that the introduction of sizable numbers of troops into Czechoslovakia during late May and June had been done "in the hope that the troops might be able to assist conservative forces in the country to regain control—perhaps in a coup."[71]

[66] Consisting of General Alexei Yepishev, Marshal Pyotr Koshevoi, Colonel General Vasily Besyarin, Colonel General Nikolai Ogarkov, and others.

[67] Michel Tatu reported in *Le Monde* on May 4, 1968, that Kosygin had been invited to Prague and might visit there on May 9.

[68] Černík press conference, Radio Prague, May 14, 1968, EE/2772/C1/1–2. Also reported in the *New York Times* on May 15 and May 18, 1968.

[69] According to Zdeněk Mlynář, interviewed by the author, June 1, 1979.

[70] Tad Szulc, *New York Times*, May 19, 1968.

[71] U.S. Department of State, Director of Intelligence and Research, *Intelligence Note 634*, August 13, 1968.

Marshal Yakubovsky, in a major *Pravda* article appearing on May 14, made clear his own position that maneuvers and the development of further cooperation in the military sphere were an integral part of the struggle against imperialist subversion. He stated that "joint exercises play a particularly important role in Warsaw Treaty defense coordination. . . . The member states of the Warsaw Pact in the interests of the further strengthening of their defense capability have carried out, are carrying out and will continue to carry out exercises of their unified Armed Forces." He concluded by saying that "the struggle against imperialist ideological subversion, the exposure of anti-Marxism and various types of antisocialist elements . . . and the assignment to strengthen the fraternal friendship and cooperation of the peoples and armies of the socialist states have acquired primary significance at the present time."[72]

In contrast to those who pressed for maneuvers as a possible prelude to stationing troops, it appears that there were others in the Politburo who opposed any such escalation before other alternatives had been exhausted. There were also those who opposed supporting a conservative comeback because they felt it was still possible to work with Dubček and because they thought the results of the regional party conferences in Czechoslovakia demonstrated that the chance of a conservative comeback had severely diminished.[73] To encompass these two opposing views, it was apparently decided (a) to press for maneuvers and discuss the stationing of troops; (b) to determine whether the conservatives were likely to recoup their positions, with or without Soviet help; (c) to continue negotiations with the Dubček government in an effort to reach a political solution without crisis escalation; and (d) to send Grechko and Kosygin to Prague as representative of these two views. The reduced length and informal nature of Kosygin's visit suggests that whereas a political solution may still have been favored by the Politburo as a whole, accommodation with the Dubček leadership and acceptance of the reform movement was no longer seriously envisaged by the majority.[74]

The official purpose of Grechko's visit was "to become acquainted

[72] *Pravda*, May 14, 1968.

[73] Tad Szulc, *New York Times*, May 19, 1968; and Brezhnev's statements at the post-invasion Moscow negotiations, in Mlynář, *Nachtfrost*, pp. 206, 299.

[74] The view that Grechko and Kosygin went to Prague as representatives of two opposing Politburo factions is supported by Mlynář, *Nachtfrost*, p. 206; and in an *Observer Foreign News Service Report*, no. 25215, May 30, 1968. The view that the greater size and authority

with the new command of the Czechoslovak People's Army, to exchange experiences, and to discuss questions of interest to both
sides."[75] Negotiations with the Soviet military delegation centered
on combat preparedness, and the Soviets were reported to have
argued that the military efficiency of the Warsaw Pact's defenses
vis-à-vis the West was being adversely affected by the reform
movement.[76]

The military delegation gave Czechoslovak reporters the opportunity of questioning Marshal Yepishev about the May 5–6 *Le
Monde* report alleging he had pledged that the Soviet army would
respond to a call to save socialism in Czechoslovakia. He replied to
journalists that the story was "utterly stupid." Smrkovský later said
that he and Yepishev had "laughed a lot" about the reports and that
Yepishev had questioned the "intentions of those who spread such
rumors."[77]

Marshal Grechko also sought to reassure the Czechs on this
point. Emphasizing his concern with military matters alone and
distancing himself from the views of some of his other military colleagues, Grechko was quoted as saying "the solution of the internal
problems of the Czechoslovak People's Army is the internal affair of
Czechoslovakia."[78] This did not prevent him, apparently, from arguing that joint maneuvers should be held in Czechoslovakia and
that the permanent stationing of Soviet troops on that country's
western border was a necessary measure to counter NATO's development of flexible response strategy. Not only was the Czechoslovak army thought to be incapable of holding a defensive line in the
event of a massive NATO conventional attack, but also the Pact's
ability to launch any surprise offensive into West Germany would
be thwarted by the necessity of first moving Soviet troops into
position alongside Czechoslovak forward units. Moreover, the
absence of nuclear sharing arrangements in the pact meant that
Czechoslovakia, as the only WTO member contiguous to the West
that did not have Soviet troops on its territory, was also the weakest

of Grechko's delegation reflected the enhanced status of the hard-liners in the Politburo was
also expressed by Harry Schwartz, *Prague's 200 Days*, p. 152.

[75] *Keesings Contemporary Archives*, June 9–15, 1968, p. 22744.

[76] John Erickson, in V. V. Kusin, ed., *The Czechoslovak Reform Movement 1968*, p. 42.

[77] *L'Humanité*, May 21, 1968.

[78] *Rudé právo*, May 19, 1968. The Yugoslav press agency, Tanyug, credited Grechko with
saying that while the USSR would not interfere in Czechoslovak affairs, nevertheless anti-
Soviet statements in the media did not contribute to friendship (Tanyug, May 19, 1968,
EE/2775/C/2).

link in terms of nuclear preparedness. The only solution to this problem was either to supply the Czechoslovak army with tactical nuclear weapons on a two-key basis or to put nuclear missiles into Czechoslovakia entirely under Soviet control. Not surprisingly, the Soviet military preferred to maintain complete control, and evidently both Grechko and Kosygin pushed for this position in their separate negotiations.[79]

One of the strongest indications that troop stationing was discussed came when a spokesman for West German foreign minister Willy Brandt announced during the Grechko-Kosygin visits on May 22 that the Soviets were pressing for the stationing of 10,000 to 12,000 non-Czech troops on Czechoslovak soil.[80] Dzúr categorically denied that any such request had been made, a denial welcomed by a West German official spokesman, who noted however that "up to now, a denial has come only from Czechoslovakia."[81] As reports suggested at the time, troop stationing could have been discussed as one of the various solutions to current problems of combat preparedness; and if the Soviets did not formally request stationing, then Dzúr's statement would technically be true. Certainly, the Czechoslovaks were anxious to assure their own population that such a subject was not even on the agenda.[82] This may also explain why the Czechs were able to report that in the May 20 meeting between Dubček and Grechko "full unity" was achieved on all questions discussed.[83]

Both Grechko and Kosygin discussed the proposed maneuvers in their separate talks with Czechoslovak leaders. Grechko's visit was scheduled to end on May 21; and in a statement issued on that day, General Dzúr confirmed that the two sides had agreed to hold

[79] Lawrence L. Whetten, "Military Aspects of the Soviet Occupation of Czechoslovakia," p. 60; Prague Radio, May 21, 1968, in RFE, *Research, East Europe, Czechoslovakia,* May 22, 1968; Michel Tatu in *Le Monde,* May 23, 1968; David Floyd in *The Sunday Telegraph,* October 6, 1968.

[80] *Die Presse* (Vienna) May 21, 1968; *Daily Telegraph,* May 17, 1968; *The Guardian, The Times,* and *New York Times,* May 23, 1968; and also *Neues Deutschland,* May 23, 1968.

[81] ČTK, May 22, 1968, EE/2778/C/1, for Dzúr denial; and *International Herald Tribune,* May 25–26, 1968, for West German response.

[82] Michel Tatu, *Le Monde,* May 23, 1968; A. Šnejdárek also maintains that in May troop stationing was discussed within the Czechoslovak Ministry of Foreign Affairs as a possible solution to developments in the strategic field, but that this idea had been rejected because the Soviet ability to interfere in internal affairs would inevitably be increased. See Šnejdárek's remarks in Kusin, *Czechoslovak Reform Movement 1968,* p. 52. Also see Robinson, "Czechoslovakia," p. 165, and Thomas W. Wolfe, *Soviet Power in Europe, 1945–1970,* p. 171.

[83] *Morning Star* (London), May 21, 1968.

maneuvers on an unspecified date in the summer. Dzúr underlined Prague's continued reluctance by stating that "there would
be several fair-sized maneuvers, but no large-scale exercises with
big contingents of troops were being planned."[84] Following this
statement, the Soviet delegation suddenly announced that it was to
extend its visit one day to attend a Czechoslovak Military Council
session on "fighting efficiency and the build-up of the army."[85] The
official report issued the following day indicated that there were
still outstanding differences.[86]

At the council session Grechko raised the question of "concrete
measures" for the improvement of the Warsaw Pact political and
military command structure and the issue of maneuvers. Although
no communiqué was issued, the official report of the meeting
stated that "concrete measures were agreed upon for the further
strengthening of cooperation and friendship within the Warsaw
Treaty."[87] In fact, the two sides had apparently not agreed on the
Soviets' maximum objective in this field: the creation of a strengthened Political Consultative Committee to coordinate bloc foreign
policy.[88] They did apparently agree on measures to increase the
staff of the Warsaw Pact's permanent mission in Prague. This mission had suffered most from the defection of General Šejna, the
Czechoslovak liaison chief for the pact. The strengthening of this
mission was expected to increase the influence of Soviet military
officers such as General Zhadov, the first deputy chief inspector of
the Soviet Ministry of Defense and the deputy head of the WTO
mission. He was also known for his negative appraisal of the reform
movement.[89]

A further sign of disagreement is the terse language of the re-

[84] ČTK, May 21, 1968, EE/2777/C/1.
[85] Radio Bratislava, May 21, 1968, reported in RFE, *Research, East Europe, Czechoslovakia*, January 22, 1969.
[86] ČTK, May 22, 1968, EE/2778/C/1.
[87] ČTK, May 22, 1968, EE/2778/C/1; *Pravda*, May 23, 1968.
[88] *New York Times*, May 25, 1968.
[89] *Lidová democracie*, June 5, 1968, reprinted a *New York Times* article alleging that it
was Zhadov who had issued Šejna a diplomatic passport allowing him to leave the country.
This produced an official Soviet Foreign Ministry protest (*New York Times*, May 12, 1968).
Smrkovský confirmed, after his visit to the USSR in June, that the Soviets had been particularly worried about anti-Soviet reporting in the Czechoslovak media, including the "rumors
that a Soviet general helped Šejna in his flight to the United States" (*Rudé právo*, June 16,
1968). Zhadov, as early as February 1968, is also said to have remarked to a Czech officer in a
barracks in Leitmeritz: "Negative forces wish to remove socialism in Czechoslovakia. But
the Soviet army also controls the armies of the allied lands and will help" (quoted in Otto
von Pivka, *The Armies of Europe Today*, p. 90).

port: the Czechoslovaks had merely "informed" the Soviets "about the planned solution of the topical problems of the Army as it is suggested in the ministry's Action Program," and that the Soviet delegation in response had "informed" the Czechoslovak side about the Soviet "armed forces build-up, this year's exercises and the planned measures in both military training and the sphere of political work."[90]

It was only on May 24, after Grechko had left but while Kosygin was still in Czechoslovakia, that the ČSSR minister of national defense announced: "Joint command-staff exercises will be held in June on the territories of Czechoslovakia and Poland. The staffs of all services of the forces of the Warsaw Treaty countries will take part in the joint exercises. The aim is to test cooperation and command under conditions of present-day operations and to improve the preparedness of the troops and staffs."[91]

Although the timing of Kosygin's visit came as a surprise, all reports suggest he was well-received and that negotiations were, in Foreign Minister Hájek's terms, "rational and realistic."[92] The initial announcement that Prime Minister Kosygin, responding to the previous invitation of the ČSSR government, had arrived for a health cure at Karlovy Vary and for a "continuation of the exchange of views . . . on questions of interest to both sides" was made two hours after Czechoslovak leaders and Soviet Ambassador Chervonenko had gone to the airport to meet his plane.[93] On the following day, May 18, Dr. František Kouril, an official government spokesman, announced that after initial talks, Kosygin would be going for a ten-day cure to Karlovy Vary where talks on economic questions would continue. Kouril also announced that Kosygin would be giving a press conference at the end of his stay.[94] Late in the same day ČTK released a statement from "authorized Czechoslovak sources" that "the talks were developed at the initiative of both sides and a solution to a number of concrete economic questions arising from the traditional economic relations of the two countries and the current requirements of the Czechoslovak economy is being approached." Then, in a sentence widely interpreted as proof of Kosygin's pro-reform attitude, it was stated that "the discussion of

[90] ČTK, May 22, 1968, EE/2778/C/1.
[91] Prague Radio, May 24, 1968, EE/2780/C/1.
[92] Hájek, *Dix ans après*, p. 83.
[93] ČTK, May 17, 1968, EE/2774/C/1; *New York Times*, May 18, 1968.
[94] Prague Radio, May 18, 1968, EE/2775/C/1.

political problems also showed that the path of the further development of socialism upon which Czechoslovakia has embarked is meeting with understanding among Soviet leaders."[95] This impression was confirmed the following day by Josef Smrkovský in *Rudé právo*: "Gradually, although not everything is satisfactory, the CPCz is succeeding in overcoming fears or reservations about developments in Czechoslovakia which could and still can be observed among some of Czechoslovakia's traditional friends and allies. This has been borne out in several recent talks, with Luigi Longo, Nikezić, during the recent Moscow talks and—which is especially important—in the current friendly talks with Aleksei Kosygin."[96] It is interesting that neither of the two statements referred to Grechko's delegation as proof of improved understanding. Furthermore, Smrkovský's account is notable for its recognition of the disunity within the bloc over the interpretation of Czechoslovak events.

Kosygin himself did nothing to assuage this perception of him as basically sympathetic toward the reform movement. On May 19, he gave the interview to the Hungarian paper *Magyar Hirlap*, analyzed previously, in which he reported with "satisfaction" that "the stand of the Soviet Union and the Hungarian People's Republic is uniform in the evaluation of every fundamental problem of international life."[97] Kosygin's statement was widely reported in Czechoslovakia and interpreted in the context of Kádár's known championship of the reform movement at the May 8 bloc summit. During his stay at Karlovy Vary, Kosygin made a point of mixing with holiday crowds, allowing himself to be photographed with his granddaughter. He was also quoted as saying that "excellent conversations" were taking place between the two sides.[98] On May 22, during an appearance on Czechoslovak television, he stated that he personally regarded "the Czechs and Slovaks as our great friends" and that it was "very pleasant to take a rest among people who have the same opinions as I do." Kosygin added that these "are not just banal words. . . . After all, we have gone over a long path of struggle together and our parties are fighting on the same front."[99]

If the atmosphere of the talks was friendly, there is less spe-

[95] ČTK, Prague Radio, May 18, 1968, EE/2775/C/1.

[96] *Rudé právo*, May 19, 1968.

[97] *Magyar Hirlap*, May 19, 1968, reported by MTI, May 19, 1968, EE/2775/A2/1.

[98] *Le Monde*, May 23, 1968.

[99] Czechoslovak Television, May 22, 1968, from Robinson, "Czechoslovakia," p. 166 and Valenta, "Soviet Foreign Policy Decision-Making," p. 343.

cific information as to their agenda and structure. Smrkovský was quoted on May 21 as saying that the Soviet Union's main worry was that events in Czechoslovakia would "threaten the socialist order itself and violate the alliance of the Warsaw Treaty" and that the Kosygin talks were concerned less with general political problems and more with "concrete questions."[100] Kosygin held three sets of negotiations including his initial talks on the day of his arrival. On May 25 he held talks with Dubček, Černík, Smrkovský, and others at Karlovy Vary, and on the next day he went to Prague for an unscheduled visit with Svoboda. Although he had not attended the Soviet military negotiations, Ambassador Chervonenko was listed as present at all of Kosygin's talks with Czechoslovak leaders.

Economic matters figured prominently in the public announcements about the substance of the talks. The meeting held on the day of Kosygin's arrival, according to a ČTK statement, had dealt with "a number of concrete economic questions arising from traditional economic relations between the two countries and the current requirements of the Czechoslovak economy."[101] This was thought to refer to the long-standing request for a massive loan to revitalize the Czechoslovak economy. Ota Šik, who was present at the second meeting at Karlovy Vary, stated that economic matters were subservient to political considerations,[102] and indeed this would support the view expressed unofficially in Prague at the time that Kosygin had made it clear the USSR was in no hurry to grant such a loan.[103]

As for noneconomic issues, Kosygin apparently was instrumental in gaining Czechoslovak acquiescence to strictly limited staff exercises beginning in June. Smrkovský quotes Kosygin as saying that the Czechoslovak reforms were "dangerous for the Warsaw Pact" and that Czechoslovakia should accept the stationing of Warsaw Pact troops. After this proposal was rejected, Kosygin reportedly insisted that the Czechoslovaks strengthen security on the western borders, permit regular Warsaw Pact inspections of these arrangements, and agree to the holding of the pact's June maneuvers in Czechoslovakia.[104]

On the reform movement itself, Czechoslovak sources reported

[100] *Le Monde, L'Humanité*, May 21, 1968.

[101] Tad Szulc, *New York Times*, May 19, 1968.

[102] According to Valenta, "Soviet Foreign Policy Decision-Making," p. 345.

[103] Tad Szulc, *New York Times*, May 27, 1968.

[104] Quoted in Adolf Müller, *Die Tschechoslowakei*, p. 266; and Levy, *Rowboat to Prague*, p. 229.

Kosygin to be basically sympathetic but worried that forces of both the left and the right might take advantage of current instability. He urged the CPCz leadership to allow only Communists to fill key government positions, especially in the security services and urged them not to legalize any opposition groups. He is quoted by Ota Šik as warning that the situation was becoming dangerous: "Don't you see the developments in your country are playing into the hands of your enemies?"[105]

The pressures exerted on the Czechoslovak leadership by Kosygin and others throughout May certainly seem to have affected the results of the CPCz Praesidium meeting held on May 21–22, which rejected the formation of new political or quasi political groupings, including KAN, K 231, and the Social Democratic party. The Praesidium also discussed the final draft of the agenda for the forthcoming Central Committee plenum, and included in it not only questions of cadre changes and restrictions on political organizations but also the Šejna defection and the need for greater press censorship.[106] The plenum resolutions were to include a formulation attacking antisocialist and anti-Soviet tendencies, and as Smrkovský later said: "The fact is that the pressure from abroad, from the Soviet Union, also helped to get that formulation in."[107] While Kosygin was still in Czechoslovakia, the Dubček leadership signaled the seriousness of its intention to prevent any further erosion of the CPCz's position by sanctioning a Ministry of the Interior announcement on May 24: "Organized activity purporting to be that of a political party" would be considered illegal.[108]

Kosygin is reported to have discussed all of these matters, including the holding of an extraordinary party congress, with the Czechoslovak leadership. Pavel Tigrid maintains that in fact an agreement was reached insuring the CPCz's monopoly of power; the continuance of democratization; the convocation of an early congress; the suspension of Novotný from the party; the conduct of Warsaw Pact staff exercises; and the maintenance of Czechoslo-

---

[105] Quoted by Valenta, "Soviet Foreign Policy Decision-Making," p. 345. Also see Levy, *Rowboat to Prague*, p. 229.

[106] *International Herald Tribune, New York Times*, May 24, 1968. This Praesidium meeting is also referred to in Josef Smrkovský, *An Unfinished Conversation*, p. 13; Jiří Hronek, ed., *ČSSR: The Road to Democratic Socialism*, p. 78; and RFE, *Research, East Europe, Czechoslovakia*, January 22, 1969.

[107] Smrkovský, *An Unfinished Conversation*, p. 14.

[108] Quoted in Galia Golan, *Reform Rule in Czechoslovakia*, p. 163.

vakia's relations with the Warsaw Pact and CMEA.[109] Yugoslav sources stated that "Kosygin's talks hence . . . were of help to both sides and eliminated various misgivings."[110]

It is not known whether Kosygin was told specifically that the extraordinary congress was being planned for September. Certainly by the time Czechoslovak leaders met with Kosygin, there was general agreement in the Praesidium on an early convocation. It is less clear whether the CPCz Praesidium had actually set the date.[111] Yet there were good reasons why Dubček should have discussed convening an early congress with Kosygin. First, any Communist leadership still claiming to be allied to the USSR would at least have to inform the Soviet leadership before taking action on an issue of this magnitude. Second, many regarded the decision to call an early congress as an opportunity to stabilize the situation and reassert the controlling interest of the Dubček core against both extremes of the left and the right. In this way, some would argue, Dubček could have used the decision to call the congress as proof that he was taking firmer control. Thus *Pravda* of August 22 stated: "It was hoped that the Praesidium of the CPCz Central Committee would use the preparations for the 14th Extraordinary Party Congress, scheduled for September 9, to put an end to the defamation of cadres. But this did not happen." Václav Král, director of the Czechoslovak Institute for the History of the European Socialist Countries, in an account of the 1968 crisis published in the USSR, used phrases that slightly altered the *Pravda* version: "The May plenary meeting decided to convene, in September, an extraordinary congress of the party. This decision would have been

[109] Pavel Tigrid, quoted by H. Gordon Skilling, *Czechoslovakia's Interrupted Revolution*, p. 250.

[110] Tanyug, June 4, 1968, cited in Valenta, "Soviet Foreign Policy Decision-Making," p. 372.

[111] According to a speech made by Bil'ak in September 1969, after the May 4 Moscow conference, Dubček decided that an August plenum should be held (see Skilling, *Czechoslovakia's Interrupted Revolution*, p. 252 n. 98). According to Indra, the decision to hold the congress in August or September was made on May 25, in the second half of the day, at a meeting between Dubček, Bil'ak, Černík, Sádovský, and himself (*Pravda pobezhdaet*, p. 190). Yet this account is not entirely convincing since the Czech leaders were preoccupied with Kosygin until almost three o'clock and Bil'ak had attended a meeting with Shelest and Shcherbitsky in Uzhgorod on that day to celebrate Ukrainian-Czechoslovak Days of Culture. From there, Bil'ak was reported to have spent four days, from May 25 to 29, with Shelest in the Ukraine. Therefore, if the May 25 meeting took place, it is highly unlikely that Bil'ak was present. For Bil'ak's movements see U.S. Department of State, Director of Intelligence and Research, *Research Memorandum, RSE-127*, August 16, 1968.

justified if the healthy forces in the party took the preparation
for the congress into their own hands. But just the opposite occurred."[112] This is the attitude the Soviets and hard-liners came to
adopt. It is not at all clear that their immediate reaction to the
Czechoslovak decision was so measured, for irrespective of the Soviet calculation of the conservatives' ability to reassert control, the
decision to set the congress deadline for September 9 certainly increased the salience of time.

On May 24, Kosygin left Karlovy Vary and returned to Prague
for talks with President Svoboda. The next day he left for Moscow
following a lunch that Černík had hurriedly organized. It is not
known why Kosygin cut short his stay by two days, returning to the
USSR without giving his promised press conference and without
providing even an informal statement on the visit. That no communiqué was issued is understandable since the visit to Czechoslovakia was not a state occasion. This may also explain why no
mention was ever made of it in any of the official Soviet or Czechoslovak accounts of the period.

Kosygin's visit undoubtedly had improved relations by convincing the Dubček leadership that at least some Soviet leaders were
reacting to the Prague Spring "with understanding." In return for
Kosygin's pledge to support their case in Moscow, the Prague leaders conceded to requests for maneuvers and for restrictions in
opposition groupings. Perhaps because of Kosygin's image as a
dove, his arguments were instrumental in persuading the CPCz
Praesidium of the need to include in the resolutions for the forthcoming Central Committee plenum a formulation about combating
antisocialist tendencies. This recognition by Dubček and others
of the need to conduct a resolute "struggle on two fronts" set the
tone for the May CPCz Central Committee plenum and greatly
strengthened Kosygin's own argument that the Czech leadership
did in fact seek to rein in antisocialist elements and improve relations with Moscow.

Of the reasons for Kosygin's return, it has been suggested that
he left because of the failure of his mission to convince Dubček of
the need for immediate and resolute actions against the press, political demonstrations, and illegal political groups.[113] It is also possible that "he did not wish his presence to influence the Central

[112] Václav Král, Lessons of History, p. 97.
[113] New York Times, May 26, May 27, 1968; The Sunday Telegraph, October 6, 1968.

Committee session."[114] Some reports suggested that he may have been called back to Moscow[115] or that he decided to return early because of information he received about the increased activity of leaders not so favorably inclined toward Czechoslovakia. Whatever the real reason for his return, the contrast between the size and nature of the Grechko and Kosygin missions certainly indicates that the majority in the Politburo was negatively disposed toward the Prague Spring, an impression supported by the activities of leading Soviet conservatives during this same period.

MEETINGS WITH CZECHOSLOVAK CONSERVATIVES

In early May the Soviets had decided to assess whether the conservatives were capable of making a comeback in Czechoslovakia, with or without Soviet help. In accordance with this decision (*number 14*), the number of meetings with this group increased. Implementation of a more active role for Moscow's East European allies (*decision number 13*) was also evident during this period. On May 9, a meeting of Alois Indra, CPCz secretary; Edward Gierek, PUWP Politburo member and Silesian party first secretary; and Leonid Kulichenko, party secretary for Volgograd, took place on the Polish-Czechoslovak border. Kulichenko was later to receive the Czechoslovak parliamentary delegation led by Josef Smrkovský, and he was among those who cautioned Smrkovský against speaking so openly to Soviet audiences about the Prague Spring. Kulichenko also delivered a hard-line speech at the July CPSU Central Committee plenum. During the May 9 meeting on the border, which coincided with the southward movement of Soviet troops toward Czechoslovakia, Indra spoke at a rally honoring Czechoslovak-Polish friendship; he argued that despite efforts to combat "imperialist intrigues," the situation was becoming more dangerous. "Imperialism and its agents are trying to break the unity of the socialist countries. We stand for . . . increasing military strength within the Warsaw Pact organization."[116] Polish television reported with approval Indra's statement: "There can be no question of the creation of an opposition bourgeois party in Czecho-

[114] Josef Maxa, *Die Kontrollierte Revolution*, p. 136, as quoted in Valenta, "Soviet Foreign Policy Decision-Making," p. 350.
[115] *New York Times*, May 26, 1968.
[116] TASS report, May 9, 1968, SU/2766/C/3. A previous speech by Indra had also been favorably reported in *Pravda*, April 30, 1968.

slovakia, of leading the republic away from the road of socialist construction and alliance with the Soviet Union" and with other socialist countries. "Let us not forget," said Indra, "that we live in a world full of conflict and disquiet, that there are still forces which would like to carry out their revisionist program."[117] Gierek, for his party, condemned those forces in both Czechoslovakia and Poland that had attempted to weaken the leading role of the party. Yet, interestingly enough, he praised the resolve of the CPCz to "consolidate the unbreakable unity and friendships of the ČSSR with the USSR, the PPR and the other countries of our socialist community" and its internal efforts "to consolidate and enrich the achievements of your republic."[118] If one considers that this statement was made three days after the Polish government had taken the unusual step of formally protesting the Czechoslovak reporting of Polish developments, Gierek's failure to condemn the reform movement, particularly in the light of Indra's speech, might suggest his more moderate view of events in Prague.

An important aspect of this period in Czechoslovakia was the difference between Czech and Slovak attitudes on the reform movement. At both the popular and official levels, the Slovaks considered issues of regional autonomy and federalization to be more important than democratization. This plus the generally more conservative Slovak national tradition (clerical and populist in character) dampened the rise of the more extreme views current among Prague's intellectual circles. Moreover, it meant that Slovak leaders, like Husák, could gain in popularity by concentrating on the national question, without having to take a firm stand on democratization.[119] For this reason, efforts by the Soviet Union and her East European allies to assess the strength of conservative opinion in Czechoslovakia as a whole were concentrated to a considerable degree on Slovakia.

In mid-May, East Germany's ambassador to Prague, Peter Florin, spent a week consulting with various conservative leaders in Slovakia. Accompanying Florin was a GDR specialist in radio propaganda, Karl Eduard von Schnitzler, who joined in meetings with Barbírek and Bil'ak. The East Germans were undoubtedly instrumental in setting up the postinvasion Radio Vltava, which beamed

[117] RFE, *Polish Press Survey*, May 22, 1968.

[118] *Trybuna ludu*, May 10, 1968.

[119] For more on Czech-Slovak differences during this period see Skilling, *Czechoslovakia's Interrupted Revolution*, pp. 241–48.

pro-Soviet Czech broadcasts from East Germany, but it is not known whether this in particular was discussed by the Czechoslovak central leadership, who despatched President Svoboda to Bratislava on May 22 for a three-day visit aimed at dissuading the conservatives within the Slovak Central Committee from blocking liberal reform. Svoboda was followed at the end of May by Černík, Goldstücker, and others who also sought to win over Slovak support.[120]

On May 25, Shelest and Shcherbitsky met Bil'ak and Barbírek in the Slovak border town of Vysne Nemecke (Uzhgorod) at the beginning of a week of cultural exchanges between Czechoslovakia and the Ukraine.[121] Shcherbitsky delivered a speech on this occasion that was considered quite moderate: "We sincerely wish our Czechoslovak friends . . . new successes and victories in fulfilling the decisions of the Thirteenth Congress of the CPCz, in implementing the party line in the construction of a developed socialist society, in the struggle against all enemies of peace, progress and socialism." He made no mention of any threats to the leading role of the CPCz and thanked the Czechs and Slovaks for the positive role their partisan units had played in the liberation of Belorussia and the Ukraine after the war.[122] It was Shcherbitsky, the Brezhnev protégé, and not Shelest, who then went on to Slovakia for a further series of rallies and meetings in connection with these "days of Ukrainian culture."[123] It is not unlikely that Shcherbitsky was acting as an envoy for Brezhnev, providing him with a disinterested report about the strength of conservative opinion in the country and particularly in Slovakia.[124] It is interesting in this connection that Shcherbitsky, the Ukraine premier and CPSU Politburo candidate member, chose to head the delegation to Bratislava, while his subordinate, Peotr T. Tronko, deputy premier for the Ukraine, was sent to Prague.[125] This is a further indication of the level of activity taking place in Slovakia in the last two weeks of May.

Although Shcherbitsky led the Ukrainian delegation to Bratislava, Shelest was also active during this time. Bil'ak represented the Czechoslovaks in the parallel exchange in the Ukraine; thus he

[120] *New York Times*, May 23, 1968; Schwartz, *Prague's 200 Days*, pp. 154–55.

[121] Prague Radio, May 25, 1968, EE/2781/C/3.

[122] *Pravda Ukrainy*, May 26, 1968.

[123] Prague Radio, May 28, 1968, EE/2783/C/9.

[124] U.S. Department of State, Director of Intelligence and Research, *Research Memorandum, RSE-127*, August 16, 1968.

[125] Prague Radio, May 27, 1968, EE/2783/C/9.

was able to have a number of meetings with Shelest during his stay from May 25 to 29.[126] The subject of their conversation is not known. On May 31, however, at Bil'ak's intervention, the proposed congress of Ukrainians and Ruthenians planned to be held in Prešov was called off.[127]

The Ruthenians had, like other national minorities, witnessed a cultural renaissance in 1968. But this increased cultural awareness manifested itself partially in a revival of Ukrainian nationalism among the Ruthenians. Party leaders in the Ukraine and particularly in its Western oblasts were especially threatened by the dual message of liberalization and nationalism imparted by the Ruthenian minority. The use of Ukrainian language broadcasts over Radio Prešov and increased border contacts, of the type Bil'ak agreed to cancel, were specific examples of the unacceptable "spillover" of the Prague Spring that Shelest was concerned to prevent.[128]

Other meetings and contacts during the closing days of May included a visit to Moscow by the Czechoslovak minister of culture and information, M. Galuška, who met with Voronov, Demichev, and Katushev, in addition to opening an exhibition devoted to Czechoslovak culture.[129] The Soviet embassy in Prague was also particularly active in eliciting letters and petitions from party organizations in various Prague factories. Petitions expressing support for the greater unity of the socialist bloc were passed on to Moscow and formed part of the continuing efforts of Chervonenko and Udaltsev to convince the Soviet leadership about the worries of

[126] U.S. Department of State, Director of Intelligence and Research, *Research Memorandum, RSE-127*, August 16, 1968.

[127] V. V. Kusin and Z. Hejzlar, *Czechoslovakia 1968–1969*, p. 48.

[128] The effect of Czechoslovak events in the Ukraine was indicated by a prison letter, dated May 3, from Vyacheslav Chornovil, the dissident Ukrainian nationalist who wrote that "historical experience shows that two paths have become discernible in socialism: that along which Yugoslavia, and now Czechoslovakia, are feeling their way, and that of Stalin and Mao Tse-tung" (quoted in Michael Browne, ed., *Ferment in the Ukraine*, p. 171). It was also reported at this time that twelve Ukrainian writers, including Viktor Nekrasov, had been threatened with disciplinary action following their protest against the closed trials of a group of Ukrainian intellectuals charged with anti-Soviet activity (*New York Times*, May 4, 1968). Worry over the political "health" of inhabitants in the region also increased, as evidenced by the announcement that in late May a plenum of the Lvov obkom was held that discussed "shortcomings in ideological-indoctrination work with youth" (*Pravda Ukrainy*, June 1, 1968). Also see Grey Hodnett and Peter J. Potichnyj, "The Ukraine and the Czechoslovak Crisis," p. 78–79; and Skilling, *Czechoslovakia's Interrupted Revolution*, pp. 605–06 for a fuller account of Ukrainian objections to Ruthenian activities in Czechoslovakia.

[129] *Pravda*, May 31, 1968; U.S. Department of State, Director of Intelligence and Research, *Research Memorandum, RSE-127*, August 16, 1968.

"honest Communists."[130] Soon after, during an official visit to the USSR, Smrkovský complained to Brezhnev personally about the activities of Chervonenko and Udaltsev: "Comrade Brezhnev, these two representatives of the Soviet Union are doing an ill service to our friendship. They're not informing you correctly."[131]

It is not known definitely whether the Soviet embassy was also actively involved in the leaflet campaign by Novotný supporters just prior to the May plenum, although it has been alleged that the printing presses at the offices of the journal *Problems of Peace and Socialism*—a bloc journal controlled by Moscow—were used. Yugoslav radio first reported "an organized appearance of the conservative forces." Belgrade reported that this included signed and unsigned leaflets demanding a return to the old situation, with some factory organizations also calling for an abandonment of economic reforms, an end to the "dictatorship of the intelligentsia," and a return of "tested Communists."[132] A particularly venomous anti-Semitic letter, date-marked May 28 and addressed to Edward Goldstücker, was published in *Rudé právo* along with allegations by Goldstücker that the letter had originated from Stalinist elements within the embattled Ministry of the Interior.[133] Drahomír Kolder, himself in the conservative wing of the party, also referred to Stalinist activities when he personally declared: "I favor isolating all leftist conservative attempts and influences and therefore I am taking a stand against everything that can put them back on their feet. . . . Their aspirations are well known from various 'leaflets' written by would-be genuine Communists, written in a primitive style and playing on backwardness of the lowest level. The May Plenum of the CPCz Central Committee condemned these actions which bring out the powerlessness, bitterness, and fury of yesterday's obdurate people."[134]

The meetings between Czechoslovak conservatives and their Soviet and East European counterparts and the leaflet campaign to stir up popular opinion against the Prague Spring lent credence to

[130] Two of these letters, both dated May 22, and addressed to the Soviet embassy in Prague, have been published as part of the official collection of documents coedited by the Soviet and Czechoslovak Ministries of Foreign Affairs (*Sovetsko-Chekhoslovatskiye otnosheniya, 1961–1971*, pp. 219–221).

[131] Smrkovský, *An Unfinished Conversation*, p. 23.

[132] Belgrade radio, May 28, 1968, EE/2783/C/1; Pelikan, *Ein Frühling*, p. 235.

[133] *Rudé právo*, June 23, 1968.

[134] *Rudé právo*, June 21, 1968.

the charges of Smrkovský and others that the conservatives were themselves holding "meetings, gatherings of activists, in fact illegal factional activity."[135] This opened up the prospect that the May Central Committee meeting might be used by these conservatives for a power struggle. One can certainly assume that Chervonenko kept Moscow, and Brezhnev personally, informed of these developments.[136] Although Novotný was known to have had contacts with the conservative faction,[137] there is no hard evidence to suggest that he actually orchestrated these pre-plenum activities.

MOSCOW INCREASES MILITARY PRESSURE

May was the most active month of the entire crisis in terms of meetings between Soviet and Czechoslovak leaders. The content and results of the meetings are not all known, yet from their trend one may conclude that they were mainly initiated by the Soviet side to seek more information and to elicit Prague's agreement for maneuvers and a more cautious approach to reform. At the same time, differences in the style and speeches of the Soviet leaders is evidence of contending interpretations and priorities within the Soviet leadership. Also increased activities of the more conservative members of both the CPSU Politburo and the CPCz Praesidium reinforces the view that both Dubček and Brezhnev were moderates trying to maintain the unity of the center against the extremes of both right and left, although Dubček's inner loyalties lay with the reformers and Brezhnev's with the conservatives.

By the end of May, however, it seemed that forces in the Soviet leadership were less evenly balanced. Negative views on the Prague Spring were being expressed with relative freedom, and conservative activities were prominent; their sheer lack of activity indicates the weakness of pro-Prague forces. Nevertheless, the activities of Kosygin and the statements of Moskalenko and Grechko about noninterference perhaps point to the continuing support, at

---

[135] Smrkovský, *An Unfinished Conversation*, p. 14.

[136] *Der Spiegel*, no. 34 (August 21, 1978). Mikhail Voslensky, who was in the CPSU Central Committee in 1968, claims that in a discussion with Chervonenko on March 23, 1968, the Soviet ambassador stated that he reported directly to Brezhnev.

[137] Ibid., for Voslensky's report that Chervonenko had stated in March that despite Novotný's past mistakes, he was still "a friend." Dubček reportedly complained to Chervonenko at the end of April about the latter's continued meetings with Novotný (*International Herald Tribune*, *Daily Telegraph*, April 24, 1968, and RFE, *Research, East Europe, Czechoslovakia*, January 22, 1969).

least within an influential core of the leadership, for a nonmilitary solution to the political crisis.

After Kosygin had cut short his visit on May 25 to return to Moscow, there ensued a period of five days prior to the opening of the CPCz Central Committee during which the Soviets could assess the results of the Grechko and Kosygin visits as well as the reports coming in from other information channels. On May 29, General M. I. Kazakov arrived in Prague to prepare the WTO maneuvers. The Prague government had agreed only on May 24 to hold June maneuvers in Czechoslovakia, so it seems reasonable to assume that between the day of Kosygin's return to Moscow (May 25) and the beginning of the border crossing (May 30) a Politburo decision was made. Judging only from subsequent events, it would appear that the decision was taken on May 26 or 27, since Kosygin returned to Moscow late on May 25 and Kazakov arrived in Prague on May 29 with a staff that probably would have taken 24 to 48 hours to assemble.

The decision (*number 15*) authorized the movement of troops into Czechoslovakia for the June WTO maneuvers. Routine authorization of a military order of the day would not normally have to come from the Politburo; but the political element of the decision involved escalation of the crisis to an unprecedented high level, for troops of a different type and in numbers greater than those to which the Czechoslovak authorities had agreed were authorized to cross the border on the very day the CPCz plenum convened.

The decision to move troops into Czechoslovakia, therefore, clearly represented a form of minatory diplomacy, a stark reminder to all that the Soviet Union could not, and would not, remain disinterested in Czechoslovak affairs.[138] It conceivably also could have represented another compromise decision incorporating the lowest common denominator in approaches to the crisis. Military preferences for large-scale maneuvers to test Czechoslovak combat preparedness were met by agreeing to override the compromise decision reached with Kosygin in Prague on May 24. Interventionist opinion was assuaged by increasing military presence in such a way that conservatives in Prague could interpret it as a sign of support for their views. Noninterventionists could be pleased

---

[138] This interpretation of the early appearance of Soviet troops was shared by Zdeněk Mlynář in author's interview with him, June 1, 1979; by Pavel Tigrid, *Why Dubček Fell*, p. 68; and by Hájek, *Dix ans après*, pp. 84–85.

that the CPCz Central Committee plenum was going to be allowed to expel Novotný and that the policy of strengthening Dubček's position against both the left and the right might yet be continued.

On May 29, General Kazakov arrived in Prague with an integrated command staff and a Soviet army liaison unit to make the initial arrangements for the maneuvers. On the same day, some Soviet units started moving into Czechoslovakia, apparently without informing Prague. Pavel Tigrid maintains that "the first news came from provincial Party and administrative organs, asking what line they should take."[139] On the following day the press secretary of the Czechoslovak Ministry of the Interior, J. Kudrna, in a statement on Prague Radio confirmed that some Soviet troops had begun to cross the border, many of them apparently at points not previously agreed to by the two sides.[140] Neither Kudrna nor the spokesman for the Czechoslovak Ministry of National Defense was able to specify the numbers involved, although the latter did initially say that in addition to preparatory staff "some units and primarily signal troops of the Soviet army will gradually arrive." The numbers involved would depend on the size of the maneuvers, which, according to the spokesman, had not yet been definitely set.[141] On May 30, *Literární listy* reported that General Zhadov, a Soviet liaison officer and the deputy head of Warsaw Pact headquarters in Prague, had been visiting military units throughout Czechoslovakia; and at one of them he was reported to have pledged that the Soviet military was ready to do its duty if called upon by loyal Communists. It was only on May 31 that General Dzúr finally conceded that Kazakov was indeed in the capital, although the number of foreign troops would still be limited to communication and auxiliary units supporting staff.[142] But then only two days later on June 2, coinciding with Western reports that Soviet tanks and armored vehicles had been sighted,[143] Major General Josef Čepický conceded in a *Práce* interview that "it is possible there will be some tank squads." Nor did he rule out the presence of aircraft. Prchlík, in his famous press conference of July 15, summed up the situation: "None of the competent Czechoslovak

[139] Tigrid, *Why Dubček Fell*, p. 67.
[140] Prague Radio, May 30, 1968, EE/2785/C1/7.
[141] ČTK, May 30, 1968, EE/2785/C1/8; RFE, *Research, East Europe, Czechoslovakia*, May 31, 1968.
[142] *The Times*, June 1, 1968.
[143] *New York Times*, June 6, 1968.

officials has had, or even now has, any idea as to how many soldiers of the friendly armies have been, and how many still are, on our territory."[144]

THE PRESSURES SUBSIDE

Fortunately, the CPCz plenum went smoothly, and whatever intentions the conservatives may have had, no comeback materialized. The plenum adopted five basic documents and carried out a number of cadre changes that resulted in the resignation of Antonín Novotný, Bohumír Lomský, Martin Vaculík, Rudolf Cvik, and other conservatives and the promotion of two noted progressives, Bohumil Šimon and Zdeněk Mlynář. In addition to declaring that an Extraordinary Fourteenth Party Congress would be convened on September 9, the plenum passed a resolution on the current situation and the party's future course that represented a shift away from absolute commitment to some fundamental aspects of the reform movement. The plenum reaffirmed the leading role of the party as the first principle of socialist construction and undertook to insure that any reform of the constitution, the legal system, or the National Front would take place within a socialist context. The party was committed to prevent violations of law and order and was warned that "the socialist character of power and of the social order should not be threatened from any direction, either by rightist, anti-Communist tendencies, or by conservative forces."[145] Dubček in his concluding report stressed that the danger from the right was not counterrevolutionary but the possibility that "a wave of spontaneous and disintegrating tendencies could assume an anti-communist direction and administration."[146]

The May plenum was interpreted as a victory for the moderates, for those who saw in the plenum proof of a willingness on the part of the CPCz Praesidium to wage a united and resolute struggle against both right and left—but primarily against the right. For this reason, the decisions to expel Novotný and call the Extraordinary Fourteenth Party Congress was less worrying to the Soviets, and the perception of threat in Moscow subsided for some time.

[144] Tanyug, July 16, 1968, EE/2824/C1/5.
[145] Prague radio, June 1, 1968, EE/2786/C/6–11.
[146] Quoted in Skilling, *Czechoslovakia's Interrupted Revolution*, p. 257. Also see Golan, *Reform Rule*, pp. 220–21.

The Soviet decision to reduce tensions with Prague was influenced primarily by events within Czechoslovakia. Yet other factors in the external environment may also have been taken into account. Within the Soviet bloc, East Germany's previously intransigent attitude to the Prague Spring appeared to soften for a short while. The GDR leadership supported the results of the Grechko and Kosygin talks and attempted to play down the growing impression that the GDR had been responsible for unnecessarily fanning the crisis. An East German news agency (ADN) dispatch published in *Neues Deutschland* on May 24 declared that in regard to

> the building of socialism in Czechoslovakia which is in part proceeding under conditions different from ours, the leadership of our party and state is guided by the principle of proletarian internationalism. These are also the concerns of the Czechoslovak working class, the Czechoslovak Communist party and its Central Committee under the leadership of its first secretary, Comrade Alexander Dubček. . . . The task is to . . . develop socialist democracy in accordance with the new level of development. . . . How the tasks are to be solved is the business of the Czechoslovak Communist party—as far as we are concerned, we are confident that they will solve the tasks successfully.[147]

Furthermore, Ulbricht, who had been in Moscow since the May 9 meeting, was joined on May 29 by a top-level GDR delegation for three days of talks with the Soviet leaders. The communiqué emphasized "the complete unity of views existing between the CPSU and the SED on questions of the theory and practice of communist and socialist construction" and reaffirmed their mutual desire to "strengthen the solidarity of the countries of the socialist commonwealth." In a phrase that once again brought the November 1968 International Communist Conference to the forefront, both parties reaffirmed that "they will take all steps for its successful preparation and implementation; and they express the certainty that it will be an important stage in rallying the communist and workers' movement and all the forces of socialism and democracy in the struggle against imperialism and for peace and progress for the ideals of communism."[148]

Renewed emphasis on the November meeting was a feature of Soviet statements during those phases of the crisis where tensions were on the decline. Not only was there a pointed reference to it in

[147] *Neues Deutschland*, May 24, 1968.
[148] *Pravda*, June 1, 1968.

the joint communiqué, but the editorial in the first June issue of *Kommunist* was devoted to the meeting. The article emphasized the need for solidarity on issues of common interest to the movement and made a number of positive gestures in the direction of the European Communist parties. Criticism was reserved entirely for the Chinese.[149]

The Soviet decision to reduce pressure on the Prague leadership may also have been influenced by wider changes in the international situation pertaining to Soviet relations with both China and the United States. On May 20, the Soviet first deputy foreign minister, V. V. Kuznetsov, delivered a speech at the United Nations announcing his government's readiness "to reach an agreement on practical steps for the limitation and consequent reduction of the strategic means for delivering nuclear weaponry."[150] Although President Johnson had been seeking these talks, and previously had signaled his enthusiasm to the Soviet leadership, the next day, the under secretary of state, Nicholas Katzenbach, made a major speech on Sino-American relations. He stressed that America did not seek to threaten China's security and that should China "wish for improved relations, the United States will be happy to respond positively."[151] Fearing Sino-American rapprochement, the Soviets stepped up their campaign against the Chinese, asserting in an editorial in *Kommunist*, for example, that "China seeks to put the USSR and the USA on a collision course to provoke a nuclear conflict and take this opportunity to enhance its domination in the international arena."[152] Hostility toward the Chinese and fear that they might enter into an anti-Soviet alliance with the Americans certainly spurred the Soviets to make concessions in their own relations with Washington. The worsening of relations between Moscow and Peking revived the old arguments that dogmatism is a greater danger than revisionism. As such, the threat from China was temporarily seen as more serious than the threat from Czecho-

---

[149] "Neodolimaya tendentsiya k edinstvu," (Editorial), *Kommunist*, no. 9 (June 1968), p. 86.

[150] Newhouse, *Cold Dawn*, p. 103.

[151] United States Information Service, American Embassy, London, *Text of Under-Secretary of State Katzenbach's Address to the Press Club on Communist China*, May 22, 1968.

[152] "O politicheskom kurse Mao tsze-duna na mezhdunarodnoi arene," (Editorial), *Kommunist*, no. 8 (May 1968), p. 97. Similar views had been expressed in another editorial in the previous issue, which appeared in the first half of May, "O kharaktere kul'turnyi revolyutsii v Kitaye," *Kommunist*, no. 7 (May 1968), pp. 103–115.

slovakia, and the China issue served to put the Prague Spring on the back burner for the time being. It was widely rumored in Moscow that Boris Ponomarev actively argued that any use of military force in Czechoslovakia would cement the Sino-American rapprochement that the Soviets were seeking to prevent.[153]

Only in the Ukraine during the first days of June did articles appear that continued to condemn the situation in Prague. *Pravda Ukrainy*, for example, published an article on June 4 stating that "the imperialists are seeking to undermine the solidarity of socialist countries from within, using for this purpose revisionist, nationalist, Zionist, and other hostile elements." This was especially the case in Czechoslovakia, according to *Pravda Ukrainy*, where these "hostile elements under the guise of 'democratization' and 'liberalization' are using every means to weaken the leading role of the Communist Party."

Press articles published in Moscow did not wholeheartedly support the view of the Ukrainian party press. On June 8, a week after the conclusion of the CPCz plenum, the first major report of its findings appeared in *Pravda*. Although reporting Dubček's speech in neutral terms, the analysis of the debates at the plenary session clearly showed a continuing anti-reform bias:

> The participants in the plenary session made many critical remarks about the press, radio and television. . . . On the other hand, there appeared in the speeches of some participants in the plenary sessions a tendency to underestimate the danger posed by antisocialist forces and attempts to foist off a dubious theory about a "new model" for the socialist society.[154]

Nevertheless, *Pravda* reported Dubček's decision to convene the Fourteenth Party Congress in September and appeared to support renewed efforts to combat both "the rightist forces, who are trying constantly to discredit the party as a whole" and similarly "the conservative forces in the party" who are seeking to "return to the situation which existed until January 1968."

The appearance of this article on June 8 points to a Politburo decision (*number 16*), probably taken on June 6 at the regularly scheduled Politburo meeting, to defuse the crisis and support the

---

[153] Author's interview with Dimitri Simes, Washington, November 16, 1979. Simes was a staff member of Moscow's Institute for World Economy and International Relations at the time.

[154] *Pravda*, June 8, 1968.

Dubček leadership in its efforts to control both leftist and rightist tendencies. They may also have discussed at this time the forthcoming negotiations with the Czechoslovaks about a loan.

It is likely, however, given the length of time between the end of the plenum and the appearance of the *Pravda* article, that the Politburo was split on the attitude it should take to the crisis. It would appear that the decision ultimately involved a concession to conservative opinion, particularly among the Ukrainian and military leadership, insofar as the military buildup in Czechoslovakia in excess of preagreed requirements continued. Moreover, the Soviets made it clear that the crisis had not come to an end: they were merely adopting a wait-and-see attitude. Should the resolutions of the May CPCz plenum not be carried out, the situation would have to be reevaluated. Yet for the moment, the Soviet leadership had good reason to hope that the Czechoslovaks were putting their own house in order. As *Pravda* was subsequently to state: "At the May plenary session of the CPCz Central Committee, it was admitted that the chief danger to the cause of socialism in Czechoslovakia comes from the right. This seemed to give grounds for hoping that the leaders of the CPCz Central Committee would pass from words to deeds."[155]

Furthermore, Brezhnev is reported to have told the Czechoslovak delegation during the postinvasion negotiations that the Soviet leadership initially had considered a military solution in May. "But then," he continued, "it seemed that this would not be necessary. The first swallow appeared—the plenary session of the Central Committee of the CPCz."[156] In return for continued vigilance, therefore, the moderates in the Politburo succeeded in persuading their opponents to postpone the use of military force. Yet although the first swallow may have brought spring, that spring was to prove short-lived.

[155] *Pravda*, August 22, 1968.
[156] Mlynář, *Nachtfrost*, p. 206.

CHAPTER SEVEN

Phase Two:
June 6–27

The second phase of the crisis period was differentiated from the preceding and succeeding phases primarily by the fact that no escalation of tensions occurred. But gone were the honeymoon days of early 1968. Conservatives and moderates remained polarized both in the Soviet Union and Czechoslovakia. Kremlin leaders anxiously watched events in Prague, hoping, as *Pravda* later put it, "that the Praesidium of the CPCz Central Committee would use the preparations for the Extraordinary Fourteenth Party Congress, scheduled for September 9, to put an end to the defamation of cadres."[1] There was no longer any question that the Czechoslovaks would have to call a halt to many major aspects of the reform movement in order to meet minimum Soviet conditions for noninterference. But it was a quiet phase, in that for these few weeks in June the Soviets decided to give the CPCz leadership the benefit of a doubt and allow them to get on with putting their own house in order.

THE SOVIETS OBSERVE THE PRAGUE EVENTS

There were many events in Prague during June of which the Soviets might have approved. The conservatives in Czechoslovakia found it slightly easier to publish their views; Viliam Šalgovič, an old Novotný supporter, was appointed deputy minister of the interior, a position that would allow him eventually to play a key role in facilitating the Soviet invasion; and the CPCz and the National Front issued a joint statement against restoration of the Social

[1] *Pravda*, August 22, 1968.

Democratic party. And indeed there were some indications that the Soviets had more confidence in Czechoslovak ability to bring the situation under control. Economic negotiations held in Moscow from June 10 to 12 with the Czechoslovak deputy prime minister, Lubomír Štrougal, fared better than previously expected. The Soviet Union seemed ready to aid the recovery of the Czechoslovak economy through the delivery of a number of installations,[2] with some reports from Prague even suggesting that the Soviet Union was willing to extend a loan provided Czechoslovakia did not seek further funding from the West.[3] Prime Minister Kosygin was responsible for the economic negotiations on the Soviet side, and the relatively favorable results of these negotiations indicate the general, if short-lived, Soviet desire to take pressure off the Czechs at this time. Even more, the results reveal Kosygin's own efforts to demonstrate to Prague the benefits of making the concessions agreed to in his May visit to Karlovy Vary and Prague.

Certainly there were still those in the Soviet leadership whose views on Czechoslovakia were less than sanguine and who remained to be convinced of the CPCz leadership's commitment to clamp down on right-wing and anti-Soviet activity. However much Soviet leaders may have been impressed by the fine words uttered by Dubček and others at the May-June CPCz plenum, they still looked for concrete deeds in Prague to prove the real intentions of the Czechoslovak leadership. Unfortunately, these deeds were not forthcoming, and indeed those within the Soviet leadership who doubted the intention or capability of the CPCz Praesidium to use the preparations for the Extraordinary Fourteenth Congress to end antisocialist activities had ample opportunity at the beginning of June to reinforce their pessimism. Laws prepared for enactment by the National Assembly at the end of June covered rehabilitation and material compensation of all political prisoners wrongly convicted between 1948 and 1965. Also censorship, which had been suspended de facto since the spring, was to be declared illegal. The revitalization of the National Front and the preparations for the Fourteenth Congress also occupied reformist circles in early June; a most important issue was the election of delegates to the congress, since it would be these delegates who then would elect the Central Committee. The Prague Spring was clearly at a critical

[2] Galia Golan, *Reform Rule in Czechoslovakia*, p. 40.
[3] RFE, *Research, East Europe, Czechoslovakia*, June 14, 1968.

stage. It was being transformed from a spontaneous, unorganized, and rather superficial revolution from above into a deeply rooted and institutionalized model of society that would not easily be reversed.

It was crucial therefore at this juncture that Moscow be reassured that the reforms would not harm socialism in Prague but rather strengthen it, and that they were not intended as a model for any other socialist society. Unfortunately, the visit to the USSR from June 4 to 15 by a Czechoslovak parliamentary delegation headed by Josef Smrkovský seems to have had almost the opposite effect. The delegation held talks with Soviet leaders and toured Russian towns for discussions on the reform movement. Soviet officials apparently were extremely worried about the effects on the Soviet population of Smrkovský's speeches about the Prague Spring. Smrkovský recounts that after three days of his tour, when he was preparing to fly to Riga, he received a new escort, Mikhail Zimyanin, who as the former ambassador to Prague and a current Central Committee member and editor of *Pravda*, had considerable influence in the party hierarchy. According to Smrkovský, Zimyanin told him that in his speeches he should not mention "the problems of the day in Czechoslovakia, those problems that we [the Czechoslovaks] call democratization." Zimyanin pointed out "that the Soviet people weren't so well informed, they weren't acquainted with these matters and to explain them thoroughly at such gatherings was impossible, and just to touch on them—that would confuse people."[4]

As Smrkovský continued his tour, other events in Prague reinforced Soviet worries. On June 5, for example, *Lidová democracie* reprinted an article from the *New York Times*, alleging that Czechoslovak General Šejna, who had defected to the West following his implication in a plot to prevent the ousting of Novotný, had actually received a diplomatic passport from a Soviet general, allowing him to flee the country. The general named was none other than the controversial Zhadov, deputy to General A. M. Kushchev, the permanent Soviet representative of the WTO with the Czechoslovak army (Zhadov's activities in promising Czechoslovak conservatives the support of the Soviet army were detailed in chapter 6). The allegation was denied officially on June 10 by TASS, which also reported that the Soviet Foreign Ministry formally had

---

[4] Josef Smrkovský, *An Unfinished Conversation*, pp. 16–17.

protested to the Czechoslovak ambassador in Moscow about the matter.[5]

Other aspects of the security situation also gave Soviet leaders cause for concern. Despite the appointment of Šalgovič as deputy minister of the interior, that ministry, and the conservatives within it, lost considerable power after the May CPCz plenum. Following a two-day session of the National Assembly's Defense and Security Committee, it was announced that the functions of this committee vis-à-vis the Ministry of the Interior were to be increased.[6] On the same day, June 6, the Czechoslovak government transferred jurisdiction for the administration of prisons from the Ministry of the Interior to the Ministry of Justice. The government also formally approved the abolition of censorship and the Central Publishing Board, and the Ministry of Culture and Information was instructed to prepare draft laws to strengthen the protection of individuals against false testimony.[7]

Josef Pavel, the Minister of the Interior, also disclosed at this time that there was continued resistance within his own ministry to implementation of the Action Program. He is said to have expressed surprise at the number of Soviet agents working within the ministry; and he increased the purge of these agents, mostly Czechoslovak citizens, by continuing their salary but taking away their entry passes to the ministry.[8] The "screening" of ministry personnel continued throughout June, and it was expected that more dismissals would be added to the 250 cited by Pavel as having already left the ministry for involvement in previous "unlawful acts."[9]

In addition to these threats to what the Soviets call "the organs of state power," Foreign Minister Hájek also delivered a report to the National Assembly's Foreign Affairs Committee on June 11 in which he stated that Czechoslovak participation in the Warsaw Pact and CMEA did not mean that the process of reducing formality and rigidity would be stopped. Reform was clearly necessary to reverse the low standards brought about through the inter-

[5] TASS in English, June 10, 1968, SU/2793/A2/1; and *Pravda*, June 11, 1968.

[6] Prague Radio, June 6, 1968, EE/2791/C/2.

[7] ČTK, June 6, 1968, EE/2791/C/1.

[8] Pavel Tigrid, *Why Dubček Fell*, p. 64. The large number of agents working for the Soviets within the Czechoslovak Ministry of the Interior was confirmed by Zdeněk Mlynář in the author's interview with him on June 1, 1979.

[9] ČTK, June 6, 1968, EE/2791/C/2; *New York Times*, June 7, 1968; *Morning Star*, June 8, 1968.

national division of labor. As a small state, Hájek believed that Czechoslovakia had different foreign policy concerns from the Soviet Union, and in future Prague would place greater emphasis on the problems of Central and Southeastern Europe. On the German question, Prague would continue to support the 1967 Karlovy Vary agreement, but, according to Hájek, there was a need to take greater cognizance of the fact that "a realistic appreciation of realities and prospects in Europe was making headway in the ruling circles of the FRG."[10]

MOSCOW LOOKS TO BERLIN AND WASHINGTON

This was not the most propitious moment for Hájek to make such a positive statement about relations with the Federal Republic, since it was at this very time that a crisis between the GDR and the USSR came to the surface over the latter's own attempts to improve relations with Bonn. On June 7, Ulbricht delivered a blistering attack on the West German policy of building bridges, which he maintained was designed purely to subvert the socialist countries from within. He could not understand why the Soviets were improving relations with Bonn at the very time that the Federal Republic was luring Czechoslovakia away from the bloc, since "it should be clear to everyone why the West German imperialists are so greatly interested in events in Czechoslovakia."[11] Although Ulbricht's speech inexplicably was not published even in East Germany until June 21, West German foreign minister Brandt appeared to be replying to it on June 10 when he condemned the political pressures being exerted by Warsaw Pact states to prevent Prague's rapprochement with the Federal Republic.[12] The following day, allegedly in response to the promulgation of emergency laws in Bonn, the East Germans announced the introduction of pass and visa requirements for all transit traffic between West Berlin and the Federal Republic.

The Soviets knew that a new crisis in Berlin would end any remaining hopes for improved relations with Bonn, and also might jeopardize the chances of a breakthrough on strategic arms limitation talks with Washington. On June 4 President Johnson had an-

---

[10] ČTK, June 11, 1968, EE/2795/C/4.

[11] *Neues Deutschland*, June 21, 1968.

[12] Ministry for All-German Affairs, *Texte zur Deutschlandpolitik*, vol. 2, Bonn, 1968, p. 160, quoted in N. Edwina Moreton, *East Germany and the Warsaw Alliance*, p. 15.

nounced in Glassboro, New Jersey, the site of constructive talks with Kosygin the year before, that the U.S. was ready to negotiate on arms limitation and that "we are moving toward other agreements."[13] Johnson was to give a major speech at the United Nations on June 12, and thus the Soviets had good reason to worry that any new Berlin crisis, caused largely by Ulbricht's desire to prevent both Prague and Moscow from improving relations with Bonn, would spill over and affect the possibility of a breakthrough on Soviet-American relations.

THE SOVIETS SEEK A BILATERAL MEETING

With all these factors in mind—Smrkovský's speeches, the *Lidová democracie* article, the security situation in Prague, the pressure from Ulbricht, and above all the failure of the Dubček leadership to match words with deeds following the May-June plenum—a decision (*number 17*) was taken by the Politburo to seek a further bilateral meeting between Soviet and Czechoslovak leaders. This decision was probably made on June 11, while both Štrougal and Smrkovský were still in the USSR. In view of deteriorating events, the Politburo authorized Brezhnev to write to Dubček seeking immediate bilateral negotiations. A statement by *Pravda* on July 22 affirmed that the Politburo had "repeatedly proposed in June and in the first half of July that a bilateral meeting of delegations of our parties be held."[14] It was at this time that the first such request was made, as later confirmed by Czechoslovak leaders. Husák, in a speech on August 19, 1969, stated:

> On 12th June last year the CPSU leadership, alarmed by the developments in Czechoslovakia, proposed a meeting with our party leadership at any place on Soviet or Czechoslovak territory, or on the border, to talk about the matters alarming them, the dangerous developments in Czechoslovakia and their impact on the entire socialist system. Our party leadership did not accept this offer and rejected this invitation for various reasons, such as conferences, holidays, and so forth. We are such a great power that in such a difficult situation we need not negotiate with one of the biggest powers on earth, need not negotiate with friends and comrades and can afford calmly to refuse—to become isolated and heighten the tension.[15]

[13] *Weekly Compilation of Presidential Documents* 4, no. 23 (June 10, 1968): 903.
[14] *Pravda*, July 22, 1968.
[15] Speech by Husák at a Prague Party *aktiv*, August 19, 1969, EE/3157/C/13.

Bil'ak in an interview also confirmed the substance of Husák's remarks, adding that the Politburo authorized Brezhnev to write a
personal letter to Dubček and that he had had the opportunity to
read it himself on June 15. Bil'ak maintained that Brezhnev was
prepared to meet Dubček either alone or as part of a larger bilateral meeting at any place that Dubček cared to designate. Bil'ak
confirmed that Dubček turned down the request for the reasons
cited by Husák.[16]

Dubček's refusal to meet Brezhnev appears to have had a major
effect in Moscow. Zdeněk Mlynář reported that during the postinvasion negotiations, Brezhnev repeatedly stated that he had defended Dubček within the Politburo as a "reliable comrade" who
was basically pro-Soviet in outlook and capable of defending and
maintaining the leadership of the party and the unity of the bloc.
Yet when Dubček stopped consulting with Moscow before making
major changes, Brezhnev also began to agree that Dubček was
weak, unreliable, and unwilling to curb the anti-Soviet and antisocialist manifestations of the Prague Spring.[17]

MOSCOW RESPONDS TO DUBČEK REFUSAL

On June 13, at their regular Thursday afternoon meeting, the Politburo would have received Dubček's negative reply. They would
probably also have received the morning reports from Prague and
thus learned that the latest edition of *Literární listy* contained two
major articles: one by O. Machatka on the execution ten years earlier of Hungarian leader Imre Nagy (this article seriously affected
the atmosphere surrounding Dubček's visit to Budapest, which
also began on June 13); and another by Antonín Liehm, calling for a
new constitution to be endorsed by a referendum. "After its final
adoption," Liehm argued, "political life would develop within a new
framework which I would not venture to predict at this juncture."[18]

In the light of these developments, the Politburo apparently authorized the publication of the first personal attack to appear in the

[16] *Rudé právo*, September 3, 1969, as contained in *Pravda pobezhdaet*, pp. 143–44. This
account was repeated in the July 16, 1970, *Rudé právo* article "Why was Alexander Dubček
excluded from the ranks of the CPCz?" and was also in *Pravda pobezhdaet*, p. 361.

[17] Zdeněk Mlynář, *Nachtfrost*, p. 299.

[18] *Literární listy*, June 13, 1968. Liehm was subsequently to state that "I don't think it
took too much reading between the lines to get my meaning. I stood for a multi-party democracy without equivocation." From his interview with G. R. Urban in the latter's, *Communist Reformation*, p. 101.

Soviet press on a current Czechoslovak leader. This was a reply by Academician F. V. Konstantinov to the speech delivered by Čestmír Císař to commemorate the 150th birthday of Karl Marx.[19] Since the speech had been made at the beginning of May, the timing of the Soviet reply must indicate a clear break with the previous decision to cease polemics. Císař's views were condemned as revisionist and compared with those previously expressed by Kautsky, Martov, and the Russian Mensheviks. Making it clear that the criticism applied not just to Císař but to the entire reform leadership, Konstantinov stated that "it is difficult to understand people who strive to propagate Marxism and at the same time try to present Leninism as a phenomenon connected solely with Russian conditions." Yet in a reflection of continued Politburo worries over China, Konstantinov made an even harsher attack on Mao Tsetung, demonstrating that there were still those within the leadership who believed that the Prague Spring was not as threatening as China's domestic and foreign policy.[20]

Also probably on the agenda of their July 13 meeting was the Soviet response to President Johnson's major speech at the UN on June 12, in which he appealed for an improvement in superpower relations. Johnson stated that despite differences between the two countries, "we urgently desire to begin early discussion on the limitation of strategic, offensive and defensive nuclear weapon systems." Johnson went on to express his hopes that a lasting period of détente between the two countries would ensue that would "establish a pattern of disarmament, in space, in science, in the arts, and—I hope—ultimately in a broadening area of politics."[21] He made no reference to the Berlin situation in his speech on June 12 or in another speech he made the following day, indicating the priority he was placing on obtaining a breakthrough in relations with the Soviets. This may have led moderates in the Politburo like Kosygin to argue that no military moves should be made in Czechoslovakia that might jeopardize this golden opportunity. At the same time, the hard-liners with some justification would also have been able to argue that if the U.S. administration was not going to respond to pressures on Berlin, it was hardly likely to worry about Czechoslovakia.

---

[19] Published in *Rudé právo* on May 7, 1968.

[20] *Pravda*, June 14, 1968.

[21] *Weekly Compilation of Presidential Documents* 4, no. 24, (June 17, 1968): 955–57.

In the light of these events, especially Dubček's refusal to meet Brezhnev, it seems likely that the Politburo also discussed a possible change of leadership in Prague. At this stage, the Soviets were pinning their hopes on finding someone to replace Dubček within the current Praesidium who could command a majority and maintain support within the country. They believed that there was support for the Soviet position in Czechoslovakia; the difficulty was in getting the Praesidium to rely on and mobilize that support to defeat the rightist forces.[22]

Accordingly, it would appear that at their July 13 meeting, the Politburo took two basic decisions. One (*number 18*) was to seek bilateral talks and to keep Soviet military units in and around Czechoslovakia at their current level of preparedness. The second (*number 19*) constituted a measured escalation of the crisis and reflected the increasingly strong opinion that the Czechoslovak body politic was "rotting from the head down" insofar as top leaders themselves rather than isolated groups of students or intellectuals were held chiefly responsible for the continuing momentum of the reform movement. In response to this view, the Soviet leadership decided to publish the first press attack on a named Czechoslovak leader to signal the strength of Soviet displeasure with the activities and views of certain of the Praesidium members, and also to activate a mass campaign at the grass-roots level in the USSR and Czechoslovakia to show the Prague leadership precisely where they could turn for support to defeat antisocialist elements. As part of this decision, the Politburo appears to have discussed the desirability and possibility of finding an alternative leader to Dubček, someone not necessarily from the conservative wing, but one who could bring matters under control. Of course, it is impossible to know the extent of Soviet discussions, but it is known that Brezhnev the very next day did in fact explore the possibility of replacing Dubček with Josef Smrkovský.

---

[22] Husák, in a speech delivered on September 25, 1969, offered a similar interpretation of this period: "The right-wing and antisocialist forces went fully into counterattack in June 1968. There can be no dispute on the fact that our party, the working class, had adequate strength to prevent the onslaught of the right-wing and antisocialist forces which were disrupting the party, the society, the state and the economy, paralyzing the bodies of socialist power and threatening the foundations of the socialist system. There was enough strength to prevent the anti-Soviet campaign—for instance, around the maneuvers of the allied armies in the framework of the Warsaw Treaty, and the like—of course, under the sole condition that the Praesidium would draw conclusions from its own experience and from the consultations with united parties, if it assessed the situation in a united way and worked energetically" (from ČTK, September 28, 1969, EE/3190/C/17).

SMRKOVSKÝ MEETS BREZHNEV

On June 14, Smrkovský and his delegation met with Soviet leaders before returning to Prague. A public account of that meeting was provided by Josef Zednik, the vice-chairman of the Czechoslovak National Assembly, who stated that in the course of discussions, Brezhnev had been moved to tears, swearing that the USSR had no intention of interfering in Czechoslovakia's internal affairs. The Soviet Union, Zednik reports Brezhnev as saying, had never forced collectivization on Poland in the 1950s, so why should it interfere in Prague's reforms? That Brezhnev referred to Poland and not to Hungary is highly instructive of the attitude he was taking to events in Czechoslovakia. Brezhnev also admitted that the Soviets had committed errors in their relations with Prague, but he stressed that he personally "had never given instructions for anything to be done one way or another." [23] Referring to the more extreme published attacks, such as Shiryamov's article on Tomáš Masaryk (*Sovetskaya Rossiya*, May 14), the Soviets stated, according to Smrkovský, that "certain consequences have been drawn so as to prevent any possible repetition of this kind of occurrence." [24] Podgorny, also present along with Grishin and Katushev, had noted many positive features of the reform movement but expressed his regret that the mass media "do not always speak up in a way designed to strengthen friendship between our countries." [25] Podgorny is also said to have lectured the delegation on how ungrateful the Czechs and Slovaks were: "Your economists should do some calculating and explain on your radio and television that . . . the Soviet Union sends grain to Czechoslovakia even at times of bad harvest when we have to buy from the capitalist countries with our gold." [26]

Despite this outburst, Smrkovský reported that the general mood of the meeting was cordial. At the end of the meeting, Brezhnev asked Smrkovský to stay for a private tête-à-tête. At this time Brezhnev "reiterated his anxiety, his dissatisfaction with the way things were going with us" and suggested, in. the words of Smrkovský, that Dubček "wasn't the right man for the job." Brezhnev apologized to Smrkovský for the Soviets' earlier negative as-

[23] Interview weith Josef Zednik, vice-chairman of the National Assembly, *Lidová democracie*, June 17, 1968.

[24] Smrkovský interview with *Svobodné slovo*, ČTK, July 3, 1968, EE/2813/C/1–2.

[25] Interview with Josef Zednik, *Lidová democracie*, June 17, 1968.

[26] Alan Levy, *Rowboat to Prague*, p. 231.

sessments of him, an error Brezhnev put down to "lack of information." Now they had come to appreciate his long contribution to the party. Smrkovský recounts that Brezhnev "put it as if I should bear the responsibility for an about-turn in our affairs." Smrkovský continues:

> I was dismayed by the talk, because I knew what he was offering me. Now how to refuse so that the form was acceptable but the answer quite clear. So I defended Dubček. Not just our policy, but Dubček too. How he was developing quickly—of course it was a lot all at once, but he would manage and he would turn into a genuine leader of the Party. I simply refused the offer which had, in effect, been made to me.[27]

Smrkovský claims to have recounted this offer to Dubček, Černík, and Svoboda following the Soviet invasion. Mlynář concurs that Smrkovský and others, including probably Černík, were approached to see whether they would replace Dubček, this being the general strategy of the noninterventionists within the Soviet leadership at this time. Smrkovský, because of his reform views, had been described by Brezhnev at Dresden as "not a promising political figure";[28] but this did not apparently matter in Moscow, for, according to Mlynář, if he had accepted "he would have been like putty in their hands."[29] And in any case, Smrkovský's admission during his tour of the USSR that it was indeed difficult to defend some of the articles being published in the Czechoslovak press may have given Brezhnev reason to believe, or at least hope, that Smrkovský's liberalism was only skin-deep.

POLARIZATION IN PRAGUE: SOVIET WORRIES

In the two weeks following Smrkovský's return from Moscow, the polarization between left and right continued in Czechoslovakia. An article by Josef Jodas expressing conservative fears that socialism was endangered in Czechoslovakia[30] prompted a reply by Ota

---

[27] Smrkovský, *Unfinished Conversation*, p. 17.

[28] According to Radoslav Selucký's interview with Smrkovský in May 1968, cited in Radoslav Selucký, "The Dubček Era Revisited," p. 40.

[29] Author's interview with Mlynář on June 1, 1979.

[30] *Obrana lidu*, June 8, 1968. *Pravda*, August 22, 1968, quoted from this article, noting that "Comrade Jodas, an old underground Communist, only with difficulty found an opportunity to publish his protest against the actions of the rightist, antisocialist forces that were trying to monopolize the mass news media."

Šik on June 18 entitled "A Communist Should Not Obscure Facts."[31] Šik's warnings to the population about the threats to the reform movement from the ultraconservatives were reiterated by Edward Goldstücker, who published the text of an anti-Semitic hate letter he had received the previous month, accompanying it with the recommendation that the party should be purged of all those time-servers who "while speaking as the defenders of the interests of the working class, the nations and the party" in fact have nothing but "contempt" for them.[32]

Calls for the legalization of political groups outside the National Front gathered momentum. By June 18, over seventy requests for legal registration by political groupings had been received at the Ministry of the Interior.[33] Although decisions on most of these groups were delayed indefinitely, it worried Moscow that they were allowed to operate in limbo without being suppressed.[34] Of particular concern to the Soviets was the fact that despite the CPCz Praesidium's decision to the contrary, the Social Democratic party had been allowed to establish a preparatory committee to plan the party's reinstitution and had laid the basis for the subsequent formation of party branches throughout the country.[35] Because of the popularity the Social Democratic party enjoyed among the working class prior to Communist rule, the Soviets naturally were keen to prevent its reappearance as an organized and independent force. A subsequent *Pravda* editorial drew attention to the fact that on June 12 a document of the Social Democratic Preparatory Committee had declared the merger of the CPCz in 1948 "invalid," and that from June 1968 onward the Social Democrats "began to operate, and to operate against the Czechoslovak Communist party."[36]

The argument about opposition parties broadened into a debate on socialism and democracy and on the "improvement of socialism," to which the Soviets and their allies took extreme exception. The leading editorial in the June edition of *International Affairs*

---

[31] *Rudé právo*, June 18, 1968.

[32] *Rudé právo*, June 23, 1968.

[33] Golan, *Reform Rule*, p. 83.

[34] Press Group of Soviet Journalists, *On Events in Czechoslovakia* (Moscow, 1968), p. 75 [commonly referred to as "the White Book"].

[35] According to Golan, *Reform Rule*, p. 155. Soviet worries about the Social Democratic party were also expressed in the White Book, *On Events in Czechoslovakia*, p. 84.

[36] *Pravda*, August 22, 1968.

(Moscow) attacked the views of Zbigniew Brzezinski, who had delivered a lecture in Prague on June 14 supporting the efforts to "improve socialism." According to *International Affairs*:

> Throwing a light on the "improvement of socialism" formula, we find that the idea is to substitute for scientific Socialism the "Socialism" that has been practiced by some Scandinavian leaders for several decades, and that is currently being preached by the British Labour leaders. . . . In its fight against Socialism, the monopoly bourgeoisie . . . has tried to breathe life into old, bankrupt Social Democratic theories, it has seized upon and advertised the Right-wing opportunist and revisionist views. . . . It is obvious, therefore, that all this talk of . . . "improvement of Socialism," etc., is designed to facilitate the penetration of bourgeois ideology into the Socialist countries.[37]

Another defender of this view was Erik Honecker, a member of the East German leadership, who published an article in *Pravda* on the GDR experience, typically entitled "Socialist Democracy in Action." Honecker claimed that socialism and democracy were inseparable, with the building of socialism made possible only through consistent application of Marxist-Leninist principles of democratic centralism and the leading role of the party. He dismissed the "hysterical cries of some people concerning freedom of opinion and the press" and insisted that true democracy was based on society's demands on the individual, rather than vice versa.[38]

The following day, *Izvestia* carried a long article by V. Platkovsky on the role of opposition parties in Communist society that echoed the May 18 article by Miloslav Scholtz in *Rudé právo*. Dr. Scholtz had rejected the formation of opposition parties on the grounds that "the number of parties is not the decisive factor for the development of real socialist democracy." Platkovsky agreed, reiterating the crucial leading role of the Communist party and adding: "Lenin warned of the danger of special maneuvering by the enemies of socialism who demand 'merely' the removal of Communists from bodies of power and administration. . . . Therefore, he declared uncategorically that 'the dictatorship of the proletariat is impossible except through the Communist Party.'"[39]

The notion of a real plurality of parties within the National Front had been discussed for some time in Czechoslovakia. The Front

[37] "Foreign Politics and Ideological Struggle at the Present Stage," *International Affairs* (Moscow), no. 6 (June 1968), p. 5.

[38] *Pravda*, June 24, 1968.

[39] *Izvestia*, June 25, 1968.

had long since ceased to be a genuine forum for policy innovation, discussion, or opposition as all of the non-Communist groups or parties represented in the Front were entirely controlled by the Communist party. The Front acted neither as a forum of policy making nor even as a loyal opposition. But there were many suggestions for change, including one from the Front's chairman, František Kriegel, which appeared in *Rudé právo* on June 19: policy-guidance functions, said Kriegel, increasingly should shift from the Communist party to the National Front. Kriegel did not envisage the Front ever including antisocialist parties, but should the non-Communist parties ever unite, the CPCz could easily be defeated within the existing Front. The likelihood of this happening increased with the rehabilitation of politicians from parties now in the Front who had led opposition to the Communists prior to 1948.

It was also during this period in June that the public debate began over the revised CPCz statutes that were to be presented to the September congress. In addition, legislation was being drafted to protect freedom of the press, and a law on judicial rehabilitations was finally passed by the National Assembly on June 25. And in the Ministry of the Interior, Pavel's continuing struggle to rid his ranks of conservatives met with some success when he dismissed three deputy ministers and demoted two others, including Miloš Jakeš, the influential head of the party's Audit and Control Commission.[40] Three new deputy ministers were appointed on June 21.[41]

Not just the events in Prague met with attention in the USSR. Following the success of the "Days of Ukrainian Culture" in May, the Prešov area of Slovakia had hosted a large number of visits and exhibitions. On June 17, the first exhibition of Ukrainian art held since 1931 opened in Košice, and later that week the Prešov Philosophical Faculty hosted an international seminar on "The Development of Ukrainian Studies in Socialist Countries." The seminar group decided to publish a bulletin and organize further conferences, with the next seminar planned for June 1969 on the explosive subject of "Ukrainian National Consciousness." The group agreed that ideally institutions in the Ukraine itself should take the initiative for organizing an association, but in case the "Ukrainian comrades" did nothing, the responsibility for maintaining links and

[40] *Sunday Telegraph*, June 23, 1968; RFE, *Research, Czechoslovakia*, June 24, 1968.
[41] V. V. Kusin and Z. Hejzlar, *Czechoslovakia, 1968–1969*, p. 55.

activities would rest with Prešov.[42] It goes without saying that although such a development may indeed have been welcomed by Ukrainian nationalists and dissidents, it was anathema to the Ukrainian party leadership. Shelest in particular responded with more outspoken statements such as those in early July that marked the fiftieth anniversary of the founding of the Ukrainian Communist party (as discussed in chapter 8).

POLEMICS WITH PRAGUE LEADERS

Publication of Konstantinov's attack on Císař served as the opening shot in a new round of polemics in which Moscow and Prague departed from previous practice and exchanged personal attacks on leading figures. Prague radio, for example, in response to Konstantinov, noted that he had served his apprenticeship as a philosopher under Stalin and concluded that "according to many views, Academician Konstantinov is not one of those philosophers prominent for the high standard of their rhetorical concepts."[43] Císař's own reply to Konstantinov came on June 22; after accusing the Soviet theoretician of misquoting and distorting his original meaning, he rejected the Soviet view that all non-Leninist interpretations of Marx should be condemned as revisionist.[44]

The personal attacks on Prague leaders continued in the Soviet press with the article in *Komsomolskaya pravda* criticizing the editors of the Prague weekly, *Student*. This article was the first on Czechoslovakia to appear in the Komsomol paper following the demotion at the beginning of June of the Komsomol's first secretary, S. P. Pavlov, a political ally of Shelepin and Semichastny. Shelepin, it will be remembered, had identified himself with Suslov's thesis that dogmatism was a greater danger than revisionism and had also spoken out in favor of Kosygin's economic reforms in the USSR.[45] And Semichastny's star had been on the decline ever since he was replaced as head of the KGB by Yuri Andropov in June 1967. As for Pavlov, he was put in charge of the Physical Culture Committee and his position at the head of the Komsomol was taken over by E. M. Tyazhelnikov, known for his ultraconservative views. The editors of *Student* were accused of being interested only in "full

[42] Grey Hodnett and Peter J. Potichnyj, "The Ukraine and the Czechoslovak Crisis," pp. 65–66.
[43] Prague Radio, June 14, 1968, EE/2797/C/1. Also see ČTK, June 15, 1968, EE/2797/C/1.
[44] *Rudé právo*, June 22, 1968.
[45] *Trud, Pravda*, February 28, 1968.

freedom for political demagogy, for the most extreme, far-out expression of one point of view, and for the persecution and defamation of all those who think differently, who are all defined in advance as retrograde."[46] Ivan Sviták, a regular contributor to *Student*, was described as someone who "attacks Marxism, the Communist party, and the dictatorship of the proletariat with almost maniacal bitterness." Sviták's views were classified as "primitively anarchic."[47]

The playwright Václav Havel was singled out for criticism by the Soviet trades union newspaper, *Trud*, for advocating the depoliticization of the Czechoslovak Union of Writers. *Trud* interpreted this as meaning both "full freedom for any views, including anti-socialist ones, and no obligation on writers to defend proletarian ideology."[48] Reflecting the sympathies felt by some members of the Soviet Writers' Union for the reform movement, an open letter from Jan Procházka was published in full in that Union's newspaper, *Literaturnaya gazeta*. The letter attacked the inefficiency of socialized agriculture, claiming that "agriculture should feed people, not serve a doctrine." Procházka continued: "Maybe I am not acquainted with Marxism, for I should be able to understand why such a brilliant theory brings absolutely opposite results. Our Moscow friends . . . cannot convince me that one model of farming can be ideal for the Ukraine, the Himalayas and Czechoslovakia." In reply *Literaturnaya gazeta*'s editor made his own views known when he described Procházka's ideas as "cheap principles" that departed from Marxism-Leninism and did an ill-service to socialism.[49]

Throughout this period the only article to express views mildly favorable to Prague appeared in *New Times* on June 21, when its Prague correspondent D. Volsky published a three-page report outlining the current policies of the Dubček regime.

MESSAGE FROM THE PEOPLE'S MILITIA

In the midst of this exchange of polemics, a national *aktiv* of 10,000 People's Militia members met in Prague on June 19 and was addressed by both Dubček and Šimon. The meeting sent a letter of greeting to the USSR via Ambassador Chervonenko, reaffirming the basic principles of socialist construction and calling for closer

[46] *Komsomolskaya pravda*, June 21, 1968.
[47] Ibid.
[48] *Trud*, June 21, 1968.
[49] *Literaturnaya gazeta*, June 26, 1968.

Soviet-Czechoslovak ties. The letter continued: "We disagree with and disassociate ourselves from the irresponsible actions of some journalists who, borrowing various fabrications from the Western press, seek to undermine our friendship."[50] Because of the status of the People's Militia as the armed wing of the party and the organ designed as the ultimate guarantor of the party's leading role, Dubček's presence at the meeting and his support for the fraternal greetings sent to the Soviets clearly were welcomed in Moscow as a step in the right direction.

This meeting in Prague coincided with mass meetings in factories, party cells, and militia units throughout the USSR all of which expressed solidarity with the working people of Czechoslovakia and sent thousands of letters and cables to Dubček and the head of the Czechoslovak People's Militia. The letters and cables were more or less standardized in form, and many appeared in the Soviet press. One typical letter from Kiev, for example, expressed the conviction that imperialism inevitably would fail "to drive a wedge in relations between our countries. . . . By rallying its ranks around the Communist party, the Czechoslovak people demonstrate their unshakeable will to crush all those who attempt to threaten the building of socialism in the ČSSR."[51]

The participation of Soviet embassy personnel in the People's Militia meetings in Prague, the emphasis of these meetings on Soviet-Czechoslovak friendship, the common format of all the resolutions passed in the factory gatherings in both the USSR and Czechoslovakia, and the simultaneity of the meetings certainly indicate that Moscow orchestrated this campaign and that it implemented decision *number 19*: to mobilize conservative grass-roots pressure on Dubček to slow down the reform movement, to strengthen the leading role of the party, to end the purge of cadres from organs of state administration, and to stop attacks on the Soviet Union.

CONTACTS WITH WASHINGTON

In the midst of the People's Militia campaign, the Politburo was also involved in far more important discussions on strategic arms limitation. On Saturday, June 15, Soviet first deputy foreign minister Kuznetsov met with U.S. secretary of state Rusk in New York.

---

[50] *Pravda, Izvestia*, June 21, 1968; *Rudé právo*, June 25, 1968.

[51] *Izvestia*, June 25, 1968. Similar articles appeared in the Soviet press every day of that week, with the campaign lasting well into July.

Their discussions centered not only on strategic arms limitation but also on the Middle East, the Nonproliferation Treaty and Berlin. Informed sources reported that Rusk had made it clear that Washington was not going to risk a new crisis over Berlin if it threatened to postpone a breakthrough on arms limitation talks.[52]

Johnson's enthusiasm would have strengthened the hand of those in the Politburo who also favored disarmament talks. Yet resistance to any improvement in relations with Washington was strong, as demonstrated by a major *Pravda* article by Viktor Mayevsky, interestingly entitled "Necessary Reminders," that appeared on June 19. In a clear polemic with Soviet proponents of improved East-West contacts, Mayevsky reminded the doves that there were four basic impediments to any improvement in relations with Washington: the American aggression in Vietnam, U.S. support for Israel, the American and NATO arms build-up, and finally, U.S. trade discrimination against the Soviet bloc. Through the use of phrases such as "we believe" and "we repeat," Mayevsky created the impression that he was speaking on behalf of at least a strong coalition within the leadership. He concluded on a pessimistic note:

> If the USA is really interested in the genuine development of Soviet-American relations, it will meet with a response from the Soviet Union. But, *we repeat*, there are substantial obstacles in the way, above all, the American aggression in Vietnam. It would be unrealistic to believe that American-Soviet relations could be improved, regardless of the solution of major international problems [italics Mayevsky's].

Ambassador Dobrynin attested to major divisions within the Politburo when he informed U.S. national security advisor Walt Rostow at the end of the month that the Politburo had finally established a "united position" only "after long travail."[53] Whatever objections individuals within the leadership may have had to expanding cooperation with the United States, they were apparently overruled at the Politburo meeting on Thursday, June 20, when the dominant mood appears to have been in favor of improvement in Soviet-American relations. Accordingly, Kosygin was authorized (*decision 20*) to proceed with contacts, and the next day he wrote to President Johnson expressing the hope that it would be possible

[52] *New York Times*, June 15 and 17, 1968.

[53] Rostow, *Diffusion of Power*, p. 387; and author's interview with Rostow, Austin, Texas, July 25, 1980.

"more concretely to exchange views" on arms limitation.[54] This meeting must also have given final approval to the major report on Soviet foreign policy delivered on June 27 by Foreign Minister Gromyko to the Supreme Soviet. His speech, "The International Situation and the Foreign Policy of the USSR,"[55] repeated all the "reminders" mentioned in Mayevsky's *Pravda* article only to refute them, thereby indicating the depth of division within the Politburo on this subject. Nevertheless these divisions had been overcome, at least temporarily, and he was able to announce that the "Soviet government is ready for an exchange of opinions on the mutual limitation and subsequent reduction of strategic means of delivery of nuclear weapons, both offensive and defensive, including anti-ballistic missiles."

Although conceding the basically aggressive nature of imperialism, shown particularly in Vietnam, Gromyko's report took issue with a number of Mayevsky's arguments and indicated the current thinking that dominated the Politburo. While accepting that NATO was spending more on arms, Gromyko maintained that American influence was in fact declining, as proved by her setbacks in Vietnam. He rejected the idea that the arms race was a "fatal inevitability"; and here the report's conclusions were aimed not at the Pentagon but at hard-line Soviet military planners. In a remarkably frank contribution to top leadership debates, Gromyko stated:

> Human reason rebels at the fact that the genius of scientists, the knowledge of engineers and production organizers, the skilled hands of workers, the talent of leading cultural figures and tremendous material funds are still being squandered on the production of weapons of destruction and annihilation. The peoples have the right to demand an end to this insanity. . . .
>
> To the worthless theoreticians who try to tell us, as they do all champions of disarmament, that disarmament is an illusion, we reply: *by taking such a stand you fall into line with the most dyed-in-the-wool imperialist reactionary forces and weaken the front of struggle against them.*[56]

Gromyko also appealed for a negotiated Israeli withdrawal from occupied Arab territories; attacked "the Mao Tse-tung" group for deliberately aggravating relations against the wishes of the Soviet Union; and called on Bonn to base its Eastern policy on the recog-

---

[54] Lyndon B. Johnson, *The Vantage Point*, p. 485.
[55] Text in *Pravda*, June 28, 1968.
[56] *Pravda*, June 28, 1968 (Gromyko's emphasis).

nition that "the question of the frontiers of Germany was settled by the Second World War, and settled finally." Nevertheless, Gromyko confirmed that the Soviet leadership was prepared for "a continuation of the exchange of views with the FRG on the renunciation of the use of force."

Although expressing moderate views on East-West relations, Gromyko's report reflected the greater intransigence of the Soviet leadership on bloc affairs. It affirmed that imperialist subversion was the greatest threat to the strength and cohesion of the bloc and stated that "for the CPSU Central Committee and the Soviet Government and for the Soviet people, there is nothing more sacred in the field of foreign policy than the consolidation of the community of socialist countries. The defense of the gains and of the unity of the socialist states is our sacred duty, to which our country will be loyal despite any trials." It was evident that Gromyko had Czechoslovakia in mind when he confirmed the Soviet commitment to the absolute immutability of bloc borders: "Those who want to wrench even a single link out of the socialist community are blind and are planning in vain, however. The socialist community will not permit this. The community of socialist states is a single entity."

The clear authority of Gromyko's statement on the bloc, its harsh and unambiguous tone, and phrases such as "sacred duty," "nothing more sacred," and "despite any trials" demonstrated both the Soviet recognition of risk and the acceptance of high cost to maintain Czechoslovakia as a loyal member of the socialist bloc. However much relations between Washington and Moscow might improve, the Soviet leadership had clearly decided that such improvement would never be at the expense of Soviet control over bloc affairs, and in the weeks ahead it would become difficult, if not impossible, to prevent the crisis in Czechoslovakia from adversely affecting attempts at improved East-West relations. And clearly, the escalating crisis in Prague would be used by those in the Politburo and in the military leadership who were still hostile toward strategic arms limitation to torpedo any efforts to improve ties with Washington.

DEBATES IN MOSCOW

This enunciation of the dominant foreign policy line took place against the backdrop of two major and continuing debates on domestic policy in Moscow, both of which were linked to the events in Prague and served to shape the Soviet decision-makers' percep-

tions of the reform movement. The first issue was the rehabilitation of Stalin; and related to this was the debate between the party
and the growing dissident movement over censorship and intellectual freedom. The question of Stalin's place in Soviet history had
been fiercely argued since his death, with his contribution clearly
receiving more favorable appraisal after Khrushchev was ousted.
In June 1968 a book was published entitled *The General Staff During the War*, by General Sergei Shtemenko, who praised Stalin's
wartime leadership. In a review of the book, *Krasnaya zvezda*
commented that the General Staff had not been so unprepared for
the Nazi invasion as some historians believed. The attack had not
thrown the General Staff into disarray, thanks primarily to Stalin,
who had remained in the Kremlin throughout, refusing to evacuate
the Staff headquarters to underground shelters in Kirovskaya
Metro.[57] Shtemenko, who had been demoted by Khrushchev for
his loyalty to Stalin, was soon to regain some of his former prominence. He was to become the chief of staff of the Warsaw Pact only
three weeks before the invasion of Czechoslovakia.

In mid-June a meeting of the party cell within the Moscow Union
of Writers heard speeches suggesting that bourgeois propaganda
was doing "everything in its power to reduce the life-asserting revolutionary effect which Soviet literature has on the mass of the people."[58] Soon after, the fifth congress of the ultraconservative Zna-
miya Society sent a message to party leaders, vowing to strengthen
ideological work and declaring that "having failed to break the
forces of the new world in a frontal attack, the imperialists are
using roundabout maneuvers in an effort to undermine socialism
from within."[59]

This debate came to a head on June 26, when a major editorial in
Literaturnaya gazeta entitled "The Ideological Struggle, The Writer's Responsibility" made it clear that the current campaign was
not merely idle sloganeering but reflected a split within the Secretariat of the Writers' Union and the Soviet intelligentsia at large
over censorship and the writings of Alexander Solzhenitsyn. The
editorial compared Solzhenitsyn with such "renegades" as Svetlana
Stalin and reminded readers that Solzhenitsyn had spent time in
prison for "anti-Soviet activity." His appeal for the abolition of cen-

---

[57] TASS, June 20, 1968, SU/2803/B/1. Also see the article by Paul Wohl, "Stalin Personality Cult Dusted Off," *Christian Science Monitor* (London edition), June 15–17, 1968.

[58] *Soviet News*, June 11, 1968.

[59] *Soviet News*, June 18, 1968.

sorship was rejected as an "attack on the fundamental principles guiding Soviet literature."

Reflecting the splits within the Writers Union, however, the article also referred to the letter sent by the novelist Venyamin Kaverin to Konstantin Fedin, the president of the Writers' Union, in January. In the letter Kaverin had lamented that "there is hardly a single serious writer who does not have in his desk a manuscript that has been submitted, considered, and forbidden," and suggested that Fedin personally had overruled other Secretariat members to stop Solzhenitsyn's *Cancer Ward* from publication.[60] The editorial in *Literaturnaya gazeta* claimed that Kaverin had "distorted the attitude of some Secretariat members" and condemned him for failing to challenge the authenticity of the letter, despite the fact that he has "heard it recited almost every day by foreign 'voices.'"

Yet Kaverin's statement that there were board members who supported Solzhenitsyn could not have been "distorted" since this same issue of *Literaturnaya gazeta* also published the full text of Solzhenitsyn's open letter protesting the publication of *Cancer Ward* in Britain and Italy without his consent. Furthermore, at the very time that *Cancer Ward* was being circulated, according to Kaverin, from hand to hand throughout Moscow in "thousands of galley proofs,"[61] another manuscript by the nuclear physicist and Academician Andrei Sakharov was also being debated. Entitled "Thoughts on Progress, Peaceful Co-existence and Intellectual Freedom," the essay contained outspoken criticism of many aspects of Soviet (and Western) society and envisaged a process of convergence of the Soviet and American systems that would lead to total disarmament, the solution of the Third World's poverty problems, and the creation of a world government by the year 2000. In the introduction Sakharov commented that the essay was a product of the anxiety felt by the Soviet scientific-technological intelligentsia "over the principles and specific aspects of foreign and domestic policy." He rejected the current "loud demands that the intelligentsia subordinate its strivings to the will and interests of the working class," which he claimed really meant "subordination to the will of the party or, even more specifically, to the party's central apparatus and its officials," and asked: "Who will guarantee that

[60] The text of the letter appeared in the *Christian Science Monitor*, (London edition), May 23, 1968.

[61] Ibid.

these officials always express the genuine interests of the working class as a whole and the genuine interests of progress rather than their own caste interests?" In particular Sakharov condemned Sergei P. Trapeznikov, the director of the Science Department of the Central Committee; as long as such men occupy key positions, he said, "it is impossible to hope for a strengthening of the party's position among scientific and artistic intellectuals."

Turning to the question of intellectual freedom, Sakharov remarked, "we are all familiar with the passionate and closely argued appeal against censorship by the outstanding Soviet writer A. Solzhenitsyn," which has shown "how incompetent censorship destroys the living soul of Soviet literature." He continued:

> The same applies, of course, to all other manifestations of social thought, causing stagnation and dullness and preventing fresh and deep ideas. Such ideas, after all, can arise only in discussion, in the face of objections, only if there is a possibility of expressing not only true but dubious ideas. . . . After fifty years of complete domination over the minds of an entire nation, our leaders seem to fear even allusions to such a discussion.

The essay also condemned "backsliding into anti-Semitism in our appointments policy" and attempts to rehabilitate Stalin. Sakharov praised "the historic role of Khrushchev" in the struggle for de-Stalinization and appealed for a restriction in the activities of neo-Stalinists, proposing that the CPSU should implement the decision, apparently taken in 1964 and forestalled by the overthrow of Khrushchev, for the symbolic expulsion of Stalin from the party.

Then in a major challenge to the orthodoxy that true socialism springs from the Soviet model and all else is heresy, Sakharov indicated that the basis for hope lay in the reform of the Soviet system along the lines currently being explored in Prague:

> Today the key to a progressive restructuring of the system of government in the interests of mankind lies in intellectual freedom. This has been understood, in particular, by the Czechoslovaks, and there can be no doubt that we should support their bold initiative, which is so valuable for the future of Socialism and all mankind. That support should be political and, in the early stages, include increased economic aid.[62]

The challenge presented by Sakharov and by a large and progressive wing of the Soviet intelligentsia who clearly supported the

---

[62] The essay was signed in June 1968 and was reprinted in the *New York Times* on July 22, 1968. It was also published as a book, *Progress, Coexistence and Intellectual Freedom* (London: Andre Deutsch, 1968).

Czechoslovak experiment as an evolutionary model for their own society was extremely threatening to the ideological legitimacy of the Soviet leadership. The challenge had to be answered, and on June 19, P. N. Demichev, a Politburo candidate member and a party secretary with responsibility for ideological work and education, delivered a speech subsequently published in the Soviet press and, in expanded form, in the July issue of *Kommunist*. The occasion was a meeting of heads of social science departments at higher education institutes. Demichev launched a scathing critique, without however mentioning Sakharov by name, of theories of convergence and the "deideologization" of science that "sow the illusion that the path to the truth lies through repudiation of class positions." With Trapeznikov himself chairing the meeting, Demichev claimed that contrary to Sakharov's opinion, "the party, after criticizing pedantry and dogmatism and in overcoming both the consequences of the cult of personality [Stalinism] and subjectivist mistakes [under Khrushchev], has created favorable conditions for the further development of theory." Demichev also dealt with the question increasingly raised by progressive circles both in Moscow and Prague, namely, the relationship between the working class and the intelligentsia. He insisted that "the working class constitutes the chief social force of the socialist system and its main support. . . . Our foes have a direct interest in putting the intelligentsia against the working class, in detaching those engaged in mental labor from the working class. Indeed, this is understandable: the bourgeoisie would like to break up the moral-political unity of the peoples of the socialist countries."[63]

The linkage between intellectual dissent and the events in Prague had become quite clear in June, and no doubt the upheavals in the Komsomol added to this perception. It seemed obvious that any accommodation with the Prague Spring would lead to demands for similar reforms at home. Indeed, as evidenced by Sakharov, Solzhenitsyn, and the debate in the Writers' Union, this was already happening.

THE SUMAVA MANEUVERS

While the politicians in the Kremlin attempted to deal with domestic dissent and also keep the Prague leadership in line, the military were involved in the Sumava maneuvers, which formally

---

[63] *Pravda* and *Izvestia*, June 20, 1968, and *Kommunist*, no. 10 (July 1968), pp. 14–36.

began in Czechoslovakia on June 20. As already noted, Soviet troops had entered the country in the last days of May. Throughout June, Soviet military commanders toured the country assessing the political mood of the people and the morale of the army. Prague radio, for example, reported on June 19 that Soviet officers had held discussions the previous day with political workers in the Czechoslovak army. The officers were "showing great interest in current affairs in Czechoslovakia. For this reason," the commentator continued, "the directorate of the exercises has made arrangements with Czechoslovak civilians and military organs to organize a program of party political work for Soviet soldiers in the days ahead."[64] Prague radio, perhaps for reasons of diplomacy, did not clarify who was hoping to educate whom.

Marshal Yakubovsky arrived in Prague to command the exercises on June 18. On his arrival, he gave an interview to *Rudé právo* indicating that the scope of the current exercises had been widened to include commanders and staff of all arms of the services, including also supply and communications staff from the USSR, Czechoslovakia, the GDR, Hungary, and Poland. The exercises themselves had been extended to the territory of Poland, Czechoslovakia, the GDR, and Western regions of the USSR and would test cooperation and command among the forces in modern conditions.[65]

During his stay, Yakubovsky contributed several articles to the Soviet and Czechoslovak press on the history and importance of military cooperation between the USSR and Eastern Europe. He asserted that in the current "unusually complex international situation" a high standard of combat readiness was a "cardinal law." In particular, the West German "revenge-seekers" were eager to "settle accounts" with the GDR, Czechoslovakia, and Poland. Under such circumstances the "morale factor" was increasingly important, and "particular significance must be attached to the Communist education of the soldiers of the fraternal armies, to ensure their unshakeable faith in the ideas of Marxism-Leninism and their passionate hatred of the class enemy."[66]

It was precisely this issue—the political reliability of the Czecho-

[64] Prague radio, June 19, 1968, EE/2801/C/4.

[65] TASS, June 17, 1968, EE/2799/C/3.

[66] *Krasnaya zvezda*, June 23, 1968. Yakubovsky also wrote an article in *Krasnaya zvezda* on June 15 and gave an interview to the Moscow correspondent of *Rudé právo* which was summarized by TASS on June 17, 1968, EE/2799/C/3.

slovak army—that assumed importance in the maneuvers. Because of the near impossibility of "proving" such an issue one way or the other except in actual combat conditions, the maneuvers themselves became an additional source of aggravation in Czechoslovak-Soviet relations.

Ill-feeling was also created because Prague leaders had difficulty in gaining access to those Soviet marshals in Czechoslovakia for the exercises. It was rumored, for example, that Černík, on trying to telephone Yakubovsky, was told that he would have to go through Moscow to talk to the Soviet marshal.[67] And yet on June 28, Yakubovsky held talks openly with Bil'ak in Bratislava and indeed was the guest of honor at a lunch given by the Praesidium of the Slovak Central Committee.[68] Rumors abounded that Soviet forces had brought their families and were making arrangements for the permanent stationing of troops, that their numbers were in the tens of thousands rather than the hundreds,[69] and so forth. It even became known that Czechoslovak intelligence had intercepted a conversation between Yakubovsky and Kazakov in which the former had stated that Soviet forces would remain "at least until 20 September," the planned closing date of the Fourteenth Congress. "After that," Yakubovsky is reported to have said, "we shall see."[70] Prime Minister Černík issued a denial that Soviet troops would be staying in the country for this length of time,[71] but the Soviet High Command was silent. Given Prague's obvious lack of knowledge about

[67] David Floyd, *Sunday Telegraph*, October 6, 1968.

[68] ČTK, June 28, 1968, EE/2810/A2/1.

[69] In addition to units that arrived at the end of May, the MND press spokesman, Josef Čepický, stated on June 6 (Prague radio EE/2790/C/1) that support, supply, and communication units would supplement the command positions. In the course of the maneuvers from June 20 to 30, the following statements were made about force levels: ČTK (June 21, EE/2803/C1/1) announced that marking troops, motorized infantry units, and a task unit would be entering Czechoslovak territory for the exercises. On the same day, Černík (Prague radio, June 21, EE/2803/C1/2) denied reports that the numbers of Soviet soldiers had risen to 30,000. On June 26, Prague radio (EE/2807/C/4), confirmed that small numbers of Soviet army aircraft "have been stationed on several Czechoslovak airfields to mark combat activities in the air." On June 27, Prague radio (EE/2810/A2/1), mentioned cooperation between "armored and motorized rifle units with the airforce and artillery." On the next day, Josef Čepický in *Obrana lidu* rejected rumors that the staff maneuvers had been transformed into full-scale exercises with troops: "Talk of mass participation of troops is absurd. I repeat again that the men are counted in the hundreds." It was stated in July that a large number of signals experts had been involved and that the total number of foreign troops had reached 16,000 with 4,500 vehicles, 70 tanks, and 40 airplanes used (*Sunday Telegraph*, July 14, 1968; *New York Times*, July 17, 1968).

[70] Tigrid, *Why Dubček Fell*, p. 68.

[71] Černík denial, Prague radio, June 21, 1968, EE/2803/C1/2.

the extent of the exercises and of the real intentions of the Soviets, inevitably the atmosphere deteriorated. Instead of the exercises bolstering the strength of pro-Soviet forces in Czechoslovakia, they only served to further isolate the conservatives and increase anti-Sovietism.

Fears in Czechoslovakia that these were no ordinary maneuvers were shared in the West. The U.S. State Department concluded that "when the Soviets introduced sizeable numbers of troops in Czechoslovakia, they seemed to have done so in the hope that the troops might be able to assist conservative forces in the country to regain control—perhaps in a coup."[72] The Command of NATO's Central Army Group similarly concluded that while "Sumava" was indeed "more of a Command Post Exercise (CPX) than a full-strength field maneuver," nevertheless "we judged this particular exercise to be a rehearsal of a planned invasion, but more specifically to serve as a dire warning to the Czech Praesidium that they had better mend their ways or else."[73]

The Czechoslovaks did not mend their ways, however. The brief interlude following the May CPCz Central Committee plenum came to an end with the publication in Prague on June 27 of the "2,000 Words." By themselves the "2,000 Words" may not have shattered the peace, but coming at the end of a month of tension, polemics, negotiations, dissent, and minatory maneuvers, it was perhaps inevitable that the Soviets should have regarded this as the last straw. They branded the statement a counterrevolutionary platform, and any hope of maintaining the moderate wait-and-see tactics of early June evaporated, so bringing this phase of the crisis period to an end.

[72] U.S. Department of State, *Intelligence Note 634*, August 13, 1968.

[73] General James H. Polk, "Reflections on the Czechoslovakian Invasion," p. 32.

CHAPTER EIGHT

Phase Three:
June 27–July 28

THE "2,000 WORDS" AND THE SOVIET REACTION

On June 27 a statement written by Ludvík Vaculík entitled "2,000 Words to Workers, Farmers, Scientists, Artists and Everyone" appeared in leading Prague papers.[1] The statement was signed by over sixty persons including leading Prague intellectuals, scientists, and writers. It supported the reform movement and the Communist party's leading role, but expressed fears that the Prague Spring was "still threatened" by "the revenge of the old forces." It demanded the removal of remaining conservatives, advocating "public criticism, strikes and boycotts of their doors" to remove them from office. It encouraged the population to continue with the process of revival at the grass roots and not to become apathetic. Dealing directly with "the possibility that foreign forces may interfere with our internal development," Vaculík stated that although restraint and diplomacy were required to prevent these "superior forces" from being used, nevertheless "we can assure our government that we will back it—with weapons if necessary—as long as it does what we give it the mandate to do."

The Soviet response was unequivocal, and as such it indicated that Moscow may have had some advance warning of the manifesto's publication. It so happened that Mikhail Zimyanin, the editor of *Pravda* and a former ambassador to Czechoslovakia, had arrived in Prague on June 26. Smrkovský recounts that he met Zi-

---

[1] The English text is reprinted in Robin Alison Remington, ed., *Winter in Prague*, pp. 196–202. It was published on June 27, 1968, by *Mladá fronta*, *Literární listy*, *Práce*, and *Zemědělské noviny*.

myanin early on the morning of the twenty-seventh even before Smrkovský had himself read the manifesto. Zimyanin, Smrkovský remembers, "let fly at me, what did I think of it, it was outrageous. . . . Zimyanin was indignant, he told me it was a call for counter-revolution."[2] Smrkovský was not the only Prague leader who first heard about the existence of the "2,000 Words" from Soviet sources. Dubček is said to have received an irate personal call from Brezhnev about the manifesto before Dubček himself had read it.[3] The Soviet embassy in Prague, therefore, does seem to have received advance notice about the "2,000 Words." And, of course, Zimyanin would have been able to give Moscow his own immediate high-level assessment.[4]

Brezhnev must have decided (*decision 21*) on the morning of June 27 that the situation was serious enough to require an immediate explanation and assurance from Dubček. It is unlikely that the Politburo would have been convened formally to agree to Brezhnev's call. Such communication between Moscow and Prague was becoming more frequent; and although Brezhnev may have been aware of the views of other leaders, it is likely that this was an ad hoc and informal decision designed primarily to gain further information and to communicate the leadership's amazement that the statement had been published in the first place. In an apparent reference to Brezhnev's early-morning call to Dubček, *Pravda* later stated:

> The leadership of our party called A. Dubček's attention to the danger of this document as a platform for further intensification of counterrevolutionary actions. He replied that the Praesidium of the Central Committee was discussing this question and that the severest appraisal of the statement would be given and the most resolute measures taken. But aside from a liberal verbal denunciation, no practical measures really followed.[5]

The CPCz Praesidium did indeed discuss the question later that day and issued a strong condemnation of the "2,000 Words," as did the National Front and the government. The Praesidium stated that "if the people who signed the declaration think . . . that their

---

[2] Josef Smrkovský, *An Unfinished Conversation*, p. 15.

[3] According to William Shawcross, *Dubček*, p. 168.

[4] According to Edward Goldstücker, interviewed by the author on October 24, 1977, Zimyanin was the person most responsible for the exaggeration of the significance and importance of the "2,000 Words" in Moscow.

[5] *Pravda*, August 22, 1968.

attitude will be helping the development of our political life, then they are quite mistaken." Showing itself to be basically in agreement with the Soviet assessment, the Praesidium concluded that "the political platform on which the declaration is based opens the way for the activation of anti-Communist tendencies and plays into the hands of extremist forces which could provoke chaos and a situation fraught with conflict."[6]

Yet following the Praesidium's strong condemnation, several individual leaders made statements expressing their own, often quite different, views about the "2,000 Words." Dubček, Šik, Kriegel, Černík, and Smrkovský all basically maintained that although the good intentions of the signatories could not be doubted, they were "naive" or "romantic" to believe that the appeals for extra-party action would not be met with a strong reaction from conservative forces.[7] The Soviets were particularly sensitive to the fact that Praesidium members were defying the principles of democratic centralism by making statements contrary to the line that had been agreed to and established. The major *Pravda* editorial issued on July 11 specifically stated that "unfortunately, some Czechoslovak leaders have made ambiguous statements attempting to minimize the danger of the '2,000 Words' statement and declaring that the fact of its promulgation 'need not be dramatized.'"[8]

The manifesto certainly highlighted and exacerbated the splits between reformers and conservatives within the CPCz Praesidium. Referring to the activities of Dubček, Černík, Kreigel, and Smrkovský, Drahomír Kolder later alleged that "the primary principles of democratic centralism were violated by these members of the Praesidium of the CC CPCz. In my opinion, this was the basic reason for the growing apprehension of the fraternal parties."[9] One of the most outspoken condemnations came from General Samuel Kodaj in a speech to the National Assembly describing the manifesto as an "appeal to counterrevolution" and calling for the criminal prosecution of its signatories.[10] Moscow favorably reported Kodaj's speech, noting that he had "justifiably called the '2,000 Words' a 'call

---

[6] *Rudé právo*, June 29, 1968.

[7] *Rudé právo*, June 30, 1968; *Zemědělské noviny*, June 30, 1968; *Rudé právo*, July 1, 1968; and Smrkovský's "1,000 Words" in *Rudé právo*, July 5, 1968.

[8] I. Alexandrov, "Attack on the Socialist Foundations of Czechoslovakia," *Pravda*, July 11, 1968.

[9] Interview with D. Kolder, *Rudé právo*, September 10, 1969.

[10] *Svobodné slovo*, June 28, 1968.

for counterrevolution.'"[11] In addition, Indra was instructed by the Praesidium to telex its position to all the subordinate party offices, which were at that time preparing to hold district conferences to elect delegates to the Fourteenth Party Congress. This he did, but, Smrkovský said, Indra "wrote the message according to how he understood the Praesidium's discussion."[12] In his telex, Indra warned that "a counterrevolutionary situation" was in the making, leading to "anarchy . . . and the destruction of the state."[13]

The Praesidium statement, the subsequent leadership debate, and Indra's telex intensified public interest in the "2,000 Words," and if anything the party's heavy-handed reaction probably increased popular sympathy for the manifesto. At the district and regional conferences, delegates criticized the party reaction and responded by electing an overwhelming majority of delegates who were committed to the reform program. Indeed as *Rudé právo* later stated, "approval or rejection of the '2,000 Words' was in many cases a criterion for election or nonelection of the proposed delegate to the regional conference or congress."[14] Moreover, the conferences acutely reflected the depth of support within the party itself for rapid and far-reaching reform. Thus, for example, the practice of appointing disgraced officials to ambassadorial posts was criticized; multiple-candidate elections were instituted at some sessions; and a number of district party committees were entirely reconstituted. In addition, several conferences demanded the recall of party functionaries and criticized the work of high party officials. The regular rotation of leading party officials was also proposed, and some conferences introduced secret balloting of delegates with the result that in a number of regions incumbent first secretaries came out at the bottom of the list.[15] Moreover, only about one third of the candidates proposed for the new Central Committee were among its current members; many leading conservatives were dropped altogether. At this stage it began to appear that conservatives such as Kolder, Bil'ak, and Indra would not be reelected at the Fourteenth Party Congress. At the Bratislava

[11] Alexandrov, *Pravda*, July 11, 1968.

[12] Smrkovský, *An Unfinished Conversation*, p. 15.

[13] The telex message was published in *Student*, July 10, 1968, as quoted in H. Gordon Skilling, *Czechoslovakia's Interrupted Revolution*, p. 277.

[14] "Why was Alexander Dubček Expelled from the Ranks of Our Party?" *Rudé právo*, July 17, 1970, in *Pravda pobezhdaet*, p. 358.

[15] ČTK, June 29, 1968; Prague radio, June 29, 1968; Prague radio, June 30, 1968, all as quoted in EE/2810/C/1–3.

municipal meeting, Husák, who had not previously been a particularly prominent figure in Slovakia, launched an attack on "the old team," arguing that Slovakia lagged behind the Czech lands in implementing the Action Program. Progress would be impossible, Husák asserted, without a "consistent purge" of the leadership in Slovakia. Yet he was critical too of Czech neglect of Slovak demands for autonomy, and he urged that the Slovak Communist party (the CPS) should break with tradition and hold its party congress *before* the Fourteenth Party Congress met in September "so as to adopt a firm standpoint" on federalism.[16] Slovak leaders such as Bil'ak were now under pressure both from liberal reformers in Prague and from Slovak "nationalists" eager for more autonomy.

As a result of these conferences, the salience of time for the conservatives in Czechoslovakia and their Soviet supporters became particularly marked. Hope faded that the period of preparation for the Fourteenth Party Congress would put an end to "the defamation of cadres," as the Soviets called it. On the contrary, the conferences showed that the rank and file in the CPCz were eager to dismiss those conservatives who were blocking rapid reform. Moreover, the time available for any decisive intervention had been shortened from September to the end of August, when it now seemed the CPS Congress would meet. Thus by the end of June the Soviet leaders had good reason to question whether the "healthy forces" in Czechoslovakia still had the capability to maintain control without "external assistance."[17]

Rumors about the activities of conservative forces certainly circulated at this time, and they were no doubt monitored in Moscow in an attempt to judge the precise strength of these forces and the likelihood of their regaining control. *Nová svoboda* published a report on June 29 alleging that Indra was organizing the conservatives within the Central Committee to stage a comeback prior to the September Congress. *Literární listy* reported on July 4 that

[16] *Smena*, July 7, 1968, quoted in Skilling, *Czechoslovakia's Interrupted Revolution*, pp. 279–82.

[17] Soviet worries were further increased at the end of June and beginning of July by Prague's announcements that the government had acceded to demands for the formation of workers' councils that would have considerable powers, including the right to dismiss and appoint factory directors. Such councils would open the way for the grass-roots participation envisaged in the "2,000 Words." Also at this time it was agreed that an independent Czech National Council should be formed to discuss with Slovaks the draft laws on federation passed in June. The purpose of the council was openly stated to be the representation of a "Czech national consciousness" (Skilling, *Czechoslovakia's Interrupted Revolution*, p. 476).

there were plans for the People's Militia to occupy key offices as a prelude to a special Central Committee plenum that would elect a new Praesidium. A statement on the "2,000 Words" by various artists' unions maintained that powerful conservative forces were "regrouping" and using the "2,000 Words" as an "excuse to encourage hysteria and nervousness . . . [in order] to disintegrate the unity of the progressive forces." The statement concluded: "We have good reason to be sure that had not the '2,000 Words' been published, the conservatives would have found another pretext."[18] As another commentator stated, the only threat of a counterrevolution came from conservative forces.[19] The leaflet campaign mounted by conservatives also heightened tension at this time, leading Edward Goldstücker to ask the People's Militia "to work vigorously at stamping out propaganda efforts which make them look like a *putsch* organization."[20] The presence of Warsaw Pact forces and the activities of Bil'ak in meeting with Yakubovsky, and reportedly also traveling to the Ukraine for secret talks with Shelest,[21] did little to assuage the public from believing that the conservatives were indeed plotting a comeback. The admission on June 28 by the Czechoslovak deputy minister of the interior, J. Rypel, that Soviet advisors continued to work as liaison officers within the Ministry could not have added to public confidence in the loyalty of the organs of state power to the reform movement.[22]

The reaction in Moscow bordered on alarm. Following Brezhnev's frantic call to Dubček on June 27, there were several days of calm before the storm while a consensus emerged as to the best course of action. The one decision taken on June 30 (*number 22*) was to keep Soviet troops in Czechoslovakia for the time being. The maneuvers were to end on that date, but without explanation TASS killed a story on the scheduled completion of the exercises.[23] On June 30 TASS reported that "the military staff and command exercises of the Warsaw Pact countries ended today on the territory of Czechoslovakia." *Pravda* on July 1 also reported that the

[18] *Literární listy*, June 27, 1968. English text in Oxley et al., *Czechoslovakia*, pp. 271–72.
[19] *Reportér*, July 10–17 and 17–24, 1968.
[20] *Rudé právo*, June 23, 1968. On July 3, the People's Militia denounced the attacks on Goldstücker, and the following day, R. Horčic, chief of staff of the People's Militia, published a statement of loyalty to the Dubček leadership in *Rudé právo*.
[21] Steiner, *The Slovak Dilemma*, p. 179.
[22] *Práce*, June 28, 1968.
[23] *International Herald Tribune*, July 4, 1968; also *Daily Telegraph*, July 4, 1968.

maneuvers had ended, as did the press agencies in Hungary, Poland, Czechoslovakia, and East Germany. But TASS in Russian, at 2250 GMT on June 30, carried a service message stating that the report on the termination of exercises should be killed. TASS in English 0531 GMT, July 1, also rescinded the earlier report.[24] This indicates that a decision was made after *Pravda* had gone to press early on Sunday evening. Since the East European press agencies erroneously went ahead with the report, it is unlikely that the decision came from WTO headquarters or from Yakubovsky's staff in Czechoslovakia where East European correspondents were attached. Apparently a last-minute political decision was made in Moscow.

Czechoslovak journalists confirmed that speculation over the prolongation of the Soviet troops' stay had begun "last weekend" with the killing of the TASS story.[25] No information is available, however, to suggest who was responsible for the decision to extend the troops' stay, but one can assume that the military command had been involved along with top party officials. That the TASS story was not replaced by another statement suggests that the Politburo as a whole had not yet decided what course to take. Yet events in the coming days would support Zdeněk Mlynář's opinion that although the May CPCz Central Committee plenum had brought the doves to the fore in the Politburo, the "2,000 Words" once again tipped the balance in favor of the hawks.[26]

THE INTERVENTIONIST MOOD HARDENS

The appearance of the "2,000 Words" coincided with Gromyko's announcement that the USSR was prepared to enter into a serious diplomatic dialogue on a relaxation of East-West tensions. One result of the manifesto's appearance was evident by the beginning of July: détente had definitely taken a back seat to the larger and more immediate issue of the Czechoslovak crisis. The effect of the "2,000 Words" was not to end efforts to bring about an agreement on arms limitation but rather to reduce the importance of these efforts to the Soviet leadership and to strengthen the position of those who opposed any accommodation with "Western imperialism"; for, conservatives could argue, Western governments were

[24] See Roy William Stafford, "Signalling and Response," p. 77 n. 9.
[25] *International Herald Tribune*, July 4, 1968.
[26] Zdeněk Mlynář, *Nachtfrost*, p. 212.

supporting "counterrevolutionary tendencies" in Prague. Although Kosygin did advise President Johnson in the last days of June that the Soviet Union was prepared to announce on July 1 that Soviet-American talks on the limitation of strategic weapons and ABM systems could go ahead "in the nearest future,"[27] the announcement received almost none of the customary Soviet publicity. Similarly, Kosygin's speech at the signing of the Nuclear Nonproliferation Treaty (NPT) received very poor coverage in the press, and although Gromyko, Suslov, Voronov, Grechko, and Ponomarev attended the signing ceremony, Brezhnev and Podgorny were conspicuous by their absence. Kosygin described the NPT as a "big success to the benefit of peace" and expressed the hope that the treaty would bring about further "concrete results in the area of disarmament awaited by all the peoples of the world,"[28] but in general the speech was short and perfunctory. He did not detail either the background to the treaty or current Soviet contacts with the West. Although Kosygin's statements may have favored increased contacts on disarmament, the tone of the speech was cautious and low keyed, possibly reflecting Kosygin's awareness that the time was not entirely propitious for a major statement on détente.[29]

An editorial in *Izvestia* on July 1 backed the more optimistic aspects of the Kosygin line and hailed the NPT as a breakthrough for the Soviet "policy of peace." In a remarkable reference to the importance of maintaining public support for foreign policy initiatives, *Izvestia* proclaimed that "the main condition for the steady growth of the international prestige of the Soviet Union . . . lies in the organic connection between the will of the people and the actions of the Soviet government." Then in a statement that reflected "Russia first" sentiments and contained none of the usual references to the USSR's internationalist duties—about which Prague had been so frequently reminded—*Izvestia* concluded that Soviet foreign policy should be "subordinated to the state interests of the Soviet people, to insuring the inviolability of our ground frontiers,

[27] L. B. Johnson, *The Vantage Point*, p. 485.

[28] *Pravda*, July 2, 1968.

[29] Kosygin's enthusiasm may have been somewhat dampened by the concurrent downing of a U.S. plane carrying 214 troops bound for Vietnam. The plane went off course and was brought down off the Soviet Kurile Islands. Despite Chinese mockery and North Vietnamese displeasure, the plane was immediately released, thereby further substantiating the view that the Soviets on the whole favored improved Soviet-American relations (*Hsinhua News Agency*, July 5, 1968; *Financial Times*, July 15, 1968; *International Herald Tribune*, July 12, 1968).

coastlines, and airspace, to protecting the dignity of the Soviet flag, the rights and security of Soviet citizens."[30] Neither Kosygin nor *Izvestia* made any reference to the formulation of the April Central Committee plenum that a phase of intensified international class war existed in which a weakened but therefore more cunning and dangerous imperialism was seeking to subvert the socialist bloc.

By contrast, the next morning's *Sovetskaya Rossiya* contained a sharply worded editorial proclaiming proletarian internationalism as the highest Soviet aim. Several passages in the editorial appeared to be direct rebuttals of the arguments made by *Izvestia* and Prime Minister Kosygin. Soviet workers were striving not only for their own country but for the future of humanity throughout the world. The duty of the Soviet people, according to Lenin as quoted by *Sovetskaya Rossiya*, was to do the most "in one country for the development, support, and arousal of revolution *IN ALL COUNTRIES*."[31]

Another sign of hard-line opinion, this time within the Soviet military, was an article in *Kommunist vooruzhennykh sil*, the journal of the Main Political Administration, headed by General Yepishev. The article appeared to be a polemic with Gromyko's condemnation on June 27 of those "sorry theoreticians" who claimed that disarmament was an illusion. The article argued that "so long as aggressive forces exist" a country's security will depend on the constant renewal of even the latest types of weapons. "This is one of the most important laws of military construction in conditions of the existence of aggressive military blocs." With clear implications also for the military situation in Czechoslovakia, the article declared that given present military doctrine, "there might be no time to build up forces" during a war and that it is now necessary "even in peacetime to have a stable superiority over the probable adversary."[32] This was one of the essential arguments used to convince the Czechoslovaks that the permanent stationing of troops was necessary.

These remarks were not just a polemic with Gromyko; they contributed to a wide-ranging and divisive debate over military doctrine in the Warsaw Pact. The Czechoslovak military certainly participated in the debate, and indeed in a document published on

[30] *Izvestia*, July 1, 1968.

[31] *Sovetskaya Rossiya*, July 2, 1968 (emphasis in original).

[32] Quoted by Victor Zorza, *The Guardian*, July 2, 1968.

July 2 in *Lidová armada*, they made suggestions for reform that could only have caused alarm in other member countries. The document, "On the Czechoslovak State Interests in the Military Sphere," was prepared unofficially by a group within the Gottwald Military Academy. The group declared its allegiance to the Warsaw Pact but stated that Czechoslovakia should respond to changes in military strategy "as a partner, and not as a sacrifice to a development on which we have no influence." In particular, the group maintained, crises in Europe leading to "a situation between war and peace" have "catastrophic effects" on the Czechoslovak economy, and hence Czechoslovakia should take all measures to avoid such situations. By advocating "an active foreign policy within the alliance" and seeking the "normalization of relations" with West Germany, it was later alleged that this and other documents prepared by the academy were in fact promoting a policy of neutrality. Even without such an extreme interpretation, it is not difficult to assess the impact that publication of the document had in Moscow.

Sharing the views expressed by *Sovetskaya Rossiya* and *Kommunist vooruzhennykh sil*, the Ukrainian party leadership lent its support to the interventionist cause. The appearance of the "2,000 Words" coincided with the preparations for the fiftieth anniversary of the first congress of the Ukrainian Communist party. Although the celebrations formally began on July 5, the speeches must have been prepared well in advance, and a number of articles about the event began to appear at the end of June. The anniversary afforded the Ukrainian leadership an unusually good opportunity to express their views on a wide range of issues including the Prague Spring. The perceived link between events in Czechoslovakia and the Ukraine was clearly reflected in the statements by party leaders. Yu. V. Il'nitsky, the first secretary of the Transcarpathian *oblast'*, which borders directly on the ČSSR, explicitly attacked the spreading of hostile anti-Soviet and "revisionist" views by the mass media in Czechoslovakia.[33]

Shelest aired his views on a number of occasions at the beginning of July. A consistent feature of all his statements was the linkage both between domestic and foreign policy and between the problems facing ideological work in the Ukraine and the larger threats to the unity of the Communist bloc. He clearly and consistently supported the resolutions of the April CPSU CC plenum, calling for a struggle against "enemy ideology" within the Ukraine

---

[33] *Pravda Ukrainy*, June 29, 1968.

and the bloc; and he warned that "striving to avoid the implementation of internationalist duty would only result in reverses and even failures. The CPSU, carrying out the legacy of Marx and Lenin, repeatedly and consistently struggles for the unity of the socialist camp . . . and the consistent implementation . . . of the principles of proletarian internationalism."[34] His most outspoken statement appeared in *Pravda* on July 5 when he declared that the Communist party of the Ukraine "has always and will always carry out an implacable struggle against any manifestations of right and 'left' opportunism, revisionism and reformism, *wherever* they might appear. [Shelest's italics]" In a clear reference to events in Czechoslovakia, he continued:

> We cannot and never will agree with those pseudo "theoreticians" who, forgetting about the class nature of socialist society and the sharp struggle against imperialism and reaction, strive to assert and propagandize farfetched and lifeless "models of socialism," abstract humanism and abstract democratization. . . .
> Bourgeois propaganda in its struggle against Communism . . . fabricates the vile myth that Leninism is a specifically Russian phenomenon not applicable to other countries. Its aim is clear . . . to weaken the fraternal internationalist link between the socialist countries. For us Communists of the Ukraine, who have passed through the great school of class struggle against internal and external enemies, the danger is clearly seen of the position taken by individual Communists in some fraternal parties when they fall for the bait of bourgeois propaganda and its yes-men opportunists of various stripes.

Then in a polemic with opponents of intervention, Shelest enunciated his own view of the principles on which a truly Leninist foreign policy should be based:

> It is impossible to agree with those who reduce proletarian internationalism to the mere recognition of the independence and equality of nations. It is not difficult to understand that to uphold only this aspect of internationalism and to ignore the other, no less important side—the necessity for unification, union, and mutual aid of socialist nations, would only lead to separatism and self-isolation.[35]

It is easy to discern the differences in the views of Shelest and Kosygin. Equally interesting is the article written by Shcherbitsky,

---

[34] P. Ye. Shelest, "Boevoi otryad KPSS," *Voprosy istorii KPSS*, No. 7 (July 1968), p. 16.
[35] *Pravda*, July 5, 1968. Similar views were expressed by Shelest in his speech before the Ukrainian Central Committee plenum on July 5, as reported in *Pravda Ukrainy* and *Radjanska Ukraina* on July 6, 1968. Shorter versions of the speech were also carried by *Pravda* and *Izvestia*.

which appeared in *Izvestia* on July 5, the same day that Shelest's article was carried by *Pravda*. Shcherbitsky concentrated far more on the steady and nondramatic progress made by the Ukrainian people in the last fifty years and made only perfunctory references to the "struggle against right and 'left' opportunism, revisionism, nationalism and chauvinism." His comments on foreign policy were less emotional than Shelest's, and he avoided making any connection between external and internal policy, confining himself to support for the April plenum's resolution on combating imperialist subversion and expressing confidence in the Central Committee's ability to "strengthen the unity of all the forces of socialism and democracy in their struggle against imperialism and for peace and progress." No mention at all was made of proletarian internationalism, mutual aid, or the dangers posed to the unity of the camp or the socialist orientation of some fraternal parties.

The secretary in charge of the Ukrainian party's propaganda department, F. D. Ovcharenko, also published an article in early July to mark the party's fiftieth anniversary. Whereas Shelest had been successful in placing a lengthy article only in *Voprosy istorii KPSS*, a journal of relatively small circulation, Ovcharenko's article appeared in the party's premier journal, *Kommunist*. The author devoted himself almost entirely to a rather bland description of the development of the Ukrainian party, admitting however that imperialist reaction and "its yes-men in our party" have taken on "an openly anti-Soviet character."[36] Yet he made no mention of any spillover from Czechoslovakia or of proletarian internationalism.

Much has been written about "the Ukrainian factor" in the internal leadership debate over Czechoslovakia, but it would certainly not be possible to conclude from speeches delivered at the beginning of July that the Ukrainian party leadership was united in favor of intervention. Shelest's views were uncompromisingly hard line, as apparently were Il'nitsky's, but the same certainly could not be said of Shcherbitsky. Less is known about Ovcharenko except that he had been actively involved with Shelest in suppressing manifestations of intellectual dissidence.[37] The reference by both She-

[36] F. D. Ovcharenko, "Boevoi otryad Leninskoi partii," *Kommunist*, No. 10 (July 1968), p. 46.

[37] The novel *Sobor* by the Ukrainian writer Oles' Honchar, which received favorable coverage when it appeared in January 1968, increasingly was criticized. At the end of June, Honchar was summoned to a meeting with Shelest and Ovcharenko who reportedly warned him against bourgeois attempts to shake the unity between the CPSU and the intelligentsia

lest and Ovcharenko to splits and disagreements would seem to indicate a subtly diverse approach to the processes taking place in
Czechoslovakia.[38] One might also conclude from this that there was
an active and urgent debate going on in the party as a whole,[39] an
impression supported by the arrival in Moscow of a top-level Hungarian delegation.

CONSULTATION WITH THE HUNGARIANS

The "2,000 Words" appeared on June 27, the same day that a Hungarian party and government delegation led by János Kádár arrived
in Moscow. It could not have escaped notice that the last time a
full-scale Hungarian party-state delegation paid an official visit to
the USSR was in July 1963 at the very time the Sino-Soviet dispute
was erupting over the publication of the letters exchanged between the Soviet and Chinese Central Committees. In 1963, as in
1968, the Soviets had ceased to be satisfied with general and ambiguous support from other Warsaw Pact members for the Soviet
stand. A common and publicly enunciated attitude by the Pact had
become necessary to back the Soviet leadership, and Hungary's
position had become particularly crucial. As a country with Soviet
forces on its territory, it could not afford the luxury of Rumanian-
style defiance; as a people who had experienced the bloodshed of
the 1956 uprising, they knew that cooperation with the Soviet
Union was the only path available; but most crucially, as a party
that had followed an increasingly moderate and reformist path, the
HSWP had a central role to play, not only in mediating between
the Soviet and Czechoslovak leaderships, but also conceivably in
helping to resolve the splits within the Politburo itself. Any continued support for the Prague Spring by the HSWP would favor
the noninterventionist stand, whereas recognition by those leaders

---

(RFE, *Communist Areas, USSR*, July 1, 1968). The novel, which portrays both the positive
and negative features of industrial life but condemns bureaucratism, was praised in Czechoslovakia at the very time it was being suppressed in the Ukraine. Dr. Orest Silynskyi, writing in the journal *Dukla*, noted that "all over the world a philosophical debate is taking place
on the tragedy of present-day man, who is suppressed by institutions, authorities and pro-
hibitions he has himself created. In his book the Ukrainian writer gives examples of this
tragedy which slowly disintegrates the human soul within the framework of socialist practice, and overcomes the intellectual upheaval which is at present taking place in our country" (RFE, *Communist Areas, USSR*, July 16, 1968).

   [38] This view is supported by Grey Hodnett and Peter Potichnyj, "The Ukraine and the
Czechoslovak Crisis," pp. 82–86.
   [39] A view supported by Mlynář, *Nachtfrost*, p. 212.

who had been through the Hungarian "counterrevolution" of similar tendencies in Czechoslovakia would do more than any other
action to favor the interventionist argument. Hungary's vice-
premier, Lájos Fehér, was later to confirm that the Hungarians'
own views of the comparison between 1956 and 1968 had been elicited by Moscow and "being desirous of helping, we reiterated our
experience which cost us so many sacrifices." Whatever sympathies the Hungarians may have initially felt for the moderate aspects of the reform movement, by July "the right-wing and reactionaries in Czechoslovakia succeeded," according to Fehér, "in
creating greater legal ground for themselves than they did in Hungary towards the end of the summer and the beginning of the autumn of 1956."[40]

When the Hungarian leaders left for Moscow, they were identified as one of the East European regimes still favorable to the
Prague Spring. Nevertheless the appearance of O. Machatka's article in mid-June praising Imre Nagy had undoubtedly affected the
Hungarian attitude.[41] During Dubček's mid-June visit to Hungary,
Kádár had stated that the HSWP would indeed favor efforts by the
CPCz to "overcome various obstacles hindering socialist development." The Hungarians frankly recognized certain negative trends
in Czechoslovakia, but Kádár reaffirmed their policy of noninterference, stating that the CPCz obviously "knows the situation better than anyone else."[42] The Hungarian mood appeared to harden
further by the end of June. On the day before Kádár's arrival in
Moscow, a belated response in the Hungarian party newspaper to
the Machatka article stated that "wrong views" must be combatted
by more than argument: "It is necessary to fight against the class
enemy with state powers."[43] The "2,000 Words" was condemned by
most Hungarian spokesmen, although the reform movement con-

[40]"Replies to Questions Relating to the Events in Czechoslovakia. Address by Comrade
Lájos Fehér, Member of the Political Committee of the HSWP, Vice-Chairman of the Council of Ministers, Broadcast on August 30, 1968," *Information Bulletin of the Central Committee of the HSWP*, no. 4 (October 1968), p. 16.

[41]*Literární listy*, June 13, 1968. Prchlík, in his famous interview of July 15, admitted that
while the Hungarians "very positively assess the whole content of our social process" nevertheless "they harbor certain apprehensions about the intensity of certain antisocialist manifestations of which, in their opinion, the most important was the material which was published in *Literární listy* on the day of the visit of our party-government delegates and which
refers to the case of Nagy. This article has exasperated and worried them" (text in Remington, *Winter in Prague*, p. 219).

[42]*Rudé právo*, June 15, 1968.

[43]*Népszabadság*, June 27, 1968; *Rudé právo*, June 28, 1968.

tinued to receive more objective coverage in Hungary than in any other bloc country, with the exception of Rumania and Yugoslavia.[44]

Little is known of the negotiations between the Soviets and the Hungarians. Despite the obvious importance attached to the trip by the Soviet press and leadership—an audience of 6,000 was mustered for a Kremlin rally on July 3 to celebrate Soviet-Hungarian friendship—comparatively little time was spent at the negotiating table. Except for June 28 and a few hours on July 3, the Hungarian delegation spent the whole time on trips to Volgograd (June 29 and 30) and Tallin (July 1 and 2). Reports suggested, however, that there were considerable differences of opinion between the two sides and that pressures had been exerted on the Hungarians to adopt a firmer stance on the Czechoslovak events.[45] Yet the communiqué of the talks did not reflect any such differences and merely reaffirmed the unshakable nature of Soviet-Hungarian friendship. It also avowed that the two sides had attained a "complete identity of views" in the course of their talks, which had been conducted in the "spirit of fraternal friendship and mutual understanding." It can certainly be assumed that Czechoslovakia headed the agenda, and although the communiqué makes no specific reference to the events in Prague, the speeches delivered by Kádár and Brezhnev at the Kremlin rally reveal attempts to reach agreement on interventionist principles.

In his speech, Kádár stated that "a tireless struggle must be waged" against bourgeois attempts "to preach the building of socialism in any one country apart from other socialist countries, and even the building of socialism without communists." He declared that there is no such thing as "anti-Soviet communism" and stated that

[44]The Hungarian press reported the substance of the "2,000 Words" and the CPCz Praesidium's condemnation of it, with *Magyar Hirlap* on June 30 calling the manifesto a "regrettable political interlude" and expressing the "sincere hope" that the manifesto would not prevent Dubček from pursuing a "principled, well-considered and planned" course toward goals that best serve the "real interests" of "our good friends, the Czech and Slovak peoples" (RFE, *Research, East Europe, Hungary*, July 2, 1968). On July 7, 1968, an article fully summarizing the "2,000 Words" appeared in the County Gyor party daily, *Kisalfold*, appealing to the authors of the manifesto to show their "good intentions" by revising their original stand and adopting a more constructive approach (RFE, *Research, East Europe, Hungary*, July 17, 1968). Radio Budapest on June 29 also described Czechoslovak intellectuals as carrying out a "passionate experiment" on behalf of socialist humanitarianism. Yet the existence of hard-liners in the Hungarian leadership should not be overlooked. Terence Varna, the foreign editor of *Népszabadság* called the "2,000 Words" a call to counterrevolution (RFE, *Research, East Europe, Hungary*, October 28, 1968).

[45]*New York Times*, August 4, 1968.

"irrespective of which country this struggle unfolds in," the HSWP "expresses full solidarity . . . with those defending the rule of the working class and the cause of socialism against the encroachments of dogmatists, revisionists and the class enemy." In a final statement, omitted by Rudé právo in its report of the speech,[46] Kádár declared: "We understand the meaning of this struggle, and we are prepared to render every kind of international assistance."[47]

Although Kádár's statements undoubtedly reflect a more negative assessment of the reform movement than he had made previously and clearly imply that international assistance might ultimately have to extend to military means, the Hungarian position was still not entirely interventionist. Kádár did assert that it was the duty of Communists "to use power to defend the cause of socialism" once "our class enemies resort to organized and violent action and attack the foundations of the socialist system." But at the same time, in a reference to a Stalinist theory that was being rejuvenated in hard-line Soviet circles, Kádár stated: "We reject the theory that the class struggle automatically sharpens with the victory of socialism," although he did admit that "under certain conditions, the struggle does grow sharper and assumes more complex forms." He did not mention Czechoslovakia by name, however, and he was careful to assert the continued necessity of a struggle on two fronts "against both rightist and leftist distortions." Furthermore, he did not say that socialism was actually threatened anywhere in the bloc except in China. And finally, in contradiction to the joint communiqué published at the end of his visit, he described the views of the Soviet and Hungarian sides as "similar" rather than "identical."[48]

BREZHNEV SEEKS CONSENSUS

At the same Kremlin rally, Brezhnev delivered a major foreign policy speech, relayed live, that contained several indications that the Soviet leader's position had hardened.[49] It was particularly noteworthy for its unusually harsh condemnation of the United States. Only three days after Kosygin's speech, the signing of the Non-

[46] Rudé právo, July 4, 1968.
[47] Pravda, July 4, 1968.
[48] As quoted by Soviet News, July 9, 1968.
[49] The speech was relayed live from the Kremlin and carried on Moscow radio, July 3, 1968, SU/2813/C/1-7.

proliferation Treaty, and the announcement of imminent talks on strategic arms limitation, it seemed rather out of place for the CPSU first secretary to be denouncing the United States as "the social and political system which engenders political banditry and arouses contempt and revulsion throughout the world. A rotten society, a degrading society, a decomposing society—this is what the USA is called even by those who recently praised the American way of life." It is difficult to tell whether Brezhnev was making a critical statement about the views of any of his own colleagues, but his own reference to the Nonproliferation Treaty and the arms limitation talks were certainly much more guarded than Kosygin and Gromyko's had been the previous week. Nowhere did he repeat the Gromyko formulation that the USSR was ready to improve relations with the United States and work together to solve outstanding international problems. On the contrary, speaking of efforts to bring about a negotiated settlement to the Vietnam war, Brezhnev accused Washington of "procrastinating in every way with regard to concrete steps towards peace."

Assessing the international situation, Brezhnev seemed to find a crisis wherever he looked: "France has become an arena for the most acute and unprecedented class battles"; "Britain is in the grip of an acute financial crisis." West Germany's recently introduced emergency laws he compared to the legislation that "in Nazi Germany served to put the country's whole life on a military basis," and he repeated the usual forecast that "Bonn's revanchist policy, even when dressed up as its so-called new Eastern policy is doomed to failure."[50]

On events within the socialist camp, Brezhnev definitely adopted a harsher note than previously. Recognizing the diversity of forms that Communist construction could take, he also recalled "the trials" Hungary had faced in 1956 "at the time of the furious attack on Hungary's socialist positions by the forces of internal and international reaction." The Hungarian Communists had prevailed by "relying on the support of the working class and most of the people, on the fraternal international alliance with the other socialist countries." Brezhnev's positive appraisal of the actions of Soviet troops in 1956, coupled with his statement that as internationalists "we cannot and never will be indifferent to the fate of socialist construc-

[50]This same pessimistic interpretation of the "crisis of capitalism" was repeated by Brezhnev in a speech to an all-union congress of teachers on July 4, 1968. The text is in *Pravda*, July 5, 1968.

tion in other countries," strongly indicates that the Soviets were actively considering military intervention as an alternative strategy. On the nature of socialist construction, Brezhnev was explicit, outlining what he believed were the common principles uniting socialist countries regardless of the variety of forms among the different states. "There is not and cannot be socialism," according to Brezhnev, "without the common ownership of the means of production; there is not and cannot be socialism without the involvement of the broadest masses of the people in the government of the society and the state. There is not and cannot be socialism without the Communist party, which is consistently guided by Marxism-Leninism and proletarian internationalism, playing the leading role."

Brezhnev admitted that "the apologists of the bourgeois order are ready to don any pseudosocialist mantle and try under a nationalist cloak to rock and, as they say, 'soften up' socialism and to weaken the fraternal links between the socialist countries." Yet he made no specific mention of Czechoslovakia, and his prescription for dealing with these "apologists" would apply as much to domestic dissent as to problems in Czechoslovakia. "The task ahead," he stated, "is to intensify our efforts as never before in our offensive against bourgeois ideology and to instill in the working people Communist conviction, Soviet patriotism and proletarian internationalism." He may also have had in mind the preparation of Soviet public opinion for a possible invasion by instilling in his audience an awareness of Russia's special duties and obligations.

He also appeared to be contributing to the debate raised by the *Izvestia* claim that the success of Soviet foreign policy depended on an "organic connection between the will of the people and the actions of the Soviet government." Brezhnev's emphasis was entirely different. Soviet foreign policy derived its success from its principled basis and not from its reflection of popular will. It was clearly the task of party workers to ensure that public opinion supported foreign policy initiatives, only in this way achieving the necessary "organic connection."

Yet the militant nature of Brezhnev's speech should not be overstressed. Although the tenor of his remarks was undoubtedly harsh, Brezhnev's actual prescriptions were on the whole moderate. He reaffirmed the USSR's "clear and consistent" support for disarmament negotiations; he maintained that the "creation of an effective system of collective security in Europe, in which the

GDR and the German Federal Republic, having full rights, should both participate, is of great importance to the Soviet Union"; and he repeatedly emphasized the value of frequent bilateral and multilateral contracts within the socialist bloc "for discussing comprehensively and working out collectively our joint line on the main issues of our time." He noted the importance of consultation both on a bilateral basis and within the framework of the Warsaw Pact, CMEA, and the forthcoming international Communist conference which, he stated, "is destined to play a great role."

On balance, the outcome of Kádár's visit as reflected in the communiqué and the speeches of the two leaders pointed to the Hungarian acceptance of the use of force as a last resort if the CPCz did not bring negative influences under control. On the Soviet side the need for a unified bloc approach to all questions, including Czechoslovakia, clearly emerged, as did their need for increased consultation and coordination. If Brezhnev himself now believed that the threat to Communist construction in Czechoslovakia had increased, as his remarks seemed to imply, nowhere did he indicate that all alternative methods of dealing with the crisis had been exhausted. On the contrary, his emphasis on bloc cohesion and the value of negotiation was very much in accord with Kádár's statement that the best way to overcome bloc difficulties was to "strengthen and develop the socialist countries' organizations and all forms of bilateral and multilateral cooperation."[51] Thus the visit of the Hungarian delegation seemed to have been successful in helping to create a consensus in favor of continued, if urgent, negotiation to avoid the use of force. These results bore fruit in the series of letters that the CPCz leadership received from the five fraternal parties following Kádár's departure on July 4.

MOSCOW URGES MULTILATERAL TALKS

By the time Kádár departed, the Soviets had agreed on their next course. They, in concert with Hungary, Bulgaria, Poland and East Germany, would ask the CPCz leadership to attend a multilateral conference for the purpose of strengthening bloc cohesion and reminding the Czechs that no socialist country could remain indifferent to the negative processes taking place in Prague.

[51] Kádár's speech, July 3, 1968, SU/2813/C/7.

There is no definite indication of when the decision (*number 23*) was taken. But it is likely that the June 30 decision (*number 22*) to rescind the report announcing the end of Pact maneuvers spurred a search for alternatives that led to agreement (probably on July 1 or 2) to further postpone the withdrawal of troops and seek an urgent multilateral meeting with the CPCz leadership and other bloc states. The need for joint consultations appears to have been discussed with the Hungarian delegation on July 3 and was certainly generally reflected in the communiqué and the speeches of Kádár and Brezhnev. Even if a Politburo meeting formally made the decision, the numbers present would have been diminished, for Kirilenko, Shelest, Shcherbitsky, and Rashidov were known to be out of Moscow,[52] and Polyansky, Demichev, Kunaev, Masherov, Mzhavanadze, and Kulakov were not mentioned in the Soviet press as present in the capital during the first days of July. Brezhnev, Kosygin, Podgorny, and Voronov (all of whom with Gromyko and Lesechko, the Soviet ambassador in Budapest, conducted the negotiations with the Hungarians) were in Moscow, as were Mazurov, Pel'she, Shelepin, a number of important Politburo candidate members, and other influential leaders such as Andropov, Grishin, Grechko, and Gromyko.[53]

The first letters from Moscow, Poland, and East Berlin arrived in Prague on July 4 with the Bulgarian and Hungarian versions arriving by July 6.[54] The actual letters were never officially released, but Yugoslav sources stated that "some of these letters, such as the East German and the Bulgarian, are really in the form of an ultimatum" to attend a bloc meeting.[55] Smrkovský confirmed that the five letters were couched so as to suggest that they were in fact "a summons to give an account of themselves."[56] All the letters were critical of Czech events, and all took the "2,000 Words" as their point of departure; Some reports even suggested that Ulbricht went so far as to offer the services of his own army and police

[52] Kirilenko headed a party delegation to Italy from June 26 to July 10 (*Pravda*, July 11, 1968); Rashidov was in Tashkent, participating in an Uzbek Central Committee plenum (*Pravda Vostoka*, June 22, 1968, and *Pravda*, July 5, 1968); Shelest and Shcherbitsky were at the Ukrainian party plenum (*Izvestia*, July 5, 1968, and *Pravda*, July 6, 1968).

[53] TASS, July 4, 1968, SU/2813/C/1; U.S. Department of State, *Research Memorandum*, *RSE–127*, August 16, 1968.

[54] The sequence with which the letters arrived was confirmed by Smrkovský, ČTK, July 6, 1968, EE/2816/C/4.

[55] Belgrade radio, July 13, 1968, EE/2822/C1/12.

[56] Smrkovský, *An Unfinished Conversation*, p. 19.

force to put down the counterrevolution in Prague.[57] Foreign Minister Hájek has revealed that the offensive tone of the "invitation" was emphasized in the official Czechoslovak response, which specifically stated that the very "tenor" of the letters had further convinced the Czechoslovak leadership that other bloc states were insufficiently informed about the situation in Prague.[58]

Pressure on Dubček to accept the "invitation" was extremely strong. Ambassador Chervonenko reportedly delivered a special letter to Dubček, informing him—incorrectly as it happened—that the other delegations were in fact already on their way to Warsaw to begin the bloc meeting.[59] According to Smrkovský, the special letter from Chervonenko arrived at the same time that the Soviet invitation was received, and this suggests that the Chervonenko letter probably was delivered on July 4. Dubček then received a telephone call from Brezhnev early on July 8 asking the Czechoslovak leadership to attend a meeting on July 10–11, an offer Dubček later maintained he declined to discuss without specific Praesidium authorization.[60]

Despite pressure for an immediate response, Dubček did not convene a Praesidium meeting until four days after the receipt of the initial letters. This delay was partly due to the dispersion of the leadership at the various regional party meetings being held throughout the country. When the Praesidium eventually did meet on July 8, it accepted the principle of further discussions but attached two conditions: first, any multilateral conference would have to be preceded by a further round of bilateral consultations on Czechoslovak soil; second, any bloc convocation would have to be enlarged to include Rumania and Yugoslavia.[61]

Dubček communicated this decision to Brezhnev by telephone at 8:30 P.M. on July 9.[62] Brezhnev is said to have been particularly interested in ascertaining if the decision not to attend a multilateral

[57] Michel Tatu, *Le Monde*, July 20, 1968; also see *Frankfurter Allgemeine Zeitung*, July 11, 1968.

[58] Jiří Hájek, *Dix ans après*, p. 87.

[59] Smrkovský, *An Unfinished Conversation*, p. 19.

[60] Dubček's speech of September 26, 1969, to the CPCz Central Committee, as contained in Shawcross, *Dubček*, p. 296; also U.S. Department of State, *Research Memorandum*, *RSE–127*, August 16, 1968.

[61] Michel Tatu, *Le Monde*, July 20; also Husák's speech on September 25, 1969, to the CPCz Central Committee (ČTK in English, September 28, 1969, EE/3190/C/18) and Smrkovský, *An Unfinished Conversation*, p. 19.

[62] Dubček's speech to September 1969, CPCz Central Committee plenum in Shawcross, *Dubček*, p. 286.

meeting had been ratified by all the members of the Praesidium, including particularly Drahomír Kolder.[63] Brezhnev clearly knew of Kolder's memorandum that there was "a raging counterrevolution" in Czechoslovakia which if left unchecked could lead to a "political catastrophe."[64] Jiří Pelikán maintains that the Soviet strategy at that time was to promote a split in the Praesidium that would force Dubček to call a special meeting of the Central Committee to discuss the response to these letters.[65] As the conservatives had far more influence in the Central Committee than they did in the Praesidium, the letters and their allegations about raging counter-revolution might have received a more favorable hearing in the Central Committee. Unfortunately for the conservatives, however, Kolder's attempt to obtain Praesidium approval to convene the Central Committee failed.[66]

Seen from Moscow, the situation in Czechoslovakia appeared to be especially ominous. Not only had the Praesidium flatly refused to give into bloc demands for negotiations, but the Soviets could no longer be sure that conservatives within the Czechoslovak Praesidium and Central Committee had any chance of even expressing their views, much less making a comeback. Then, at the very time Kolder failed to force the convocation of the conservative-dominated Central Committee, the Prague City Party Committee, dominated by liberals, went into permanent session.

UNCERTAINTY OVER TROOP WITHDRAWAL

Refusal of the Dubček leadership to attend the Warsaw meeting was not the only issue worrying Moscow. Soviet leaders also had to decide what to do with all the Soviet and bloc troops still in Czechoslovakia following the official end of staff exercise "Sumava." Marshal Yakubovsky's headquarters and a Soviet army communications center installed at Ruzyně Airport just outside Prague were not dismantled following the maneuvers (and indeed the facilities at Ruzyně ultimately were instrumental in landing Soviet airborne forces during the invasion). Privately, Czechoslovak military authorities, aware that the Soviets had spent much of the last month

[63] Michel Tatu, *Le Monde*, July 20, 1968.
[64] Kolder's memorandum, submitted on July 11, was published in *Tribuna*, September 10, 1969, and quoted in Skilling, *Czechoslovakia's Interrupted Revolution*, p. 289 n. 106.
[65] Jiří Pelikán, *Ein Frühling*, pp. 250–51.
[66] *Pravda pobezhdaet*, pp. 160–61.

drawing up detailed plans of all military facilities and air bases, became convinced that the Soviets were preparing for an invasion
should they be forced to withdraw.[67] Far from a military deescalation in early July, ships of the Soviet Baltic fleet moved into the
Atlantic, placing themselves astride Europe's supply routes with
North America, in case NATO should contemplate any resistance
to a possible Soviet invasion of Czechoslovakia later on.

The Soviet decision to kill the TASS story announcing the end of
maneuvers on June 30 gave rise to Czechoslovak fears that Moscow
had every intention of keeping its forces in the country to achieve
the de facto stationing of troops. Such fears were not allayed when
Czechoslovak journalists were denied entry to a briefing by Yakubovsky at the official end of the exercises. Rumors circulated
that Yakubovsky had concluded that the poor performance of the
Czechoslovak army necessitated a further round of maneuvers.
When Czechoslovak commanders protested that further exercises
were not possible until after the harvest, Yakubovsky is reported to
have replied that in that case Soviet troops would have to stay until
autumn.[68] Czechoslovak military authorities responded by announcing publicly on July 2, in a statement issued by the army's
official spokesman, General Čepický, that all foreign troops would
leave Czechoslovakia within the next two or three days.[69]

Soviet troops did not leave, however, and Brezhnev, at a July 8
Moscow reception for graduates of military academies, appeared to
support the arguments previously voiced by military leaders Yepishev, Konev, and Yakubovsky that the Prague Spring was affecting the morale and fighting capability of the Czechoslovak army.
Brezhnev stated:

> It is not to be wondered at that our enemies, in their attempts to
> weaken the socialist community or its unity resort to ideological sabo-
> tage which is also aimed at the armed forces of the individual socialist
> countries. And if imperialism is now carrying out attacks on the au-
> thority of the socialist armies and is seeking to weaken their links
> with the people, this demonstrates once again to all Communists and
> to the working class how important it is to protect this authority and
> strengthen those links. . . . The Warsaw Treaty countries have al-
> ready gathered much and manifold experience in military coopera-
> tion. With the aid of this experience, we will continue constantly to

[67] Otto von Pivka, *The Armies of Europe Today*, p. 90; Pelikán, *Ein Frühling*, p. 249.
[68] *New York Times*, July 17, 1968, quoting diplomatic sources from Warsaw.
[69] Prague Radio, July 2, 1968, RFE, *Research, Czechoslovakia*, July 10, 1968.

strengthen our collective defense and improve the machinery of co-operation between the fraternal armies.[70]

Brezhnev's failure to make any mention of the success of the Pact maneuvers that had just ended in Czechoslovakia and that were intended, after all, to test military cooperation and coordination between Pact armies is a rather notable omission.

Grechko, speaking on the same occasion, did not repeat any of Brezhnev's formulations about the ideological sabotage of fraternal armies. And although he too refrained from making any specific comment on the recent maneuvers, he did state that previous maneuvers of the fraternal armies "had proved the beneficial influence of the friendship and mutual understanding of the officers' corps of the Warsaw Treaty countries on dealing with common tasks." This certainly was a more optimistic appraisal of the current state of military cooperation than seemed warranted by the dispute between Moscow and Prague over Soviet withdrawal. Reminding the cadets that last April's Central Committee plenum called for "high political vigilance" against bourgeois propaganda, he still made no reference to imperialism's effort to subvert socialism from within. Instead, he singled out "above all" American imperialist activities in Vietnam and only then mentioned "the revanchist aspirations of leading circles in West Germany." Finally, whereas Brezhnev emphasized the duty of the armed forces to defend "the security of the Soviet Fatherland and the extensive socialist commonwealth," Grechko made no mention of the commonwealth, concluding his speech with the "Russia first" statement, "We have all that is necessary . . . to defend the Homeland."[71]

In Czechoslovakia, the controversy over withdrawal continued. Čestmír Císař in an interview on July 9 was adamant in his insistence that Soviet troops were about to leave Czechoslovakia and that they definitely would not be staying until the end of September.[72] General Dzúr supported this, adding that "specialized analyses" and technical repairs were still being made, but that all staff and troops would leave after the completion of this work.[73] Dzúr also revealed that only 35% of the foreign troops had left Czechoslovakia, and he hinted at difficulties in the negotiations with the

---

[70] Moscow radio, July 8, 1968, SU/2817/C/3.
[71] Izvestia, July 9, 1968.
[72] ČTK, July 9, 1968, EE/2818/C/3.
[73] Ibid.

Soviets for withdrawal when he said that "we believe they will understand us."[74]

The next day, July 10, General Prchlík was asked in the course of a television interview why Soviet troops had not withdrawn despite Čepický's statement. Prchlík responded: "If General Čepický said that, obviously such a plan was under consideration. And since it did not materialize, apparently a new situation has arisen." When asked at what time the Czechoslovak military authorities would have a definite date for withdrawal, Prchlík replied: "Tomorrow I will be wiser than I am today."[75] On the same day, an angry telephone exchange took place between Dubček and Brezhnev, with eyewitnesses saying that Dubček pounded the table while addressing the Soviet leader.[76] The Czechoslovaks were not going to settle for anything approaching de facto stationing, and clearly a decision would have to be made in Moscow.

THE JULY 10 MEETING

Three interrelated decisions (*numbers 24, 25,* and *26*) were in fact made on July 10. The first decision was to defuse the situation surrounding the maneuvers by agreeing to withdraw at least some Soviet troops. At 10:00 P.M. on July 11, Czechoslovak radio stations broadcast a communiqué of the WTO Joint Staff High Command stating that troops currently in Czechoslovakia would "gradually" be returning to their respective countries in accordance with a timetable worked out by the maneuvers' staff.[77] The TASS version of the communiqué, published in *Pravda* on July 12, failed to make any reference to the gradual withdrawal of troops. It confined itself instead to stating that the various tasks set before the participants had been fulfilled. It was also rather unusual in singling out the presence of Dubček, Svoboda, Černík, Smrkovský, and Dzúr at the analysis of the exercises held by Yakubovsky without listing any of the other participants. Finally, the article made no specific reference to the dates the maneuvers were held, stating only that they took place "in June and July." No explanation was ever given for these disparities, but everything points to some indecision in the military establishment about the withdrawal of troops.

[74] ČTK, July 9, 1968, RFE, *Research, Czechoslovakia*, July 10, 1968.
[75] Czechoslovak television, July 10, 1968, RFE, *Research, Czechoslovakia*, July 11, 1968.
[76] Kenneth Ames, "Reform and Reaction," p. 48.
[77] ČTK, July 11, 1968, EE/2820/i; RFE, *Research, Czechoslovakia*, July 12, 1968.

It seems likely that the telephone call from Dubček prompted Brezhnev's participation in the decision to withdraw, making this a joint decision by high military and party leaders. An editorial in *Krasnaya zvezda* on July 12 entitled "The Invincible Friendship of Warriors" attempted to dispel the various rumors surrounding the maneuvers. The article stated that the purposes of the exercises had been to perfect coordination between allied armies, increase combat readiness, and promote friendship and that all these objectives had been achieved. Attacking the various "imperialist fabrications" circulating about the maneuvers, *Krasnaya zvezda* asked: "What, for instance, is the good of the clumsy attempt by Western anti-Soviet propagandists to depict the joint exercise as a means of forcing the USSR's own strategic concepts on its allies?"

It is likely that Grechko was involved in the decision to withdraw Soviet troops; it is also possible that he had a hand in the *Krasnaya zvezda* article, the phrasing of which seemed to label anyone who favored de facto stationing (including Yakubovsky) as a "Western anti-Soviet propagandist." An unexplained change in Grechko's schedule further suggests that he and the rest of the Soviet High Command—as opposed to the Warsaw Pact High Command—began to play a more pronounced role in military decision making for Czechoslovakia. On June 30, it was announced both on Soviet radio and in the newspapers, that Marshal Grechko would begin an official visit to Algeria on July 9. His departure, however, was postponed without explanation. All the remaining military maneuvers conducted after July 9 were commanded not by Warsaw Pact officers but directly by the Soviet High Command in collaboration with individual East European military establishments.[78] It would appear therefore that *decision 24* involved not only formal ending of the Warsaw Pact maneuvers in Czechoslovakia headed by Yakubovsky and Kazakov, but also—and more importantly— the transfer of operational control for any future exercise or military actions to the Soviet High Command, under Grechko's direct supervision.

The Czechoslovak authorities responded with considerable re-

[78] Maneuvers held after July 9 included Soviet, Polish, and East German ships in operation "Sever" (North), commanded by S. Gorshkov, Soviet admiral of the fleet; operation "Skyshield," controlled by Marshal Batitsky of the Soviet Air Force; and operation "Memel," involving the movement of Soviet reservists and their equipment to the areas surrounding Czechoslovakia. The maneuvers that began on August 11 and culminated in the invasion were also commanded by Soviet officers headed by General Pavlovsky of the Soviet Army.

lief to the announcement of troop withdrawals. General Prchlík, answering further questions on television, asserted: Any "stationing of troops" by one state on the territories of other states was done "always in agreement with these states—I stress *after* an agreement with these states." When asked whether "guarantees were really given this time" that allied troops would leave Czechoslovakia by the agreed deadline, Prchlík responded: "I see the guarantee in the fact that it is an official, obviously well-advised and responsible statement by the commander of the Warsaw Treaty, and I personally do not doubt that this military word will be kept by the commanders."[79]

OSTPOLITIK REJECTED

At the same time that the Soviet leadership was trying to reach agreement over the withdrawal of Pact troops, another decision (*number 25*) was made: to abandon the secret negotiations with the Bonn government over the renunciation-of-force agreement. Despite the statement by Foreign Minister Gromyko on June 27 that "the Soviet government is ready for a continuation of the exchange of views with the FRG on the renunciation of the use of force," the promulgation of emergency laws in West Germany, coupled with Bonn's growing friendship with Prague and the commensurate deterioration in relations with East Germany, made it almost impossible for any Soviet leader to argue in favour of *Westpolitik*. It was clearly inconsistent to blame West German "revanchists" for inciting counterrevolution in Prague and at the same time negotiate with Bonn to strengthen security in Europe. Even Gromyko's speech had contained an icy denunciation of Bonn's *Ostpolitik*, and several Soviet leaders, including Brezhnev, increased their criticism of West German efforts to divide the socialist bloc. This theme was expressed in newspaper articles during the first week of July[80] and until July 10, when the Soviet leadership conclusively decided to end the exchange of letters with West Germany.

On July 11 the Soviets began the unilateral publication of the previously secret documents involved in the exchanges, and from the published evidence it would appear that negotiations found-

---

[79] Prague radio, July 11, 1968, EE/2820/C/2; and Bratislava television, July 11, 1968, EE/2820/C/3.

[80] *Izvestia*, July 6, 1968.

ered on two main issues: Soviet demands that Bonn conclude identical, and presumably simultaneous, renunciation-of-force agreements with all East European states, including the GDR, until
which time the USSR would maintain its right of intervention in
West Germany; and the demand for a significant reduction in the
Federal Republic's presence in West Berlin.[81] Both these requirements were consistent with East German attitudes. Gomułka, too,
evidently opposed signing a nonaggression pact with Bonn until
the Federal Republic recognized the Oder-Neisse line as the western boundary of Poland. Thus Gomułka had his own reasons for
supporting Ulbricht's opposition to secret Soviet-West German relations, and the abandonment of those relations represented a victory for both these bloc leaders and for the hard-liners in Moscow.
The issue of Bonn's ties with Czechoslovakia was useful ammuni-
tion for this coalition. Thus conservatives had succeeded in forcing
Moscow to abandon, for the time being, any hopes of "détente" in
Europe, and the "German threat" to the unity of the bloc and to
socialism in Czechoslovakia became a major and increasingly important theme for the public expression of concern over the reform
movement in Prague.

PRAVDA SIGNALS CONSENSUS

Decision number 26 was to proceed with the publication of a major
Pravda editorial entitled "Attack on the Socialist Foundations of
Czechoslovakia." Published on July 11, it represented the Soviets'
harshest official denunciation of the Prague Spring to date. Signed
by I. Alexandrov, the article clearly had Politburo endorsement, as
confirmed by Kosygin two days later during his press conference in
Stockholm. Asked by journalists to explain the Soviet view of the
democratization process in Czechoslovakia, he advised them to
read the Alexandrov article, saying, "It reflects our assessment of
the events now taking place in Czechoslovakia."[82]

Previous analyses of the Alexandrov article have pointed to the
more unyielding elements of the piece as indicating that the hawks
were in the ascendancy. Although the dominant impression left by
Alexandrov was indeed that Soviet patience was running out, a care-

[81] This evidence is discussed in N. Edwina Moreton, "The Impact of Détente on Relations between the Member States of the Warsaw Pact," pp. 148–49.

[82] *Pravda*, July 15, 1968.

ful dissection reveals that the article was in fact a blend of the various views on Czechoslovakia being expressed by Soviet leaders.

To begin, the article contained an explicit comparison between the tactics used by "counterrevolutionary elements" in Czechoslovakia and those used twelve years previously in Hungary. To the extent that there were any differences between 1956 and 1968, the editorial maintained, "the tactics of those who would like to undermine the foundations of socialism in Czechoslovakia are even more subtle and insidious." This was the first time that the Politburo had specifically endorsed elements of the theory of "quiet counterrevolution," which was to gain prominence as an argument by hard-liners in favor of invasion. It was most fully enunciated after the invasion in the September 11 *Pravda* article by Kovalev (also the author of the so-called Brezhnev doctrine). According to this theory, it is not necessary to wait for blood in the streets before going to the aid of good Communists; indeed the leaders of each new counterrevolution, aware that open revolt, as in 1956, had in the past only provoked overwhelming military response, would become ever more subversive and insidious. Defenders of socialism, therefore, should take action not solely in response to an irrevocable breakdown in law and order but when the socialist foundations of a society are being undermined.

Second, the Alexandrov article made veiled reference to Smrkovský, Kriegel, and others who had censured the "2,000 Words" for its "political romanticism"[83] without however condemning it as counterrevolutionary. The article seemed to express regret rather than anger about this: "Unfortunately, some Czechoslovak leaders have made ambiguous statements attempting to minimize the danger of the '2,000 Words.'" This mild rebuke was in contrast to much harsher articles that appeared at the same time in both *Literaturnaya gazeta* and *Sovetskaya Rossiya*, with the former specifically accusing František Kriegel of having "expressed solidarity . . . with works of this ilk."[84] The "2,000 Words" was condemned in itself, but the main thrust of the harsher elements of the Alexandrov article was that support for the "2,000 Words" had proved that this document was "not an isolated phenomenon, but evidence of the increasing activity in Czechoslovakia of rightist and

[83] See Smrkovský's "1000 Words" in *Rudé právo*, July 5, 1968.
[84] Article by "Zhurnalist," *Literaturnaya gazeta*, July 10, 1968; also *Sovetskaya Rossiya*, July 12, 1968.

overtly counterrevolutionary forces obviously linked with imperialist reaction."

The article reprinted excerpts from the bloc press, drawing from the Bulgarian *Rabotnichesko Delo* the statement that "our public cannot remain indifferent when the foundations of socialism are under attack in a friendly, fraternal country." The Hungarian party newspaper *Népszabadság* was quoted as advising that "those who are speaking out against the people's rule, against the socialist system and its legal order must be fought by the most effective means required in the present situation." This latter statement can certainly be construed as Hungarian advice to the CPCz to employ immediate administrative measures to put an end to antisocialist activities—it cannot in itself be interpreted as Hungarian support for an invasion.

On this issue, the final sentence of the Alexandrov article promises that "the working class and all Czechoslovak people can always count on the understanding and complete support of the people of the Soviet land." A commitment ultimately to use force if necessary to maintain socialism may be implied from this, but other aspects of the article clearly indicate that the Politburo did not as yet believe that all other alternatives had been exhausted. Thus, the article was careful to detail the fact that "the healthy forces" in Czechoslovakia had condemned the "2,000 Words," noting that the CPCz Praesidium, the Slovak Central Committee, the CPCz regional party organizations, the Czechoslovak government, the National Front, the National Assembly, public organizations, and various enterprise collectives had all "expressed sharp criticism" of the document. In the penultimate paragraph, the article concludes that "the peoples of the Soviet Union and other socialist countries . . . express confidence that the Czechoslovak Communists and all the working people in the ČSSR, being deeply interested in strengthening the country's socialist foundations, will succeed in dealing a decisive rebuff to the reactionary antisocialist forces." Not yet had a consensus emerged in the Politburo that the "healthy forces" were insufficient to deal with the situation inside their own country, although there was apparent agreement that "counterrevolutionary forces," in the words of Alexandrov, were making "fierce attacks against the foundations of socialist statehood" and that these forces had to be stopped, one way or the other.

That the developing consensus in the Politburo represented a balance between contending views can be seen more clearly when one considers the subjects *not* included in the Alexandrov article. There was no mention at all of "proletarian internationalism," dealt with at such length by both Brezhnev and Shelest earlier in the month (Shelest recently had included "mutual aid" as a vitally important element of proletarian internationalism).[85] Nor was there any reference to the possible use of the military as a legitimate form of "mutual brotherly aid," as proposed by Grishin in April.[86] Imperialism in general and the Western press in particular were condemned for their interest in supporting antisocialist forces in Czechoslovakia, but the Alexandrov article is notable for making no specific mention of "Bonn's revanchist policies," criticized earlier in the week by Brezhnev and frequently condemned by the Soviets. Finally, although the 1956 Hungarian uprising was discussed and Hungarian opinion comparing the events in Prague and Budapest quoted, there were many more hard-line statements on this subject made in both the USSR and the bloc that Moscow could have quoted had a more militant consensus emerged in the Politburo. Brezhnev's own view, stated the previous week, that the Hungarian Communists had prevailed in 1956 by relying on, among other things, "the fraternal international alliance" was not explicitly mentioned. Nor, interestingly enough, did Alexandrov quote any of the more extreme articles appearing in the East German or Polish media, even though some of these articles were being reprinted verbatim in the Soviet press at this time.[87] *Decision number twenty-six*, therefore, committed the entire Politburo to this general line: The situation in Czechoslovakia threatened the socialist foundations of that country, and future action of some type by the USSR and its allies might be necessary to help deter antisocialist forces; for the time being, however, it was agreed that the CPCz had the capability to deal adequately with the situation.

There were still, however, some Soviet leaders who felt that the Czechoslovak authorities lacked the will to stop antisocialist excesses and failed to appreciate the seriousness with which the situation was seen elsewhere in the bloc. Brezhnev's own speech only days earlier had been more hard-line than the Alexandrov article,

---

[85] Both published in *Pravda*, July 5, 1968.

[86] *Izvestia*, April 23, 1968; *Leninskoe znamya*, April 23, 1968.

[87] A *Neues Deutschland* editorial of July 13, 1968, claimed for example that "the political offensive of imperialism is directed against Czechoslovakia, but thereby also against the vital interests of the GDR and of all the states of the socialist community." This appeared in *Pravda* on July 14, 1968, with the words "of the GDR and" removed, however.

and it must be concluded that Brezhnev now counted himself as one of these leaders. The general line actually appears to have been the lowest common denominator, in which invasion was held as an option but was still not inevitable. With Brezhnev's public proclamation that counterrevolution in Hungary had been averted by Soviet military assistance, the possible became the probable. His conversations with Dubček and the Czechoslovak refusal to attend a multilateral meeting appear to have made Brezhnev much more pessimistic about the chance for a peaceful solution to the conflict. As a result, almost from the moment the decision (*number 26*) was taken to commit the Politburo to the Alexandrov line, that line was under incredible pressure. It was becoming clear that an impasse had been reached, and one side or the other would have to break it.

OBSERVERS FEAR INVASION

Continued Czechoslovak refusal to attend the Warsaw meeting produced a discernible escalation of tension, and a number of incidents led observers to conclude that an invasion was actively being considered in certain quarters. In one such incident on July 12, an arms cache of American-made weapons deposited in five rucksacks was found near Sokolovo in Western Bohemia. It was subsequently stated by Interior Minister Pavel that the arms had been planted and that the incident had been intended as a provocation designed to "prove" U.S. backing for counterrevolutionary forces.[88] Furthermore, Czechoslovak sources later in the month made it known that the weapons had been of mixed origin—possibly including some of East German manufacture—that the Soviet and Bulgarian press agencies reported the cache before the Czechoslovak authorities had revealed its existence, and that although the Soviet report quoted local eyewitnesses to the discovery, none could be found.[89] It was also alleged that Warsaw Pact troops had conducted maneuvers in the Sokolovo area only days before the cache was uncovered.[90]

In a second incident, the promised withdrawal of Pact troops, which began on July 13, was abruptly halted on the next day, with reports circulating in Prague that planeloads of "Soviet tourists"

[88] Quoted in RFE, *Research, Czechoslovakia*, July 23, 1968. Also Mlynář, *Night Frost in Prague*, p. 170.

[89] *Práce*, July 22, 1968; *Zemědělský noviny*, July 23, 1968.

[90] L. Bittman, *The Deception Game*, pp. 194–95.

were arriving at various Czechoslovak airfields and reporting directly to Soviet units.[91] Yakubovsky informed the Czechoslovak government that any withdrawal would not now take place before July 21.[92] He appears to have been concerned that any use of Soviet troops to achieve political objectives in Prague would become immeasurably more difficult if those troops were forced to withdraw and then reenter Czechoslovakia in a clear invasion of sovereign territory. From the military standpoint, it was far better to delay withdrawal, even if it fostered Czechoslovak resentment; for to have to intervene at a later date across Czechoslovak frontiers posed enormous military and political problems. Procrastination was, therefore, the military's strategy until the political leadership formally decided what it was going to do.

Prchlík was not the only leader who feared an imminent invasion. Kádár met with Dubček and Černík on the Czechoslovak-Hungarian border on July 13, both to encourage them to attend the Warsaw meeting and to warn the Czechoslovaks that in their absence, some participants might press for an invasion. As Prchlík reported the encounter, Kádár told Dubček and Černík that although the Hungarians "harbor certain apprehensions about the intensity of antisocialist manifestations," they "very positively" assess the overall objectives of the reform movement and they "are resolved to act in Warsaw in such a manner that nothing is adopted there which would further aggravate the dispute as well as nothing which would involve a violation of our [Czechoslovakia's] state sovereignty."[93] Other statements by Hungarian leaders at the time confirmed their general support for the Czechoslovak position. Foreign Minister János Péter, in an address to the Hungarian National Assembly on July 13, declared: "I should like to express the hope that the current internal process in Czechoslovakia will . . . make a contribution to raising the international prestige of the socialist world."[94] During the same debate, János Gosztonyi, the editor in chief of *Népszabadság*, the same newspaper quoted by *Pravda*'s Alexandrov two days previously, stated: "Is there a counterrevolution in Czechoslovakia? The answer is, not at all." Despite

[91] According to Lt. Gen. Prchlík on July 15, quoted by Tanyug, July 16, 1968, EE/2824/C1/5.

[92] Tanyug, July 17, 1968, EE/2824/C1/5.

[93] Prague Radio, July 15, 1968, quoted in Remington, *Winter in Prague*, p. 219. The Yugoslav News agency Tanyug also reported the meeting on July 13, 1968; also the *Times*, July 16, 1968.

[94] MTI, July 13, 1968, EE/2823/A1/3.

the fact that "antisocialist forces have become livelier in Czechoslovakia, . . . Hungarians remain convinced that the Czechoslovak sister party will carry out the cause of socialism to triumph in its country."[95]

Statements from Yugoslavia and Rumania also made it clear that the danger of invasion was perceived as imminent and real. President Tito had granted an interview to Egyptian journalist Mohamed Heikal, which was due to be published in Heikal's column in *al-Ahram* on July 19. Heikal then received an urgent telegram from Tito asking that the section of the interview dealing with Czechoslovakia be released immediately. This was done on July 13, with Tito quoted as saying: "I do not believe that there exist in the USSR people so shortsighted as to resort to a policy of force to resolve Czechoslovakia's internal questions. . . . Moreover, I do not believe that there is anything about the present situation in Czechoslovakia which constitutes a threat to socialism."[96]

President Ceauşescu of Rumania took the occasion of a visit to, of all places, a tractor factory to deliver this warning against invasion: "Our people, the Rumanian Communist party, do not share the view of those who are alarmed over what, allegedly, is happening in Czechoslovakia, and would like to intervene to bring Czechoslovakia on a particular socialist road. We have full confidence in the Communist party of Czechoslovakia, and we are convinced that . . . they will know how to build socialism in Czechoslovakia in accordance with their hopes and aspirations."[97]

So great was the concern of Euro-Communist parties that Waldeck Rochet, head of the French party, flew to Moscow with two Italian Communist party representatives, Giancarlo Pajetta and Carlo Galuzzi, thus marking the first time that the two largest Communist parties in Europe had acted in concert against a Soviet policy. French Communist party sources leaked a story to the Western press three weeks later to the effect that Rochet's trip had been prompted by a definite warning that the Soviets had assembled a puppet government which they were preparing to install as soon as Dubček could be toppled either by military pressure or by a palace coup.[98] By the time the delegation arrived in

[95] MTI, July 13, 1968, EE/2823/A1/4.

[96] Mohamed Heikal, *Sphinx and Commissar*, pp. 204–05; Tanyug, July 13, 1968, EE/2822/i.

[97] Agerpress, July 15, 1968, EE/2823/A1/2.

[98] *Sunday Telegraph*, quoting French Communist Party sources, August 11, 1968. The PCF statement issued following the invasion confirmed that Rochet had warned the Soviets

Moscow on July 14, however, Soviet leaders had already left for hurriedly arranged talks in Warsaw, and as a result they were able to see only Suslov and Zagladin, Ponomarev's deputy in the International Department.

All the evidence, therefore, points to a discernible and sudden reverse in the Soviet attitude toward invasion. The general line reflected in the Alexandrov article apparently had been perceived by the hard-liners as merely a consolidation before a further and immediate round of escalation.

KOSYGIN IS OUTMANEUVERED

Prime Minister Kosygin left for Sweden on the morning of July 11, accompanied by First Deputy Foreign Minister Kuznetsov and L. M. Zamyatin. From beginning to end, his trip to Sweden was overshadowed by events in Moscow, Warsaw, and Prague. His plane touched down late, officially explained by a late takeoff from Moscow. Then as soon as he landed he announced that although he had intended to stay until Sunday, July 14, he would now be returning to Moscow on July 13. Throughout the three days, he was preoccupied with Czechoslovakia, and on several occasions when speaking about events in Sweden he inadvertently substituted Czechoslovakia. He did, however, find time before leaving Sweden to hold a press conference for Western journalists. When asked whether events in Czechoslovakia were the cause of his early departure, Kosygin replied: "It is because our time is limited . . . and because we have concluded our work somewhat ahead of schedule that we are leaving Sweden today." The entire press conference was published in *Pravda* on July 15, after Kosygin's return from Sweden and while Czechoslovakia's fate was still being decided in Warsaw. The fact that the following question from an Associated Press correspondent was published in *Pravda* along with Kosygin's full answer is therefore all the more remarkable:

> *(Question)*   Mr. Chairman, do you consider that the leading role of the Communist party of Czechoslo-

---

against invasion (*L'Humanité*, August 23, 1968; *New York Times*, August 23, 1968). Also see the transcript of the meeting between Rochet and Dubček on July 19, 1968, in which Rochet warned that the situation was not only serious, but "extremely dangerous" (*L'Humanité*, May 18, 1970). Also a U.S. State Department Intelligence Note (No. 563) marked "secret" from the Director of Intelligence and Research to Secretary of State Rusk on July 17 stated that Rochet had indeed argued against intervention.

vakia is now seriously endangered, and do you consider military or political intervention [*vmeshatel'stvo*] in Czechoslovak affairs possible under certain circumstances?

(*Answer*)   Our country and our party have long marched in struggle and friendship side by side with the Czechoslovak people and the CPCz. The fight against German fascism in the Second World War cemented the friendship between the Czechoslovak and Soviet peoples and strengthened the trust and unity between the CPCz and the CPSU. We are confident the CPCz will yield its leading role to no one. An attack on the socialist base of Czechoslovakia would meet with an effective rebuff from the Czechoslovak people and Communists. We are also confident that no force exists that can destroy the friendship between our two peoples. The Soviet Union and Czechoslovakia are allies in the Warsaw Treaty. We have mutual obligations deriving from this treaty, and we shall fulfil them without reservation.[99]

Kosygin's pointed reference to the obligations deriving from Soviet membership in the Warsaw Pact was particularly interesting since the terms of the Warsaw Pact Treaty sanctioned the entry of Soviet troops onto Czechoslovak territory only in the event of a direct military attack on Czechoslovakia by the Federal Republic of Germany, or forces allied with it. The only question that did not appear in the *Pravda* account related to the continued Soviet military presence in Czechoslovakia. When asked whether this constituted a form of military pressure, Kosygin dismissed the question, stating this was an issue that "bothered the Western press but not the Czechoslovaks."[100] In other respects, the conference was reported in full, leaving the Soviet public with the clear impression that Kosygin, at least, did not see any reason why the CPCz could not deal adequately with the situation.

On his return from Sweden on July 13, Kosygin was met at the airport by Voronov, Mazurov, Pel'she, Andropov, Grishin, Ponomarev, and Gromyko. Suslov presumably was meeting with Rochet; and Brezhnev, Podgorny, Shelest, and Katushev had already departed by train for Warsaw. The extent of Kosygin's exclusion

[99] *Pravda*, July 15, 1968; also *SWB*, July 14, 1968, SU/2322/C1/3.
[100] *New York Times*, July 13, 1968; and *Christian Science Monitor*, July 16, 1968.

from the decision to go to Warsaw was further illustrated by the TASS statement printed on the front page of *Pravda* on July 14:

> On July 12 the delegation of the Soviet Union left Moscow for Warsaw for participation in a meeting of leaders of socialist countries, the composition of which included . . . L. I. Brezhnev (head of the delegation) . . . N. V. Podgorny . . . *A. N. Kosygin* . . . P. Ye. Shelest . . . K. F. Katushev. On July 13 the delegation arrived in Warsaw [emphasis added].

Of course, it is known that Kosygin was not on the train to Warsaw, and indeed he did not arrive until July 14, the day the formal conference actually started. What is even more remarkable than erroneously listing Kosygin's name among the others was that directly below the TASS announcement on the front page of *Pravda* was the text of the joint Soviet-Swedish communiqué, the first sentence of which stated that Kosygin had been in Sweden from July 11 to 13. If the careful *Pravda* reader failed to pick up this discrepancy, further proof was given elsewhere on the page that Kosygin could not possibly have been on the train when it left Moscow, or even picked it up en route to Warsaw. Two articles giving detailed accounts of Kosygin's movements in Sweden and his flight back to Moscow told the reader that Kosygin's press conference in Stockholm had taken place "in the second half of the day" after an official lunch. He could not have arrived in Moscow, therefore, before early evening, and in any case, probably after the rest of the delegation reached Warsaw. These articles, combined with the publication of the press conference the following day, demonstrated not only that there was no truth in the TASS story but also, and more importantly, that although Kosygin had been excluded from the decision to go to Warsaw, he had sufficient support to signal publicly that counsels were divided in the Kremlin.

HARD-LINERS REGROUP

There seems little doubt that the decision to proceed with the immediate convocation of the Warsaw meeting was taken without Kosygin's participation, and very possibly without his foreknowledge. There are in fact two decisions that can be traced. First, the Soviet leadership decided (*decision 27*) on July 11 to reassert the need for a meeting and duly organized a joint letter from the "five" that was delivered, according to Dubček, "on Thursday, July 11, in the late hours." Although Dubček stated that the letter urged the

CPCz Praesidium to participate in the Warsaw conference, he was adamant that "the new day for this conference was not mentioned in the letter."[101] Thus, at the Praesidium meeting on July 12, the Czechoslovak leadership felt no immediate pressure and reiterated its desire for bilateral talks. The Praesidium was later to state that their meeting had been superfluous since the Soviets, without informing Prague, had already fixed the date of the meeting for July 14. And indeed they claimed not to have been informed of the date until July 13 when the news agencies reported the arrival of the CPSU delegation in Warsaw.[102] Most Czechoslovak leaders subsequently agreed that the failure to attend the Warsaw meeting had been a "fatal mistake," with others, including Bil'ak and Husák, alleging that Dubček had been told the date of the meeting and had failed to inform the Praesidium. Either way, the Soviet decision (*number 28*) to hold the meeting on July 14 must have been made on either July 11 or 12.[103]

The Warsaw meeting was almost certainly called to formulate a bloc consensus for inclusion of military measures as one of the possible—and increasingly likely—alternatives for dealing with the crisis. The Central Committee of the CPSU would also need to be consulted; and given the amount of time required for the organization of a full plenum, for the preparation of speeches and for provincial leaders to fly to Moscow, it would seem likely that the decision (*number 29*) to convene the plenum was made on July 11 or 12, before Brezhnev, Shelest, Podgorny, and Katushev left for Poland —and while Kosygin was still in Sweden. The plenum eventually opened on July 17, less than twenty-four hours after the Soviet delegation's return from Warsaw.

There were several important pillars of support for intervention. One was Shelest and his supporters within the Ukrainian leadership. Some of these, including Yu. V. Il'nitsky (first secretary of the Transcarpathian *oblast'*) and A. P. Botvin (a member of the Central Auditing Commission and head of the Kiev City Party Committee) recently had published explicit attacks on the reform movement and its effect on the Ukraine, claiming, as Botvin did, that recently in the Ukraine "people are even ready to reiterate the decadent

[101] Dubček's speech to July 19, 1968, CPCz CC plenum, in Remington, *Winter in Prague*, p. 245.

[102] Czechoslovak Reply to the Warsaw Letter, ibid., p. 242.

[103] Hájek, *Dix ans après*, p. 112; Mlynář, *Nightfrost*, p. 167; Bil'ak, *Pravda pobezhdaet*, p. 145; and Husák's speech to CPCz CC plenum, September 25, 1969, EE/3190/C/18.

petty 'theories' of enemy propaganda about the necessity of a 'democratization' and 'liberalization' of socialism."[104]

A second group included the republican and important provincial (*oblast'*) party secretaries and Central Committee functionaries responsible for ideological indoctrination and control, a task that was becoming increasingly difficult. Hard-line sentiments on Czechoslovakia within the top leadership were reported by Western intelligence as shared "to the point of alarm by the regional Party leaders on the Union Republic and Oblast' (province) level, many of whom are Central Committee members." The report went on to state that "these men, being in direct charge of the population, would have to worry about Czech contagion at the grass-roots level, and they consequently are a very conservative lot on the whole."[105] Judging from the newspaper articles written by members of this group and from their input into Central Committee plenums—where men such as Grishin (Moscow), Kulichenko (Volgograd), Snechkus (Lithuania), and Voss (Latvia) delivered hard-line speeches against Czechoslovakia—many of them were indeed worried to the "point of alarm." This group was composed of party secretaries with many different motivations, however. Some, in charge of non-Russian areas, particularly the Ukraine and Baltic republics, were concerned about the revival of anti-Russian nationalism in their regions. Some from the Russian Republic viewed Czechoslovak pronouncements about the inapplicability of the Soviet model to their own historical circumstances as examples of anti-Russian sentiments and opposed them for that reason. Western intelligence sources noted that "some local leaders are even faced with revived Russian nationalism against the Czechs,"[106] and given the upsurge of what Alexander Yanov has called the "Russian New Right" during 1968, the importance of grass-roots Russian na-

[104] *Pravda*, July 13, 1968; Il'nitsky, *Radjanska Ukraina*, July 6, 1968. Botwin may have been referring to an article in *Literaturna Ukraina* on July 2, 1968, entitled "Friendship and Brotherhood Should Become Stronger." Writing on the "Ukrainian Days," which had recently been held in the Prešov region of Czechoslovakia, the author had quoted exclusively and exhaustively from the Czech press on this festival as proof that Czechoslovak-Ukrainian friendship was continually growing. The *New York Times* also reported on July 18, 1968, that Shelest himself had stated "the previous week" that liberal influences from neighboring Czechoslovakia had stirred demands among young Ukrainian workers for reforms.

[105] U.S. Department of State, *Research Memorandum, RSE–127*, August 16, 1968.

[106] Ibid. A samizdat publication appeared in Moscow in 1969 entitled "The National Shame of Great Russians," which acknowledged the power of Great Russian nationalism at the highest levels as a motivator of the decision to invade. The piece is reprinted in Stephen Cohen, ed., *An End to Silence*, pp. 293–96.

tionalist feeling against the Czechs and its support and encouragement right up to the highest levels should not be discounted. If
Yanov is to be believed, Polyansky was its chief but not sole patron
within the Politburo.[107] Others, represented by party secretaries
Kirilenko, Demichev, and Pel'she, were concerned about the
effect of Czechoslovak reforms of the party structure on their own
ability to control the intelligentsia and the internal workings of the
CPSU in the face of possible similar demands for revision of the
cadre system, democratic centralism, inner-party democracy, and
so on. Demichev recently had identified himself openly with a
hard line toward Czechoslovakia in his article in *Kommunist* entitled "The Building of Socialism and the Tasks of the Social Sciences."[108] He first rejected the notion of "ideological pluralism"
within Marxism, attacking it as a cover for a fundamental challenge
to the party's monopoly of ideology (p. 17) and labeling it as a veiled
form of "anti-Sovietism," which had become "the common platform of all the revisionists and unites them with professional anti-
Communists" (p. 18). He continued with a long section on the development of the relationship between various classes in a socialist
society, maintaining that the Western interest in Czechoslovakia
was further proof that "the bourgeoisie would like to break the
moral-political unity of the peoples of the socialist countries."
(p. 26). On the issue of the development of socialist democracy,
Demichev condemned those who "slander . . . the leading role of
the Communist Party," and he offered a strong reminder to any
possible supporters of the Czech experiment:

> Historical experience has already shown that expatiations about de-
> mocracy and "liberalization" are used by counterrevolution as a
> smokescreen for attempts to liquidate the conquests of socialism and
> socialist democracy. We remember how, during the Hungarian events
> of 1956, under these slogans counterrevolution caused the bloody car-
> nage of Communists [p. 27].

Given the nature of Podgorny's speech on Czechoslovakia the
following week and his known close contacts with Ulbricht (he was
in East Germany from June 30 to July 2 to celebrate Ulbricht's
seventy-fifth birthday), it can probably be assumed that Podgorny
counted himself among the hard-liners. Publication in *Sovetskaya*

---

[107] Alexander Yanov, *The Russian New Right*, pp. 15, 60.
[108] P. N. Demichev, "Stroitel'stvo kommunizma i zadachi obshchestvennykh nauk," *Kommunist*, no. 10 (July 1968), p. 27.

Rossiya and *Literaturnáya gazeta* of harsher denunciations of Czechoslovakia than had been included in Alexandrov formulations showed that although the hard-liners were indeed strong, they were not powerful enough to sway the entire Politburo—at least not without outside support. And this was where East German and Polish pressure became so important as the two main external pillars of support for military intervention.

The views of the KGB and Ministry of the Interior heads are not known, although certain specific developments in Czechoslovakia at this time could not have been viewed very favorably by security chiefs in any of the bloc countries. The first was the revelation by Czechoslovak Interior Minister Pavel that six members of the KGB were working in his ministry as "liaison officers" and that a Czechoslovak state security officer was similarly assigned in the USSR.[109] Pavel's claim came at a time when Czechoslovak agents of the KGB increasingly were being purged from the Ministry of the Interior. In another development, Major General Peprny, the commander of the Czechoslovak border guards, stated that in the first six months of 1968, 513 persons, 40 percent from the GDR, had been apprehended while trying to cross to the West. Although he admitted this was a larger number than usual, he reaffirmed the official policy of removing the barbed wire along the Czech-Austrian border.[110] These developments as well as the controversy over the document produced by the Gottwald Military Academy, the Prchlík interview, and Pavel's open allegation that the arms cache had been planted as a provocation must have convinced security chiefs that some, if not all, of their counterparts in Prague were politically unreliable and would have to be replaced.[111]

THE WARSAW MEETING

Brezhnev, Podgorny, Shelest, and Katushev arrived in Warsaw early in the afternoon of July 13.[112] It is not known how many of the other bloc leaders were already in Warsaw by this time, but the

---

[109] Prague Radio, July 7, 1968, EE/2816/C/4.

[110] ČTK, July 12, 1968, EE/2821/C/8.

[111] For a systemic analysis of the military-security issue, see Karen Dawisha, "Soviet Security and the Role of the Military: The 1968 Czechoslovak Crisis," *British Journal of Political Science* 10 (1980): 341–363.

[112] The Polish agency announced the delegation's arrival at 13.05 GMT (July 13, 1968, EE/2821/i), also incorrectly listing Kosygin as having arrived.

Soviet delegation, without Kosygin, would have had the opportunity for at least a day of preconference talks with Gomułka and the other Polish leaders. It is highly likely that some of the other East European leaders had also arrived to discuss the strategy they would adopt before the conference formally opened. Since it became known that the ultimate Warsaw Letter came out of two preliminary drafts presented by the Poles and the Soviets, these presumably were discussed at this time, again in the absence of Kosygin.[113]

The tone of the meeting was set by a tough editorial in *Trybuna ludu* appearing July 14, the morning of the Conference. The article focused on the possibility that Czechoslovakia might leave the Warsaw Pact, warning that the entire Communist alliance was at stake and that "none of our countries can reject this responsibility and its obligations." *Trybuna ludu* complained that "hostile forces" were trying to push Czechoslovakia "on a liberal-bourgeois road, to disown it [socialism], to subvert the socialist order and to oppose Czechoslovakia's alliance with the fraternal socialist countries." The article went on to assert that "if in a socialist country the forces of reaction endanger the basis of socialism, this undermines the interests of other socialist countries." In advocating any particular course of action, however, the editorial was less specific. If the Polish leadership declared that "a decisive rebuff to the forces of reaction and imperialist maneuvers in Czechoslovakia is of vital interest to all fraternal nations," it did not go so far as to suggest that "fraternal assistance" was required. The editorial stated: "We believe that the Czechoslovak Communist party will find this rebuff among the working class and among all the progressive and really democratic forces in the country." It did, however, possibly leave its options open by stating that "our party fully backs those ready to oppose enemy forces to assure the favorable socialist development of Czechoslovakia and to strengthen friendship and unity with fraternal socialist states."

By the time the formal session began on Sunday morning, July 14, Kosygin had arrived in Warsaw. His attitude suggested, according to Erwin Weit (one of the official interpreters at the session who subsequently defected and wrote his memoirs), that he was "very worried."[114] He and the other participants could not have been pleased by the implications of the cable they received from

[113] Author's interview with Zdeněk Mlynář, June 1, 1979.
[114] Erwin Weit, *Eyewitness*, p. 211.

the Czechoslovak Praesidium: "In the interests of the international ties which link our Communist parties, no measures should be taken which might have an unfavorable impact on the complex situation in Czechoslovakia."[115]

At the conference, Gomułka made the opening speech, obtaining agreement that no chairman be elected and that no official report of the proceedings be kept. The Polish leader maintained that despite previous Czechoslovak assurances that antisocialist manifestations would be eliminated according to an agreed time limit, this promise had not been kept, and indeed the publication of the "2,000 Words" and the support it had received from some party leaders showed the situation to be much worse now than before. Further, the sweeping cadre changes being made were in fact only disguised attacks on the party and had to be stopped. Although clearly stating that "in no circumstances can we allow the counterrevolution to be victorious," he upheld the line set out in the *Trybuna ludu* article by stopping short of advocating direct military assistance.[116]

Kádár spoke next, providing a report of his meeting with Dubček in which Kádár had been told by Dubček that he was in complete control. Kádár agreed that there were a number of worrying antisocialist tendencies in Czechoslovakia and supported the sending of a strongly worded joint letter (thereby indicating that this course of action had already been discussed in the preconference session), but remained true to the assurances of support he had given to Dubček in their recent meeting by stating that "any decision over and above this could lead to serious consequences in the whole world communist movement, and also inside Czechoslovakia."[117]

At this point, Weit claims that Ulbricht interrupted Kádár, impatiently shouting in his high-pitched voice: "If you think, Comrade Kádár, that you are helping the cause of socialism with your objections and reservations, then you are making a big mistake. And you have no idea what will happen next. Once the American-West German imperialists have got Czechoslovakia in their control then you will be the next to go, Comrade Kádár. But this is something you can't or won't understand."[118]

---

[115] Dubček, *Rudé právo*, July 19, 1968.

[116] Weit, *Eyewitness*, pp. 198–200.

[117] Ibid., p. 201. Kádár is also said to have taken a moderate stance. Willy Brandt, *People and Politics*, p. 212.

[118] Weit, *Eyewitness*, p. 201.

Ulbricht's speech was predictably hard-line and particularly pessimistic about the capability of "honest Communists" in Czechoslovakia to make a comeback without external support. Of primary concern to Ulbricht was that the West German leadership, in its efforts to isolate and weaken the GDR, was placing great hope on Czechoslovakia's defection to the Western camp, which would expose the GDR's southern flank. The problem with the current situation was that "willingly or unwillingly" several of the Czechoslovak leaders had become "servants of world imperialism." Furthermore, Ulbricht was keenly aware of time limitations. If the CPCz were allowed to hold an extraordinary congress in September, there would be an entirely new (and, by implication, more liberal) Central Committee, and the five would be faced with a qualitatively different and more complex situation. With this sense of urgency, Ulbricht pressed the others to accept his own conclusion that "we must react before this party congress can take place."[119] U.S. government intelligence, as early as July 18, also noted a sharp debate on this subject, concluding that "there was disagreement at the Warsaw meeting over the timing of any military action, perhaps with the Hungarians arguing for greater patience."[120] Ulbricht not only favored an invasion but also, according to Weit, suggested that the Slovaks might be "stirred up," thereby providing an excuse for an intervention.[121]

Todor Zhivkov, the Bulgarian party leader, supported Ulbricht's hard-line stance, explicitly asserting that it was necessary to provide the ČSSR with assistance to defeat counterrevolution, "military assistance not excluded."

Brezhnev was the last speaker of the five, adopting a hard-line position in his assessment of the situation in Prague, but falling short of openly advocating military intervention. The Soviet leader made no analysis of the "German threat" or the extent to which Czechoslovakia was being used by imperialism to divide the socialist camp. Rather, he was almost exclusively concerned with the reform movement itself, in particular the attacks on two fundamental principles of socialism: democratic centralism and the leading role of the party. Brezhnev's greatest concern was that the CPCz lead-

[119] Ibid., p. 202.

[120] U.S. Department of State, *Intelligence Note 564*, July 18, 1968.

[121] Weit, *Eyewitness*, p. 216. Willy Brandt in an interview on July 18, 1968, also claimed that Ulbricht had acted as the "firebrand" at the Warsaw meeting (*Daily Telegraph*, July 19, 1968).

ership was no longer in control of the reform movement, and for this reason he appeared to doubt the trustworthiness of promises offered by Czechoslovak leaders. Without explicitly advocating invasion, Brezhnev did state that whenever the unity, strength, or existence of the socialist commonwealth was endangered, it was the duty of others to eliminate the source of that danger. Thus it was the duty of the bloc to assist the Czechoslovak working class so that "the counterrevolution will not succeed in Czechoslovakia."[122]

At the end of the speeches and discussions, in which only the heads of delegations reportedly took part, the conference elected a drafting committee to work out a joint letter to be sent to the CPCz Central Committee. The final letter was based on the two earlier drafts brought to the conference table by the Polish and Soviet delegations, revised to meet the views of the entire group.

Once the final version had been drawn up, it was agreed that the letter was to be addressed to the CPCz Central Committee, rather than to the Praesidium. This was probably done in the hope that such a move would force the convocation of a special session of that conservative-dominated body, thereby assuring that the letter would be given a full hearing by the "responsible" authorities while at the same time giving a needed boost to the "healthy forces" in the party. It was also decided not to publish the letter for four days, so as to give a proper amount of time for the Czechoslovak authorities to consider it without the pressure of public opinion.[123] Gomułka openly stated another reason for not publishing it immediately, namely, that to do so would allow the Euro-Communists ("who do not even agree with us in such obvious facts as the existence of a counterrevolution in Czechoslovakia") "to learn its contents and give them time to organize themselves so that they can continue to support the revisionists within the Czechoslovak Communist Party and back up their positions."[124]

The Warsaw Letter, as it came to be known, appeared in *Pravda* on July 18. It boldly informed Prague that as events in Czechoslovakia threatened both the socialist foundations of that country and the unity of the entire bloc, "it is no longer your affair alone." After providing a lengthy account of previous efforts made by the USSR and other bloc states to warn the CPCz leadership of the wider re-

[122] Weit, *Eyewitness*, pp. 207–09.
[123] Ibid., p. 215.
[124] Ibid.

percussions of the course it was pursuing, it asked a pointed question: "Is it possible that you fail to see that the counterrevolutionaries have taken one position after another from you and that the party is losing control over the course of events and is retreating more and more under the pressure of anti-Communist forces?" Then, in a clear shift away from the view expressed in the Alexandrov article of July 11 that Czechoslovakia can always count on "the understanding and complete support" of the USSR, the Warsaw Letter stated unequivocally that "it is not only your task but ours too to deal a resolute rebuff to the anti-Communist forces and to wage a resolute struggle for the preservation of the socialist system in Czechoslovakia." It then outlined specific demands—the tasks required to defend "the rule of the working class." The first was "a resolute and bold offensive against rightist and antisocialist forces and the mobilization of all means of defense created by the socialist state," clearly implying that the full weight of police and administrative measures immediately be used to crack down on anyone expressing antisocialist views.[125] The next demand was "a cessation of the activities of all political organizations that oppose socialism," the K 231, KAN, and related groups that were organizing outside the framework of the National Front. Third, censorship was to be immediately reimposed over the mass media. And finally, the Warsaw Letter demanded "solidarity in the ranks of the party itself on the fundamental basis of Marxism-Leninism, steadfast observance of the principles of democratic centralism and struggle against those who through their activities assist hostile forces." This was clearly the most central and contentious demand, for it not only passed judgment on the activities of certain party members and leaders by claiming that they were aiding "hostile forces" but also denounced any aspirations for political reform of the party itself as being contrary to Marxism-Leninism.

After setting their demands, the signers appealed to the "healthy forces" in the country, who "are capable of upholding the socialist system and dealing a defeat to the antisocialist elements." Seen together with the last demand and the stated fear that "the party is losing control," it becomes clear that the primary worry of the five was not so much that counterrevolutionary elements existed in the

[125] U.S. Department of State, *Intelligence Note 564*, July 18, 1968, interpreted this passage to imply that measures should be taken toward "the enhancement of the power of the secret police."

country as that they existed in the party itself—and indeed at the very top of the party, within the leadership. Thus, the appeal was no longer to Dubček personally or to the CPCz Praesidium, but to "healthy forces" wherever they might exist in the country and in the party. The final paragraph of the letter made the position of the five clear: "We express our conviction that the Czechoslovak Communist party, realizing its responsibility, will take the necessary measures to block the path of reaction. In this struggle you may count on the solidarity and comprehensive assistance of the fraternal socialist countries." The threat of military intervention was still not explicit, but the formulation "comprehensive assistance" had never before been used in a bloc communiqué and thus represented both an escalation and an implied willingness to use all means, including military, to put Czechoslovakia back on course.

Although the Warsaw Letter clearly represented an escalation in tensions, there were still certain conciliatory elements in the letter that showed moderate opinion had not entirely been overturned. First, the signatories reassured the CPCz that they "have not had and do not have any intention of interfering in affairs that are purely the internal affairs of your party and your state." The problem, of course, was in finding any aspect of the reform movement that the five considered to be purely the internal affair of the CPCz. They evidently decided there were three (and by implication only three) such areas: The first was "the rectification of errors and shortcomings, including the violations of socialist legality that took place" in the past. Second, the five declared "we do not interfere with the methods of planning and administration of Czechoslovakia's national economy or with the actions aimed at perfecting the economic structure and developing socialist democracy." This would extend, presumably, to cover most aspects of Czechoslovakia's planned economic reform, although it gives no explicit approval to aspects of the "market socialism" favored by Ota Šik or to any measure that would reorient Czechoslovakia's foreign trade more toward the West. Finally, the five positively affirmed that they would "welcome adjustment of the relations between Czechs and Slovaks on the healthy foundations of fraternal cooperation within the Czechoslovak Socialist Republic." It might be assumed that the five would favor any measure that increased the influence of the generally more conservative Slovaks over the Czechs, who had always been seen as more liberal and Western oriented. This therefore was a concession to Bratislava at the expense of Prague.

At the conclusion of the conference TASS issued a communiqué stating only that the participants "unanimously adopted a decision on the question under discussion."[126] The Warsaw meeting, to the extent that it ended in unanimity, certainly was not characterized by a single and resolute commitment to one course of action. Informed sources, for example, reported that Hungary flatly refused to subscribe to a second ultimatum being sent to Prague that demanded a multilateral conference within the next two weeks, following a series of bilateral talks between Prague and each of the five. The other four signatories informed Prague over the next few days through separate channels of this second demand.[127]

The Warsaw meeting served as yet another forum for consensus building and consultation. The Soviet Union gained approval for its position that any action taken against Czechoslovakia would be a joint action. The meeting committed all bloc parties to the single perspective that there was a counterrevolution in Czechoslovakia that had to be brought under control one way or another. Finally, in the event of the CPCz's failure to take sufficient measures to restore the situation, "comprehensive assistance" would be provided by all the parties to the Warsaw Letter. With the Warsaw Letter, both of the essential elements of the so-called Brezhnev doctrine were established: the subordination of national interests to the (Soviet-defined) interests of the international Communist movement, and not only the *right* but the positive *duty* of socialist states to come to the defense of socialism, wherever it might be threatened and irrespective of the source of that threat. Once it had been accepted in principle that any measures could be justified to defend socialism in another country, and once it was agreed that socialism was in fact threatened, the top decision makers only needed to be convinced that all other alternatives for dealing with the situation had been exhausted and that military force was the only remaining option. As the U.S. State Department was to conclude in a priority telegram to its mission in NATO and to all European diplomatic posts at the end of the Warsaw meeting: "Soviets and hard-line allies have constructed public rationale for direct intervention in Czechoslovak affairs, although Moscow's hope prob-

[126] *Pravda*, July 17, 1968.

[127] *New York Times*, July 19, 1968. U.S. Department of State, *Intelligence Note 564*, July 18, 1968, also concurred that the Warsaw Letter was "only part of the correspondence from the five to Czechoslovakia" with the parties also insisting "on other bilateral meetings and a joint summit within two weeks."

ably remains that situation can be controlled without such action."[128] It only remained to be seen whether Czechoslovakia would put its own house in order.

THE CPSU CENTRAL COMMITTEE PLENUM

Having arrived back in Moscow by train on July 16, the Soviet leadership convened an extraordinary plenum of the CPSU Central Committee to discuss the results of the Warsaw meeting. As mentioned previously, the decision to convene the meeting was probably made before the departure of the Soviet delegation to Warsaw, probably on July 12. If this was the case, then Kosygin could not have been privy to the decision to convene the July plenum, just as he was not privy to the decision to convene the April plenum.

The plenum was opened by Brezhnev, who presented for discussion and approval a document entitled "Results of the Meeting in Warsaw of Delegations of the Communist and Workers' Parties of the Socialist Countries."[129] Following Brezhnev's introduction, fourteen speeches were given, and it is instructive to list the speakers in the order given by the official communiqué: Shelest, Grishin, Kunaev, L. C. Kulichenko (first secretary of the Volgograd obkom), Yu. V. Il'nitsky (first secretary of the Transcarpathian obkom), N. M. Gribachev (secretary of the board of the Writers' Union), V. S. Tolstikov (first secretary of the Leningrad obkom), A. I. Shibaev (first secretary of the Saratov obkom), A. E. Voss (first secretary of the Central Committee of the Latvian Communist party), V. I. Konotop (first secretary of the Moscow obkom), V. I. Degtiarev (first secretary of the Donetsk obkom in the Ukraine), M. V. Keldysh (president of the Soviet Academy of Sciences), A. Yu. Snechkus (first secretary of the Central Committee of the Lithuanian Communist party), and S. G. Lapin (general director of TASS).[130]

Although the texts of their speeches were never revealed, various analyses have pointed to a strong coalition between Ukrainian interests, party secretaries concerned about the spillover of the reform movement, and officials involved in the control of the intelligentsia and the media. Taking the Ukrainian element first, the

[128] U.S. Department of State, *Telegram 202635*, July 15, 1968, to U.S. Mission, NATO.

[129] *Spravochnik Partiinovo rabotnika*, vol. 8 (Moscow: Izdatel'stvo politichoskoy literatury, 1968), p. 12.

[130] Ibid.

views of Shelest are well known; and it is most interesting that he was the only member of the Warsaw delegation, with the exception of Brezhnev, to give a speech at the plenum. Il'nitsky had spent his entire career as a party official in the Transcarpathian *oblast'*, that area incorporated into the USSR in 1945 from Czechoslovakia. Il'nitsky would have been particularly worried about spillover from the reform movement since the inhabitants of his region had historical and linguistic ties with Czechoslovakia. On several occasions during July, Il'nitsky publicly criticized the reform movement, emphasizing the deep impression that life under the "'democracy' and 'freedom' of Masaryk and Beneš" had made on the inhabitants of his region.[131] The difficulty of persuading the people of the *oblast'* that the Prague Spring was in fact counterrevolutionary could not have been made easier by the ability of inhabitants in Transcarpathia to pick up Czechoslovak radio and television stations, and indeed Il'nitsky was later to complain of the harmful influence on existing nationality tensions in Transcarpathia of "foreign radio stations and television studios."[132] It is extremely significant that Il'nitsky gave a speech at the plenum, since he was not a member of the Central Committee. Therefore, as Hodnett and Potichnyj state, "he must have been invited to dramatize the danger of Czechoslovak influence upon the Ukraine." It is difficult to disagree with their conclusion that "this is an extremely important point, for it reveals better than almost anything else possibly could that the majority in the Politburo wanted or needed to convince the Central Committee of the seriousness of the Czechoslovak threat to the Soviet Union's south-western flank."[133] One might add, however, that the lineup of speakers suggests the purpose of the meeting was not to overcome a traditional division between the Politburo and the Central Committee but to override the vertical splits between contending groups, all of whom had patrons in the Politburo and supporters in the Central Committee. Certainly the absence from the speakers list of the other members of the Warsaw delegation—Kosygin, Podgorny and Katushev—and the similar exclusion of other policy elites who deal with foreign affairs indicates the strength of the coalition that was being developed

[131] *Pravda Ukrainy*, July 29, 1968; also *Radjanska Ukraina*, July 6, 1968.

[132] "Nashe Znamya—internatsionalizm," *Kommunist Ukrainy*, no. 1 (1969), pp. 85–93, as quoted by Hodnett and Potichnyj, "The Ukraine and the Czechoslovak Crisis," p. 145.

[133] Ibid., p. 86.

and in particular the power at this time of Shelest and the Ukrainian contingent.

Also with the Ukrainian contingent were Degtiarev and Konotop. The first secretary of the Moscow obkom, Konotop was Ukrainian by ethnic origin. Only the previous day he had returned from Czechoslovakia, where he was at the head of a Moscow *oblast'* delegation. His arrival in Prague occurred shortly after his very liberal counterparts there, the Prague City Party Committee, had decided to go into permanent session, a development that the Soviets felt threatened the guiding principle of democratic centralism. Konotop, according to U.S. intelligence conclusions, reported to the Central Committee on the "counterrevolutionary activities" of this group.[134]

Of the other speakers, Voss and Snechkus also represented republics that had had their fair share of nationality problems. Although leader of the Latvian party, Voss was not a Central Committee member, probably because his predecessor Arvid Pel'she, a full Politburo member and head of the Party Control Committee, was responsible for representing the interests of the Baltic states in Moscow. Latvia had gone through a major nationality crisis under Khrushchev. In 1959, a number of top officials accused of nationalism had been purged. Pel'she took up his post as head of the Latvian party soon after and had since been promoted on the basis of having demonstrated his special loyalty to the Soviet Union's nationality policy.[135] Voss himself does not appear to have played a major role in the months leading up to the invasion of Czechoslovakia, except for a meeting with Smrkovský when the latter visited Riga during his tour of the USSR in June. Following the invasion, Voss was quoted as admitting that the situation in Latvia had become particularly dangerous during 1968, when "the revisionists and nationalists" were using a program of "democratic and humanist socialism" as a smokescreen for "the restoration of capitalist society."[136] Just as nonmember Il'nitsky was almost certainly invited to support the view of Shelest, Voss's presence can be most satisfactorily explained in terms of representing the views of his Moscow patron, Pel'she.

[134] U.S. Department of State, *Research Memorandum, RSE-127*, August 16, 1968.

[135] Juris Dreifelds, "Latvian National Demands and Group Consciousness Since 1959," in George W. Simmonds, ed., *Nationalism in the USSR and Eastern Europe*, pp. 136–56.

[136] A. E. Voss, *Politicheskoye samoobrazovaniye*, no. 9 (September 1968), pp. 22–30, as quoted in Valenta, *Soviet Intervention*, p. 60.

Lithuanian party boss Snechkus was in a slightly stronger position insofar as he at least was a member of the Central Committee.
He had also gone on record prior to the July plenum in favor of a
"tireless struggle against nationalism and revisionism." "Lithuania"
he claimed, "together with other Baltic republics, had become an
object of bitter attacks by imperialist propaganda."[137] For Snechkus,
this claim was not idle polemicizing, for during this time a mass
movement was taking root in Lithuania among groups of Catholic
priests protesting restrictions on the printing of Bibles and religious literature, the entry of students to seminaries, and related
church issues. The party hierarchy appeared to be almost helpless
in preventing its spread; by 1972, for example, an appeal to the
United Nations against religious persecution had been signed by
17,000 people from Lithuania.[138]

The other speakers were either provincial and city party secretaries or officials in charge of maintaining party orthodoxy over intellectual life. Several had been directly involved in the development
of the Soviet positions on the reform movement. Kulichenko, for example, had gone to Prague with Brezhnev, Shelest, and Katushev
in February for a bilateral meeting and had also participated in the
April plenum debate on Czechoslovakia. He had conferred with
Indra and Gierek on May 9 at the Czechoslovak-Polish border, and
he had hosted both Smrkovský's delegation at the beginning of
June and Kádár's delegation at the end of June during their respective visits to Volgograd. As for Grishin, he had been highly active
in advocating a hard-line approach to Czechoslovakia, as witnessed
by his April 22 speech, and in fact he was the only Soviet leader,
with the exception of Brezhnev, to participate in the debates on
Czechoslovakia at all three Central Committee plenums held in
1968 (Shelest also addressed all three plenums, but at the October
meeting he spoke not in the foreign policy debate but in the agricultural debate). Tolstikov had also participated in the April debate, and with Leningrad as one of the foci of the continuing signa-
ture campaign against the trial and imprisonment the previous
January of Ginzburg and Galanskov, it could be expected that
Tolstikov and the representatives of TASS, the Writers' Union, and
the Academy of Sciences would all be strong adherents of a harsh

---

[137] A. Yu. Snechkus, *Kommunist* (Lithuania), no. 6 (June 1968), pp. 3–7, as quoted
in ibid.

[138] Peter Reddaway, "The Development of Dissent and Opposition," in Archie Brown and
Michael Kaser, eds., *The Soviet Union Since the Fall of Khrushchev*, pp. 137–38.

stand against "imperialist ideological subversion," particularly if it came from a neighboring socialist state.

Support for the Prague Spring by Andrei Sakharov and other Soviet intellectuals threatened to further complicate the authorities' efforts to clamp down on dissent, and it appeared to confirm Soviet fears of spillover. Soviet efforts to gain support among leading intellectuals for a campaign against Czechoslovakia had not been an overwhelming success, and indeed it was only on July 23, a full month after the publication of the "2,000 Words," that *Sovetskaya kultura* managed to find seven National Artists who would sign an article explicitly condemning it. General Petro Grigorenko, who by that time had been identified with dissident causes, subsequently wrote that the "2,000 Words" had been secretly translated into Russian— Czech newspapers were no longer sold openly—and circulated widely among the intelligentsia who generally followed developments in Prague "as if [they] were all a fairy tale." [139] The party ranks had only recently been purged of all those members (almost all of them intellectuals) who had signed letters protesting the illegality of the Ginzburg-Galanskov trial, but a group of over a hundred writers had notified the Writers' Union Secretariat that if even one signatory were expelled from the Writers' Union, they would all resign. [140] Among this group was the writer A. Ye. Kosterin, who later in July was to resign from the party in protest over Soviet attempts to repress the Prague Spring. [141] It was not surprising, therefore, that the day after the close of the plenum the Propaganda Department of the Central Committee issued a directive on the need for much more work in instilling "ideological conviction among the Soviet intelligentsia." [142]

This strong connection, first drawn at the April plenum, between domestic ideological control and the threat to that control posed by the events in Czechoslovakia was further reinforced by the July plenum. It has been pointed out that Podgorny, Katushev, and Kosygin, the other participants in the Warsaw meeting, were not called on to discuss its results at the plenum. It is also noteworthy that none of the leaders concerned with foreign policy and the international Communist movement spoke, most notably, of course, Suslov and Ponomarev, both of whom were interested in

[139] Petro Grigorenko, *Memoirs*, pp. 357–59.
[140] Peter Reddaway, ed., *Uncensored Russia*, pp. 83–89.
[141] *New York Times*, July 30, 1968.
[142] *Pravda*, July 19, 1968.

the effects of the Warsaw Letter on the plans for the November International Communist Conference. Neither Gromyko nor
Grechko (who had finally departed on July 15 for Algeria) was on
the list of speakers, despite their participation in the April debate
and despite the fact that any decision concerning Czechoslovakia
would have immense consequences for their respective spheres
of activity. The list of speakers, therefore, strongly suggests a narrowing of the focus on Czechoslovakia; increasingly it was seen
through the prism of its impact on ideological control and orthodoxy at home and in the bloc. It also suggests an intensification of
the perceived threat of the Prague Spring; and the apparent inability of all those known for their more moderate views to participate in the plenum debate indicates a marked increase in the
strength of the coalition favoring a hard line to counter that threat.
Furthermore, the structure of the debate, with its preponderance
of middle-level officials as opposed to top Politburo members or
party secretaries, represents an attempt to broaden the base of
support for a hard-line policy. This represents a further stage in
consensus-building, an unambiguous welding of the party to a particular view of Czechoslovakia and to a particular course of action.

TASS announced on July 17 that a resolution had been "adopted
unanimously" by the plenum stating that the Central Committee
"completely approves" the activity of the Politburo and "highly ap-
preciates and unanimously endorses" the results of the Warsaw
meeting. Specifically, it backed "the conclusions reached" at Warsaw, including the need to ensure "the consolidation of the socialist
system on the basis of the principles of proletarian internationalism
and the conclusions on the need for resolute efforts in support of
the cause of socialism in Czechoslovakia."

It stopped short of discussing what "resolute efforts" might be
required, but in an attempt to reinforce the weight of the Warsaw
Letter, the resolution stated that the Central Committee "expresses confidence that the letter of the fraternal parties, adopted in
Warsaw, will meet with understanding and support on the part
of the Communist party and the peoples of Czechoslovakia as an
expression of sincere, friendly international help . . . and will contribute to the strengthening of friendship between the peoples
of Czechoslovakia and the Soviet Union and the entire socialist
community."

The next paragraph clearly indicated the direct connection between the Prague reform movement and the threat to ideological orthodoxy at home. The resolution, in a far from optimistic formulation, stated that the Central Committee "considers it necessary to continue in every possible way to consolidate the unity of the party and the people, to extend ideological work and to popularize the great teaching of Marxism-Leninism in all spheres."

By unanimously supporting the Warsaw meeting conclusions about the need for "resolute efforts" to aid the cause of socialism in Czechoslovakia, the Central Committee endorsed the position expressed in the Warsaw Letter that counterrevolutionary tendencies existed in Czechoslovakia as well as the need for action by the community as a whole to restore Czechoslovakia to the socialist path. Whereas the April Central Committee plenum resolution had merely endorsed the Dresden meeting decisions on greater bloc unity, the July plenum resolution went several steps further: it openly named Czechoslovakia, declared socialism to be threatened there, publicly encouraged the CPCz to heed the advice offered in the Warsaw Letter, and supported the need for "resolute efforts" based on the principle of proletarian internationalism if all else failed.

From the standpoint of preparing the party rank and file for a possible invasion, the July plenum resolution went as far as could be expected without explicitly calling for military measures. Yet there is no evidence that an actual invasion was even discussed. Indeed, it is unlikely that it would have been, even if such plans were well advanced. Although key members of the Central Committee were obviously influential in supporting a decision to invade, the plenum as such with its 360 full and candidate members was too formal and public a forum to discuss such a highly secret military plan. Rather, the function of this plenum was to provide whatever legitimization the Politburo—the body formally accountable in party statutes to the Central Committee—might require for any eventuality, including an invasion. For the time being, however, the Soviets would wait and see how the Czechoslovak leadership responded to the Warsaw letter, although as Western intelligence concluded: "while there is no indication at present of an imminent use of force against Czechoslovakia, this step could come with little or no warning."[143]

[143] U.S. Department of State, *Intelligence Note 564*, July 18, 1968.

THE CZECHOSLOVAK REACTION

Although the five signatories had addressed their letter to the CPCz Central Committee in the hope that this would allow conservatives the opportunity to use that forum to recoup their strength, Dubček did not immediately convene a special plenum. The official reply was composed by the CPCz Praesidium on July 17, and only then on July 19, after it was made public, was it discussed and endorsed at an extraordinary CPCz Central Committee plenum, whose ranks had been swollen by a number of liberal nonmembers.

The Praesidium reply conceded that there might be some "extremist tendencies," some "antisocialist activities" or even on occasions "violation of the principle of democratic centralism." It rejected, however, any justification for "calling the present situation counterrevolutionary, invoking a direct threat to the basis of the socialist system or claiming that Czechoslovakia is preparing a change in the orientation of our socialist foreign policy or that there is a concrete danger of our country breaking away from the socialist community." Conceding that "voices and tendencies appear in the press . . . which do not coincide with the positive endeavors of the party," the Praesidium nevertheless refused to reintroduce administrative measures to deal with the situation, replying that "we consider the solution of these questions to be a long-term task."

They also bluntly made clear their view of the Warsaw meeting: "We think that the common cause of socialism is not advanced by the holding of conferences at which the policy and activity of one of the fraternal parties is judged without the presence of their representatives." The reply ended by urgently reiterating the desire of the CPCz leadership to hold bilateral talks as a prelude to "a common meeting of the socialist countries."[144] Husák was later to describe the CPCz Praesidium's negative reply to the Warsaw Letter as "one of the gravest mistakes in our internal and particularly our international relations."[145] Yet with this reply and the renewed call for bilateral talks, the ball was once again in Moscow's court.

[144] Text in Remington, *Winter in Prague*, pp. 234–43.
[145] Husák's speech at the CPCz Central Committee plenum, September 25, 1969, EE/3190/C/19.

THE CONSIDERATION OF ALTERNATIVES

By the time the CPSU Central Committee concluded its session on July 17, reaffirming the party's support for the results of the Warsaw meeting, the CPCz Praesidium had already rejected the letter of the five, forcing Moscow to react fairly quickly. The broad variety of options discussed indicated a widening search for alternatives as the crisis escalated into this crucial stage. The various and often conflicting actions advocated by different leaders included the following:

1. Support for the French Communist party's plan to convene an immediate international party conference to discuss Czechoslovakia

2. Use of the "good offices" of Waldeck Rochet and other Communist leaders to mediate between Prague and Moscow

3. Moderation of overt political pressure on Prague in an effort to calm the situation and allow the Dubček leadership to regain firm control

4. Pursuit of bilateral talks with the Czechoslovak Praesidium as a prelude to a multilateral conference of leaders from socialist countries

5. An increased public campaign against Prague in an attempt not only to signal to the CPCz leadership the seriousness of Soviet intent, but also to prepare Soviet public opinion for any eventuality and to create a climate more conducive to a military intervention

6. Renewed demands for immediate concessions by the Czechoslovak authorities in the area of security and in the military sphere, including cadre changes and stationing of troops

7. Increased military preparedness for a full invasion that could be mounted at short notice, even if all Soviet and bloc troops currently still in Czechoslovakia had first to be withdrawn.

These various alternatives were all debated and examined in the days following the return of the Soviet delegation from Warsaw and the receipt of Czechoslovakia's negative response to the Warsaw Letter. Seven separate decisions can be identified and are analyzed below. They can be summarized here as follows:

July 17, decision 30: The Central Committee affirms the need for a nationwide campaign to familiarize the Soviet public with the Warsaw Letter and to mobilize public opinion against counterrevolutionary tendencies in Czechoslovakia.

July 17, decision 31: Brezhnev seeks bilateral talks with Czechoslovakia.

July 19, decision 32: After Prague rejects Brezhnev's appeal, the CPSU Politburo publicly reaffirms the call for bilateral talks.

July 20–21, decision 33: The Politburo fails to endorse Rochet's call for a European Communist conference to discuss Czechoslovakia.

July 20–21, decision 34: The Politburo (presumably with military participation) decides to send a formal letter to the Czechoslovak government demanding the immediate stationing of Soviet troops in Czechoslovakia.

July 20–21, decision 35: The Politburo (with the participation of at least Gromyko and Grechko) agrees to proceed with a full-scale invasion of Czechoslovakia before August 26, unless Dubček agrees both to end the reform movement and to allow the permanent stationing of Soviet troops on Czechoslovakia's western border. Accordingly the Politburo (a) authorizes the military to make final preparations; and (b) instructs the foreign minister to ascertain the likely Western response.

July 22, decision 36: The Politburo agrees to hold bilateral negotiations with the CPCz Praesidium on Czechoslovak soil, at Čierna nad Tisou.

THE RENEWAL OF POLEMICS

The CPSU Central Committee plenum of July 17 had affirmed the need for a countrywide campaign both "to strengthen the unity of the party" and to reaffirm the support of the Soviet people for the results of the Warsaw meeting. In effect, *decision 30* involved both the convocation of nationwide party *aktivs* to mobilize party cadres and the start of a massive press campaign. These measures were designed to inform the Soviet public of the extent of leadership concern and to create a political climate that would put pressure on Prague and at the same time prepare the public for a possible invasion. As *Pravda* stated on July 19, "the Communists and all the working people of Czechoslovakia can be sure that the CPSU, the Soviet government and our people are ready to render them all necessary assistance in defending socialist gains."

Party *aktivs* were held on July 18 in Moscow, Leningrad, and all the capital cities of the various Union Republics, with Grishin, Tolstikov, Shelest, Mzhavanadze, and other party leaders as speakers.[146] These served as the first round in a series of party meetings designed to mobilize the rank and file. *Pravda*, on July 22, noted with satisfaction that the extent of support by Soviet Communists

---

[146] *Pravda*, July 19, July 20, 1968.

for the Warsaw Letter was demonstrated by "the resolutions adopted at meetings of the Party *aktiv* and the numerous letters from the working people that are being received by the Party Central Committee and newspaper offices."

The need for party unity was never more apparent than in the days immediately following the Central Committee plenum, when almost all the top political and military leaders were engaged in feverish activity to either promote or avert a final decision to prepare for a full-scale invasion. That decision, discussed in detail below, was made during a weekend meeting of an expanded Politburo on July 20–21, but in the days and hours before that meeting, there was a very high level of both public and behind-the-scenes activity.

JULY 17–20: MULTI-TRACK APPROACHES

Brezhnev and the Bilateral Talks

On his return from Warsaw, Brezhnev spent most of his time trying to persuade the Dubček leadership to agree to bilateral talks. He sent a personal letter to the CPCz Praesidium which was delivered by Ambassador Chervonenko on Wednesday night, July 17, while the Praesidium was still in session trying to decide on its reply to the Warsaw Letter. Chervonenko arrived at the Central Committee building to find the Prague and the world press corps camped in the anteroom outside the Praesidium chambers. He was ushered in for talks which lasted over an hour, during the course of which Smrkovský slipped out and said "victory" to waiting reporters and secondary party officials. Dubček, too, emerged after Chervonenko had left, exclaiming "it is hard to repair the errors of twenty years."[147]

In his note, Brezhnev struck an extremely conciliatory tone, reportedly stating that the Warsaw Letter had not been an ultimatum. The Soviet Union merely wished to warn Prague that groups hostile to socialism were gaining in strength. Brezhnev sought direct bilateral talks between the CPSU Politburo and the CPCz Praesidium and evidently proposed that they be held the coming Friday, July 19, in the Slovak town of Košice.[148] There is some evidence that Brezhnev had sent an earlier note on the same day suggesting Moscow as a venue, but Dubček had rejected this

[147] Henry Kamm, reporting from Prague, *New York Times*, July 19, 1968; Alan Levy, *Rowboat to Prague*, pp. 262–63.

[148] Levy, pp. 262–63.

site, as well as Kiev, Lvov, and Uzhgorod.[149] If this is the case, then Chervonenko's arrival, direct from Moscow's Central Committee plenum, would have assumed an air of even greater urgency.

Only after receiving these new proposals from Brezhnev, regarded in Prague as a triumph for their point of view, did Dubček decide to convene a special Central Committee plenum. It was packed with liberals who were not members of the current Central Committee, although many had been elected as delegates to the forthcoming congress. Armed with a vote of support for the Praesidium's negative reply to the Warsaw Letter, Dubček could then negotiate with Moscow from a position of strength.

Brezhnev's proposed date of June 19 for a bilateral meeting was too soon for the Czech side, and they sought a postponement. This may have appeared in Moscow as an attempt to stall for time once again, the invitation to attend talks was reaffirmed, this time by the Politburo as a whole (*decision 32*), and published in *Pravda* on July 20. It was revealed that "the Politburo . . . sent a letter to the Praesidium . . . on July 19, 1968, proposing that a bilateral meeting be held." The article disclosed that the Soviet leadership had repeatedly sought such a meeting in the weeks prior to the Warsaw enclave, but that "the Czechoslovak comrades postponed it indefinitely every time." The letter sent to the Dubček leadership specifically suggested that the "full membership" of the CPSU Politburo and the CPCz Praesidium participate, but conceded that if Dubček considered this "impossible" then Moscow would accept a meeting of delegations "with the largest possible representation." The Politburo proposed that the meeting be convened on July 22 or 23 in Moscow, or "if it is more convenient for the Czechoslovak comrades, in Kiev or Lvov."

By issuing the invitation publicly, Moscow was putting tremendous pressure on the Czechoslovak leadership to accept, especially since it was they who had specifically called for bilateral consultations in their own reply to the Warsaw Letter. The change in Soviet attitude on the venue for the talks, with the Politburo letter reverting to the initial demand that the talks be held on Soviet territory, may just have been a bargaining ploy, but it is possible that the full Politburo did not agree to Brezhnev's own proposal to accept the Czechoslovak preference for Košice. Yet the agreement to

---

[149] Ibid. Levy claims there were two notes; Kamm, *New York Times*, July 19, 1968, refers to the venues.

accede to Prague's request that the talks be held on Czechoslovak soil was in itself a victory for the moderates; and considering that the previous communication with the CPCz Praesidium had been at Brezhnev's own initiative, it can be counted as a victory for his own policy preferences. He may have been aided in achieving Politburo agreement to bilateral talks by the fact that Shelest was in Kiev on July 19 addressing the Kiev Party *aktiv* on the results of the Central Committee. It may not be entirely coincidental that the article announcing Shelest's absence from Moscow on July 19 was placed directly below the TASS communiqué stating the Politburo's decision on bilateral talks.[150]

The motive behind the Soviet proposal that the meeting be between the entire CPSU Politburo and the CPCz Praesidium has been variously ascribed to the Soviet desire to ensure conservative representation on the Czechoslovak side and to the demands of Politburo members for full participation. Twenty conservatives had failed to attend the CPCz Central Committee plenum held on July 19, thus declining to go on record in support of Dubček's reply to the Warsaw Letter. This was a clear signal to Moscow that there was a hard, if diminishing, core of opposition to liberal policies that could be manipulated by the Soviets. By this time, Praesidium members Bil'ak, Kolder, Švestka, Rigo, Barbírek, and Piller had all been identified as having reservations about Dubček's handling of the Warsaw meeting and the reply to the Warsaw Letter; and Moscow had every reason to seek the participation of these leaders in any negotiations.

The decision to seek a full Politburo-Praesidium meeting could also have been motivated by various internal political considerations on the Soviet side. Western intelligence reported that those Politburo members "not in complete agreement" with the current handling of the crisis favored a full Politburo delegation.[151] Hardliners may have agreed, knowing that the results of any bilateral meeting would then be open to less argument by those who had not attended. Whatever the motives, the decision to hold a joint Politburo-Praesidium enclave did mark a significant departure from past practice. It indicated that as the crisis escalated, the Politburo tended to increase the size of the decisional unit to ensure

---

[150] *Pravda*, July 20, 1968.

[151] U.S. Department of State, *Intelligence Note 576*, July 22, 1968; and U.S. Department of State, *Telegram 206938* to all European Diplomatic Posts, July 23, 1968.

both fuller participation and shared responsibility. This tendency was clearly supported by Brezhnev, who had been calling for a full Politburo-Praesidium meeting from his first letters to Dubček on July 17. Brezhnev's own preference for full participation reflected his leadership style and no doubt his desire for collective responsibility if the talks produced no results and thereby precipitated an invasion.

Suslov Seeks Euro-Communist Mediation

As discussed previously, a delegation consisting of Waldeck Rochet, the French Communist party chief, and Giancarlo Pajetta and Carlo Galuzzi, two Italian Communist party representatives, arrived in Moscow on July 14, having received a "definite warning" from unspecified sources that the Soviets had assembled a puppet government they were preparing to install as soon as Dubček could be toppled.[152] The Euro-Communists met Suslov and V. V. Zagladin, Boris Ponomarev's deputy in the International Department of the Central Committee, and they warned the Russians that they would oppose a Soviet intervention. Indeed Pajetta stated after his return that he had also told the Soviets that the Italian party would only attend the November International Communist Conference provided the principle of noninterference in the internal affairs of other parties was strictly upheld.[153] Pajetta also confirmed that prior to their departure from Moscow, they were informed of the contents of the Warsaw Letter. In response, Rochet sought, and apparently received, the endorsement of Suslov and Zagladin for a proposal to convene an immediate European Communist Conference to discuss Czechoslovakia. According to a secret State Department memorandum on July 17, it was Soviet "assertions of deep concern which in turn led him [Rochet] to propose a European CP conference on the Czechoslovak situation."[154] Several other sources have indicated that, at the very least, Suslov and Zagladin did not oppose this initiative.[155] Within hours of Rochet's return to Paris on July 17, a PCF Politburo communiqué formally proposed "a meeting of Communist and Workers' parties of Eu-

---

[152] Sunday Telegraph, quoting French Communist party sources, August 11, 1968. Also see n. 98 above.

[153] International Herald Tribune, July 18, 1968.

[154] U.S. Department of State, Intelligence Note 563, July 17, 1968.

[155] International Herald Tribune, July 20–21, 1968, quoting "reliable diplomatic sources in Vienna"; Christian Science Monitor, July 20–22, 1968.

rope in the coming days" to discuss the Czechoslovak situation "and the problems arising from it."[156]

Suslov and Zagladin also apparently encouraged Rochet to visit Prague. State Department sources calculated that Moscow had "consciously generated concern over its willingness to use force to enlist parties sympathetic to the Dubček regime in mediating efforts which could include pressure on the Czechoslovak leaders to exert greater control over liberalization."[157] Having just sustained a major electoral defeat in the June elections, the PCF was particularly concerned about the domestic consequences of a Soviet intervention, particularly given the pro-Soviet sympathies of the party's inner core. Consequently, on July 19, Rochet visited Prague and sought Czechoslovak support for his proposal. Dubček, however, was far from enthusiastic: "We have not said no to a meeting between parties of the socialist countries, and we are not saying no to a European conference. We simply say that bilateral meetings are necessary first and that . . . the object of any collective meeting must not be the examination of the situation of any single party."[158] After Rochet's return to Paris on July 21, the PCF issued a communiqué stating that although support for the proposal had been received from fourteen Communist parties, it had been decided that as long as there was the possibility of bilateral talks between Moscow and Prague, the planned Euro-Communist conference would not be held.[159]

Soviet intentions and actions regarding this episode are extremely difficult to discern. Evidence suggests that Suslov and Zagladin did not immediately seek to dissuade Rochet from publicly proposing a conference. There are at least two possible explanations for this initial support. On the one hand, they may have calculated that the Czechoslovaks might attend such a gathering and that Moscow would be able to control its results. If this was their calculation, they were wrong on both counts, as evidenced by Dubček's reaction to the proposal and the negative response of the majority of Euro-Communist parties to the harsh tone of the Warsaw Letter. This response may in itself have dampened initial Soviet enthusiasm for Rochet's proposal, leading Moscow to pressure

---

[156] *L'Humanité*, July 18, 1968.

[157] U.S. Department of State, *Intelligence Note 563*, July 17, 1968.

[158] *L'Humanité*, May 18, 1970, released the text of the conversation between Rochet and Dubček.

[159] *L'Humanité*, July 22, 1968.

the PCF to abandon the idea. Alternatively, Suslov and Zagladin may have hoped that the Politburo would have been forced to respond to a PCF invitation and in the process at least be made aware of the ramifications of the escalating crisis on the CPSU's standing in the world Communist movement. In this vein, the Moscow correspondent of *Práce* reported that "in talking with certain people these days, one becomes aware that they are disturbed by the different points of view adopted by the Communist parties of Western Europe and by those of certain socialist countries. . . . People are beginning to wonder if this letter from Warsaw has not divided the Communist movement instead of unifying it."[160]

Despite Rochet's repeated insistence that he had come to Moscow at his own initiative and that he was solely responsible for proposing a European Communist meeting, the TASS dispatch of his departure, printed in *Pravda* on July 18, stated not only that he had been seen off at the airport by Suslov and Zagladin but that he had been in Moscow "at the invitation of the Central Committee," a statement vigorously denied by Rochet. This led some commentators, including some who quoted PCF sources, to suggest that hard-liners in Moscow were attempting to discredit Suslov and others by implying that behind-the-scenes scheming was taking place while other Soviet leaders were in Warsaw.[161] In this connection it is interesting to note that the head of TASS, S. G. Lapin, was one of the hard-line speakers at the Central Committee plenum convened on July 17; hence he may not have been adverse to releasing such a statement.

Ponomarev in the Shadows

It has been suggested, notably by Jiri Valenta, that Boris Ponomarev, the head of the International Department, supported Suslov and Zagladin in welcoming the Rochet initiative.[162] Certainly, Ponomarev worked closely with Suslov in planning the November International Communist conference and was likely to have calculated the negative effect of an invasion on the success of the conference. There is really no evidence, however, to suggest that Ponomarev backed this initiative. Indeed if this had been the case, one might have expected Ponomarev himself, rather than his dep-

[160] Quoted by Michel Tatu, *Le Monde*, July 25, 1968.
[161] *New York Times*, July 23, 1968.
[162] Jiri Valenta, *Soviet Intervention in Czechoslovakia*, pp. 67–69.

uty, to have joined Suslov in meeting with Rochet. Moreover, it has been claimed, in evidence presented by Valenta himself, that Ponomarev sent confidential letters to all West European Communist parties making it quite clear that Moscow would regard the convening of such a conference as a hostile act.[163] Ponomarev's motivations in this incident can therefore be described at best as murky and at worst something between opportunism and double-dealing.

Kosygin Acts Alone

Having been excluded from the decisions to go to Warsaw and to convene a special CPSU Central Committee plenum, Kosygin was hardly in the strongest of positions. He was unable to air his views at either the Warsaw meeting—which was dominated by delegation heads—or the plenum. He did, however, find yet another way of publicly signaling his dissent from hard-line opinion. Taking advantage of the presence in Moscow of Czechoslovakia's Deputy Premier Hamouz for the Thirty-fifth Session of the CMEA Executive Committee, Kosygin received Hamouz personally on July 18. He pointedly issued a press statement reporting the meeting as friendly and saying he saw no reason why economic cooperation should not be expanded. Czechoslovak Prime Minister Černík immediately responded: "We took note today with pleasure of a press statement according to which Premier Kosygin stated that the Soviet Union would continue to fulfil its obligations and that from the Soviet side nothing stood in the way of further cooperation in all spheres."[164] The extent of Kosygin's isolation was shown, however, by the fact that the Soviet press, though noting that a meeting between Kosygin and Hamouz had taken place,[165] did not reprint the press statement that he issued. It was only published in the Czech press.[166]

Podgorny and Voronov Contend

If Kosygin had difficulty in finding a forum for his views the same was certainly not true for others in the Politburo. On July 19, two Politburo members, Podgorny and Voronov, gave speeches to the

---

[163] Valenta's interview with Franz Marek, then a Politburo member of the Austrian Communist party, *Soviet Intervention*, p. 68.

[164] Prague Radio, July 19, 1968, EE/2827/C/9.

[165] TASS, July 18, 1968, SU/2826/A2/4.

[166] ČTK, July 18, 1968, RFE, *Research, Czechoslovakia*, July 19, 1968.

Russian republic's Supreme Soviet. The occasion was the bestowal on that republic of the Order of the October Revolution. Present at the session were all the full and candidate members of the Politburo except Shelest, Mzhavanadze, and other republic party secretaries whose presence would not be expected at such an "all-Russian" occasion. Brezhnev and Shelepin were also absent, but the one really surprising absentee was D. S. Polyansky, the first deputy prime minister and the former chairman of the Council of Ministers of the Russian republic. Polyansky has been identified as one of the primary patrons of the resurgence of right-wing Russian nationalism that began during 1968,[167] and his absence from a meeting devoted to the glorification of Mother Russia must support rumors that he was quite ill during this time.[168]

Voronov, in a speech published in *Pravda* on July 20, dealt almost exclusively with the achievements of the Russian republic. Only in concluding did Voronov mention that delegates to the Supreme Soviet session had "entirely endorsed the resolution of the plenum of the CC CPSU, the results of the meeting in Warsaw . . . and the letter of the fraternal parties to the Central Committee of the Communist party of Czechoslovakia." But apart from these assurances, Voronov did not make any statements about Czechoslovakia.

Podgorny's speech was in marked contrast to Voronov's. In the first place, perhaps because he was a Ukrainian, Podgorny had felt obliged to express his filial affection for the great Russian people, and this he did, glorifying their "rich culture . . . their stoicism, their persistence, their courage and heroism" and thanking them for giving the country both Vladimir Ilyich Lenin and the Bolshevik party. Then, launching into a lengthy tirade about the current struggle between imperialism and socialism that was manifesting itself most clearly in Czechoslovakia, he continued:

> Here, with the active support of imperialism, right-wing, antisocialist forces—remnants of the defeated, exploiting classes, revisionist and nationalist elements are subjecting the very foundations of socialist construction to fierce attacks.
>
> Having taken advantage of measures carried out to improve the operation of the party and government, and to correct existing mistakes and shortcomings, demogogically concerning themselves with the slogan of "democratization," they seek to discredit the Communist

---

[167] Yanov, *The Russian New Right*, p. 15.

[168] *New York Times*, July 23, 1968, reported that Polyansky had not been seen in public for weeks.

party of Czechoslovakia and to deprive it of its leading role, and to discredit Marxist-Leninist teaching. Hostile external and internal forces clearly seek to push Czechoslovakia off the path of socialism, and to tear her from the socialist community.

The representatives of Communist and Workers' parties who met recently in Warsaw expressed the decisive will to strengthen the socialist system, its unity and cohesion. They firmly declared that they would never consent to the historical victories of socialism being threatened, to imperialism making a breach in the socialist system by peaceful or nonpeaceful means from within or without.

Our party, our people, sincerely believe that the Communist party of Czechoslovakia, the working class . . . are able to block the path of reaction. . . . Our Czechoslovak friends . . . need not doubt that Communists, all Soviet people, fulfilling their internationalist duty, will render them the utmost aid and support in this.[169]

Podgorny's speech may possibly have been a public reflection of a raging debate within the leadership around the issue of invasion. It almost certainly was designed to increase the political pressure on Czechoslovakia and to create a climate within the USSR more accepting of invasion should that course be necessary. In such circumstances the role and attitude of the military assumed great importance.

The Marshals Return to Moscow

The unexpected return to Moscow on July 19 of Marshals Grechko and Yakubovsky raised fears that a change in Soviet military policy toward Czechoslovakia was in the offing. Marshal Grechko had only just begun his much-postponed visit to Algeria on July 16, with the Arab press reporting that he was due to stay there until July 21.[170] He cut short his visit, however, and returned to Moscow on the evening of July 19.[171] On the same day, Marshal Yakubovsky left Prague by air for Moscow[172] in the midst of reports that Soviet troop withdrawals from Czechoslovakia had once again been promised by Moscow.[173] On July 20 *Krasnaya zvezda* published an editorial eulogizing the 145,000 Russian soldiers who had given their lives in the liberation of Czechoslovakia from Nazi Germany. The newspaper, which as the organ of the party committee in the Minis-

[169] *Pravda*, July 20, 1968.

[170] *Egyptian Gazette*, July 16 and 17, 1968.

[171] *Times*, July 20, 1968; and Prague Radio, July 20, 1968, EE/2827/C/12.

[172] Prague Radio, July 19, 1968, EE/2827/C/12.

[173] *International Herald Tribune*, July 23, 1968.

try of Defense was under the control of Yepishev and not Grechko, reported that Soviet soldiers were "deeply disturbed by the intrigues of antisocialist forces in Czechoslovakia" and would increase their combat readiness and vigilance. It is likely that both Grechko and Yakubovsky arrived in Moscow after this article was written and possibly even after it had gone to press. The editorial condemned a "hostile campaign" unleashed by the Czechoslovak press against the recent WTO staff exercises, and it accused that press of saying "not a word about why or for what purpose the armed forces of the aggressive NATO bloc, to which the revanchist forces of West Germany belongs, are holding maneuvers near Czechoslovakia's borders." The article alleged that antisocialist elements "are attempting to . . . undermine the truism that Czechoslovakia can maintain its independence and sovereignty only as a socialist country and as a member of the socialist commonwealth." *Krasnaya zvezda* concluded by promising that "Soviet fighting men have rallied their ranks ever more closely around their Leninist party and its Central Committee and are demonstrating their readiness to continue standing vigilant guard over socialism."[174]

The interesting aspect of this last statement was that Marshal Grechko had not been given the opportunity to rally his own ranks around the Central Committee. As a full Central Committee member, he was eligible to attend, but he was in Algeria during the plenum. And it was Yepishev and not Grechko who addressed the Party *aktiv* in the Ministry of Defense, which unanimously endorsed the Warsaw Letter.[175]

JULY 17–20: MILITARY SECURITY ISSUE
TAKES PROMINENCE

While Grechko was still in Algeria, a press campaign began, signaling a rise in the importance of the military security issue. Several articles alleged the existence of a Western plan to subvert Czechoslovakia. One of these articles, published by *Pravda* on July 19, purported to quote directly from a secret CIA and Pentagon plan for the "ideological sabotage" of Czechoslovakia as a prelude to the "'liberation of East Germany and Czechoslovakia.'" The plan advised agents working in Czechoslovakia to monitor "the degree of

[174] *Krasnaya zvezda*, July 20, 1968.
[175] *Krasnaya zvezda*, July 21, 1968.

the opposition forces' penetration of the Communist party," and "of Czechoslovakia's state security agencies, military intelligence and her counterintelligence services." In the words of *Pravda*, "the conduct of direct aggression is to begin when, in the opinion of the plans' authors, ideological sabotage has created the 'requisite situation.'" The situation "demands all-out vigilance and solidarity from the peoples of the socialist commonwealth, the strengthening of their defense might and readiness to deal a resolute rebuff to aggressive assaults on the positions of socialism."

An article on the same day exposed the secret arms cache that had been found on July 12 near Sokolovo in Western Bohemia. Czechoslovak minister of the interior Pavel had already stated that the rucksacks of arms had been clumsily planted there as a "provocation," and rumors in Prague attributed the cache to East German machinations, but *Pravda* went ahead with the story on July 19. The article claimed that the arms had been brought from the FRG by "Sudetan revanchists" and that "the complement of seized weapons fully conformed to the needs of an insurrection and could be used for actions by small groups of rebels."

The appearance of these articles was almost certainly designed to convince any recalcitrant leader that the security situation had deteriorated markedly and that Western military and intelligence services, even if they were not initially responsible for the reform movement, had by now developed a clear and sophisticated plot to aid the insurgents and infiltrate into the very heart of the Czechoslovak state security system. Naturally, under such conditions, attention was focused on Czechoslovakia's border security, but also and more particularly on the political situation within the key organs of state security, namely the Ministry of the Interior, the Ministry of Defense, and the party's eighth department. And unfortunately almost wherever the leaders chose to look, they were alarmed by what they saw.

Prchlík Plans Resistance

While the five were still holding their enclave in Warsaw, Lieutenant General Prchlík, reacting to the continued failure of the Pact High Command to withdraw its forces from Czechoslovakia and to the news of the Warsaw meeting, gave a press conference. Prchlík deplored the emergence of a factional grouping within the Pact, witnessed, as he saw it, by the current meeting in Warsaw. He criticized the work of the state security system, which, under

Novotný, had been oriented away from counterespionage toward internal security, and he proposed that the responsibility for controlling the security forces and the military be shifted from the party to the state. For this purpose the recently established Military and Security Affairs Committee of the National Assembly should be further strengthened, and a state defense council should be established to discuss "the necessary conditions for working out a Czechoslovak military doctrine."

Prchlík made other references to the need for an independent doctrine, strongly implying also that any Soviet military intervention to achieve the permanent stationing of troops would have no legal basis within the framework of existing bilateral or multilateral agreements. He stated: "I myself have taken interest in the problem as to whether there are any provisions in the Warsaw Pact which would entitle the other partners to arbitrarily station or place their units on the territory of the other member states. I have studied all the available materials, but I have not found such a section in any of them." In response to questions about what guarantees existed to prevent a violation of Czechoslovakia's state sovereignty, Prchlík's reply was ambiguous: "In my opinion, we have only one way out and that is . . . to insist that we shall not permit a violation of our state sovereignty . . . and that we shall uncompromisingly demand that all pertinent provisions of our treaties are respected." Prchlík made other proposals for the reform of the WTO structure to alter an unequal situation. As he described the existing structure, the Pact's "command is formed by marshals, generals, and officers of the Soviet Army and the other armies have only their representatives in this joint command."[176]

Prchlík also complained that the Czechoslovak leadership and the military authorities had been kept in the dark about both the recent maneuvers and the promised withdrawals. That Yakubovsky had "failed to fulfil his promise [to withdraw] given to . . . Dubček and Černík" could not be ignored. The troop withdrawals scheduled for July 13 had been canceled by Yakubovsky and were now set for July 21. Only 1,500 troops had left Czechoslovak territory, according to Prchlík, and Yakubovsky's entire headquarters with its equipment was still in the country. Prchlík complained that "none of the competent Czechoslovak officials has had, or even now has,

---

[176] Prague Radio, July 15, 1968, quoted from the text in Remington, *Winter in Prague*, pp. 214–20.

any idea as to how many soldiers of the friendly armies have been, and how many still are, on our territory."[177]

Prchlík's press conference was explosive enough in its content and possible repercussions. But there were additional indications that Prchlík's call for resisting any "violation in our state sovereignty" was in fact a call to develop plans for military resistance. Jiří Pelikán later stated that Prchlík "and some of his collaborators submitted to the party Praesidium an alternative plan for the case of an invasion, suggesting how some military defense action could be carried out." According to Pelikán, "this plan was immediately withdrawn before it was even discussed because it was considered a provocation." But, as Pelikán states, "there were people in the Praesidium who probably informed the Soviet leadership about this matter."[178]

It is less clear whether the Prague leadership actually discussed other forms of civil, nonviolent resistance. An additional investigation carried out by Prchlík following his press conference revealed that Soviet military units had installed electronic jamming devices on Czechoslovak soil to which, in the words of Michael Stepanek-Stemmer (a colonel in the army and President Svoboda's advisor and press officer), "Czechoslovak military experts and supervising bodies had no access."[179] As a result, Stepanek-Stemmer claims, the Dubček leadership, against the votes of Kolder, Indra, Švestka, and others, decided to "take countermeasures" so that in the event of invasion the leadership could ensure their contacts with the public. Stepanek-Stemmer continues: "A few days later Dubček in fact succeeded as a result of an excited telephone discussion with Moscow in persuading the Soviet leadership to dismantle the Soviet military jamming appliances and remove them from Czechoslovakia."[180] After this Stepanek-Stemmer claims, "the Czechoslovak mass media officially halted their preparations for the eventuality of any

[177] Tanyug, July 17, 1968, EE/2824/C1/5.

[178] Pelikán in V. V. Kusin, ed., *The Czechoslovak Reform Movement 1968*, p. 58; also see Pelikán, *Ein Frühling*, p. 260; Erickson in Kusin, *Czechoslovak Reform Movement 1968*, p. 46; Valenta, *Soviet Intervention*, pp. 75–76; Shawcross, *Dubček*, pp. 178–79; and Galia Golan, *Reform Rule in Czechoslovakia*, p. 230. The Czech press also hinted that plans for resistance had been drawn up, as in ČTK, July 27, 1968; *Zemědělské noviny*, July 30, 1968; and *Reportér*, January 16, 1969.

[179] Michael Stepanek-Stemmer, *Die tschechoslowakische Armee*, p. 45.

[180] This report is supported by an article in the *Daily Telegraph*, July 17, 1968, that the Czech army had discovered four radio transmitters and several jamming installations which they had ordered dismantled.

military intervention from the east."[181] As is known, however, a lot of unofficial media preparation continued and bore fruit after August 20.

Purges in the Interior Ministry

Prchlík was not the only leader giving interviews in Prague that were alarming to Moscow. On July 16, V. Šalgovič, Pavel's deputy in the Ministry of the Interior and a proponent of a pro-Moscow line, announced in an interview that most of the department heads, as well as a number of regional heads, in the Directorate of State Security had been dismissed.[182] Official Yugoslav sources commented that this current purge "which took place last weekend" was "still going on" and was aimed at strengthening the power of the progressives. These same sources went on to state that "the underground activity of conservative forces—such as distribution of leaflets, the content and purpose of which are strikingly similar to the campaign of some neighboring countries against Czechoslovakia—is also being linked with some people who are now being removed."[183] Also at this time further dismissals of Soviet advisors or liaison officers were rumored.[184] Pavel Tigrid has maintained that these purges in the Ministry of the Interior "were the subject of several alarmist reports sent by the Soviet liaison officers to the High Command of the Warsaw Pact. They only served to reinforce Moscow's growing fears at the dangerous weakening of its influence in the Czechoslovak army and security forces." Černík was later to state, according to Tigrid, that these factors were "the drop which made the cup brim over."[185] Certainly Soviet worries were evident in the alarmist article published in *Pravda* on July 19, alleging that a key objective of the CIA's plan to subvert Czechoslo-

---

[181] Michael Stepanek-Stemmer, *Die tschechoslowakische Armee*, p. 45.

[182] Prague Radio, July 16, 1968, EE/2825/C/2, and Bratislava Radio, July 23, 1968, EE/2834/C/2. Šalgovič also stated that since 1956, 257 leading officials in State Security had been dismissed for their complicity in the Stalinist trials. Most of these dismissals had taken place in the past few months, and Michel Tatu reported in *Le Monde* on July 20, 1968, that in the latest purge, twenty-nine high functionaries had been removed. In addition to those removed by Pavel, the Security and Defense Committee of the National Assembly also reportedly removed thirteen leading officials "mainly in the sector of state security" at this time, according to a Reuters report from Vienna quoted by the *Daily Express*, July 26, 1968.

[183] Tanyug, July 17, 1968, EE/2825/C/3.

[184] Pavel Tigrid, *Why Dubček Fell*, p. 64, maintains that during the summer 150 agents of the Soviet security forces, mostly Czechoslovak citizens working as Soviet advisors, were purged.

[185] Ibid., p. 65.

vakia was to ascertain "the degree of the opposition forces' penetration of Czechoslovakia's state security agencies" in order to achieve "the recruitment of agents to carry out subversive schemes."

Border Security

Border security also continued to worry Moscow and the East European allies. Czechoslovak admission that more arrests than usual had been made of persons, many of them from the GDR, trying to cross illegally to the West[186] led the East German authorities to the extreme measure of erecting barbed wire fences along their own borders with Czechoslovakia.[187] It was also reported that after July 24 both the USSR and the GDR stopped issuing tourist visas to their own citizens for holidays in Czechoslovakia.[188] Moscow, of course, was not only worried about the ease with which people could cross to the West; they were also concerned about the increased numbers of Western tourists in Czechoslovakia, many of whom were journalists and officials visiting Prague on tourist visas but who nevertheless received access to Czechoslovak decision makers. Most worrying to the Soviets was Prague's apparent willingness to encourage such contacts, especially with West Germany. It was certainly true that several high officials made informal visits to Prague in the spring and summer months: Zbigniew Brzezinski, the architect of the U.S. policy of "building bridges"; a group of deputies from Bonn who visited Prague in May to establish parliamentary contacts; Walter Scheel, leader of the West German opposition Free Democratic party, who had talks with Foreign Minister Jiří Hájek; and Karl Blessing, president of the West German Federal Bank, who was a weekend guest of Otto Pohl, president of the Czechoslovak National Bank. Czechoslovak protestations that such officials were in Prague in a purely private capacity were not made more credible by assertions in the Western press on July 16 that Scheel and Blessing "were standing in for others whose visits at the moment would be an embarrassment to the liberal regime in Prague."[189] *Pravda* was quick to respond, observing that "Bonn's politicians are also hurrying to Prague, both overtly and incog-

[186] ČTK, July 12, 1968, EE/2821/C/8; and *Observer Foreign News Service*, July 24, 1968, no, 25419.

[187] *The Times*, July 24, 1968.

[188] *International Herald Tribune*, July 26, 1968.

[189] *The Guardian*, July 16, 1968; and Adolf Müller, *Die Tschechoslowakei auf der Suche nach Sicherheit*, p. 259. Müller also cites Brandt's foreign policy adviser Bahr and Helmut Schmidt as visitors.

nito. . . . The favorite means of crossing the Czechoslovak border is to proclaim oneself a tourist. The 'guests' from the West are delighted. How easy it has become now!"[190]

Two other security matters concerned the Soviets at this time. One was the impending publication of the report of the Piller Commission on the political trials of the fifties. Although the report was not ready in July, a series of articles by Karl Kaplan, the chief researcher for the commission, appeared at this time alleging, among other things, that Soviet advisors had acted independently of the Czechoslovak authorities. Piller is said to have warned party leaders that the report contained such "shocking facts that its distribution could seriously shake the authority of the CPCz and some of its chief representatives."[191] Its publication was postponed, but, as H. Gordon Skilling states, "there is little doubt that the sum and substance of the document . . . were well known to Soviet authorities."[192] The second issue involved the Piller Commission's recommendation that the political police be disbanded. According to Antonín Liehm, the Dubček leadership approved this measure "three or four days" before the meeting at Čierna. This decision, in Liehm's opinion, played an important role in the Soviet conclusion that an invasion would be necessary if the talks failed.[193]

The Prchlík affair, the purges in the Ministry of the Interior, and the evidence of a more liberal attitude toward border security—all of these, combined with public support for Dubček's reply to the Warsaw Letter from the Peoples' Militia, the Ministry of Defense, and a number of army and police officers throughout the country, heightened the perception of threat in Moscow. The almost total collapse in the power of conservative forces within the military and security apparatus heightened the "siege mentality" of those who remained and contributed to the view in Moscow that measures had to be taken to prevent a total rout of "healthy forces."

INCREASED TIME PRESSURE

The time available for taking action to protect the "healthy forces" was affected appreciably by the announcement from Bratislava on July 18 that the Slovak Central Committee plenum had decided to break with tradition and hold their own Slovak Party Congress be-

[190] Pravda, July 22, 1968.
[191] Skilling, Czechoslovakia's Interrupted Revolution, p. 410.
[192] Ibid., p. 411.
[193] Liehm in Kusin, ed., Czechoslovak Reform Movement 1968, p. 61.

fore the Extraordinary Fourteenth Party Congress. This was to insure a unified Slovak stand on federalization proposals to take forward to the CPCz Congress, but it also would allow a "consistent purge" of the Slovak Central Committee and Praesidium, in the words of Gustáv Husák, the proposal's main supporter.[194]

This was an extremely important event; it meant that the Soviets were now working toward a deadline not of September 9 but of August 26, the date the extraordinary congress of the Slovak Communist party would open in Bratislava. After that congress, the Soviets could expect many of the conservatives, possibly including Bil'ak, to have lost their party positions. Thus any "fraternal assistance" offered by the Soviets in response to a call by "healthy forces" would have to come before August 26. After that date, an invasion would become a much more difficult operation politically, for Soviet forces would have to be used not in support of a "palace coup" but to put private citizens in power, in the process flouting even further the legitimacy of the very Communist party organizations the invasion would be mounted to support.

POLITBURO DECISIONS: JULY 20–21

All available evidence points to a crucial meeting of the Politburo, with the probable participation of other key military and political leaders, during the weekend of July 20–21. Three decisions were adopted including the key strategic decision to prepare for a full-scale invasion of Czechoslovakia. The evidence for this conclusion is strong, although circumstantial and inferential. It is presented below in the course of the analysis.

The first issue to be decided that weekend was the response to Rochet's call for a European Communist conference. The possible motivations of Suslov, Zagladin, and also Ponomarev were discussed above. If Suslov and Zagladin harbored hopes that such an initiative would succeed, by the weekend it had become clear that this was unlikely both because of objections from other Soviet leaders and because of Dubček's own insistence, in the course of talks with Rochet on July 19, that such a conference would be undesirable "for the time being" and should be preceded by bilateral talks.[195]

Suslov was reported to have agreed to drop his demand for a

[194] Skilling, *Czechoslovakia's Interrupted Revolution*, p. 281.
[195] *L'Humanité*, May 18, 1970, for transcript of talks between Rochet and Dubček.

conference in return for a commitment to bilateral talks with the Czechoslovaks.[196] Presumably Brezhnev, who had been seeking such bilateral talks since the beginning of the week, would have agreed, and so would have Kosygin. The Politburo duly agreed (*decision 33*) not to proceed with the PCF call for a European Communist conference, and the commitment to at least one further round of bilateral talks was renewed. Ponomarev, as discussed above, informed all those European Communist parties supporting the Rochet proposal that Moscow would regard the convening of such a conference as a hostile act.[197]

Also apparently discussed during the meeting was the status and disposition of those Soviet troops still in Czechoslovakia. Prague's resentment and tension over the repeated postponement of troop withdrawal was exacerbated by the constant revelations in the Czechoslovak press that jamming equipment had been discovered, that the Soviet military headquarters had not yet been dismantled, that the postexercise evaluation of the performance of the ČSSR armed forces had concluded they were unable to hold a defensive line for the requisite seventy-two hours, that the Prague leadership had no direct access to Soviet military personnel still in Czechoslovakia, and so on.

The next promised deadline for the withdrawal of Soviet troops was July 21, and clearly a decision had to be made. One option was open refusal to withdraw, thus sparking off an immediate political crisis. Such an option would have forestalled bilateral talks, and its success would have depended on political collaborators being in place and ready to stage a palace coup. As long as Soviet troops were still in Czechoslovakia, such an operation, if it succeeded, would be low cost, both politically and militarily; and this military option had been at the forefront of Soviet calculations since the end of May, when Soviet troops crossed into Czechoslovakia on the very day that the CPCz plenum convened.

---

[196] *Christian Science Monitor*, July 20–22, 1968.

[197] Valenta, *Soviet Intervention*, p. 68. As stated by Antonín Liehm, Rochet "ran . . . into Russian objections—objections he apparently regarded as a grave set-back, so much so that the eventual collapse of his health and the end of his political career have been variously ascribed to it" (Antonín Liehm, "Eurocommunism and the Prague Spring," in G. R. Urban, ed., *Communist Reformation*, p. 99). Rochet fell ill in 1969, never to recover. In an interview in *Le Figaro*, February 24, 1977, Socialist leader Guy Mollet states that he had talked to Rochet in July 1968 after his return from Prague and the collapse of his proposal for a conference: "After his return from Prague, Rochet was no longer the same man. He was in the process of dying over Czechoslovakia."

Time was running out, however, and the strength of the conservative forces in the ČSSR was being undermined to the extent that the contingent of Soviet troops still in Czechoslovakia might not be sufficient to achieve even minimum political objectives.

A second military option was therefore considered, and because of the pressure of time, adopted. This was the option of a full-scale invasion of Czechoslovakia by the combined forces of the five. Judging from the extremely high level of military activity from July 23 to August 10—including the mobilization of hundreds of thousands of soldiers in the USSR, the GDR, and Poland—it seems clear that this option was only adopted at the July 20–21 meeting. It may very well have been discussed previously, and judging from the swiftness with which the mobilization was organized, coming only two days after the decision, it would indeed appear that the Soviet High Command was quite ready for this contingency. The operation of the plan included the transfer of military command from Warsaw Pact Headquarters to the Soviet High Command, the mobilization of reservists, the requisitioning of civilian transport, the placement of troops, fuel supplies, and logistical and communication equipment in a ring around Czechoslovakia, and the appointment of military commanders to handle the operation. None of these measures were taken before July 23, and they continued unabated up until August 10, when all the military forces went into a holding pattern, awaiting final instructions.

The Soviet leadership dealt with four possible options at this meeting: (1) the Rochet initiative, which it rejected; (2) bilateral negotiations, which were accepted but without great optimism; (3) the use of military forces still in Czechoslovakia to support a palace coup, also apparently rejected as unlikely to succeed; and (4) full invasion. If these were the alternatives, what were the objectives and the specific points of agreement and decision that came out of the meeting? Moving beyond the decision to reject the Rochet initiative (*decision 33*), the Politburo agreed that the deteriorating security situation in Czechoslovakia warranted immediate attention. Accordingly they decided (*decision 34*) to send an official note to the Czechoslovak leadership demanding, among other things, the immediate stationing of troops. The note, which was delivered by Ambassador Chervonenko on Monday, July 22, demanded the stationing of troops on the basis of a previous agreement with Novotný that stationing would be allowed if it became necessary. The Soviets argued that the arms cache had proved the laxness of border security and that the poor performance of the Czechoslovak armed forces in the recent maneuvers had proved their inability to hold their positions for the 72 hours required for the arrival of Soviet reinforcements. Moreover, cadre changes had made certain elements within the armed forces politically unreliable, and the note demanded that Prchlík in particular be removed.[198]

Decision 35 to prepare for full-scale invasion was almost certainly not adopted without considerable debate and dissent. The exact extent of the dissent cannot be measured, but it was known in both Eastern Europe and the West that deep divisions were expressed at this meeting and were resolved by a compromise, albeit one that favored interventionist opinion. In Washington, cables were received from both Ambassador Beam in Prague and Ambassador Thompson in Moscow that an invasion now seemed almost inevitable.[199] Secretary of State Rusk, relying on a report from Chip Bohlen in Moscow, told President Johnson that "the odds were 60 to 40 for a Soviet-led invasion."[200] As a consequence, all diplomatic leave was postponed, and a special State Department crisis unit was established to monitor events around the clock.[201]

As to the extent of division within the Kremlin, other evidence seems to support the conclusions reached in a lengthy secret report, released to the author under the U.S. Freedom of Information Act. Prepared for Secretary of State Rusk on July 22, immediately following the weekend Politburo meeting, the report is entitled "Czechoslovakia—The Pros and Cons of Soviet Military Action."[202] Examining inaction as an option, the report concluded

---

[198] U.S. Department of State, *Intelligence Note 576*, July 22, 1968; *Telegram 206938*, July 23, 1968, to All European Diplomatic Posts; Prague Radio, July 24, 1968, EE/2830/i and July 24, 1968, EE/2830/C/2; *Svobodné slovo*, July 24, 1968; Tanyug, July 23, 1968; in RFE, *Research, Czechoslovakia*, July 26, 1968; the *Times* and the *Guardian*, July 23, 1968; and the *New York Times*, July 29, 1968. Also the *Observer Foreign News Service*, July 24, 1968, no. 25420, stated that according to well-informed Yugoslav sources, the question of stationing Soviet troops on Czechoslovak territory had become "vital." Zdeněk Mlynář has also stated that at the Moscow negotiations following the invasion, "the demands of the hawks could have been satisfied by the stationing of a limited number of troops (in particular, strategic forces), and a much more modest reform movement could have been allowed to continue unhindered" (Mlynář, *Nachtfrost*, p. 298).

[199] Author's interview with Jacob Beam, November 16, 1979. Also the interview with Beam in G. R. Urban, ed., *Communist Reformation*, p. 244.

[200] Bohlen, *Witness to History*, p. 529.

[201] Author's interview with Paul Costolanski, member of the State Department's special Czechoslovakia crisis unit, November 14, 1979.

[202] U.S. Department of State, *Intelligence Note 575*, July 22, 1968.

that there had already been "grumbling from the party bureaucracy" to the effect that inaction by "the top Soviet leaders" was
the cause of the current impasse and that action therefore had to
be taken to break out of it. The impatience of the interventionists
was reflected in a July 22 *Pravda* editorial that asked, almost in exasperation: "Can it be that one should wait until the counterrevolutionary forces become master of the situation in Czechoslovakia before giving battle to them?" It appeared that even those in
the party bureaucracy who might not have favored an invasion had
by now accepted it as almost inevitable. Mikhail Voslensky, who
worked during 1968 as an adviser to the Central Committee on
Western policy and as the secretary of the Disarmament Commission of the Academy of Sciences, recounts a conversation on July 19
with V. A. Kirillin, himself a Soviet Central Committee member
and a deputy premier in charge of the State Committee for Science
and Technology, in which Kirillin stated that unfortunately "extreme measures" might be necessary against Czechoslovakia. The
same view was expressed three days later to Voslensky by another
Central Committee official, leading him to record in his diary on
July 29 that "the Moscow people" were ready to smash Czechoslovakia without reference to its effect on the Communist parties in
Europe in order to set an example for the intelligentsia in the Soviet Union.[203]

Similar pressure for invasion was being exerted from certain of
Moscow's East European allies. The East Germans typically were
most concerned, with the SED Central Committee declaring on
July 19 that "we stand firmly beside our Czech comrades in the
necessary fight."[204] In Poland, the July 19 *Trybuna ludu* openly attacked Dubček by name, the first time any organ in the bloc press
had done so, and dismissed his protestations of loyalty to Communism as "reassuring words contradicted by facts." As usual, only
the Hungarians showed any sympathy toward Prague. Hungarian
party leaders had not matched the demands of the other Warsaw
signatories for bilateral talks. They also had broken the agreement
reached in Warsaw to adopt uniform press coverage by authorizing
the immediate release of the text of the Warsaw Letter and by allowing the publication of excerpts from the CPCz Praesidium reply
to the letter. In addition, Hungary had printed the Czechoslovak

[203] *Der Spiegel*, no. 34, August 21, 1978.
[204] *Daily Telegraph*, July 20, 1968.

version of the arms cache in Bohemia alongside Soviet allegations that the weapons had been planted by "Sudetan revanchists."[205]

The secret U.S. State Department report to Rusk stated that "a decision on use of force against a Communist country would be a difficult one for the Soviet leaders" especially in light of "differences within the Politburo on what the effects of Soviet action versus inaction would be." The *New York Times* of August 9, quoting "highly placed sources in East Berlin," released a story that the Soviet Union and East Germany had come close to invading Czechoslovakia in mid-July, but that moderate elements "in the Soviet leadership succeeded in deflecting 'at the 11th hour' those who favored invasion and ultimately persuaded them to settle for the Soviet-Czechoslovak meeting at Čierna." The rationale for action passed on to Moscow by the East Germans, according to the source, was that Dubček and the reformers were like "a rotten fish that begins stinking at the head." The pretext would have been the July 19 revelations about the arms cache, which would be used as a signal for remaining conservatives in Prague to "rise up and cry for help," with the removal of Dubček and his followers as the objective. The problem in Moscow, according to this source, was that most Soviet leaders still had faith in Dubček but believed he was trying to "ride on the back of a tiger." In mid-July, the informant continued, "Moscow briefly leaned toward the East German interpretation but reverted soon to its original theory."

The U.S. report stated that invasion was being resisted by two groups. There were those who feared the negative repercussions of invasion on East-West relations and on the planned International Communist Conference; and there were those who "differ in their reading of the tactical situation—had the moment for military action arrived?" And could a puppet regime installed by force in Czechoslovakia ever be viable? Fears about the possible repercussions of an invasion on the Soviet Union's standing in the international community certainly do appear to have been discussed at this meeting, for the following week Soviet ambassadors made approaches to Western foreign ministries (discussed below). Also the Soviet leaders may have been somewhat mystified by the likely U.S. reaction to an invasion. On July 17, "qualified informants" reported that the United States had advised Moscow that East-West

---

[205] *New York Times*, August 4, 1968. The *Népszabadság* editorial was reprinted in *Pravda*, but without the last sentence.

cooperation would be imperiled by an invasion.[206] But on the next day, Secretary of State Rusk went out of his way to disclaim the report and insisted that the United States had not expressed its concern to the Russians, twice stating emphatically that "we have not involved ourselves in this in any way."[207] The following day, a State Department official appeared to backtrack by saying he was not "ruling out the possibility of a conversation between an official of the United States government and an official of the Soviet government on the subject of Czechoslovakia."[208] Then, to completely confuse the situation, the State Department maintained on July 20 that "one or two American diplomats may have informally discussed the crisis with Russians, but insist they were not instructed to do so."[209] Signals coming from Washington may well have given the Politburo reason to believe that international repercussions would be limited, even minimal, but there was still some uncertainty.

The final decision (*number 35*) of this long and complicated meeting was once again a compromise. Final preparations for a full invasion were ordered. The military would not be ready for such an extreme move until after August 10, but making the decision at this time ensured that if political negotiations failed, an invasion could be mounted before the crucial date of August 26, when the Slovak Party Congress was to convene. Although it was agreed that the Soviet leaders would pursue bilateral negotiations with the Dubček leadership, there was to be no relaxation of pressure. The official response to the CPCz reply to the Warsaw Letter was agreed to at this meeting and published in *Pravda* on July 22. The CPCz Praesidium was accused of "avoiding a thorough analysis of the actual situation in the country" and of having "ignored the fundamental questions raised" in the Warsaw Letter. The article affirmed the Politburo's united commitment to the demands laid down in the letter and essentially signaled the collective decision that "resolute action" would have to be taken if the demands were not fulfilled. A clear indication that the decision reached was at least collective, if not unanimous, was that after this meeting, not one member of the

---

[206] *New York Times*, July 18, 1968. It was later reported that these private contacts consisted of American officials calling to the attention of Soviet officials editorials and other commentary in the American press, a very low-key diplomatic effort indeed. *Washington Post*, August 24, 1968.

[207] *International Herald Tribune*, July 19, 1968.

[208] Bohlen, *Witness to History*, p. 533.

[209] *The Times*, July 20, 1968.

Politburo made any public comment on Czechoslovakia until well after the invasion—not one except Prime Minister Kosygin, who managed on July 25, in the course of a meeting with Czechoslovak minister of foreign trade, V. Valeš, to reiterate his by now purely personal view that he saw no reason why any obstacles to Soviet-Czechoslovak friendship should not be cleared up.[210] Once again, the Soviet press did not report his statement, and after this meeting his isolation seemed to be complete.

JULY 22–28

Having extended a public invitation to the CPCz Praesidium to attend bilateral talks (*decision 32*, on July 19), and having reaffirmed that decision during their weekend meeting, the Soviet leadership waited for the Czechoslovak response. Dubček once again refused to leave Czechoslovak territory; and late on July 22, the same day that the talks were originally scheduled to begin, the Politburo backed down, agreeing (*decision 36*) to negotiations on Czechoslovak soil but heartened no doubt by the Czechoslovak decision that their entire Praesidium would be represented.[211] Negotiations were to begin at the end of the month in the village of Čierna nad Tisou, on the Czechoslovak-Soviet border.

It was also on Monday July 22 that Ambassador Chervonenko delivered the Soviet note complaining officially about the deteriorating military and security conditions in Czechoslovakia and demanding the permanent stationing of Soviet troops and the dismissal of Lieutenant General Prchlík. The charges about lax border security were resisted. Major General Karel Peprny, the commander of the Czechoslovak Border Guards, commented on July 23 about Moscow's concern over the arms cache and lax border security: "I understand this concern; and I also fully understand that people should see a connection between weapons being found on our territory and the standard of the defense of our state frontier. . . . I can reasonably state that in recent years we have apprehended all violators of the frontier coming from capitalist states."[212]

Despite this denial, the Soviet note evoked widespread concern. A meeting of the National Assembly's Defense and Security

[210] *Frankfurter Allgemeine Zeitung*, July 26, 1968.
[211] TASS International Service in English, 17.04 GMT, July 22, 1968, SU/2829/i.
[212] Prague Radio, July 23, 1968, EE/2830/C/2.

Committee was convened "in view of certain doubts expressed concerning the assurance of the security of our country and its internal order."[213] A deputy minister of the interior rejected, during this session, the notion that "domestic extremists were acting in conjunction with the outside."[214] Nevertheless, the Prague leadership acceded to the Soviet demand that Prchlík be removed from his post as head of the eighth department of the Central Committee. The Soviet note also prompted a meeting in the Ministry of Defense, an account of which has been provided by President Svoboda's press officer: "It has been documented that after the military hawks in Moscow had called for and achieved the deposition of Prchlík as head of the eighth department that General Dzúr, the defense minister, had in the course of stormy meetings in the Defense Ministry decisively refused to even mention the possibility of an armed Czechoslovak defense against any military aggression from the east. The military hawks had been reliably informed that neither Dzúr, the defense minister, nor President General Svoboda would issue any such order."[215] This account is essentially confirmed by an official statement of the Czechoslovak Ministry of National Defense issued on July 26, the day after Prchlík's removal, vehemently denying rumors that military measures would be taken to counter a Soviet invasion.[216]

Nevertheless, the Czechoslovaks continued to resist Soviet pressures for the permanent stationing of troops; and although the note resulted in Prchlík's dismissal and clear signals that any Soviet military move would not be resisted by the Czech army, the Soviet victory was not complete. As a concession to domestic support for Prchlík, the strategically key department he headed was also abolished, thereby removing in one blow a powerful lever of party control over the state security services. Furthermore, Prchlík was reassigned to head the Czechoslovak military district in Eastern Slovakia on the border with the Ukraine in the area where the bilateral talks with the Soviets at Čierna were soon to open.[217]

Neither the July 20–21 Politburo meeting nor the Czechoslovak reaction to the demands and decisions resulting from that meeting did anything to lessen attacks by the Soviet and East European

[213] *Rudé právo*, July 26, 1968.
[214] Ibid.
[215] Stepanek-Stemmer, *Die Tschechoslowakische Armee*, p. 52.
[216] V. V. Kusin and Z. Hejzlar, *Czechoslovakia 1968–1969*, p. 67.
[217] *New York Times*, July 29, 1968.

press on the Czechoslovaks for the sheer "impudence" of their behavior.[218] Doubts were raised about the CPCz leadership's capability and willingness to prevent a "political catastrophe," and individual leaders were singled out in the Soviet press for denunciation.[219] The weakening of democratic centralism was of special concern, with specific mention made of the soon-to-be-published draft CPCz statutes allowing the promulgation of minority views.[220] A commentary by a military officer on GDR radio came closer than any other to calling openly for invasion. Col. Karl Dittmer stated on July 22 that "the Warsaw Pact has always proved itself a reliable instrument for preserving peace. . . . In 1956, the Soviet troops, loyal to their international obligation, rendered fraternal aid to the revolutionary forces of the people in Hungary." After quoting the example of August 1961 in the GDR when the Wall was built, Dittmer concluded with this comment on the current situation: "The efforts of the enemy are doomed to failure, because our peoples and their armies will never allow the socialist achievements of any one of our fraternal countries . . . to be risked by careless conduct."[221] This was followed on July 24 by an official statement from the SED Politburo that ever since the Warsaw meeting, there had been signs of a "menacing deterioration" in Czechoslovakia.[222] This view found support in Poland when, on July 25, the party paper, *Trybuna ludu*, stated that if anything the Czechoslovak reply to the Warsaw Letter had only increased the anxiety of Prague's allies about the willingness of the CPCz leadership to struggle against antisocialist elements.[223] An article in the Polish army newspaper *Żolnierz Polski* on July 26 went even further: "The Czech people are so bewildered by what has happened the past months that they cannot distinguish between truth and falsehoods: it is time the Czechoslovak army restored order." Three days later the military journal *Żolnierz Wolności* stated that the Polish armed forces, "faithful to their allied obligations resulting from Poland's membership in the Warsaw Pact, will do everything in their power to prevent the enemy from making a breach in the fraternal family of socialist

[218] *Krasnaya zvezda*, July 23, 1968.

[219] Prchlík in *Krasnaya zvezda*, July 23, 1968; Pavel in *Izvestia*, July 24, 1968; Šnejdárek in *Literaturnaya gazeta*, July 24, 1968; Šik by *Pravda*, July 25, 1968.

[220] *Pravda*, July 25, 1968.

[221] Radio GDR, July 22, 1968, EE/2829/C/4.

[222] *New York Times*, July 25, 1968.

[223] PAP, July 25, 1968, EE/2831/i.

countries."[224] This was the same message contained in a declaration issued by the Bulgarian Central Committee, which agreed that since the Warsaw meeting, counterrevolutionary forces had become "more active" and that the Bulgarian party, "gravely alarmed" by current developments, "will spare no efforts to strengthen the militant unity between the socialist countries."[225] Even the Hungarians were forced to admit that action had to be taken by the Czechoslovak leadership against rightist elements. The Hungarian leadership offered advice, as in this editorial from *Népszabadság*, from those who had seen it all before: "We went through all this, we saw all this, tragedy overtook us all as a result of this. If we now speak about all this we do so . . . because we want to cry out and give this warning: Comrades—bar the way to the things that in Hungary resulted in open counterrevolution . . . don't let the socialist revival cost the blood and individual tragedy of hundreds of thousands."[226]

In the midst of this crescendo of press polemics from Eastern Europe, a new round of military maneuvers was announced. A rear services exercise (code-named "Nemen") was announced prominently on the front page of *Izvestia* on July 23. It was scheduled to last until August 10 and involved the call-up of thousands of reservists and the requisitioning of thousands of items of civilian motor transport to bring Class II and III divisions to full alert. The exercises began in the Ukraine, Belorussia, Latvia, and the westernmost part of the RSFSR (Kaliningrad *oblast'*). They were then extended at the end of July into the GDR and Poland and were expanded in scope to include not just logistic equipment but also tanks, artillery, rocket launchers, and other battle equipment.[227] U.S. Embassy officials reported to Washington that farm trucks commandeered from the harvest had been called to Moscow to pick up reservists before heading West. At the same time, most of the Russian chauffeurs in the embassies in Moscow were called up and did not return until after the invasion.[228] All freight cars were

[224] RFE, *Research, East Europe*, August 1, 1968.

[225] Sofia Radio, July 26, 1968, EE/2836/C2/5.

[226] MTI, July 25, 1968, EE/2831/i; and *Daily Telegraph*, July 26, 1968.

[227] TASS, July 23, 1968, SU/2830/i; *New York Times*, July 28, 1968; *International Herald Tribune*, July 31, 1968, *The Guardian* and *Daily Telegraph*, July 24, 1968; and General James H. Polk, "Reflections on the Czechoslovakian Invasion," p. 32.

[228] Interview on November 14, 1979, with Paul Cook, special advisor to the director of the Bureau of Intelligence and Research, U.S. State Department, who was in the U.S. embassy in Moscow in 1968.

requisitioned by the military, and both the summer harvest and civil transport practically came to a standstill.[229]

The man in charge of the exercises, army general S. S. Maryakhin, deputy minister of defense and chief of Rear Services, confirmed that these exercises of rear support troops were the largest ever conducted in Soviet history and that their function was to perfect communications and improve supply to the front line.[230] It was clear that in this case the front line was the border with Czechoslovakia and not Western Europe. A communications center was established just north of Cieszyn on the Polish-Czechoslovak frontier, and Russian troops began to pour into Poland, where they were stationed in areas adjacent to Czechoslovakia alongside troops that had just been withdrawn from Czechoslovakia. The movement of 75,000 Soviet troops along the GDR border with Czechoslovakia was also reported,[231] as was the publicized alert and partial mobilization of East German armed forces for three days at the end of July, justified to the troops by the need for vigilance during the preparations for the NATO exercise "Black Lion."[232] The commander of NATO's Central Army Group later confirmed as "a fact of considerable significance" that the Soviet units withdrawn from Czechoslovakia at this time (the pullout had recommenced following Dubček's agreement to bilateral talks) "did not return to home stations but remained in encampments around the Czech border."[233]

On July 25, extensive air defense exercises in the Baltic-Moscow-Black Sea triangle were announced.[234] Code-named "Skyshield," the exercises were controlled by Marshal P. F. Batitsky. Grechko visited the headquarters of the exercises, which lasted until July 31, when *Krasnaya zvezda* announced their successful completion.[235]

---

[229] *New York Times*, July 26, 1968; and Polk, "Reflections on the Czechoslovakian Invasion," p. 32.

[230] Moscow Radio, July 28, 1968, SU/2834/B/5.

[231] *New York Times*, July 28, 30, 31, 1968; *The Times*, July 30, 1968; *Christian Science Monitor*, July 30, 1968.

[232] According to the diary of an East German infantryman, excerpts of which were published in *The Times*, August 18, 1978; also David Binder's report in the *New York Times* of August 9, 1968.

[233] Polk, "Reflections on the Czechoslovakian Invasion," p. 32. Prague Radio on July 22 confirmed that 1000 military vehicles had crossed the Czechoslovak-Polish border at Nachod, whereas only 100 vehicles had crossed into the Soviet Union (RFE, *Research, Czechoslovakia*, July 23, 1968).

[234] *Krasnaya zvezda*, July 25, 1968; also Marshal Batitsky gave an interview to *Krasnaya zvezda* on the same day.

[235] Grechko's visit reported on Moscow Radio, July 29, 1968, SU/2833/i.

With these exercises the Soviet army, the navy (which had been on maneuvers in the Baltic), and the air defense forces were all mobilized along with the Polish and East German armies and their navies. The Hungarian and Bulgarian armies and Soviet forces stationed in Hungary were not, however, involved until mid-August, immediately prior to the invasion. As later events were to show, the "Nemen" and "Sky Shield" exercises effectively acted as a cover for the logistical and air build-up for the August invasion. Western military intelligence was subsequently forced to admit that the successful camouflage by the USSR of its military build-up led NATO chiefs to "misinterpret" the rear service exercise, which "was not given due weight in the intelligence estimate, both our own and those of higher headquarters."[236] A further important indicator that the key decision on military intervention had been taken prior to the beginning of the "Nemen" exercises on July 23 was the shift in the locus of command from the Warsaw Pact High Command to the Soviet Ministry of Defense. At no point in the Soviet press coverage of the "Nemen" and "Sky Shield" exercises was any mention made of the Warsaw Pact staff, even though the armies of more than one Warsaw Pact state were involved.[237]

In the midst of these military maneuvers, Grechko issued an Order of the Day on July 27, published in *Pravda*, stating that "the paramount task of the Soviet armed forces is to further raise their combat readiness." This was made necessary by the directive of the July Central Committee plenum "for further strengthening the cohesion of the socialist community on the basis of the principle of proletarian internationalism and for a resolute struggle for the cause of socialism." It is interesting to note, however, that Grechko's statement, issued on Navy Day, still put "the criminal war the USA is conducting in Vietnam" above "the attempts of international imperialism to make a breach in the socialist system and to alter the balance of forces to its own advantage" in the list of activities threatening world peace. Grechko seems to have used this occasion to once again emphasize his own view that the threat posed by America's actions in Vietnam was still more serious than the situation in Czechoslovakia.

It was also at the end of the month that two of the military commanders who ultimately would be responsible operationally for the invasion became more visible. General I. G. Pavlovsky, deputy

---

[236] Polk, "Reflections on the Czechoslovakian Invasion," p. 32.
[237] Malcolm Mackintosh, *The Evolution of the Warsaw Pact*, pp. 13–15.

minister of defense and chief of ground forces, wrote an article
in *Krasnaya zvezda* on July 26, choosing as his subject a particularly interesting and topical issue: the importance of morale, discipline, and psychological factors in an army's preparedness for war
under "the current difficult and complex conditions." General
S. M. Shtemenko, whose promotion to the chief of staff of the Joint
Armed Forces of the WTO (replacing General M. I. Kazakov) was
not announced until early August, was, however, present at a
meeting held in the Soviet Ministry of Defense on July 29. Present
at the meeting, announced by the East German news agency, were
General Heinz Hoffmann, the GDR minister of defense and probably the most influential non-Soviet military commander in the
Warsaw Pact; Marshal Grechko; Marshal Zakharov; and Generals
Yepishev, Shtemenko, and Kazakov. The Soviet press made no
mention of the meeting, presumably because Hoffman was officially "in the USSR on holiday."[238] The presence of Shtemenko was
most interesting, not least because as operations officer of the Soviet General Staff under Antonov during World War II he had been
involved in planning the 1944 putsch in Slovakia and the 1945 liberation of Prague. His impending promotion and his involvement at
this time in military meetings of Pact officers add credence to the
view that military plans for a full invasion were well advanced but
still not complete.

In addition to making final military preparations, the Soviet
leadership was still trying to assess the international repercussions
of invasion. In Washington, Ambassador Dobrynin met Secretary
Rusk; and in the presence of Chip Bohlen, the deputy under secretary for political affairs, Rusk told Dobrynin that "the Soviet government should be under no illusion regarding American attitudes. Americans still believed in the principle . . . that the people
had a right to determine for themselves the institutions under
which they were to live."[239] But, Rusk said, charges in *Pravda* that
the United States was involved in any Czech counterrevolutionary
movement were false. Dobrynin is reported by Bohlen to have lis-
tened courteously without response. Rusk had two other meetings
with Dobrynin, on July 25 and 31, in which the latter sought to
clarify the American position on Czechoslovakia and East-West relations and to state that in Moscow's view, the Czechoslovak situa-

[238] ADN, July 30, 1968, SU/2835/A2/8.
[239] Bohlen, *Witness to History*, p. 533.

tion was an "internal" Communist matter of no concern to Washington.[240] A State Department memo concluded that Moscow, in calculating the cost of invasion, "would have to expect cancellation or postponement of talks with the U.S. on strategic arms, and they may expect a step up in defense spending in the U.S. and in Western Europe."[241] But no military countermeasures of any kind were envisaged by the United States. President Johnson's personal interest in arms limitation talks was well known, and he certainly gave no indication that these talks would be canceled or postponed in the event of a crisis in Central Europe. On the contrary, at the very time that hundreds of thousands of Soviet, East German, and Polish troops were being mobilized in formations encircling Czechoslovakia, Johnson held a press conference declaring his pursuit of arms limitation talks with Moscow as the most important single effort of his office and the one he desired to succeed in most.[242]

Washington also instructed NATO headquarters "not to exacerbate the internal political struggle in Czechoslovakia by stepping up of excessive land or air patrolling and . . . to avoid any sort of incident or accidental over-flight in the sensitive area of the Czech border."[243] In the words of the U.S. ambassador to NATO, "if we have any deep-dyed plot in this matter, it is to keep well out of it."[244] On July 24, the day after operation "Nemen" was announced, the West German government, at American urging, announced that the "Black Lion" maneuvers scheduled for mid-September had been moved from an area near the Czechoslovak border to a less "provocative" venue 120 miles south west of the original site.[245] The Soviets, according to the British cabinet minister Richard Crossman, had also instructed their ambassadors in every Western capital to "test Western reactions" to an invasion,[246] and certainly there is no doubt that the dominant view expressed, according to Crossman, was that "there would be no response whatsoever and that they [the Czechs] must fend for themselves."[247]

[240] LBJ Library, *Papers of Dean Rusk*, Box 4, 1968; an interview with Dean Rusk in Stafford, "Signalling and Response," p. 100.

[241] U.S. Department of State, *Intelligence Note 575*, July 22, 1968.

[242] *New York Times*, August 1, 1968; also Johnson, *The Vantage Point*, pp. 479–486.

[243] Polk, "Reflections on the Czechoslovakian Invasion," p. 21.

[244] *Christian Science Monitor* (London edition), July 20–22, 1968.

[245] *Times*, July 25, 1968; and Stafford, "Signalling and Response," p. 101, for evidence of U.S. pressure on the FRG to relocate the exercises.

[246] Richard Crossman, *The Diaries of a Cabinet Minister*, p. 162.

[247] Ibid., p. 143.

With the repeated public assurances of inactivity by the United States and her West European allies, Moscow's leaders and military commanders could not have had any doubt that they had a free hand to deal with Czechoslovakia as they saw fit. With NATO statements of Western noninvolvement and the reassurances from Dzúr that the Czechoslovak army would not resist, two major elements of uncertainty for the military planners were removed by the end of July. As July drew to a close and the pressure of time increased, there was both a clear narrowing of options, and a lowering of risks, with Moscow putting military preparations fully in hand should bilateral talks collapse. A secret State Department memorandum prepared on July 26 concluded: "The increased readiness of Soviet forces would take on real significance should Party discussions fail to settle the crisis and Soviet leaders decide to intervene militarily."[248] On the day the Čierna talks opened, both *Pravda* and a broadcast from Radio Moscow to Czechoslovakia pointedly emphasized: "The threat to the socialist gains of the Czechoslovak working people has been intensified and the class comrades are *warning* the working people of Czechoslovakia that *there is no time to lose*."[249]

[248] U.S. Department of State, *Intelligence Note 591*, July 26, 1968.

[249] *Pravda*, July 28, 1968; Radio Moscow in Czech, July 28, 1968, SU/2834/A2/2 (emphasis added).

CHAPTER NINE

Phase Four:
July 29–August 5

THE ČIERNA NEGOTIATIONS

On Monday, July 29, the Soviet negotiating team arrived by train at the Czechoslovak border town of Čierna nad Tisou. Almost the entire top Soviet political leadership was present, including all the full Politburo members with the exception of Polyansky (rumored to be ill) and Kirilenko. Politburo candidate members Demichev, Masherov, Katushev, and Ponomarev were included, and Soviet ambassador Chervonenko also managed to find his way into the Soviet delegation. Of the Soviet party leaders who had previously been involved either in negotiating with the Czechoslovaks or in speaking about Czechoslovakia, only Grishin and Shcherbitsky were excluded from the team. Also the absence of Andropov, Grechko, and Gromyko made clear that this was purely a party conclave.

The full CPCz Praesidium was included in the Czechoslovak delegation, as was President Svoboda and M. Jakeš, the head of the party's Commission on Supervision and Auditing. But whereas the Soviets came fully prepared with advisors, complete documentation of Czechoslovak press "deviations," and even a communications system linked to Moscow and independent of Czechoslovak control, the Czechoslovak side clearly was less well prepared and more disunited. Zdeněk Mlynář relates that before the Čierna meeting, the CPCz Praesidium had met to discuss their negotiating tactics. After two hours of pointless debate, which, according to Mlynář, seemed more like "the editorial board of some magazine than an important state function," the meeting broke up, with

255

Jiří Hájek asking Mlynář in exasperation: "If this is the party leadership, I ask you, how can I be Minister of Foreign Affairs?"[1]

Brezhnev opened the negotiations at Čierna. He put on the table a thick pile of press cuttings—some from Czech and Slovak papers, others from Western publications—all commenting on recent events in Prague. It is symptomatic of information processing throughout the entire crisis that the top Soviet leaders worked from raw data and not from the briefs and summaries more typically used by their Western counterparts. Brezhnev used the clippings to cover every topic from non-Communist political activity, the leading role of the party, and press censorship to the West German "threat," bloc unity, and Czechoslovak foreign policy. In a speech lasting almost four hours, Brezhnev repeated many of the demands already made in the Warsaw Letter. He focused on the need for extensive personnel changes both in the highest echelons of the party and state and in the security services and mass media. Brezhnev also pressed the Czechoslovaks to postpone the upcoming Fourteenth Party Congress, already scheduled for September 9. Indeed Jiří Pelikán states that in addition to the demand for personnel changes, "the main pressure from Brezhnev was to postpone the Congress."[2] The issue of a free press was also at the center of Brezhnev's concerns, and at one point he is reported to have burst out: "It is madness for you to let your so-called 'free writers' dictate your policies for you. They are either hired agents of the imperialists or at least they do what the imperialists want!"[3] According to Smrkovský, Brezhnev rejected Czechoslovak protestations that the post-January course and their current negotiating position were mandated by public opinion (a petition with over a million signatures had been collected) with the rebuttal that under no circumstances could the negotiations be subjected to the pressure of a "nationalized public."[4]

Brezhnev's own observations apparently were supplemented by other members of the Soviet delegation. Suslov, for example,

[1]Zdeněk Mlynář, *Night Frost in Prague*, pp. 134–36.

[2]Jiří Pelikán, "The Struggle for Socialism in Czechoslovakia," p. 25; and Moravus, "Shawcross's Dubček—A Different Dubček," p. 209. Also the document adopted at the Central Committee CPCz plenum in December 1970 entitled "Lessons of the Crisis Development in the CPCz and Society after the 13th CPCz Congress" refers to the refusal of right-wing Czechoslovak representatives to postpone the Fourteenth Party Congress, which "would have brought them a conclusive victory" (*Pravda pobehzhdaet*, p. 38).

[3]Gordon Brook-Shepherd and David Floyd, *Sunday Telegraph*, October 6, 1968.

[4]Josef Smrkovský, *An Unfinished Conversation*, p. 20.

charged the Czechs with repeated breaches of security over the last months—he referred to Prchlík's interview and the public debate over the presence of Soviet troops—as a result of which information on Pact troop dispositions and plans had been leaked to NATO powers.[5] By the end of the morning's session, therefore, the Czechoslovak team could be under no illusions about the seriousness with which the situation was viewed in Moscow and the extent of Soviet resolve. Dubček answered Brezhnev's allegations in the afternoon, maintaining that although there had been isolated antisocialist acts, the party was firmly in control. He attempted to assuage Soviet fears by answering all of Brezhnev's charges, but this apparently had little effect, and at the end of the first day the meeting appeared to be deadlocked.

The Soviet leaders withdrew in their special train across the border for the night to the small town of Chop in the Soviet Ukraine. Some sources maintain that the Soviets used this opportunity to consult with their other East European allies. Willy Brandt, in his memoirs, contends that Soviet leaders reported each evening "to the waiting representatives of Poland and the GDR: Premier Stoph . . . repeatedly tried to urge a 'hard line' on Brezhnev in Ulbricht's name."[6]

The second day also got off to a bad start, with Brezhnev angrily brandishing that morning's edition of *Rudé právo*. He was incensed not over an editorial or an article but over an advertisement for a party secretary's post at the Czechoslovak party headquarters in Prague, in which the only qualifications required were a university degree.[7] If the Soviets had reason to be annoyed, so too did the Czechoslovaks, since on that morning *Pravda* had published a letter written two weeks earlier from ninety-nine Prague workers, members of a factory people's militia unit, who denounced their countrymen's demands for withdrawal of Soviet troops from Czechoslovakia.

Yet, according to many accounts, it was President Svoboda's strong speech in support of Dubček and the post-January course

[5] Michael Stepanek-Stemmer, *Die Tschechoslowakische Armee*, p. 78.

[6] Willy Brandt, *People and Politics*, p. 213. Smrkovský (*An Unfinished Conversation*, p. 19) is more ambiguous, stating merely that "the Soviets had all the services on their side [of the border], probably including regular contacts with their colleagues from the Warsaw meeting." Yugoslav sources had told Western journalists in Belgrade that Soviet leaders had met with Polish and East German leaders in the Ukraine, also immediately before the talks in Čierna began, according to the *Daily Telegraph*, July 26, 1968.

[7] Reported by several sources, including *Daily Telegraph*, August 1, 1968.

that most surprised the Soviet leadership. As a general who had fought alongside the Red Army in the Great Patriotic War, Svoboda commanded considerable personal respect from the Soviets, and he had never had anything but praise from the Soviet media. He described Soviet suggestions that Czechoslovakia was betraying the socialist camp as "incomprehensible." After all, there was long-standing friendship between the Czechoslovak and Russian peoples, he argued, a friendship that had been tested in battle. As for the issue of Czechoslovakia's western borders, he himself had toured the defense areas with Marshal Yakubovsky earlier in the summer; and he described how, at the end of the tour, the Soviet marshal had declared himself impressed with the morale, equipment, and battle readiness of the troops. According to one account, Svoboda then asked whether Yakubovsky was lying then or whether the Russian leaders were now accusing their own commander of stupidity.[8]

After Svoboda's speech, the talks evidently disintegrated into an uncontrolled argument. At one point Shelest made an accusation, in the words of Smrkovský, "that there were even leaflets printed in our country which were distributed in Transcarpathian Russia; they called for the separating of Transcarpathian Russia from the Soviet Union, and he held us responsible."[9] In the ensuing fracas, Shelest (and some sources say Kosygin too) made disparaging and anti-Semitic remarks about František Kriegel, calling him the "Jew from Galicia."[10] Kriegel's family had emigrated to Czechoslovakia from Galicia during the Russo-Polish War in the 1920s, and that area later was incorporated into the USSR, thereby making Kriegel particularly vulnerable to Shelest's otherwise unfounded accusations that he harbored separatist ambitions for his former homeland. At this point, the talks collapsed, as Smrkovský recounts:

> [The Soviet delegation said] a whole lot of outrageous things, which ended in Dubček getting up, and we with him, because we weren't willing to listen any longer to these insults. Dubček announced that if it was to continue like that, we would pack up and go home, we wouldn't take part any longer in proceedings of that kind. I got up,

[8] Gordon Brook-Shepherd and David Floyd, *Sunday Telegraph*, October 6, 1968.

[9] Smrkovský, *An Unfinished Conversation*, p. 21.

[10] Mlynář, *Night Frost*, p. 152. Alan Levy, *Rowboat to Prague*, p. 277, and Pavel Tigrid, *Why Dubček Fell*, pp. 84–85 both state that Kosygin also attacked Kriegel. And the *New York Times* on August 28, 1968, quoted a senior member of the Czechoslovak delegation at Čierna as saying: "Kosygin was one of the nastiest—not at all the moderate he has always been described."

too, I went over to Chervonenko who was present. I told him to take it from me in my capacity as Chairman of the National Assembly and to convey officially to his government that I would not be party to such proceedings, if that was how representatives of the ČSSR were treated, such humiliating and insulting proceedings I would not take part in. In short, the talks broke down. We rose and left the room in that railwaymen's house.[11]

After the talks broke down, Brezhnev evidently received three letters cautioning the Soviet Union against any military intervention. One was from Tito. A second, much more strongly worded emotional appeal was from Ceauşescu. The third, delivered to Kirilenko in Moscow by two Spanish Communists representing eighteen European Communist parties and transmitted to Brezhnev, demanded an end to Soviet interference in Czechoslovak affairs and threatened to call a conference to condemn Soviet behavior.[12] Such a move would have ended any hopes Moscow may have had of convening the International Communist Conference, scheduled for November and being organized by Suslov and Ponomarev. It is thought that as a result of these letters, "Brezhnev, Kosygin and in particular Suslov" became more conciliatory.[13] The Soviet leaders went to Dubček's railway car, apologizing for Shelest's behavior, saying that he had "exaggerated"; and according to Smrkovský, they tried "to reconcile everything so we would carry on with the talks next day."[14]

Wednesday's talks brought the parties much closer to a *modus vivendi*. It started with a private meeting between Dubček and Brezhnev after the latter had complained of being too ill-disposed to hold full-scale negotiations. Brezhnev's illness was widely reported to have been political and not medical. It was caused, some say, by criticism from his own Politburo, and especially from Suslov, who is said to have accused him of "speaking like Ulbricht" and to have reminded him that "the Soviet Politburo several weeks earlier rejected the forceful approach towards Czechoslovakia advo-

[11] Smrkovský, *An Unfinished Conversation*, p. 21.

[12] Adolf Müller, *Die Tschechoslowakei auf der Suche nach Sicherheit*, p. 293; *New York Times*, August 3, 1968. The tone of the Rumanian letter may also be adduced from another official note sent by Bucharest on the same day to the Polish government, stating that "as a most important demand . . . nothing should be undertaken, in any form, that would lead to the aggravation of mutual relations, to the deepening of disagreements and divergencies" (Agerpress, July 31, 1968, EE/2837/12/2).

[13] Tigrid, *Why Dubček Fell*, p. 87, confirmed by accounts given by Smrkovský, Černík, and Císař to leading journalists, *New York Times*, August 3, 1968.

[14] Smrkovský, *An Unfinished Conversation*, p. 21.

cated by East Germany's Ulbricht."[15] Mlynář adds a fascinating account of the private meeting between Brezhnev and Dubček, which is based on his reading of the 500-page transcript of the Čierna negotiations and on the account given to him by Dubček and other participants. It deserves to be quoted at length:

> As far as I know, the impression Dubček gained from this private meeting was that Brezhnev was in conflict with the "hawks" in his own Politburo (represented by Shelest, though the people really behind them were the marshals of the older generation), and was genuinely looking for a way out of the predicament that would vindicate his moderation and enable him to stand up to pressure from Ulbricht and Gomułka, who were united with the Soviet "hawks" in pushing the situation toward open conflict and a military intervention in Czechoslovakia. The real arguments behind the scenes had little to do with the public attacks against *Literární listy*, which were only the propagandist, ideological guise, but rather were based on the claim that the security of the entire Soviet bloc was threatened, and that the conditions in Czechoslovakia were impairing the defensive capability of the bloc and weakening its political unity under the hegemony of Moscow.[16]

The private meeting between Brezhnev and Dubček then broadened to include Kosygin, Podgorny, and Suslov on the Soviet side and Černík, Smrkovský, and Svoboda for the Czechoslovaks.[17] General Dzúr also flew into Čierna on Wednesday, which suggests that there was indeed discussion of troop withdrawals or stationing.[18] The Soviet delegation seemed suddenly keen to reach an agreement, with Suslov even conceding at one point that the post-January course did indeed represent a renaissance of Marxism to a certain extent. There could be "no more excommunications," he said, and "the Czechoslovak question must be settled by agreement if great harm is not to ensue for the international communist movement and its unity."[19]

By Wednesday, July 31, the negotiations, which originally had been scheduled for only one day, had been extended to four. It was announced that the meeting would end that evening, and a closing banquet was planned to demonstrate that the talks had been con-

[15]Colin Chapman, *August 21st—The Rape of Czechoslovakia*, p. 30; A. Levy, *Rowboat to Prague*, p. 279; *Daily Telegraph*, August 3, 1968.

[16]Mlynář, *Night Frost*, p. 152.

[17]Smrkovský, *An Unfinished Conversation*, p. 21; and *New York Times*, August 1, 1968.

[18]*International Herald Tribune*, August 1, 1968.

[19]Tigrid, *Why Dubček Fell*, p. 86; confirmed by many sources including the author's interviews with E. Goldstücker, October 24, 1977, and Z. Mlynář, June 1, 1979.

cluded in a conciliatory and fraternal spirit. Reporters assembled for a promised news conference but were suddenly told that it had been canceled and that the negotiations would continue for a further day. A U.S. State Department telegram to its European missions, based on information received from its embassy in Prague, confirmed that Ulbricht once again was working feverishly behind the scenes to force a unified hard-line Soviet stance. The telegram read: "U.S. Embassy source reports delay in signing Čierna communiqué caused by Ulbricht telephone call designed to frustrate agreement."[20] On the same day, *Izvestia* reprinted an extremely provocative *Neues Deutschland* article that claimed that the absence of bloodshed and open insurrection in Czechoslovakia did not prove that the situation was not counterrevolutionary: "Perhaps such notions were provoked by the 1956 counterrevolutionary putsch in Hungary, which was characterized by arson, shooting and the murder of Communists. However, a counterrevolution does not necessarily have to look precisely like this. . . . The imperialists and the antisocialist forces in the ČSSR collaborating with them are openly, systematically and deliberately applying methods different from those used in 1956 in Hungary. . . . Now they are banking on a 'quiet counterrevolution.'"

By now, both the Soviet and Czechoslovak sides were eager to end the talks. Dubček was having to communicate constantly with Prague to delay even further the imminent arrivals of Tito and Ceauşescu. And for their part, the Soviet delegation, too, could not long extend the absence of the country's entire Politburo from the capital. Rejecting pressure from the East Germans and hardliners within the Politburo, a majority (some sources say the vote was 5:4) of the leaders decided on July 31 (*decision 37*) to give the Czechoslovaks one more chance and to convene a multilateral meeting at Bratislava to sanctify the results of Čierna and reassert bloc unity.[21] Shelest, Podgorny, Shelepin, and Pel'she were reported to have taken a tough stand in Čierna and apparently disapproved of the Bratislava meeting.[22]

There is much contention about what actually was decided at Čierna. All the Czechoslovak participants remained adamant that no formal written agreement had been signed, although several leaders referred to vague promises or "undertakings." Dubček, for

[20] U.S. Department of State, *Telegram No. 213732*, August 1, 1968.
[21] F. Beer, *Die Zukunft Funkioniert Noch Nicht*, p. 355.
[22] *Christian Science Monitor*, August 22, 1968.

example, speaking in 1969, reaffirmed that there were no secret clauses and that he had presented "a report" to the Soviet leaders on "proposed methods of control of information media and on those problems of cadres to which we intend to give urgent attention during our pre-Congress Plenary session."[23] Černík, speaking in Ostrava in September 1968, explained: "We did not conclude any agreement at Čierna. We only informed the Soviet representatives of what our future procedure would be in order to prevent both right-wing and left-wing extremist action."[24] Husák, in August 1969, made no reference to anything like a written agreement, but stated that the Soviets had made "urgent demands that we should institute order in our country." At the negotiation's end, he said, "there were these conclusions, and again there were these promises made on our part to solve these or other problems."[25] Smrkovský also subsequently denied that there had been any written agreement, but he recalled certain demands: "When I recapitulated in my own mind what the Soviet comrades had concretely wanted of us—through that flood of criticism . . . it boiled down to six concrete points." These six points were, according to Smrkovský, the dismissal of Kriegel, of Císař, the banning of the Social Democratic party, of KAN, and of K 231, and the firm control of the mass media.[26]

Soviet references to Čierna also failed to mention any written agreement. The Soviets seemed to be in no doubt, however, that the Czechoslovaks had made clear and unequivocal promises to undertake various immediate measures. The August 17 letter of warning from the Soviet Politburo to Dubček referred specifically to efforts to gain "firm control over the mass media"; to stop "antisocialist and anti-Soviet publicity in the press, radio and television"; to end activities of clubs, groups and organizations that take an antisocialist attitude; to prevent any activity by a Social Democratic party; and to "take further appropriate measures, including steps to strengthen the leading publications in the interest of the

[23] Dubček's speech to the CPCz Central Committee, September 26, 1969, in William Shawcross, *Dubček*, p. 289.

[24] *Pravda* (Bratislava) September 22, quoted in H. Gordon Skilling, *Czechoslovakia's Interrupted Revolution*, p. 308.

[25] Husák speech, Prague, August 19, 1969, EE/3157/C/14–15.

[26] Smrkovský, *An Unfinished Conversation*, p. 21. These points were supported by Dubček's speech to the CPCz Central Committee, September 26, 1969, in Shawcross, *Dubček*, p. 289; and by the Foreign Minister Jiří Hájek in his account, *Dix ans après*, p. 102.

leading role of the Party and to consolidate the position of socialism in Czechoslovakia."[27] Some say appropriate measures included Czechoslovak reassurance both of loyalty to the WTO and CMEA and of support for the Soviet position at the November International Communist meeting.[28] The *Pravda* editorial of August 22, 1968, also referred to Čierna, stating that the CPCz leaders had given "assurances . . . that they would take immediate concrete measures to stabilize the situation."

There has never been any evidence that the two sides did sign an agreement. Rather, these statements appear to confirm that the two sides parted with a "gentleman's agreement." This impression is strengthened by Bil'ak, who maintains that at the end of the final Čierna meeting, Brezhnev remarked to those still in the hall: "Comrades, we are not signing any agreement. We rely on your Communist word. We expect that you will act and behave as Communists. If you deceive us once more, we shall consider it a crime and a betrayal and act accordingly. Never again would we sit with you at the same table."[29]

Despite agreeing to take various ill-defined measures, the Czechoslovaks still felt they had won a major victory for their "socialism with a human face." The Soviets had agreed that the forthcoming multilateral meeting would be held on Czechoslovak territory and that it would not discuss either Czechoslovak internal developments or the Warsaw Letter. Soviet press polemics against Czechoslovakia also would cease (Brezhnev is reported by one source to have instructed Moscow in the early hours of August 1 to halt all polemics),[30] and the Warsaw Pact troops that had entered Czechoslovakia for maneuvers would finally be withdrawn, although it is not clear whether there was agreement on a specific timetable. One source said that the two sides left the details of the withdrawal to be worked out at Bratislava.[31] It would certainly seem that the Czechoslovaks once again refused to give in to Soviet pressure for the stationing of troops and that they extracted a compromise on further Soviet troop withdrawals. According to a U.S. State Department telegram:

[27] "Letter of Warning from the CPSU Politburo, August 17, 1968," reprinted in *Studies in Comparative Communism* 3, no. 1 (January 1970): 141.

[28] *Sunday Times*, August 4, 1968, quoting "sources close to the Czechoslovak Praesidium."

[29] *Pravda zůstala pravdou*, p. 169, quoted in Skilling, *Czechoslovakia's Interrupted Revolution*, p. 307.

[30] *Times*, August 6, 1968.

[31] *New York Times*, August 3, 1968, quoting an account given to journalists after the talks by Smrkovský, Černík, and Císař.

Despite Embassy Prague informant report that Czechoslovaks have not agreed to stationing of troops under Warsaw Pact provision, Dubček and Svoboda statements on need for additional measures to strengthen Pact, as well as evasive Smrkovský remarks on departure of Soviet troops, could indicate some Soviet elements may be remaining in Czechoslovakia. Some Czechoslovak diplomats have hinted new security arrangements might provide for presence in Czechoslovakia of Warsaw Pact officers, with supporting and technical services "not exceeding few thousands."[32]

Dubček had stressed upon his return from Čierna that "our Army is not only a firm component in the defense of our socialist community but also a sufficient guarantee of the defense of our state frontiers and by the same token of the frontiers of socialism."[33] Yet as the State Department telegram points out, Dubček's failure to mention either troop presence or withdrawal is an indication of the lack of specific and firm agreement for the full and immediate withdrawal of Soviet troops. And as Colonel Stepanek-Stemmer, press officer to President Svoboda, has stated, the Soviet military attaché and other Soviet officers in Prague continued to emphasize after Čierna that "the Czechoslovak rectangle," the "cornerstone of Soviet defense" in Europe, was in no way adequately guaranteed and that "it could not remain unprotected for the foreseeable or indefinite future."[34]

In trying to assess the results of Čierna for the Soviets, several points emerge. One is that both hard-line attacks on the Czechoslovak reform movement and military maneuvers continued throughout the negotiations, making clear the uncompromising and even increasing hostility to the reform movement felt by an overwhelming majority of the leadership. Čierna was designed as a last-ditch attempt to get the Czechs to do themselves what the Soviets were otherwise prepared to undertake, however reluctantly. Undoubtedly there were divisions within the Soviet leadership about the best course to follow; so too was there indecision and wavering and changes of view among certain of the Soviet leaders during the course of the talks, particularly because of the letters received from other Communist parties which highlighted and even increased the perceived costs of an invasion. Thus reports that both the French and Italian Communist parties received assurances following Čierna

---

[32] U.S. Department of State, *Telegram No. 214637*, August 3, 1968.
[33] Prague Radio, August 2, 1968, EE/2838/C/8.
[34] Stepanek-Stemmer, *Die tschechoslowakische Armee*, p. 50.

that the USSR would not use force[35] demonstrated the prominent concern among at least some Soviet leaders for the unity of the international Communist movement, which motivated, however temporarily, the Soviet impulse to achieve a political settlement at Čierna. In essence, the understanding reached at Čierna was not a compromise but a quid pro quo—the Soviets would withdraw troops in return for concrete and immediate changes in Czechoslovak politics. The tenor of the final communiqué is itself an apt indication of the depths to which relations had sunk. As a result of problems in drafting a communiqué, the end product was very negative, confining itself to the comment that there had been a "broad, comradely exchange of opinions" and that the meeting had "proceeded in an atmosphere of complete frankness, sincerity, and mutual understanding." There was no mention of the customary "complete unity of views." Nor did the communiqué hint at any agreement on internal reforms in Czechoslovakia, saying only that the meeting "was aimed at seeking ways of further developing and strengthening the traditionally friendly relations between our parties and peoples."[36] The Soviet Politburo might have hoped for a more positive communiqué from the Czechoslovaks, but failing that, all eyes would now be on the results of the Bratislava meeting and the development of events inside Czechoslovakia.

THE BRATISLAVA CONFERENCE

The multilateral conclave called to ratify the results of Čierna and reassert bloc unity met for only one day, in the Slovak capital of Bratislava on Saturday, August 3. Present were the leaders of Czechoslovakia, Hungary, Bulgaria, Poland, the GDR, and, of course, the USSR, which was represented by Brezhnev, Kosygin, Suslov, Podgorny, Shelest, Katushev, and Ponomarev. This was the only time, with the exception of Čierna, that Suslov and Ponomarev had been part of a Soviet delegation dealing with Czechoslovakia, and it is therefore probably indicative of the greater weight their views held at this time. And although Shelest may have been ostracized at Čierna following his outbursts, which nearly wrecked the conference, he found a place in the Bratislava team, this emphasizing his continuing influence.

[35] *New York Times*, August 22, 1968, quoting "Communist sources."
[36] *Pravda*, August 2, 1968.

Both Gomułka and Ulbricht made clear from the very beginning their open hostility to the Čierna compromise and to the calling of the Bratislava meeting. Gomułka demanded to know "why it was necessary to meet again when all that needed to be said had already been said in the Warsaw Letter."[37] Ulbricht, in the first of what was to be an almost nonstop barrage of acid remarks on the situation in Czechoslovakia, asked Dubček: "I was under the impression that I was coming here on an official visit, but at the airport all I could hear was 'Dubček, Dubček.' Is it because I don't understand Czech?"[38] Evidently he believed that the crowd's failure to shout his own name was further proof that Czechoslovakia had abandoned true proletarian internationalism. Only Hungarian leader János Kádár expressed any open optimism, stating at his arrival that he was "glad to come with good cause, with good intentions, and confidence."[39]

The opening ceremonies were extremely brief, and according to Larisa Sil'nitskaya, an interpreter for the Czechoslovak delegation throughout the opening and closing sessions, Brezhnev began by announcing the decision made at Čierna that a meeting of those now present would be called to draw up a joint declaration. It was then decided that a drafting committee consisting of the first secretary, prime minister, and selected advisers and interpreters from each delegation would meet to draw up the final communiqué.[40] Suslov and Mlynář were selected as additional participants on the Soviet and Czechoslovak sides.[41] The members of the working committee withdrew to the next room and did not reemerge until 7:00 P.M. that evening.

Sources say that the delegations agreed to work from a basic Soviet draft but that the negotiations were protracted, primarily because of Czechoslovak objections and counterproposals. Mlynář, who was a participant in the negotiations, claims that the Czech delegation, often supported by the Hungarians, spent immeasurable time obtaining changes of phrasing. For example, the draft referred to only two "forces of peace" standing against the revanchist

[37] Colin Chapman, *August 21st*, pp. 34–35.

[38] Mlynář, *Night Frost*, p. 155.

[39] "Conference of the Six Communist and Workers' Parties in Bratislava," *Czechoslovak Digest* (Prague), no. 32 (August 8, 1968), pp. 11–12, as quoted in Valenta, "Soviet Foreign Policy Decision-Making," p. 525.

[40] Larisa Sil'nitskaya, "Recollections of Bratislava"; also Mlynář, *Night Frost*, pp. 151–52.

[41] Mlynář, *Night Frost*, pp. 151–52; and Tigrid, *Why Dubček Fell*, p. 90.

policies of the Bonn Government—the GDR and the West German Communist party. Against considerable opposition from Ulbricht, the Czechoslovaks managed to insert the phrase that support would also be given to "those forces [in the FRG] struggling against revanchism, militarism, and neo-Nazism and for democratic progress."[42] Some sources suggest that Ulbricht tried to get a formulation condemning "West German imperialism" inserted at this point.[43] His failure to do so suggests that Brezhnev was indeed trying to pursue a more moderate course.

The draft also stressed that "it is possible to advance along the path of socialism and communism only by strictly and consistently following the general laws governing the construction of a socialist society and primarily by strengthening the guiding role of the working class and its vanguard—the Communist parties." At Czechoslovak insistence, however, a qualifying sentence was added to the effect that "in the building of socialism, each fraternal party takes into account national characteristics and conditions."[44]

The draft also contained a section that Dubček and Mlynář objected to and that later became enshrined as the central core of the "Brezhnev doctrine of limited sovereignty." The passage in its final version read:

> It is the common international *duty* of all socialist countries to support, strengthen and defend these gains, which were achieved at the cost of every people's heroic efforts and selfless labor. This is the unanimous opinion of all the conference participants. . . .[45]

Mlynář states that he wanted to qualify the first sentence with the clause "while respecting the sovereignty and national independence of each country," and he suggested joining this clause to the second sentence with a dash. But as Mlynář recounts, Brezhnev vehemently objected, exclaiming that "the dash in this instance would go against the spirit of the Russian language!"[46] Moreover, Brezhnev went on, there was an explicit mention of "respect for sovereignty and national independence" several paragraphs later. Zhivkov, Ulbricht, and Gomułka all supported Brezhnev's formula-

---

[42] Mlynář, *Night Frost*, p. 154; *The Guardian*, August 5, 1968.

[43] *Sunday Telegraph*, October 6, 1968.

[44] Mlynář, *Night Frost*, p. 154; quotes from the Bratislava statement are from *Pravda*, August 4, 1968.

[45] *Pravda*, August 4, 1968 (emphasis mine).

[46] Mlynář, *Night Frost*, p. 154.

tion; Kádár took the Czechoslovak side. The declaration may refer to "respect for sovereignty," but nowhere does it mention noninterference in domestic affairs as one of the principles governing mutual relations. Thus the Bratislava Declaration contains all the elements of the theoretical and ideological justification of invasion—signed and sealed by all the participating states, including Czechoslovakia.

In the weeks to come, the Bratislava Declaration was evoked on numerous occasions. On the very day of the invasion, August 20, both *Pravda* and *Izvestia* praised the results of Bratislava as "a barrier to imperialist subversion." And in the final communiqué of the postinvasion Moscow negotiations, the Soviet and Czechoslovak leaders undertook resolutely to implement the joint decisions made at Čierna and the principles proclaimed at Bratislava.[47] Most importantly, the August 22 *Pravda* editorial explaining the reasons for the invasion stated that the decision had been made "in accordance with the commitments undertaken at the conference of Communist and Workers' parties in Bratislava."

Whereas it is undeniable that the Bratislava Declaration was used to legitimize the eventual invasion, it is certainly questionable whether that was the sole intention of all the non-Czechoslovak leaders who attended the conference. Even within the declaration there were important indications of moderate opinion. There was, for instance, a long section on the need to improve economic cooperation that stressed "the urgency of holding an economic conference at the highest level in the very near future," and there was a call for a European security conference. And in a passage that must have appeased Suslov, the declaration noted that "recently a good deal of work has been done in preparing for a new international conference of Communist and Workers' parties. The fraternal parties value this work highly and express the conviction that the forthcoming conference will proceed successfully and will make an important contribution to the course of consolidating all the revolutionary forces of the present day."

It is also noteworthy that a number of the participants themselves praised Bratislava as a victory for moderation. The Czechoslovak leaders uniformly echoed Dubček's statement that Bratislava "opened the door to the further room required for our socialist re-

[47] *Pravda*, August 28, 1968.

vival process."[48] Mlynář, even in retrospect, rejects the view that Brezhnev was consciously seeking a statement to justify invasion. He says of Brezhnev's motives: "I think rather that at this stage he was only covering his options and that no concrete decision to intervene . . . had yet been made."[49]

The Hungarians also gave a positive, if more guarded, appraisal of the results of Bratislava. The Budapest daily *Magyar Hirlap*, while conceding that "there were in fact differences of opinion between the five socialist countries and Czechoslovakia," described the meeting as "a blow to those who had hoped for a split in our camp."[50] Upon his return Kádár also offered an optimistic, if qualified, appraisal: "It is a very great thing that meanwhile it has been possible partly to clear up the misunderstandings and differences and partly to concentrate the attention of the six parties on what is common—even if differences in assessment may possibly have remained."[51]

The Soviets, too, portrayed Bratislava as a success, with *Pravda* declaring:

> The meetings in Čierna nad Tisou and Bratislava have reconfirmed the premise that wise, calm, thoughtful and patient discussion of complex questions on a principled basis and imbued with profound concern for the vital interests of world socialism and the International Communist movement is a norm that has justified itself in relations among the socialist countries and their Communist and Workers' parties. The CPSU has always taken and continues to take this stand and makes its contribution to the cause of solidarity and unity among revolutionary forces and the fraternal socialist commonwealth.[52]

While the Czechoslovaks were basking in the success of this favorable peripeteia, Western journalists and diplomats also took the chance to go on long-delayed holidays. Yet several quarters continued to watch the situation with concern. Yugoslav sources considered Bratislava a compromise whose success would depend on whether "the conservatives would again try to undertake, through methods of pressure, to impose their will and put a stop to

[48] Dubček, *K otazkam*, p. 243, quoted in Skilling, *Czechoslovakia's Interrupted Revolution*, p. 311; Skilling quotes similar views expressed by both Černík and Bil'ak.

[49] Mlynář, *Night Frost*, p. 155.

[50] Quoted in *The Guardian*, August 6, 1968.

[51] *The Guardian*, August 5, 1968.

[52] *Pravda*, August 5, 1968.

the development of socialism."[53] The U.S. State Department, in a lengthy telegram evaluating the results of Bratislava, also remained relatively unimpressed by all the rhetoric, noting that Soviet forces ringing Czechoslovakia were still in place, and that much would depend on whether Ulbricht and other hard-liners were genuinely placated by Bratislava. The telegram stated that "undertakings reached at Čierna and Bratislava likely to be subject of new and differing interpretations and perhaps starting point for renewed strains in Soviet-Czechoslovak relations. It seems difficult . . . to conceive of Soviets refraining from any attempts to influence internal developments as crucial Czechoslovak Party Congress approaches." For these reasons, the State Department advised its missions overseas against undue optimism: "Prior differences between Czechoslovakia and other critical regimes appear to have been papered over rather than resolved, and it is unclear how modus vivendi sanctioned at Čierna and later Bratislava will stand test of time."[54]

[53] *Kommunist* (Belgrade), August 7, 1968, quoted in Skilling, *Czechoslovakia's Interrupted Revolution*, p. 707.

[54] U.S. Department of State, *Telegram No. 215343*, August 5, 1968.

CHAPTER TEN

Phase Five:
August 5–20

AUGUST 6 POLITBURO MEETING

With the return of the Soviet delegation from Bratislava on August 5, almost the entire Soviet political and military leadership was in Moscow. This was made clear by Soviet press coverage of their return and of the funeral the same day of Soviet Marshal Rokossovsky (who had been sent by Stalin to Poland as minister of defense). Shelepin, Kunaev, Mzhavanadze, and Shcherbitsky were the only members of the Politburo or the Secretariat not mentioned as present in the capital that day.

On August 6, it was announced that the Warsaw Pact's chief of staff, General M. I. Kazakov, was to be replaced by General S. M. Shtemenko. The explanation given for Kazakov's early retirement—"for reasons of ill-health"—proved to be transparently false when he later appeared at several Western embassy social functions in apparently vigorous form. It has been suggested that Kazakov was advocating a different course of action in Czechoslovakia and that he opposed an invasion because of the long-term negative repercussions it would have on the Czechoslovak army's reliability as a member of the Warsaw Pact. It was therefore concluded that a more resolute and hard-line military leader was required for any invasion. Shtemenko, as the former chief of operations during the Great Patriotic War, not only had been responsible for planning the liberation of Prague in 1945 (Who better to conduct a repeat performance?) but had recently returned to favor as a chronicler of Stalin's positive achievements at the head of the war effort. Shtemenko, therefore, had the right political and military profile for participation in an impending invasion.[1] It is not clear whether all other Pact members were consulted in advance about this change in the Pact High Command, although the presence in Moscow of top Polish military figures for Rokossovsky's funeral would at least have allowed some consultation. Whatever the true significance of Kazakov's replacement, it is clear that during the absence of the political leadership in Čierna and Bratislava, the High Command had not been idle, and military plans for an invasion had proceeded apace.

Thus when the Politburo met in full session on August 6 to consider the results of its two meetings in Czechoslovakia, it was faced with deciding whether military action indeed would be required. Secret U.S. State Department reports reveal that the meeting had an expanded membership, suggesting the participation of military leaders.[2] The communiqué published in *Pravda* the following day in some ways represented the lowest common denominator among various views and does not in itself indicate a clear victory either for intervention or for nonintervention. The communiqué reported that the Politburo "fully approved" the activity of the CPSU delegation at Bratislava—it did not use the stronger term "unanimously." The same endorsement was not reported for the Čierna conclave. On Čierna, the Politburo simply "notes" that the Čierna meeting was "timely and of great importance for the further development and strengthening of relations" between the Soviet Union and Czechoslovakia. Such a meager assessment of the results of Čierna is clear indication that the leadership was beginning to recognize it for the fiasco that it had been. By contrast, the Politburo "highly appreciated" the conclusions reached at Bratislava that the future of socialism "lies in unflinching loyalty to Marxism-Leninism, in the cultivation among the popular masses of . . . socialistic and proletarian internationalism." The communiqué, however, did not reaffirm the Bratislava statement's recognition of various "national characteristics and conditions." Nor did it place value on "wise, calm, thoughtful and patient" negotiations in settling disputes, as

[1] For details of the change from Kazakov to Shtemenko, see John R. Thomas, *Soviet Foreign Policy and Conflict within the Politburo and Military Leadership*, pp. 7–9; Malcolm Mackintosh, *The Evolution of the Warsaw Pact*, pp. 14–15; and Galia Golan, *Reform Rule in Czechoslovakia*, p. 233. Shtemenko's book, published at this time, was entitled *General'nyi shtab v gody voiny*.

[2] U.S. Department of State, *Research Memorandum RSE-127*, August 16, 1968, Appendix A, p. vii.

had the *Pravda* and *Izvestia* editorials the previous day. It adopted instead a wait-and-see approach, putting the burden on Prague to act on the principles of the Bratislava statement. As the Politburo communiqué concluded: "The implementation of the Statement's propositions is the paramount international task of the fraternal parties." An implicit threat of military action was contained in the communiqué's assertion that the Soviet Union would do "everything in its power" to guarantee the fulfillment of the Bratislava Declaration.

No statements or speeches were made by Soviet leaders following their return to Moscow, but analysis of the communiqué and of intelligence information reaching Western governments leads one to conclude that at this meeting, the last before Politburo members left the capital for their holidays, the decision (*number 38*) was made to proceed with the invasion plans delineated during the July 20–21 Politburo meeting, and to implement those plans before the August 26 deadline unless the Czechoslovak leaders showed clear and unequivocal adherence to the Soviet interpretation of the Bratislava statement.

There is considerable evidence to suggest that on August 6 the Politburo emerged more united in its resolve to go ahead with military plans for an invasion before the August 26 Slovak plenum and certainly before the September CPCz Congress convened, should Dubček fail to take firm measures against antisocialist activities. A first piece of evidence was a telegram sent to the U.S. State Department from Tommy Thompson, the American ambassador in Moscow, indicating that there was imminent danger of invasion. As Eugene Rostow later admitted, until that point the intelligence about Soviet intentions had been mixed. But the telegram was sufficiently detailed and persuasive that it "decided the debate."[3] The head of West German intelligence received similar information. Immediately following the invasion, he alleged that the information had been suppressed by the U.S. government. The new and dynamic young chief of intelligence, General Gerhard Wessel, authorized a "leak" from his office on August 24, detailing the extent of West German foreknowledge of the invasion plans. It was claimed that "information received by early August ended all doubts that

---

[3] George Urban, "The Invasion of Czechoslovakia 1968," p. 106. This analysis was corroborated by Paul Costolanski in the author's interview with him, Washington, D.C., November 14, 1979. Costolanski calculated that Soviet alarm over the CPCz Draft Statutes was the major factor behind the August 6 decision.

the Russians would invade with massive forces." Previous delays in
making a decision had been due to a "disagreement between the
'hawks' and the 'doves' inside the Kremlin," but by early August
this had been overcome.[4] Michel Tatu, also writing after the invasion, underlines the importance of the August 6 meeting; he maintains that following the indecision within Soviet ranks at Čierna,
the "ultras," or hard-liners, forced through a decision finally committing the entire Politburo unequivocally to invasion should things
not change dramatically in Prague.[5]

The final evidence relates to the escalation of military activity.
On August 7 most of the top Soviet leaders left Moscow on vacation; and indeed between August 7 and 15, analysis of the Soviet
press reveals that eight of the eleven full Politburo members,
seven of the nine candidate members, and two of the five party
secretaries not counted elsewhere were outside Moscow. Yet military activity continued and even increased. U.S. intelligence observed that troops being withdrawn from Czechoslovakia were almost entirely reservists who had finished their three-month tour of
duty. Individual soldiers may have returned home, but their units
remained in place around Czechoslovakia and were resupplied with
new recruits.[6] Rear service maneuvers completed on August 10 were
followed immediately by expanded joint exercises of communication troops involving the "operations and unit staffs" of the Soviet,
GDR, and Polish armies.[7] This particular exercise in fact never
ended; it led directly to the invasion. A U.S. Department of State
priority telegram to its mission in NATO stated that "announcement of August 10/11 exercise in areas where Soviet troops remain
arrayed against Czechoslovak borders indicates continued resort to
potential threat of military action in order to influence developments in Czechoslovakia."[8] Western analysts estimated that the
military required two weeks from the beginning of countdown to
invasion in order to prepare their troops.[9] This countdown had be-

[4] *Sunday Times*, August 25, 1968.

[5] *Le Monde*, August 20, 1969.

[6] Author's interview with R. Baraz, leading Soviet analyst for U.S. State Department,
Bureau of Intelligence and Research, February 21, 1983.

[7] *Krasnaya zvezda*, August 13, 1968.

[8] U.S. Department of State, *Telegram No. 219344*, to U.S. Mission NATO, August 12,
1968.

[9] This was the view of the State Department's twenty-four-hour monitoring unit set up to
follow events in Czechoslovakia, as recounted to the author by one of its members, Paul
Costolanski, in Washington, November 14, 1979.

gun on July 23, after the Politburo meeting on July 20–21 authorized the military to commence final preparations. By the time Soviet leaders returned from Bratislava, the military were in position and awaiting further orders. The Politburo, acting *before* its members dispersed, authorized the military to continue full mobilization, despite the heavy financial cost—particularly now that the grain harvest in western Russia and the Ukraine was being totally disrupted. Only a few days remained before the August 26 deadline, and these would be devoted to determining whether the countdown to invasion should—or indeed could—be stopped.

EVENTS IN CZECHOSLOVAKIA

In Prague, popular skepticism about possible concessions made at Čierna and Bratislava soon gave way to euphoric preparations for the Extraordinary Fourteenth Party Congress. On August 10 the revised draft party statutes were published. Although the party would maintain its essentially unified and hierarchical structure under these provisions, minority factions would be given the right to form and to publicize their views, and balloting within the party was to be secret. Another report was also presented to the CPCz Praesidium for discussion prior to its adoption at the congress. This was the so-called Kašpar report, prepared by conservatives within the information department of the Central Committee and designed to evaluate the possible future development of the party in the period following the forthcoming congress. Its conclusions could only have further alarmed those who already feared the worst. It predicted that almost the entire Central Committee would be replaced; and far from stabilizing the situation, the congress might lead to further uncertainty over the leading role and internal cohesiveness of central party organs. Certainly the report was not optimistic that the congress in itself would rally the country around the party and put an automatic end to antisocialist elements.

The Praesidium decided at its August 13 meeting to discuss the Kašpar report at its regular session on August 20, along with a lengthy memorandum being prepared by Kolder and Indra about measures to implement the Čierna and Bratislava agreements. Meanwhile, antireformists like Kolder, Indra, Bil'ak, Švestka, and others, aware that their political days were numbered, increased their activity and concentrated their energies on warning likeminded leaders in Moscow and Eastern Europe of the need for action to forestall not only the Fourteenth Party Congress but also the Slovak Congress scheduled to commence on August 26, during which Bil'ak and other hard-line Slovaks were now certain to lose their positions.

By contrast, the leisurely pace with which Dubček appeared to be moving in curbing the press and groups such as KAN and K 231 did not give the impression that he was aware that the countdown to invasion had begun. The Soviet leaders' departure to the Black Sea and Dubček's preoccupation with preparations for the congress and bilateral meetings with East Europe leaders also contributed to a distinct lack of urgency in reformist circles.

MEETINGS WITH TITO AND CEAUŞESCU

Yugoslavia's President Tito arrived in Prague on August 9 for a two-day visit. Despite official attempts to keep his sojourn on a formal basis and Tito's own public assurances that there was no need to sign a friendship treaty between the two countries, nothing could stop the massive outpouring of jubilation created by the presence in the capital of the first leader successfully to defy the Russians and build his own national brand of socialism. The CPCz Praesidium's exhortations to the press to "take into consideration the national and international interests of the Czechoslovak people"[10] in the coverage of Tito's visit also went unheeded as the media got caught up in the popular spirit. *Literární listy*, for example, stated on August 10 that the response to Tito expressed "the yearning of the nation for its own Tito." Yet in private the Yugoslav leader strongly urged the Czechoslovak party not to abandon its leading role and to proceed more cautiously.[11]

A similar atmosphere surrounded the trip to Prague between August 15 and 17 of Rumania's President Ceauşescu. The formal purpose of his visit was to renew the bilateral treaty binding the two countries, but, like Tito, he was the subject of considerable public adulation. He too avoided fanning the flames. Some articles by Czechoslovak journalists proposed that Czechoslovakia, Ru-

[10] *Morning Star*, August 8, 1968.
[11] Pelikán in V. V. Kusin, ed., *The Czechoslovak Reform Movement 1968*, p. 318. Willy Brandt (*People and Politics*, p. 214) also stated: "Tito told me later that he had been to Moscow not long before [the invasion] and that Brezhnev had asked him to help to find a way out. I travelled to Czechoslovakia and gave the comrades some advice. By the time I returned, the Russians had already marched in."

mania, and Yugoslavia should form "a firm bloc of democracy, reason, and humanistic socialism."[12] Ceauşescu firmly discounted such notions, stating that there were "nine socialist states which have the same views on the development of relations among themselves" and that while he adhered to the principle of noninterference in domestic affairs, he also supported the strengthening of the defensive unity of the Warsaw Pact.[13] However much Ceauşescu and Dubček may have hoped that their meeting would not escalate the crisis, the terms of the new treaty and the fact that it was being signed at all (in contrast to Rumania's other bilateral treaties which Ceauşescu was still stubbornly refusing to sign) could not but enflame tensions. Unlike other bilateral treaties in force between East European states, this treaty made no mention of the FRG as a potential aggressor, and affirmed the two countries' mutual adherence to the WTO only "for the period of its validity." Then in a particularly provocative passage, Article 8 declared that "in the event of an armed attack from a state or a group of states" against Czechoslovakia or Rumania, all necessary assistance including military aid would be provided.[14] When asked whether this would include an armed attack by one member of the Warsaw Pact on another, a Rumanian government spokesman did nothing to assuage bloc fears by answering: "This will be left entirely to your interpretation."[15] This particular statement was made in early August when it first became known that such provisions were likely to be incorporated in the treaty, and thus it formed the backdrop to growing concern, particularly in East Germany. This concern was amply expressed by Ulbricht during his own hurriedly arranged trip to Czechoslovakia on August 12.

ULBRICHT–DUBČEK CONCLAVE

While Tito was still in Prague, Ulbricht was addressing the GDR Volkskammer on the outcome of the Bratislava conference, stressing that implementation of the declaration required a resolute struggle to prevent imperialism from driving a wedge between the GDR and other socialist countries. In the same speech, Ulbricht announced East Germany's readiness to negotiate directly with the

[12] *Kultúrny život*, August 16, 1968.
[13] *Rudé právo*, August 18, 1968.
[14] Bucharest home service, August 18, 1968, EE/2852/C/5.
[15] *Daily Telegraph*, August 6, 1968.

Federal Republic provided that there were no prior conditions set by Bonn and that the FRG declared itself "willing to conclude treaties on the renunciation of force in our mutual relations and on the recognition of frontiers."[16] This statement was accompanied by an increase in anti-FRG propaganda, giving rise to the interpretation that Ulbricht was interested more in reasserting his own control over the direction of bloc policy on the German question than in the successful outcome of talks with Bonn.

Ulbricht's priorities were reflected clearly in his meeting with Dubček in Karlovy Vary on August 13. The two delegations met in closed sessions (antireformists were excluded from the Czechoslovak delegation, as they were also from the meetings with Tito and Ceaușescu), but extensive leaks from the Czechoslovak side indicated that Ulbricht had particularly objected to the growth of contacts between Prague and Bonn outside the framework of united bloc policy. Dubček is said to have denied Ulbricht's right to make Prague account for its policy toward a third party, and he refused to include a stronger denunciation of the FRG than that contained in the Bratislava Declaration.[17]

Czechoslovakia's internal problems also caused heated argument. Ulbricht's impatience with Dubček's explanations about the difficulties of overcoming "past deformities" and the need for a special congress was evident in an acrimonious public exchange during a joint press conference. If the CPCz was unable to find a solution to its problems, Ulbricht asserted, it need only look to the East German political system for a model: "We are among the most stable party and state leaderships in Europe. . . . We have had a perfectly continuous development in the work of the party leadership and also in the rejuvenation of the party leadership. And this is not a matter for a party congress."[18] Ulbricht is known to have been especially concerned with whether Dubček was really willing to reassert media censorship, and at the end of the press conference he cynically expressed the hope that Czechoslovak journalists would succeed in raising their "socialist consciousness."[19]

The talks were officially described as having taken place in an "atmosphere of candor," and if further evidence were needed that the negotiations had been acrimonious, Dubček made it known

[16] ADN (East German news agency), August 9, 1968, EE/2847/A1/1.
[17] *International Herald Tribune*, August 14, 1968.
[18] Deutschlandsender, August 13, 1968, EE/2848/C/3.
[19] *Neues Deutschland*, August 14, 1968.

that Ulbricht had invited himself.[20] The Czechoslovaks refused to release a final communiqué. They agreed only to a "press statement,"[21] which the East German news agency persisted in describing as a communiqué in any case.[22]

Following the invasion, the East Germans made it perfectly clear that they had assessed the situation very negatively after Karlovy Vary: "the talks showed that the right-wing group of the CPCz was not prepared to adhere to the Bratislava agreements but that it was strengthening its dangerous right-wing course."[23] After the invasion, the East Germans insisted that the Czechoslovak leadership implement the demands made at Karlovy Vary particularly concerning the German question, and indeed they even raised the results of the August 13 Karlovy Vary meeting to the status of an agreement between the two countries: "in the same measure as the agreement between the party and state leaders of the Soviet Union and Czechoslovakia of 27 August, which we approved, is being implemented, it will be possible to implement the agreements of Karlovy Vary."[24]

Clearly the East German leadership attached great importance to the demands they made, but there is no definite evidence that Ulbricht reported immediately to Moscow on the results of this trip. The Czechoslovak leaders who negotiated with Ulbricht most certainly judged the situation to have taken a grave turn for the worse after his visit; and it was widely believed both in Prague and in Washington that Ulbricht did in fact present a highly alarmist report to Soviet officials. CPCz leaders learned after the invasion of Ulbricht's insistence that Prague had secret links with Bonn and that Rumania and Czechoslovakia had plans to leave the Warsaw Pact.[25] Indeed, information to this effect received from Moscow by Walt Rostow, President Johnson's national security advisor, was one of the factors that led him to advise the president that the crisis in Czechoslovakia was not going to be resolved peacefully and that chances of an invasion were now very high.[26]

---

[20] Deutschlandsender, August 13, 1968, EE/2848/C/3.

[21] Prague radio, August 13, 1968, EE/2847/C/1.

[22] ADN, August 13, 1968, EE/2847/i.

[23] *Morning Star*, and *Times*, August 27, 1968.

[24] *The Standpoint of the German Democratic Republic*, n.d. distributed by GDR Embassy in London, October 1968.

[25] Pavel Tigrid, *Why Dubček Fell*, p. 95; also Alan Levy, *Rowboat to Prague*, p. 296; and the *Times*, August 23 and 28, 1968.

[26] Author's interview with Walt Rostow, Austin, Texas, July 25, 1980.

THE WARSAW PACT MILITARY MOVES

While the Soviet leaders were deliberating in Moscow on August 6, Soviet marshals were involved in the rear services exercises, code-named Nemen, designed to test supply and logistics capabilities and to bring up to full strength Class II and III divisions stationed in the Ukraine and western Russia. Western and Soviet military analysts agreed that the success of any Soviet "offensive" operation would rely heavily on Soviet ability to supply their forward troops with technical and medical supplies and especially with fuel.[27] Thus *Pravda's* assessment of the exercises is informative: "Our fully mechanized rear services can supply the troops with everything they need. . . . Main pipelines have been laid across forests and rivers right behind attacking units and have supplied fuel without any breakdown in the battle situation."[28] Presumably in substance this was the report Marshal Grechko received when he visited the exercise headquarters in Minsk for talks with its commander, General Maryakhin, on August 9.[29]

East German and Polish troops also participated in the exercises; and troops from Bulgaria and Central Asia, apparently using the exercise as a cover, also moved into position on the Soviet-Czechoslovak border.[30] Another function of the exercises directly related to the preparations for the invasion was the testing of rapid troop transport capabilities. This aspect of the exercises was not revealed in the Soviet press until just before the invasion when Marshal Vershinin stated that Soviet aircraft could operate at extremely low altitudes carrying big payloads. This capability, he said, had been demonstrated during the Nemen exercises where it was proved that military transport aircraft "could now transport troops and military equipment . . . for long-distance use in a short space of time."[31]

Immediately succeeding these exercises on August 11 were joint operations of the Soviet, Polish, and East German communication troops, which in fact allowed the final establishment under Gen-

[27] See Erickson in Kusin, ed., *Czechoslovak Reform Movement 1968*, p. 62; and General James H. Polk, "Reflections on the Czechoslovakian Invasion, 1968," p. 32. Also TASS in Russian for abroad on August 8, 1968 (SU/2844/A2/1), underlined the importance of the rear service exercises in support of "offensive" operations by the Soviet army.

[28] *Pravda*, August 9, 1968.

[29] Moscow home service, August 10, 1968, SU/2845/A2/2.

[30] *Observer*, August 25, 1968.

[31] TASS, August 18, 1968, SU/2852/B/1.

eral Shtemenko of a command and signals network for the invasion.[32] In connection with these exercises, Shtemenko met with General Bolesław Chocha, the Polish vice-minister of national defense, on August 13.[33] On the same day, Marshal Grechko and General Yepishev were met in East Germany by Soviet Marshals Yakubovsky and Koshevoi where all four attended "an exercise of the Soviet forces in Germany"[34] and a meeting on August 14 with General Hoffmann, the GDR minister of national defense.[35] From the GDR, Grechko, Yakubovsky, and Yepishev flew on August 16 to southwest Poland to confer with Shtemenko and the Polish High Command on problems of "cooperation and coordination of the fraternal armies."[36] The Soviets never announced a completion date for these exercises, and this, combined with the reports that Soviet military personnel in Czechoslovakia had been put on alert on August 11[37] and that Soviet GRU (military intelligence) and KGB agents were being infiltrated into Prague,[38] was further evidence that the exercises were a cover for final invasion preparations. These preparations were accompanied by the announcement on August 15 (again *before* Soviet Politburo members had all returned to Moscow) that the reluctant Hungarians had also finally commenced joint Soviet-Hungarian maneuvers.[39]

As early as August 13, press statements by both Soviet and East European military leaders maintained that "our fighting men . . . are prepared to perform any task, including extremely complex ones,"[40] and that because of "the growth of hostile and dangerous trends in fraternal Czechoslovakia," the Pact military has declared its "readiness to support and aid the party and people of Czechoslovakia."[41] Such statements, along with the high level of military

[32] J. Keegan, *World Armies*, p. 738.

[33] PAP, August 14, 1968, EE/2849/A2/4.

[34] TASS, August 15, 1968, SU/2849/A2/3.

[35] *Pravda*, August 18, 1968.

[36] *Krasnaya zvezda*, August 18, 1968.

[37] *New York Times*, August 24, 1968.

[38] Jacob Beam, the U.S. ambassador in Prague, stated that at a reception for Rumanian President Ceaușescu on August 16, he had been told by "a leading official of the Czechoslovak Praesidium" that Prague "is filling up with Soviet agents" (quoted in Urban, *Communist Reformation*, p. 246). In the author's interview with Beam on November 17, 1979, he named Císař as the source of his information.

[39] Budapest home service, August 15, 1968, EE/2852/A2/1.

[40] "Strengthening of Combat Readiness Is Our Chief Task" (Editorial), *Krasnaya zvezda*, August 13, 1968.

[41] General Wojcech Barański, deputy chief of the Polish General Staff, "Our Common Concern and Our Common Responsibility," *Krasnaya zvezda*, August 14, 1968.

activity, clearly showed the determined readiness of the High Command for the final signal from the political leadership. They also lead one to wonder whether there was by this time so much momentum behind military preparations that it would be almost impossible to pull back from the precipice.

POLITBURO VACATION ACTIVITY

Although most of the top political leaders were officially on holiday between August 7 and 15, the recommencement on August 14 of hard-line attacks on Czechoslovakia in the Soviet press indicated that political maneuvering was still taking place.[42] According to *Pravda* reports of August 10 and 11, a meeting of the powerful Moscow regional party committee (obkom) had been addressed by Grishin and Konotop. Both had participated in inner-party debates and negotiations on Czechoslovakia, and Konotop had only recently returned from heading a Moscow obkom delegation to Czechoslovakia at the invitation of the same Prague party committee that was only one week later to be accused by the Politburo of seeking to establish a "second CC."[43] It is unlikely, therefore, that Konotop's report would have presented anything but a pessimistic, and even alarmist, picture of the situation in Prague.

News of the Moscow meeting coincided with a U.S. intelligence report that second-echelon officials in the CPSU increasingly were disturbed by the prospect of having to reorient the massive grassroots campaign in the country away from attacks on Czechoslovakia's anti-Sovietism and toward acceptance of the Čierna and Bratislava compromises. The report suggested that the failure to convene a Central Committee plenum to ratify the results of Čierna and Bratislava was attributable to leadership fears of coming under fire from hard-line elements within the second echelon:

> After their strenuous efforts to inform the Party cadres about the April and July plenums and to whip up grass-roots support for a display of massive power against Czech liberalization, some local leaders are even faced with revived Russian nationalism directed against the Czechs and explaining how the great danger of this spring has suddenly evaporated.[44]

[42] See especially the August 14, 1968, articles by "Zhurnalist" in *Literaturnaya gazeta* and one entitled "The Fundamental Features of Socialism Are Constant" in *Pravda* of the same date.

[43] "Letter of Warning from the CPSU Politburo, August 17, 1968," p. 143.

[44] U.S. Department of State, *Research Memorandum RSE-127*, August 16, 1968.

There were several reliable reports at the time that dissatisfaction among Central Committee members was such that it actually forced the leaders to return from holiday and step up the plans for invasion.[45] It has also been suggested that their aspirations may have been supported or even manipulated by hard-line Politburo members with political ambitions. Zdeněk Mlynář recounts that Brezhnev told Bohumil Šimon, who led the Czechoslovak delegation to Moscow in November 1968: "Not even I can do what I'd like; I can achieve only a third of what I would like to do. If I hadn't voted in the Politburo for military intervention, what would have happened? You almost certainly would not be sitting here. And I probably wouldn't be sitting here either."[46] As to who may have led the coalition that convinced Brezhnev that an invasion of Czechoslovakia was necessary not only for the future of socialism but also for his own political future, U.S. intelligence suggested that Shelepin "as the long-reputed leader of Moscow's 'Young Turks' may well be the disgruntled Party element's representative on the Politburo." Admitting the dearth of firm evidence on Shelepin's activities or on the views of regional party secretaries, the report nevertheless concluded that "Czech-engendered friction within the Soviet regime could be at least as great, and very possibly greater, between the ruling clique and its lower echelons as within the top council itself."

Zdeněk Mlynář also places considerable significance on political infighting within the Politburo as a cause of the change in Moscow's attitude toward Czechoslovakia:

> While I have no factual evidence, I believe that some time around August 10 a new alliance of sorts was forced between the "hawks" and some of those previously undecided, welded together, most likely, by the offer of the Secretary-General position to someone. . . . I don't know who it was—perhaps Shelepin—but I assume the stakes were no less. . . . I consider it highly probable that Brezhnev and the Politburo moderates forestalled a putsch in the Kremlin by rapidly taking the initiative and uniting with the "hawks" over the military intervention in Czechoslovakia, thus defusing the main arguments of

[45] A report from Vienna (*International Herald Tribune*, August 26, 1968) quoting "entirely reliable" sources in Eastern Europe stated that Brezhnev, Kosygin, and Podgorny had actually been called back from holiday to attend a Central Committee plenum organized in their absence. A secret CIA report written on August 21, 1968, also refers to "the convening of the Central Committee in the midst of the top leaders' vacation" (U.S. Central Intelligence Agency, Directorate of Intelligence, *The Soviet Decision to Intervene*, August 21, 1968).

[46] Zdeněk Mlynář, *Night Frost in Prague*, p. 163.

the anti-Brezhnev forces. In such a situation, nothing Dubček might have done in Prague could have averted the invasion itself.[47]

In an interview with the author, Mlynář confirmed that it was widely believed among Prague leaders, particularly in the light of what they learned in Moscow during the postinvasion negotiations, that an internal challenge to Brezhnev led by Shelepin had indeed been a major cause of the change in the Soviet position. Yet this conclusion must be tempered by the fact that final military preparations were already well under way by this time, and in any case, nothing is known of Shelepin's whereabouts between August 1 and 15. Moreover, Shelepin is one of the leaders later reported to have expressed doubts about the feasibility of military action.[48] Although his gradual political demise continued after the invasion and ended in his removal from the Politburo in 1975, it would seem that if he did challenge Brezhnev, it must have been very carefully finessed to limit the damage of failure.

Similar statements have been made about the activities of Shelest during this vacation period. Intelligence received on August 12 by President Johnson's national security adviser, Walt Rostow, stated that Shelest was pressing hard for an immediate invasion, warning that he would not be held responsible for the growing Ukrainian nationalist and separatist tendencies resulting from the Czechoslovak spillover.[49] Shelest's activities in essence were confirmed by a later report leaked from the Kremlin following his demotion in 1972. The report suggested that Shelest had been part of an ad hoc "caretaker government" in Moscow during this brief vacation period, that he had used the time to assemble a report exaggerating the extent of counterrevolutionary danger in Prague, and that he presented this report to the Politburo when it convened in Moscow at his urgent request on August 16.[50] Shelest was said to have derived much of his information from Ulbricht in East Germany, from Chervonenko and Udaltsev in Moscow's Prague embassy, and from Bil'ak and other hard-liners within the CPCz leadership fearful of their political future if "fraternal aid" were postponed too long.

Yet activity during the August 7–15 vacation period was not con-

[47] Mlynář, *Night Frost*, p. 168.
[48] Tigrid, *Why Dubček Fell*, p. 96.
[49] Author's interview with Walt Rostow, July 25, 1980, in Austin, Texas.
[50] *International Herald Tribune*, December 27, 1972.

fined to Moscow. Brezhnev, residing with other Soviet leaders, including Podgorny, in the Black Sea retreat of Yalta, continued to put pressure on Dubček. On August 9 and 13, Brezhnev is known to have called Dubček, strongly urging him to fulfill the commitments entered into at Čierna and Bratislava. Smrkovský was present at one of these conversations and records that "Dubček explained again what would be happening at the [Central Committee plenum] at the end of August, what would happen at the Congress, and that we couldn't use administrative means," such as police power and executive privilege to halt antisocialist activities.[51]

Apparently unimpressed by Dubček's assurances and no doubt aware of the growing strength of interventionist opinion within the party—opinion now supported by a military machine that was on the move—Brezhnev decided (*decision 39*) on August 13 to send a strongly worded personal letter to Dubček. As later revealed by Husák, Brezhnev "gravely pointed out the danger of developments in this country, recalling the obligation to fulfill the adopted undertakings."[52] On the same day, according to Husák, another letter was sent to Dubček, this time in the name of the Politburo, and again drawing the attention of the CPCz leadership to the nonfulfillment of earlier agreements. A later letter sent by the Politburo to Dubček on August 17 also stated that Ambassador Chervonenko "on the instructions of the Politburo" had "approached Comrade Dubček and Comrade Černík" on two occasions during this vacation period.[53] Little is known of these communications, and it is not clear who made the decisions (*numbers 40* and *41*) to send the Politburo letter and to use Chervonenko as an envoy. In the letter the Soviets once again apparently demanded the permanent stationing of troops in Czechoslovakia. On August 16 Císař told the U.S. ambassador in Prague, Jacob Beam, that Moscow had recommenced pressure for troop stationing, in addition to seeking another high-

[51] Josef Smrkovský, *An Unfinished Conversation*, p. 22. Smrkovský states that Brezhnev was calling "every day." Telephone conversations were also mentioned by Husák in his Prague speech before a Party *aktiv* on August 19, 1969, EE/3156/C/9, and by Artur Starewicz, a secretary of the PUWP in 1968, in the author's interview with him in Warsaw on August 28, 1980. The letter sent by the CPSU Politburo to the CPCz Praesidium on August 17, 1968, and published by the Czechoslovaks a year later specifically states that Brezhnev called Dubček on August 9 and 13 (*Studies in Comparative Communism* 3, no. 1 [January 1970]: 142).

[52] Husák speech at CPCz Central Committee plenum, September 25, 1969, in ČTK, September 28, 1969, EE/3190/C/20.

[53] "Letter of Warning," p. 142.

level bilateral meeting.[54] It was further reported that Hungarian party leader János Kádár, learning of the change in the Soviet position, had traveled to Yalta just before Brezhnev's departure for Moscow on August 15. Brezhnev (*decision 42*) is said to have acceded to Kádár's urgent appeal that he be allowed to mediate between Moscow and Prague.[55] These decisioins point to the continued, if fading, hopes among Brezhnev and some of the Soviet leaders that a full-scale military invasion might still be averted. By Friday, August 16, all the Politburo leaders had reassembled in Moscow. A secret CIA report dated August 21 assessed the situation as follows:

> The fragile balance in the Soviet leadership which produced the Čierna agreement has, in the space of less than three weeks, been upset in favor of those who may all along have wanted the toughest kind of policy and have made use of the time and developments since Čierna to undo the agreement.[56]

FINAL POLITBURO DELIBERATIONS

The mood on August 16, the day the Soviet leaders reassembled in Moscow, was reflected in a *Pravda* article by the influential political commentator Yuri Zhukov, who described some of the reports appearing in the Czechoslovak press as "arrogant, vulgar and vile" and demanded "a consistent and unwavering fulfillment of the Bratislava Agreement." The atmosphere in Moscow had suddenly and perceptibly hardened, and events now unfolded in a much more confused and haphazard fashion than had previously been the case. Brezhnev, returning to Moscow, decided to send yet another personal letter to Dubček. The missive, dated August 16, appealed to him once more to heed previous warnings.[57] This decision (*number 43*) reflected both Brezhnev's growing centrality and his own desire to seek a way out of the invasion—even at this late stage.

---

[54] Author's interview with Jacob Beam, November 17, 1979, in Washington, D.C. The letter was also mentioned on Czechoslovak radio, August 26, 1968, EE/2854/C/17.

[55] Michel Tatu, *Le Monde*, August 20, 1969; Richard Lowenthal, "Sparrow in a Cage," p. 26.

[56] U.S. Central Intelligence Agency, Directorate of Intelligence, *The Soviet Decision to Intervene*, August 21, 1968. Artur Starewicz, in author's interview with him in Warsaw on August 28, 1980, confirmed the basic analysis that the balance between the hawks and doves had tipped in the former's favor by the end of the vacation period.

[57] *Ezhegodnik, Bol'shoy Sovetskoy Entsiklopedii, 1969*, p. 402; "Letter of Warning," p. 142.

As previously mentioned, a Kremlin report claimed it was Shelest who called the leaders back to Moscow for an urgent Politburo meeting at which new information was presented about the growth of antisocialist trends in Prague. Reports from Chervonenko even suggested that a majority of the CPCz Praesidium would now welcome "fraternal assistance."[58] Regardless of the catalyst for the meeting, it did take place, almost certainly on Saturday August 17 with all Politburo members apparently present. Evidence indicates that despite possible reservations of several members about the timing, effectiveness, or consequences of an invasion, the Politburo agreed (*decision 44*) to proceed on August 20 with the intervention plan on the basis that events in Czechoslovakia constituted "an immediate and lasting danger to the political, military, and strategic cohesion of the camp and that its defense capabilities were thus seriously shaken and weakened."[59] It cannot be known with any certainty whether the decision was taken by vote and if so whether the vote was unanimous. It would appear, however, that several Politburo members, especially Suslov and Kosygin, opposed the decision or at least expressed serious reservations even at this point.[60]

There were a number of implementing decisions arising from the consensus that finally emerged:

[58] Michel Tatu, *Le Monde*, September 24, 1968; *Sunday Times*, October 6, 1968; *International Herald Tribune*, December 27, 1972. Tatu reported that after the failure of the invasion to produce a quisling government, Suslov blamed Chervonenko for misleading the Politburo. In the 1972 report following Shelest's demotion, a leak from the Kremlin put the blame on Shelest for calling the Politburo back to Moscow and presenting it with an overly alarmist report.

[59] Tigrid, *Why Dubček Fell*, p. 95. Tigrid based his information on a report from Černík. U.S. officials concurred that the crucial decision had taken place on August 17 (*International Herald Tribune*, November 27, 1968).

[60] Paul Cook, in the U.S. embassy in Moscow at the time of the invasion, stated it was the embassy's view that despite heated argument and reservations, the formal vote to invade had been unanimous. Other sources share this view: "informed government sources" quoted by *The Observer*, August 25, 1968, and the *Christian Science Monitor*, September 9, 1968; Dimitri Simes, who worked at the Soviet Institute of World Economy and International Relations, in "The Soviet Invasion of Czechoslovakia and the Limits of Kremlinology," *Studies in Comparative Communism* 8, nos. 1 and 2 (Spring/Summer, 1975): 179. Eugene Rostow states that a joint Anglo-American intelligence assessment concluded that the vote had been unanimous (in Urban, "The Invasion of Czechoslovakia," p. 109). Oldřich Černík told a government meeting, following his return from Moscow, that although Suslov and Shelepin had had reservations, the vote to invade had been unanimous (as reported on Prague radio, August 28, 1968, and quoted in Golan, *Reform Rule*, p. 235).

Other sources suggest that whereas there was agreement on the need for invasion, there were reservations about *when* to invade. A commentary on Prague radio (August 20, 1969, EE/3158/C/24) is revealing: "In the Soviet Union, there were those who approved of such an

Decision forty-five authorized a letter from the full CPSU Politburo to the CPCz Praesidium, setting out the precise grounds for
Soviet concern. Some Soviet leaders may have hoped that the letter would alert Dubček to the necessity for immediate action,
whereas others may have calculated that it could be used by pro-
Soviet elements within the Praesidium as the basis for an appeal to
Moscow for fraternal assistance.[61] This letter was sent to Dubček on
August 17 following the Politburo meeting (although he claimed
not to have received it until 11:00 P.M. on August 19)[62] and the text
was read out one year later over Prague Radio. It contained specific
criticisms of the CPCz leadership for failing to undertake measures
agreed on at Čierna and Bratislava including control of the mass
media and suppression of all antisocialist and anti-Soviet activity.

operation, but for a later date; as soon as people were killed and injured in Czechoslovakia,
the Soviet Union would be asked for assistance. A premature intervention could discredit
the Soviet Union. However, after extensive deliberations, the Soviet leaders arrived at the
right conclusion." The commentary also reported that Brezhnev had told Jan Piller: "After
the Hungarian experience, the blood of a single Czechoslovak Communist, of a single ordinary person, is dearer to us than the temporary loss of prestige in the world."

Other sources say the vote had not been unanimous. The most frequently mentioned
opponents of invasion were Suslov and Kosygin, with Shelepin next on the list. The Hungarian ambassador to Rome told C. L. Sulzberger (as recounted in *An Age of Mediocrity*,
p. 465) that Suslov had voted against invasion. George Brown, Britain's former foreign secretary, vouched for Kosygin's dovish credentials (*Evening Standard*, November 14 and 15,
1968). An AFP despatch from Moscow (*Le Monde*, August 23, 1968) and a story in *L'Unita*
(August 22, 1968) both claim that Kosygin, Suslov, and Shelepin had voted against.

Mikhail Voslensky (*Der Spiegel*, no. 34, August 21, 1978) stated that he had been told in
the editorial offices of *Kommunist* on October 3, 1968, that Kosygin, Suslov, and Shelepin
voted against and that both Grechko and Zakharov had expressed reservations. Voslensky
had also noted that there were rumors of Grechko's opposition earlier in the summer.

Even Brezhnev is mentioned as having strong reservations at this late stage, although it
is almost certain that in the final analysis he voted in favor. *The New York Times*, August 29,
1968, quoting a "Communist source who flew to Moscow last week from Prague," stated that
Brezhnev, Kosygin, and Suslov all had "strong reservations" about the invasion. David
Binder, quoting "highly reliable East European sources" stated in *The Times* on August 25,
1968, that Brezhnev and Kosygin had been overruled by hard-liners. Willy Brandt (*People
and Politics*, p. 214) concluded that "there are grounds for supposing that the Soviet Politburo's drastic step was resisted to the last. The voting was probably six to five. It later
seemed that Brezhnev, who may well have cast the deciding vote, was unhappy about the
decision."

As to the views of candidate, and therefore nonvoting, Politburo members, Michel Tatu
reported in *Le Monde*, August 20, 1969, that Ponomarev had also opposed the invasion and
had later been criticized in the party for having "underestimated the dangers of the counterrevolution" in Prague.

[61] *Pravda*, August 22, 1968, made specific reference to the split within the CPCz Praesidium, claiming that "a minority of Praesidium members, headed by A. Dubček, took overtly
right-wing opportunist stands" and "thwarted fulfillment of the understanding reached in
Čierna nad Tisou and Bratislava."

[62] Golan, *Reform Rule*, p. 235.

The Politburo condemned both Císař and Prchlík by name and singled out recent student demonstrations in Prague, the attacks against the workers at the Praga factory and members of the People's Militia, and the activities of the Prague City Party Committee as proof that there was a "growing threat of a counterrevolution." It ended without threatening specific punitive measures, but it did emphasize "the immediate necessity of fulfilling the obligations which we jointly accepted at the meeting of brother parties."[63]

Decision forty-six informed leading officials inside the Soviet Union and in the fraternal countries and parties of the impending invasion and its consequences. Kádár was at that time traveling to Komárno, where he held urgent and lengthy negotiations with Dubček until almost midnight on Saturday August 17. Kádár is reported to have told Dubček everything he could, short of revealing the invasion details, and to have pleaded with him in despair as they parted: "Do you *really* not know the kind of people you're dealing with?"[64] There are several indications that Kádár then reported the failure of his talks to a meeting of leaders from the five aligned bloc countries on August 18, where the decision to invade was confirmed and the principle of collective responsibility adopted.[65] Evidence on this point is scarce, however, and it is also possible that Moscow informed the leaders of the other invading states individually that in light of the failure of Kádár's mission, the decision to invade was irrevocable.[66] It appears that the Finnish government and some of the Euro-Communist leaders may also have learned of Soviet plans. The Finnish minister of defense arrived in Moscow "for a holiday" at the invitation of Marshal Grechko on Au-

[63]"Letter of Warning," pp. 141–44. The letter is also mentioned by the Russians in *Ezhegodnik, Bol'shoy Sovetskoy Entsiklopedii,* 1969, p. 402. Husák referred to the letter in his speeches on August 19 and 25, 1969, EE/3156/C/9 and EE/3190/C/20.

[64]Mlynář, *Night Frost,* p. 157. Mention of the Kádár-Dubček talks is also made in *Ezhegodnik, Bol'shoy Sovetskoy Entsiklopedii, 1969,* p. 402; Golan, *Reform Rule,* p. 235; Levy, *Rowboat to Prague,* pp. 244–300.

[65]Tigrid, *Why Dubček Fell,* p. 96. Michel Tatu, *Le Monde,* August 20, 1969, states that Kádár met with Brezhnev and "his colleagues" in Moscow; V. M. Khvostov (*Problemy istorii vneshnei politiki SSSR i mezhdunarodnykh otnoshenii,* p. 453) states that the decision "to introduce our forces into Czechoslovakia" was taken by the CPSU Central Committee and the Soviet government "together with the Central Committees and the governments of the four fraternal states." Adolf Müller (*Die Tschechoslowakei auf der Suche nach Sicherheit,* p. 302) quotes a source within the CPCz Secretariat as saying that a meeting of the five took place in Hungary on August 18. Edward Goldstücker (interviewed by the author on October 24, 1977) also maintained that a meeting of the five took place, but he stated that it was convened in Warsaw.

[66]Levy (*Rowboat to Prague,* p. 300) states Kádár was informed by Moscow on Sunday evening, August 18, that the invasion would proceed.

gust 17. The TASS despatch of his arrival simply said that after brief consultations in Moscow, he departed for Sochi.[67] Luigi Longo was also in Moscow "on holiday" at this time, and here the evidence suggests much more clearly that he had been told of the imminent invasion by Suslov and others and had tried unsuccessfully to forestall it.[68]

Within the USSR, the first public indication of things to come appeared with the August 18 *Pravda* article by Alexandrov (the universally recognized pseudonym used for important policy statements by the Politburo). Entitled "Insolent Attacks by Reactionaries," the article repeated the allegations of the Politburo letter to the CPCz Praesidium, claiming intensified counterrevolutionary activities in Prague and charging that these "insolent reactionaries" sought to "undermine the foundations of socialism, discredit the leading role of the working class and its party and cut Czechoslovakia off from the socialist commonwealth." The final paragraph ended on this ominous note:

> But the enemies' schemes are doomed to failure. The working people of Czechoslovakia, leaning on the international solidarity and support of the fraternal socialist countries as clearly and profoundly expressed in the Bratislava statement, are fully resolved to rebuff the schemes of internal and external reaction and to uphold and strengthen their socialist gains.

Closed channels were also obviously used to inform other Soviet officials of the Politburo's decision, but there is no firm evidence that party members below the Central Committee level were given anything but the most veiled and general signals.[69] There is some indication that further meetings between the Politburo and other consultative groups took place following the August 17 decision. Some reports speak of a formal but secret Central Committee plenum, others of an ad hoc meeting of key Central Committee members stationed in Moscow. Western intelligence monitored considerably

[67]TASS, August 17, 1968, SU/2851/A2/2.

[68]Longo returned from Moscow to Rome via Paris, where he told journalists that in "a short discussion" with Suslov and other "leading members" of the Soviet Communist party he expressed his dissent over the invasion plans "with great frankness" (*International Herald Tribune, Morning Star*, August 23, 1968, *Sunday Times*, August 25, 1968). Longo was reported by *Pravda* on August 15, 1968, to have arrived the previous day in Moscow for his holidays. He was met at the airport by Kirilenko.

[69]Grey Hodnett and Peter Potichnyj ("The Ukraine and the Czechoslovak Crisis," p. 78) disclose that two meetings for propagandists in the Ukraine were held on August 16 and 20. It seems more than likely that Czechoslovakia was at the top of the agenda, but it is not likely that the invasion plan was revealed.

heightened activity in and around the Kremlin during the weekend, although the absence of similar activity at the airports might suggest that party functionaries were not being called in from the provinces. Certainly the official CPSU yearbook for 1968 makes no mention of a Central Committee meeting during this period, and it is possible that the Politburo assembled leading party and government officials to inform them of its decision on an ad hoc and consultative, rather than a formal and decisional, basis.[70] It is also quite possible that some leaders still sought to prevent, or thought they could prevent, the invasion at this late stage.

Decision forty-seven sought to contain the international consequences of the invasion, certainly in the political area and perhaps also in the military sphere. To this end, Premier Kosygin on August 19 informed President Johnson that the Soviet Union was prepared to announce its readiness to host a summit between the two leaders in Leningrad beginning September 30 to discuss the limitation of strategic arms. Both leaders agreed that a simultaneous announcement to this effect would be made in Washington and Moscow on Wednesday morning, August 21.[71]

[70] Michel Tatu, *Le Monde*, August 20, 1969, speaks of a meeting of party functionaries on August 17–18, 1968. *The Sunday Times*, August 25, 1968, on the basis of West German intelligence, reports a Brezhnev meeting with Grechko, Yakubovsky, and Yepishev. Jiří Hájek (*Dix ans après*, p. 114) refers to an "unexpected meeting of the Soviet Central Committee from which nothing has ever been made known." The CIA memorandum *Soviet Decision to Intervene*, August 21, 1968, also refers to the convening of a Central Committee plenum, as does Tad Szulc in the *New York Times* on September 9, 1968, and Sir William Hayter (*Russia and the World*, p. 45), who state that the plenum met on August 20. Italian Communist officials also revealed that at 8:00 P.M. on August 20 news reached them of an impending invasion and that the news came from "the Moscow meeting of the Central Committee" (*Sunday Times*, August 25, 1968). Vladimir Maximov (in Urban, *Communist Reformation*, p. 268) has stated that "for three whole days the Central Committee was in continuous session because there was a presumption that the Czechs might fight, and that this might provoke further trouble elsewhere in Eastern Europe and in the Soviet Union." *The Sunday Times*, August 25, quoting highly placed informed sources, stated that the decision to invade was *confirmed* at an enlarged meeting of the Politburo, with as many Central Committee members present as could attend. *Süddeutsche Zeitung* and the *Daily Express* of August 20, 1968, both report rumors of an emergency Central Committee plenum beginning on August 19. *Die Welt*, August 21, 1968, also confirms an August 19–20 plenum. Paul Cook and Paul Costolanski (interviewed by the author on November 14, 1979) concur that there was a weekend meeting but state that it was essentially a greatly enlarged Politburo meeting, with Gromyko, Grechko, and other party and state notables present but not voting. George Brown, the former British foreign minister, maintains that Kosygin and other doves tried to forestall the invasion up to the last moment with an all-night meeting on August 19–20 (*Evening Standard*, November 14, 1968).

[71] *New York Times*, August 23, 1968. The date and venue for the Kosygin-Johnson summit had been discussed earlier in the summer, as confirmed by Raymond Garthoff who was then in the State Department preparing the U.S. position, in an interview by the author, March 9, 1984.

If the decision to invade was by this time firm, unanimous, and irrevocable, Kosygin's message can be interpreted as a rather cynical attempt to offer the Americans the carrot of SALT while using the stick against Prague, on the assumption that Johnson's desire for an East-West summit was such that he would not abandon it, even if it were to be announced simultaneously with the invasion.[72] There are of course other explanations of this rather strange sequence of events. One is that Kosygin did not believe the decision to invade was irrevocable and that he hoped to use Johnson's agreement to attend a summit in Leningrad as a constraint on those who favored an invasion of Czechoslovakia, which would inevitably scuttle any hopes of a summit.[73] A third view has been forwarded —that the "hawks" hoped to kill two birds with one stone. They may have agreed to approach the United States, hoping, on the one hand, to mask Soviet preparations and defuse American reactions while, on the other hand, setting back the prospects of arms control at a time when the Soviet military was only finally reestablishing its position and prestige after the setback of the Khrushchev era.[74] Of course, it is certainly possible that different Soviet leaders may have been motivated by different priorities, but the relative speed with which Soviet-American contacts on SALT were resumed after the invasion suggests a degree of unity on this issue.

It has also been suggested that on August 18 Moscow received assurances from the United States that it would not respond militarily to the Pact invasion. This allegation of American connivance, later hotly disputed in Washington, was made most clearly by Zdeněk Mlynář, who recorded that at the postinvasion Moscow negotiations, Brezhnev, in a sudden fit of irritation at Dubček's refusal to sign the "normalization" agreement, shouted at the Czechoslovak delegation:

[72] See especially Fritz Ermath, "Internationalism, Security and Legitimacy, The Challenge to Soviet Interests in Europe, 1964–1968," p. 116–17.

[73] This view was adopted by Chip Bohlen and others at the U.S. State Department and it formed one of the bases of their conclusion that the decision to invade was made only finally the day before the troops moved in (see Charles E. Bohlen, *Witness to History, 1929–1968*, pp. 531–32.

[74] This argument suggests that dissension over the invasion reflected broader disagreements over defense spending and arms control. In this respect, note *Pravda's* treatment of a speech by Politburo member Kiril Mazurov on November 6. Mazurov emphasized Moscow's continued enthusiasm for an East-West summit: "One can recall in this connection that we have expressed our readiness to negotiate with the United States on the whole complex of these questions. This positive solution, however, depends not on the Soviet side alone" (Radio Moscow, November 6, 1968). *Pravda* in reprinting this speech the next day deleted this passage altogether, suggesting continued lack of agreement on this issue.

What are you waiting for? Do you expect anything is going to happen to help you? No, there is going to be no war—you might as well take note of that. I had an enquiry sent to President Johnson asking him whether the United States would respect the Yalta and Potsdam agreements, and on 18 August I received his reply saying that as far as Czechoslovakia and Rumania were concerned the U.S. would unquestionably honor these agreements—the case of Yugoslavia, he said, would have to be the subject of negotiations.[75]

It must be said that although there could be little doubt in Soviet minds by August 20 of Washington's policy of strict noninterference, there is no other specific evidence to support Mlynář's account. Certainly Moscow's posture immediately prior to the invasion was designed, as the British ambassador to the USSR recalled, to show the Soviet Union's "anxiety to reassure the United States government that Soviet policy in Czechoslovakia had no real anti-American aim."[76] But beyond this, there is no indication of specific agreement between Moscow and Washington over spheres of influence.

The decision to invade brought the crisis period to an end. The final days before the intervention were marked not only by the heightened activity of the Politburo, the core decisional unit, but also by an enlargement of that unit and by increased consultative activity. The agreement to invade did finally emerge, in the words of Kádár, as an "unhappy necessity," and that consensus reflected a greater cohesion in the outlook of the collective leadership than had often been detected in the previous months. Yet the analyst must conclude that the frantic and diverse political activity of the final preinvasion hours was caused partly by general anxiety over the prospects of the invasion's achieving both its political and military goals and partly by continuing reservations over the timing, utility, and likely efficacy of the invasion in the first place. The outcome of the invasion was to show that these reservations were not entirely ill conceived.

[75] Mlynář, "August 1968," in Urban, *Communist Reformation*, p. 132.

[76] Hayter, *Russia and the World*, p. 122. Without specifically mentioning any secret signaling, a high U.S. official admitted as early as August 24, 1968, that NATO and the WTO adhere to unwritten "no troops arrangements" and that since Czechoslovakia lay within the "Russian sphere of influence," the U.S. "never" considered any military action in response to an invasion (*Observer*, August 25, 1968).

CHAPTER ELEVEN

Findings

DECISIONS

The crisis period was divided into five phases, with the following
major decisions being taken in each phase:

Decision Number	Date	Content
		PHASE ONE: MAY 5–JUNE 6
11	May 5	The Politburo decides to renew press polemics, conduct bilateral and multilateral bloc negotiations, and use military displays of force against Czechoslovakia as part of a campaign of minatory diplomacy. As part of this widening of alternatives, development of contingency plans for a possible invasion was also likely to have been agreed on at this time.
12	May 7	The Politburo decides to convene a summit of the five (USSR, Poland, Hungary, Bulgaria, and the GDR) the following day in Moscow.
13	May 8	The Soviet delegation to the Moscow meeting of the five agrees to greater participation in crisis management by East European leaders.
14	May 14–15	The Politburo (probably with military representation) decides (a) to press for maneuvers and discuss the stationing of troops in Czechoslovakia; (b) to determine whether the conservatives are likely to recoup their positions, with or without Soviet help; (c) to

continue negotiations with the Dubček government in an effort to reach a political solution without further crisis escalation; and (d) to send Grechko and Kosygin to Prague as representatives of these two views.

15   May 26–27   The Politburo (probably with military representation) authorizes the Soviet military to begin moving units into Czechoslovakia ostensibly for the June WTO maneuvers but actually to coincide with the May CPCz Central Committee plenum.

16   June 6   The Politburo decides to defuse the crisis and support the Dubček leadership in its efforts to control both leftist and rightist tendencies.

PHASE TWO: JUNE 6–27

17   June 11   The Politburo authorizes Brezhnev to write to Dubček seeking immediate bilateral talks.

18   June 13   The Politburo decides to seek bilateral talks and to keep Soviet military units in and around Czechoslovakia at their current level of preparedness.

19   June 20   The Politburo authorizes a nationwide campaign of solidarity with the People's Militia and the working people of Czechoslovakia and increases press polemics against Prague with the publication of the first personal attack on a Czechoslovak leader (Císař).

20   June 20   The Politburo agrees that Kosygin should write President Johnson seeking arms limitation talks.

PHASE THREE: JUNE 27–JULY 28

21   June 27   Brezhnev calls Dubček to protest the publication of the "2,000 Words" manifesto.

22   June 30   The Politburo decides to keep Soviet troops in Czechoslovakia for the time being.

23   July 1–2   The Politburo decides to seek an urgent multilateral meeting with the leaders of Czechoslovakia and other members of the five.

24   July 10   The Politburo (with military participation) agrees to formally end maneuvers and withdraw some troops from Czechoslovakia, at

the same time also apparently transferring operational control for any future exercise or military action from the WTO Headquarters under Yakubovsky to the Soviet High Command under Grechko.

25	July 10	The Politburo decides to abandon the secret negotiations with the Bonn government over a renunciation-of-force agreement.
26	July 10	The Politburo agrees to the publication of an article by I. Alexandrov entitled "Attack on the Socialist Foundations of Czechoslovakia," the harshest official denunciation of the Prague leadership yet to be made by the Soviet leadership.
27	July 11	The Politburo (minus Kosygin) agrees that the five should once again demand a multilateral meeting with Czechoslovak leaders.
28	July 11–12	The Politburo (minus Kosygin) agrees to despatch a delegation to Warsaw immediately for a bloc enclave.
29	July 11–12	The Politburo (minus Kosygin) agrees that following the Warsaw meeting, a special CPSU Central Committee plenum should be convened.
30	July 17	The Central Committee affirms the need for a nationwide campaign to familiarize the Soviet public with the Warsaw Letter and to mobilize public opinion against counterrevolutionary tendencies in Czechoslovakia.
31	July 17	Brezhnev seeks bilateral talks with Czechoslovakia.
32	July 19	The Politburo publicly reaffirms the call for bilateral talks.
33	July 20–21	The Politburo fails to endorse Waldeck Rochet's call for a European Communist conference to discuss Czechoslovakia.
34	July 20–21	The Politburo (presumably with military participation) decides to send a formal letter to the Czechoslovak government demanding the immediate stationing of Soviet troops in Czechoslovakia.
35	July 20–21	The Politburo (with the participation of at least Gromyko and Grechko) agrees to pro-

ceed with a full-scale invasion of Czechoslovakia, before August 26, unless Dubček agrees both to end the reform movement and allow the permanent stationing of Soviet troops on Czechoslovakia's western border. Accordingly, the Politburo (a) authorizes the military to make final preparations; and (b) instructs the foreign minister to ascertain the likely Western response.

| 36 | July 22 | The Politburo agrees to hold negotiations on Czechoslovak soil at Čierna nad Tisou. |

PHASE FOUR: JULY 29–AUGUST 5

| 37 | July 31 | The Soviet delegation at the Čierna nad Tisou talks decides to give the Czechoslovaks one more chance to put their own affairs in order and to convene a multilateral meeting at Bratislava sanctifying the results of Čierna and reasserting bloc unity. |

PHASE FIVE: AUGUST 5–20

38	August 6	The Politburo decides to proceed with plans for an invasion and to implement those plans before the August 26 deadline unless the Czechoslovak leaders show clear and unequivocal adherence to the Soviet interpretation of the Bratislava statement.
39	August 13	Brezhnev decides to send a letter to Dubček demanding the fulfillment of undertakings made at Čierna and Bratislava.
40	August 13	Soviet leaders send a second letter to Dubček in the name of the entire Politburo, drawing the attention of the CPCz leadership to the nonfulfillment of prior agreements.
41	August 7–15	On Politburo instructions, Ambassador Chervonenko meets Czechoslovak leaders, apparently seeking permanent stationing of troops and demanding another high-level bilateral meeting.
42	August 15	Brezhnev agrees to Kádár's urgent appeal that he be allowed to mediate between Moscow and Prague.
43	August 16	Brezhnev sends Dubček a letter appealing to him to heed previous warnings.

44	August 17	The Politburo agrees to proceed on August 20 with the intervention plan.
45	August 17	The Politburo agrees to send a letter to the CPCz Praesidium setting out the precise grounds for Soviet concern.
46	August 17	The Politburo agrees to inform leading officials inside the Soviet Union and in fraternal countries and parties of the impending invasion and its likely consequences.
47	August 17	The Politburo decides on various measures to contain the international consequences of the invasion.

DECISION MAKERS AND THEIR PSYCHOLOGICAL ENVIRONMENT

The lengthy crisis period, dissected into its five phases, revealed a high level of participation by the Soviet leadership in the management of the Czechoslovak crisis. In tracing the decisions that were made, the analyst is faced with the problem that in many cases, the difficulty lies not in discerning that a decision has been made but in divining by whom. This is particularly apparent in the crisis period when the general level of political activity was high, divisions within the leadership were apparent, and individual leaders were often dispersed in the provinces or abroad. The analyst can assume that there was both opportunity and motivation for heightened ad hoc activity by leadership factions, yet it is still very difficult to ascertain by means of *direct* evidence which leaders or groups were controlling the decision-making process and which were being excluded from it.

There are, however, a number of *indirect* indicators, including participation both in negotiations over the Czechoslovak issue and in the public debate over Czechoslovakia. Looking first at participation in negotiations, there were during the crisis period thirty-three delegations received or sent by the USSR in which Politburo or Central Committee members or military leaders were involved and in which Czechoslovakia was known to have been discussed. An analysis of participants reveals the existence of a Politburo inner core consisting of Kosygin (who was involved in no less than twelve of the thirty-three negotiations); Brezhnev (nine); Podgorny (eight); Katushev (eight); Suslov (six); Demichev (four); Voronov (three);

Shelest (three); and Ponomarev (three). Analysis of the negotiating teams also shows the very high level of military involvement, with Grechko included in six of the thirty-three delegations, Yepishev in five, Shtemenko in five, Yakubovsky in four, and Koshevoi in three.

Examination of involvement in the public debate over Czechoslovakia reveals a not dissimilar picture. There were twenty-one political leaders and twenty-seven military leaders who between them were responsible for fifty published speeches, articles, statements, and press interviews on matters relating directly or indirectly to Czechoslovakia during the crisis period. Several of the speeches were in fact delivered at closed sessions of the Central Committee or at party *aktivs*, and although they indicate leadership activity, their content cannot be assessed in the analysis of leadership views. Of the total, Kosygin was responsible for eight of the fifty, Brezhnev for six, Shelest for five, Podgorny for three, and Gromyko for two. The military once again were active in the public debate. Twenty-one of the forty-one speeches, articles, or press conferences published were made by military leaders, with Yakubovsky responsible for seven, Konev for three, Zakharov for three, and Grechko for two—excluding orders of the day printed over his name.

These two indicators support the analysis presented in the preceding chapters, which underlines the centrality in the decision-making process of Brezhnev, Kosygin, Podgorny, Suslov, and Shelest as political leaders and the generally high level of involvement of military leaders. The activities of these men have already been analyzed extensively, but it is worthwhile summarizing the similarities and differences in their views here.

Brezhnev

In Brezhnev's speeches, the views he expressed in the course of the Warsaw and Čierna meetings, and Mlynář's record of the impromptu speech Brezhnev delivered at the postinvasion Moscow negotiations, several recurring themes and characteristics appear.[1]

[1] Brezhnev: speech at Soviet-Hungarian friendship meeting in Moscow in presence of Kádár, July 3, 1968, SU/2813/C/1–7; speech at the All-Union Congress of Teachers, *Pravda*, July 5, 1968; speech at the Kremlin reception for graduates of military academies, July 8, 1968, SU/2817/C/1–5; accounts of his views, as expressed in meetings with Smrkovský on June 14 (chapter 7), at the Warsaw meeting (chapter 8), at Čierna (chapter 9), and at the postinvasion Moscow meeting (chapter 12).

One is a leadership style strongly inclined toward conciliation and collective leadership. This appears to have been the product not just of the balance of forces within the Politburo but also of his own personal orientation. Brezhnev followed opinion, he did not make it; he was neither the first of the Soviet leaders to publicly advocate the use of military means where socialism was threatened (Grishin, April 23), nor was he the last person to express confidence in the ability of the Czechoslovak people and party to deliver an effective rebuff to any attack on the socialist basis of Czechoslovakia (Kosygin, July 13). He both helped to form a political consensus and reflected that consensus; he was an architect of both the hard-line Warsaw Letter and the Čierna compromise, although he was neither the most hawkish of leaders at Warsaw (Ulbricht and Gomułka) nor the most dovish of leaders at Čierna (Suslov).

Brezhnev viewed the events in Czechoslovakia very much through the lens of the threat they posed to the ideological foundations of the socialist system. He had revealed himself to be deeply opposed to any manifestations of intellectual dissent or nationalist activities in his own country, and it was this aspect of the Prague Spring that most worried him. For Brezhnev, in the balance between dogmatism and revisionism, the latter was the greater danger. The Chinese example found little echo in his own country, but the Czechoslovak reform movement stood to exacerbate the tensions within the CPSU and between the party and the intelligentsia brought about by the harder line in cultural affairs in the post-Khrushchev period. If Brezhnev opposed invasion, as he apparently did for so long, it was not out of sympathy with the Prague Spring; it was attributable to the cautiousness of his own personal style and his abiding belief that the source of trouble in Czechoslovakia was limited to subversion by antisocialist groups and a few leaders and journalists who could easily be dealt with by administrative means. According to his own testimony after the invasion, he had long defended Dubček as a "good comrade" who could be relied upon to restore order. Only after Dubček did not implement the Čierna and Bratislava agreements did Brezhnev finally apparently agree that an invasion was necessary.

Kosygin

Analysis of Kosygin's participation in negotiations and in the public debate reveals a very high level of activity, indeed the highest of any Soviet leader. At the same time, it has been shown that Kosygin was excluded on several occasions from important decisions escalating the crisis with Czechoslovakia, including the convening of the April Central Committee plenum and the decision to hold the Warsaw meeting without Czechoslovak participation.

Looking at his speeches and the accounts of his views,[2] as expressed particularly during his one-man sojourn to Karlovy Vary in May, Kosygin emerges as a leader with a much broader vision than Brezhnev. He did not interpret the events in Czechoslovakia solely or even primarily through the attitudinal prism of the threat imposed by the reform movement to the socialist community as a whole or to the ideological basis of Soviet-style systems. That is not to say that Kosygin was sympathetic to the Prague reform per se or in toto, just that he was not opposed to the very notion of reform and that he had a much more pragmatic appreciation of the problems involved in controlling the crisis from Moscow. He, almost alone of the Soviet leaders, valued quiet diplomacy; and he may have accepted Czechoslovak reassurances that the problems being encountered in Czechoslovakia were a transient phenomenon. Certainly Kosygin could see that an invasion would jeopardize two policies to which he was personally committed: the reform of the Soviet economy, and the East-West détente. His positive attitude to an improvement in East-West relations was more than apparent from his statements in Sweden.[3] He answered questions on the German problem but did not condemn the policy of "building bridges" and called instead for an all-European security conference; he talked about the Second World War, but instead of stressing the extent of Soviet sacrifices (which he as a party *apparatchik* in besieged Leningrad would have witnessed) he concluded that the fight against fascism had "cemented the friendship between the Czechoslovak and Soviet peoples and strengthened the trust and unity between the CPCz and the CPSU." He attacked the renewed American bombing of Vietnam, but instead of interpreting it as proof of U.S. perfidy and increased aggressiveness, he stated that this was all the more reason why the Paris talks had to continue. This contrasted sharply with the view expressed by Shelepin in his April 8 speech

[2] Kosygin: interview with *Magyar Hirlap*, May 19, 1968; speech at the signing in Moscow of the Nonproliferation Treaty, *Pravda*, July 2, 1968; press conference in Stockholm, July 13, 1968, SU/2822/C1/1–6 and *Pravda*, July 15, 1968; accounts of his views, as expressed in Karlovy Vary in mid-May (chapter 6), at the Warsaw meeting (see chapter 8), and at Čierna (see chapter 9).

[3] *Pravda*, July 15, 1968; *Christian Science Monitor* (London Edition), July 13–15, 1968.

on Vietnam discussed in chapter 5. It is also remarkable that barely one week after Brezhnev had described the United States as a "rotten, decaying society" and had stated that the "crushing of reaction in Hungary" in 1956 had saved socialism there, Kosygin should praise East-West disarmament contacts as "already a great thing" and dismiss questions about Soviet troop movements in Czechoslovakia, saying that "the press is more worried than the Czechs." Thus while Kosygin almost certainly did not sympathize with the political aspects of the Prague Spring, he did express views predisposing him to minimize the threat of Prague and to maximize the negative repercussions of a Soviet invasion.

Podgorny

There are few accounts of Podgorny's position from Czechoslovak or other informed sources. Yet during the crisis period, he delivered three public speeches and gave one interview.[4] On May 6 Vladimír Koucký, the new Czechoslovak ambassador to Moscow, presented his credentials; and in the course of the welcoming ceremony, Podgorny took the unusual opportunity of wishing Czechoslovakia success "in the struggle against the intrigues of circles hostile to the course of progress and socialism." Instead of talking about the bonds of trust and unity linking the two countries, as Kosygin had done, he stated that "our peoples' socialist gains are reliably guaranteed against the encroachments of imperialism by the power of the indestructible militant alliance among the fraternal socialist countries formed by the Warsaw Pact." The following month, in an interview with a British member of Parliament, he bitterly attacked U.S. policy in Vietnam and the Middle East without mentioning the value of negotiation. He also dwelled extensively on the German problem, as he did on July 18 in the incongruous setting of a speech he delivered at the end of a Moscow visit by India's president, Dr. Zakir Hussein. (Kosygin also gave a speech at a farewell luncheon for Hussein, but he limited himself solely to Soviet-Indian relations.) Podgorny lost no opportunity to condemn U.S. policy in Vietnam and in the Middle East; and perhaps in a rebuff to some of his own more liberal-minded colleagues, he stated on the same occasion that it was "dangerous to display toler-

[4] Podgorny: speech at the welcoming ceremonies for Czechoslovak Ambassador Koucký, *Pravda*, May 7, 1968; interview with the R. H. Maurice Edelman, M. P., *Daily Express*, June 4, 1968; speech on July 9 at a luncheon in honor of the Indian president, *Soviet News*, July 23, 1968; speech at a meeting of the RSFSR Supreme Soviet, *Pravda*, July 20, 1968.

ance toward the growth of militarism, revanchism, and neo-Nazism in the Federal Republic of Germany."

The fourth speech, and the only one in which Podgorny spoke directly on Czechoslovakia, has been analyzed extensively in Chapter 8. Delivered at a meeting of the Russian republic's Supreme Soviet, it was the last public speech delivered by any Soviet leader on Czechoslovakia before the invasion. Podgorny wasted no time in expressing an extremely negative view of events in Prague, where "remnants of the defeated, exploiting classes, revisionist and nationalist elements are subjecting the very foundations of socialist construction to fierce attacks." Clearly showing himself to be an advocate of intervention, Podgorny promised "our Czechoslovak friends" the "utmost aid and support" in blocking "the path of reaction."

Suslov

Suslov gave only one public speech during the entire crisis period, but this was a major address of nearly 17,000 words marking the 150th anniversary of Marx's birth.[5] His speech was confined almost exclusively to two subjects: the unity of the international Communist movement (6,250 words) and the principles governing Communist construction (10,250). In a speech delivered at the Budapest Consultative Meeting of Representatives of Communist and Workers' Parties at the end of February,[6] Suslov had stated that the USSR attaches "fundamental importance" to the convening of a world Communist conference in November 1968 and that all tactics to postpone the conference had failed. At that time he also gave a positive assessment of changes taking place in Eastern Europe, and he concentrated his entire attack on the Chinese. It is in the context of these views that Suslov's May 5 speech should be assessed. It is also revealing to compare it with Pel'she's earlier speech in the GDR to commemorate the same occasion (given on May 2 and therefore classified as part of the pre-crisis period). As did Pel'she, Suslov dwelt on the current significance of Marxism-Leninism and emphasized the dictatorship of the proletariat, the leading role of the Communist party, and democratic centralism as the major principles underlying socialist construction. These principles, Suslov insisted, were universal, although all countries could make a creative contribution to the application of Marx's teaching to their

[5] *Pravda*, May 6, 1968.
[6] *Pravda*, February 29, 1968.

own societies. Thus Suslov would not have sanctioned much of the fundamental reform taking place in Czechoslovakia and indeed would have disagreed with much of Čestmír Císař's speech made on the same day (see chapter 6), but he did not set himself up as an opponent of reform per se.

The most interesting part of his speech was a vicious denunciation of Maoism and its divisive effect on the unity of the international Communist movement. On the basis of this speech, Suslov cannot be counted as one of those leaders who considered revisionism the major danger, nor as one who felt an equal battle had to be fought on two fronts against left-wing dogmatism (Maoism) or right-wing revisionism (the Prague Spring). Nowhere in this speech did Suslov condemn revisionism, and even his mention of "petit-bourgeois nationalism and chauvinism," which might under other circumstances have been a veiled criticism of Czechoslovakia, was specifically tied to the Maoist "perversion." Suslov therefore emerges as a leader who would be predisposed to accommodate the less radical aspects of the Prague Spring in order to maintain the unity of ranks against the Chinese. This is precisely the impression the Czechoslovak delegation at Čierna formed of Suslov.[7] It can be assumed that his priorities remained unchanged throughout the crisis period, right up to the decision to invade.

Shelest

In addition to the speech Shelest delivered at the closed session of the CPSU Central Committee in July, there are his four articles or published speeches and the statements by Czechoslovak leaders of encounters with Shelest,[8] all of which reveal that Shelest was probably the major advocate of invasion within the Soviet leadership. Concerned with maintaining a fragile independence for the Ukraine in matters of culture and nationalities policy, Shelest was acutely sensitive to the separatist tendencies within his own population that could so easily be exacerbated by the Prague Spring. Thus he condemned any movement toward liberalization in Czechoslovakia that might spill over into the Ukraine; and although he paid lip service to the necessity for an equal struggle against both right and

[7] As analyzed in chapter 9.

[8] Shelest: "Boyevoy otryad KPSS," *Voprosy istorii KPSS*, no. 7 (July 1968), pp. 7–21; articles marking the fiftieth anniversary of the Ukrainian Communist party, *Pravda*, July 5, 1968, and *Radjanska Ukraina*, July 6, 1968; speech marking the fiftieth anniversary of the Ukrainian Communist party, *Pravda*, July 6, 1968; accounts of his views as expressed at Čierna are discussed in chapter 9.

left opportunism, his most bitter denunciations were saved for the right.

Grechko and His Generals

The military high command was active not only in implementing the decision to invade but also in shaping and interpreting for the political leadership the parameters of the many strategic and military issues involved in the crisis. The entry of the military into the debate on the extent to which the reform movement per se was threatening the security of the Soviet Union and the Warsaw Pact was legitimized by the resolutions of the April CPSU Central Committee plenum, which declared imperialist subversion (rather than a direct military buildup) to be the major front of East-West conflict. By so doing, the party decreed that the military had to give priority to areas where communism was being threatened from within, such as Czechoslovakia, rather than to areas where the West might be attempting to overthrow communism by direct military action, as in Vietnam. Aid to Vietnam was of course to continue, but not on the scale of the "fraternal assistance" soon to be extended to Czechoslovakia.

If the April plenum authorized the military to enter the debate on subversion, not all the marshals appeared to agree with this reorientation of priorities. Marshal Grechko's speeches and articles in particular were notable for the lack of references to domestic processes in other socialist states; they were concerned almost exclusively with strengthening the preparedness of the Pact to deal with direct military invasions from the West. Of the military leaders, Grechko made the least mention of subversion as a weapon of imperialism.[9] For example, at a ceremony for military graduates in July at which Brezhnev delivered a wide-ranging hard-line speech, Grechko limited his remarks on subversion to the rather bland statement that "the sharpening of the ideological war makes it essential for all to display a high degree of vigilance and to expose the intrigues of bourgeois propaganda."[10] Yet denunciations of the FRG and calls to consolidate the bloc and increase combat readiness were standard features of his speeches. Grechko's failure to comment on imperialist subversion does not mean that he did not favor the invasion. If he were sufficiently convinced (and after the Šejna defection, he may well have been) that the West had also

---

[9] His most important speeches and articles in the crisis period are contained in *Pravda*, May 2 and May 9, and in *Izvestia*, July 9, 1968.

[10] *Izvestia*, July 9, 1968.

come to regard Czechoslovakia as a weak link, he may have accepted the necessity of invading primarily in order to obtain the stationing of troops. Such a position is consistent with reports that there were those within the Soviet military, including Grechko and Yakubovsky, who had used the June maneuvers to "prove" that the Czechoslovak army was incapable of holding a defensive line for the required seventy-two hours.[11] It is from this perspective that one must view Soviet concern about NATO deployments close to the Czechoslovak border and the dramatic "revelations" in the Soviet press in July and August of a NATO plan to invade and overrun Czechoslovakia in forty-eight hours before turning on Poland and the GDR.[12] That there were both military and political leaders who were concerned less about the reform movement than about security arrangements is also consistent with Mlynář's statement that in the Moscow negotiations following the invasion, "the demands of the hawks could have been satisfied by the stationing of a limited number of troops (in particular strategic forces), and a much more modest reform movement could have been allowed to continue unhindered."[13]

Whether the Czechoslovak army had the capability of holding a defensive line was related to a second issue, namely, whether the reform movement was affecting military morale and in particular whether liberal and anti-Soviet tendencies within the army had begun to erode its loyalty and reliability. Here there was a marked difference in approach between the Soviet military leaders. During his visit to Prague in May, Marshal Yakubovsky reportedly complained to Dzúr about the continuing worries within the Soviet leadership over the reform movement's effect on the morale of the Czechoslovak army. When Dzúr replied that he too was worried about low morale, Yakubovsky is rumored to have embraced him, saying "one friend has understood another!" and to have used this admission in his argument for the permanent stationing of troops.[14] In marked contrast, during his own trip to Czechoslovakia later in May, Grechko was quoted as saying "the solution of the internal

[11] *New York Times*, August 1, 1968, quoting a "member of the intelligence community in Bonn."

[12] Ernst Henry's article in *Izvestia*, August 15, 1968; and *Pravda*, July 9, 1968.

[13] Zdeněk Mlynář, *Nachtfrost*, p. 287. Mlynář rates the military influence on decision making during the crisis as being both high and tending toward the hawkish position. This is also the view of Jacob Beam, the U.S. Ambassador to Prague at that time (see J. Beam, *Multiple Exposure*, p. 188).

[14] Mlynář, *Nachtfrost*, p. 188. Also the document presented at the December 1970 plenum of the CPCz Central Committee entitled "Lessons of the Crisis Development in the

problems of the Czechoslovak People's Army is the internal affair of Czechoslovakia."[15]

Concern about the impact of "imperialist subversion" on the morale and effectiveness of the Czechoslovak army was not confined to the military leaders. Indeed Brezhnev, in a speech to military cadets on July 8, candidly stated:

> It is not to be wondered at that our enemies in their attempts to weaken the socialist community or its unity resort to ideological sabotage which is also aimed at the armed forces of the individual socialist countries. And if imperialism is now carrying out attacks on the authority of the socialist armies and is seeking to weaken their links with the people, this demonstrates once again to all Communists and to the working class how important it is to protect this authority and strengthen those links.[16]

Grechko's failure to include any similar references in his speech to the cadets indicates that he did not entirely agree with his military colleagues or with Brezhnev.

If Marshal Grechko was unable to agree fully with Brezhnev's perceived need to combat imperialist subversion, there were any number of other commanders who did. General Yepishev, the head of the Main Political Administration within the Ministry of Defense, was among the first military leaders to express concern about Czechoslovak developments, which he viewed so negatively that he was reported in May to have declared the Soviet military's readiness to intervene should an appeal come from "loyal Communists" in Prague.[17] Marshal Konev, too, was active in upholding the military's right to condemn and combat subversion, whatever its source. Konev considered it the military's duty to defend not only the frontiers of the socialist states but also the socialist orientation of those states, and this was the keynote of the speech he delivered in Prague on May 9. He declared that the USSR and its East European allies will "always firmly and reliably defend our socialist gains as well as our frontiers of the socialist camp. . . . Vigilance is particularly necessary by the ČSSR, which is the bridgehead situated right next to the capitalist world. . . . I can say outright that

---

Communist Party of Czechoslovakia and in Society after the 13th Congress of the CPCz" stressed that the reform movement had had "a particularly adverse effect on the operation and the moral-political condition" of the army after April, when the new command began to take over. See *Pravda pobezhdaet*, p. 43.

[15] *Rudé právo*, May 19, 1968; and Tanyug, May 19, 1968, EE/2775/C/2.

[16] L. I. Brezhnev, *Leninskim kursom, Rechi i Stati*, pp. 256–57.

[17] Reported by Michel Tatu in *Le Monde*, May 5–6, 1968, and *Literární listy*, May 9 and 30, 1968. *Literární listy* of May 30, 1968, also claimed that another Soviet general, said to be

events [here] cannot catch us unawares."[18] For anyone who failed to understand Konev's message, he repeated it in a speech to workers in Kladno, encouraging them to continue to strengthen militant proletarian traditions and promising that "we shall permit no one to break the fraternal ties binding our people."[19] Marshal Yakubovsky, too, was concerned about the need to combat imperialist subversion; and in an article written immediately prior to negotiations in Prague on the holding of joint WTO maneuvers, he stated his position: "The struggle against imperialist ideological subversion, the exposure of anti-Marxism and various types of anti-socialist elements, untiring work, and the work of strengthening the fraternal friendship and cooperation of the peoples and armies of the socialist states have acquired primary significance at the present time."[20]

The differences in the high command were, on the whole, less wide-ranging than those in the Politburo and the political leadership. There is no conclusive evidence that any military leader actually resisted the decision to invade, apart possibly from the Warsaw Pact's Chief of Staff, M. I. Kazakov, who was replaced by General S. M. Shtemenko on August 5. Even Grechko, although unwilling to pass judgment on the political aspects of the reform movement, was nevertheless devoted to a buildup of Soviet military strength on the Czech border with the Federal Republic. The repeated failure of negotiations on this subject and the documents from the Gottwald Military Academy calling for an independent Czechoslovak military strategy may have been quite sufficient to put Grechko into the interventionist camp.

CRISIS COMPONENTS

Brecher gives the following definition of the crisis period:

> The *crisis period* is characterized by the presence of all three necessary conditions of crisis—a sharp rise in perceived threat to basic values, an awareness of time constraints on decisions, and an image of the probability of involvement in military hostilities (war likelihood) at some point before the issue is resolved. It, too, begins with a trigger event (or cluster of events).[21]

General Zhadov (the man rumored to have issued a diplomatic passport to Šejna), made a similar promise on May 21 during a visit to Czech army barracks.

[18] Konev's speech was carried on Prague radio's home service, May 9, 1968, EE/2767/C/3 (emphasis added).

[19] Moscow radio home service, May 13, 1968, SU/2769/A2/1.

[20] *Pravda*, May 14, 1968.

[21] Michael Brecher, *Decisions in Crisis*, p. 23.

A cluster of events at the end of April and beginning of May served as the source of the crisis period. In Czechoslovakia, the calls for the early convocation of an Extraordinary Fourteenth Party Congress, the increase in press attacks on the USSR and socialist practices under Novotný, the refusal to hold full-scale spring maneuvers on Czechoslovak soil, and the spontaneous demonstrations and speeches celebrating May Day had all contributed to a heightened perception of threat to basic values in Moscow. The essential failure of the May 4 Soviet-Czechoslovak summit in Moscow to allay these fears acted as the particular trip-wire for the escalation to the crisis period.

From early May onward, the probability of involvement in military hostilities perceptibly increased. There were two main military contingencies that appear to have been developed more or less simultaneously in Moscow. The first was to use the presence of Soviet troops already in Czechoslovakia for maneuvers to support conservative elements in their attempts to stage a comeback. This option was favored until the end of July, when the Soviet leadership had to agree to the almost total withdrawal of troops as a concession to Dubček in return for his own commitment to contain antisocialist forces. The second contingency, a full-scale invasion, then gained preeminence in Soviet preparations. The plan allowed for support by conservative elements in Czechoslovakia but was not dependent on it.

Time pressure was manifest during the crisis period at several crucial points. The first such point, during Phase One, involved Soviet concern that the CPCz plenum scheduled to convene in the last days of May would be used to rout remaining conservative forces. The precipitant and unannounced breaching of the Czechoslovak border by Soviet troops well in advance of the start of the June maneuvers was planned to coincide with the CPCz plenum and reflected Soviet awareness that time was of the essence if the collapse of conservative forces was to be prevented. But the plenum committed the CPCz to a fight against antisocialist forces; and as Brezhnev later admitted, although the Soviet leadership initially had considered a military solution in May, "then it seemed that this would not be necessary. The first swallow appeared—the plenary session of the Central Committee of the CPCz."[22]

Soviet leaders had learned by the end of May that the CPCz leadership was going to convene a party congress on September 9,

[22] Mlynář, *Nachtfrost*, p. 206.

but during the low-stress Phase Two (June 6–27) this did not create particular concern; for, as *Pravda* later stated, it had initially been hoped that "the Praesidium of the CPCz Central Committee would use the preparations for the Extraordinary Party Congress, scheduled for September 9, to put an end to the defamation of cadres."[23]

At the end of June the publication of the "2,000 Words" convinced Moscow that the Dubček leadership was not going to take decisive measures against antisocialist elements, and the Soviets realized that the deadline for action was not September 9 but August 26, the date of the Slovak congress, when Bil'ak and other leading conservatives would almost certainly lose their posts. With this realization, and the publication of the "2,000 Words," Phase Three began, and time pressure once again was acute. Evidence presented in chapter 8 suggested that the Soviets came very close to a military solution at the end of July. When the decision was made to give negotiations one final chance, they warned Prague that the threat to socialism in Czechoslovakia had intensified and that therefore "there is no time to lose."[24]

Phase Four represented the short remission of the Čierna and Bratislava negotiations, but clearly it was not long before Soviet leaders decided that the negotiations had failed to resolve such fundamental issues as the future of pro-Moscow conservatives and the direction of political change as a whole, both of which were still to be decided when the Slovak Congress (August 26) and the Fourteenth Party Congress (September 9) convened. Phase Five, therefore, saw a dramatic increase in the salience of time; and the increased time pressure did ultimately force the leadership to make the decision to invade. Without such pressure they probably would have put off the decision almost indefinitely.

COPING MECHANISMS

Information

It is undoubtedly true that the Soviet leaders fundamentally overestimated both the strength of conservative opinion in Czechoslovakia and the likelihood that pro-Moscow elements within the leadership would openly appeal for military assistance and thereby legitimize the invasion. The inclination to perceive the working

[23] *Pravda*, August 22, 1968.
[24] *Pravda*, July 28, 1968.

class, the Communist party, and organizations such as the People's Militia as unswervingly pro-Soviet in their orientation was a constant feature of the Soviet ideological outlook. The conviction that any anti-Soviet manifestations were therefore the result of imperialist subversion and not symptomatic of intrinsic weaknesses either in Soviet-style socialism or in Soviet alliance management was equally characteristic of the Soviet attitude. The escalation of the crisis in Czechoslovakia served to reinforce these preexisting perceptions and misperceptions, but it was not responsible for creating them. Thus one must conclude that Soviet cognitive performance was not in essence the product of crisis-induced stress.

Cognitive performance definitely was affected by previous crisis experience, however. Until the end of July, there was a tendency for Soviet statements to compare the events in Czechoslovakia with those in Hungary in 1956. Since there was no armed insurrection and no bloodshed in Czechoslovakia, it was argued, there was no counterrevolution. But by August, the influence of the Hungarian experience had diminished, and with that diminution a mental barrier to invasion was removed.[25]

The crisis also had a discernible effect on the perceived need, and consequent quest, for information. This need was most apparent during the three high-stress phases of the crisis period: Phase One (May 5–June 6), Phase Three (June 27–July 28), and Phase Five (August 5–20). The quest for information is reflected to some degree by the number of negotiations Moscow conducted during the crisis period. Of the thirty-three negotiating sessions, thirteen were in Phase One, four in Phase Two, eight in Phase Three, two in Phase Four, and six in Phase Five. Of course, not all delegations were sent to gather information, and indeed this objective decreased as the crisis escalated. In particular, none of the negotiations in Phases Four or Five—that is, those after Čierna—was devoted to obtaining further information about the situation in Prague. Before that time, however, Moscow had been concerned about the need for further information. Brezhnev had even apologized to Smrkovský during their June 14 meeting for previous negative assessments of Prague events, putting these down specifically to "lack of information."[26]

---

[25] *Izvestia* on July 31, 1968, for example, specifically warned against thinking that all counterrevolutions would be like Hungary in 1956.

[26] Josef Smrkovský, *An Unfinished Conversation*, p. 17.

The Czechoslovaks certainly believed that a key cause of the escalation of tensions was misinformation provided to Soviet authorities by their embassy in Prague. At the height of tensions in July, the Czechoslovak-Soviet Friendship Society in Prague passed a resolution stating that the major problems being experienced in bilateral relations were "the result of insufficient objective information."[27] Dubček, too, put much of the blame for Moscow's miscalculations of the threat imposed by the Prague Spring on distorted information. As he was to write in 1974: "I still cannot believe how our allies could receive and believe obviously twisted and nonobjective information about the solution we planned for the internal troubles of our party and country."[28]

Responsible for initially receiving and processing this information was the Soviet embassy in Prague. Moscow increased its staff in the Prague embassy throughout the crisis period, recruiting more interpreters and translators to maintain contact with pro-Moscow elements (something which Dubček repeatedly objected to) and to monitor the Czechoslovak media more fully. Similarly in the Soviet Union, Slavists with a knowledge of Czech were seconded to the government from the universities for the same purpose.[29] A Soviet citizen living in Prague who worked as a translator and interpreter revealed that throughout the summer "Soviet embassy officials displayed a lively interest in everything printed in Czechoslovakia" but that the material they selected for translating was heavily biased in that it exaggerated the dangers of antisocialist activities.[30] There is some indication that following the invasion several of the Soviet leaders appreciated the extent to which they had been misinformed about the situation in Czechoslovakia. Chervonenko in particular was reported to have been criticized (some say that Suslov was especially critical)[31] for overreliance on leaders who were about to be purged and who therefore had a personal stake in exaggerating the crisis.[32]

Information was transmitted directly to Moscow, and it reached the very highest decision makers in a "raw" state. The Czechoslovak delegation at Čierna recalled Brezhnev laboriously wading through

---

[27] Prague Radio, July 20, 1968, EE/2828/C1/2.
[28] Dubček's letter to Smrkovský's widow, *The Guardian*, March 14, 1974.
[29] As attested to by Larisa Sil'nitskaya, "Recollections of Bratislava."
[30] Ibid.
[31] *Christian Science Monitor* (London edition), October 3, 1968.
[32] *Daily Express*, September 9, 1968; *The Guardian*, September 3, 1968.

a thick pile of press clippings, some translated from Czech and Slovak papers, others from Western publications. Several sources have maintained that in the Soviet system there is a greater tendency than in the West for raw data on critical issues to reach the highest Politburo level without much previous filtering or digesting.[33] This certainly happened throughout the crisis period in 1968, beginning at the end of the pre-crisis period and lasting at least up to early August when the Soviet leadership dispersed on holidays. Also during July—during the high-stress Phase Three of the crisis, when rumors abounded of an imminent Soviet invasion—receptivity to new information was noticeably increased. In May, during Phase One, Moscow had concentrated its efforts on finding out as much as possible about events *within* Czechoslovakia, but in July the focus of Soviet information gathering was considerably widened. At this time Moscow was trying to assess possible international reactions to a Soviet invasion, and as a result the leadership's receptivity to new information was at its highest.[34] After Čierna and Bratislava, however, in Phase Five, when the Soviet leaders dispersed on their holidays, both the quest for information and the receptivity of the leadership to that information were at a low.

Consultation

There were three main groups consulted during the crisis period: the East European leaders; the military; and the party Central Committee, both as an *apparat* and as a plenary organization.

The entire management of the crisis, from the pre-crisis to the post-crisis period, involved East European leaders. This involvement was in part sought by the Soviet leaders and in part forced on them by East Europeans seeking participation. It was greatest during the crisis period and led to numerous multilateral and bilateral meetings.

The military high command was also very much involved in the consultative process throughout the development of the crisis, but, as with the East European leaders, its participation was most

[33] See chapter 14.

[34] As Richard Crossman reveals in his *Diaries of a Cabinet Minister* (p. 150), he learned that at the end of July the Soviet ambassador had called on the British foreign secretary on some pretext but in fact to discuss Western reactions to a possible invasion of Czechoslovakia. As Crossman states, "I found out later that the Russians had given their ambassadors in every capital instructions to make an identical approach in order to test Western reactions."

marked during the crisis period per se. From the beginning of the crisis period the military constituted an active pressure group seeking the achievement of specific objectives: the holding of maneuvers in Czechoslovakia and the permanent stationing of troops near Prague's border with the Federal Republic. Certainly the salience of military objectives and preparations for invasion was at its peak during the high-stress phases (One, Three, and Five), and therefore the importance of military advice increased concomitantly in these periods, reaching its peak in Phase Five. There was clearly a high level of participation by military leaders (Grechko, Yepishev, Yakubovsky, Shtemenko, Konev, Zakharov, and Koshevoi being foremost) in negotiations and in public debate on Czechoslovakia. Indeed such was the importance of military issues in the Soviet perception and handling of the crisis that individual military leaders were on several occasions actively involved in decision-making as such rather than as part of a more passive consultative process.

The third major group involved in the consultative process was the second echelon of the party. This group was amorphous and itself divided into numerous and conflicting factions grouped around departments or individuals. Much data has been presented in the various chapters of the crisis period about the activities of the second-echelon party secretaries who, on the whole, acted as advocates of a hard line against ideological subversion at home and abroad. The leadership was obliged to consult them, although the absence of a Central Committee plenum following the Čierna and Bratislava compromises was one indication that formal consultation with this group decreased after reaching its peak in Phase Three. Informal and ad hoc consultation continued, however, and evidence presented in chapter 10 indicates that it reached a high point immediately prior to the invasion.

Decisional Forums

The data on decisional forums has already been presented in the first two sections of this chapter, but briefly they can be summarized as follows. The basic unit throughout the crisis period remained the Politburo, which occasionally was enlarged to include representation of military and other (notably Gromyko's) views, presumably on a nonvoting basis. An inner core within the Politburo, consisting of Brezhnev, Kosygin, Podgorny, Suslov, and Shelest, was active in the management of the crisis, with Brezhnev's level of involvement particularly high and increasing in Phase Five. Although there was evidence of a high level of participation by Kosygin, his obvious opposition to a military solution meant that attempts were made, sometimes successfully, to exclude him from the decision-making process or at least to diminish his influence. On the whole, disunity within the decision-making group was most marked in public during July, that is during the high-stress Phase Three. Yet there is ample indication that even if the formal Politburo vote of August 17 (*decision 46*) to invade Czechoslovakia was unanimous, several leaders had deeply felt and long-lasting misgivings about the decision. It cannot, therefore, be concluded that the cohesiveness of the Politburo increased dramatically as the crisis escalated.

Consideration of Alternatives

Examination of the Soviet decisions reveals that the search for and evaluation of alternatives was highest in Phases One and Two. This process gradually decreased until by the middle of Phase Three, after the Warsaw meeting, there were really only two alternatives that were being seriously considered: that the Dubček leadership be convinced through negotiation to put its own house in order; or that the five aligned bloc members employ military means. Before that time, various alternatives had been explored: political exhortations and pressure, positive and negative economic incentives, the permanent stationing of troops as a limited and sufficient objective; the use of these troops to support a comeback by Czechoslovak conservative elements; and the disposition of Pact troops in and around Czechoslovakia as a form of minatory diplomacy designed to warn Prague of the consequences of inaction against anti-socialist elements. These alternatives as well as the use of third-party intermediaries ranging from Ulbricht to Kádár to Rochet to Tito were all employed without effect. Dubček's failure to implement the Čierna and Bratislava agreements in a manner consistent with Soviet perception represented the final exhaustion of alternatives, and except for last-minute appeals by Brezhnev and Kádár, Phase Five saw a marked diminution in the search for alternatives.

The military details of the plan were minutely calculated, as will be discussed in the next chapter. Overwhelming force was used to cover every conceivable contingency. On the political level, the invasion plan envisaged the smooth transfer of power from Dubček and the CPCz Praesidium to a revolutionary workers' and peasants'

government formed, according to Soviet calculations, from a majority of the existing Praesidium and from other key government
functionaries. The major tasks of the new government would be
not only to request, and therefore legitimize, fraternal assistance
but also to carry out all the administrative measures—arrests,
purges, censorship, and so on—necessary to start Czechoslovakia
on the long road to "normalization." All indications are that at the
political level the Soviets had not established alternative plans
should the revolutionary workers' and peasants' government collapse or not be formed. And of course, it was this lack of contingency planning that caused a near catastrophe when the political
side of the invasion went woefully astray.

PART FOUR

The
Post-Crisis
Period

CHAPTER TWELVE

August 20–27

THE INVASION PLAN

It is generally recognized that the invasion was a military success. During the night of Tuesday, August 20–21, using a combination of air and road approaches, the Soviets mounted an impressive combined arms operation which put upwards of twenty front-line divisions from five Warsaw Pact countries into Czechoslovakia in a matter of hours.

Beginning at 2300 Central European time, 1:00 A.M. Moscow time, units of the Twenty-fourth Soviet Tactical Air Army took control of Prague's Ruzyně airport and other airports throughout the country and guided in hundreds of tank- and troop-carrying Antonovs. By this time, the ground operation was well under way. Four Soviet tank divisions and one East German division moved to occupy Karlovy Vary, Plzeň, and Usti nad Labem and to seal the Czechoslovak border with West Germany. Five more Soviet divisions, accompanied by one East German division, encircled Prague and established the headquarters for General Ivan Pavlovsky, Soviet deputy defense minister and commander of Soviet ground forces, who was to take charge of all occupation forces in Czechoslovakia. Polish troops also moved across their border with Czechoslovakia to occupy positions alongside Soviet soldiers, in Ostrava and other cities in Eastern Bohemia, Northern Moravia, and Central Slovakia. Four Russian divisions rolled from the military district in Transcarpathia into Eastern Slovakia, taking Košice, while Soviet, Hungarian, and Bulgarian troops breached the southern border to occupy Bratislava, Brno, and the remainder of Central and Western Slovakia and Southern Moravia. By the morning of

Wednesday August 21, the country's road and communications network was in their hands. The Czechoslovak army had been neutralized, although it never appeared that organized military resistance was contemplated. All the purely military objectives had been achieved.[1] Now it remained to transform military power into political control, and in this process the invasion plan proved to be most perilously deficient.

All the major accounts of the political aspects of the invasion agree that the Soviets appear to have had the following intentions: A majority of the CPCz Praesidium, which was meeting at the time the troops started invading, would back a call for immediate fraternal assistance to put down the threat of counterrevolution; and this majority, combined with other leading state and party officials, the most crucial being the president of the republic, would constitute a revolutionary workers' and peasants' government and would begin work on purging the party and state apparatus of reformist elements. The invasion, therefore, was to have been legitimized by Czechoslovak leaders themselves who would also be responsible for taking the various "administrative measures" required. As far as the attitude of the population was concerned, the sheer number of military personnel involved suggests that the Soviet High Command was taking no chances should there be pockets of resistance. At the same time, they clearly expected a tidy and speedy transfer of power within Czechoslovakia and were not particularly well equipped to cope with the passive resistance and general collapse of authority that in fact occurred.

THE COLLAPSE OF THE INVASION PLAN

Zdeněk Mlynář reveals that a group of full and candidate members of the CPCz Praesidium "chiefly consisting of Bil'ak, Indra, Kolder and Jakeš, but to which Švestka, Piller, Lenárt and Kapek also belonged (and which counted on the support of Rigo, Barbírek and perhaps even Voleník), promised the Kremlin that they would engineer a domestic political justification for legalizing the inter-

---

[1] Military details are derived from *Sunday Telegraph* (Gordon Brook-Shepherd and David Floyd) October 20, 1968; Otto von Pivka, *Armies of Europe Today*, pp. 91–92; Philip Windsor and Adam Roberts, *Czechoslovakia 1968*, pp. 107–9; Erickson in V. V. Kusin, ed., *Czechoslovak Reform Movement 1968*, p. 31; *Frankfurter Allgemeine Zeitung*, August 26, 1968; and *New York Times*, September 10, 1968.

vention."[2] The group agreed at a meeting on the morning of August 20 that at the Praesidium meeting that afternoon they would use the memorandum prepared by Kolder and Indra on the so-called Kašpar report as a vehicle for passing a negative assessment of developments in the country that then could be used as the basis for legitimizing the intervention.

The meeting began at two o'clock that afternoon under the chairmanship of Dubček, and immediately the members of the Praesidium got involved in a lengthy procedural wrangle over which item to take up first on the agenda. The collaborationists obviously wanted to discuss the Kolder-Indra memorandum first, but they were defeated by those, including Dubček, who felt that the preparations for the upcoming Fourteenth Party Congress should be taken up first. Most accounts suggest that Dubček did not suspect a link between the Kolder-Indra memorandum and the intervention. What he did suspect was that this position paper would lead to a discussion of the letter he had received from Brezhnev only the day before, the existence and contents of which still had not formally been made known to the Praesidium. Any debate over the Brezhnev letter would have split the leadership, with the collaborationists possibly using any Praesidium reply as a de facto request for fraternal assistance.[3] Although a majority would not have issued an open request for armed intervention, the collaborationists still hoped to muster a majority in the Praesidium for a resolution supporting a negative assessment of the situation in Czechoslovakia. They could then have used the authority conferred on them by the majority vote to mobilize co-conspirators in the state organs, such as Oldřich Pavlovský, Šalgovič, Sulek, and Karel Hoffmann, to issue an open request for assistance. After this, with the arrival of the armies, a revolutionary workers' and peasants' government under the leadership of Indra would be formed; and its "revolutionary tribunal" would swing into action.[4]

The first act of a revolutionary workers' and peasants' government was to have been the signing of an appeal legitimizing fraternal assistance. One of Mlynář's many interesting revelations is that

[2] Zdeněk Mlynář, *Night Frost in Prague*, p. 201.

[3] Mlynář, *Night Frost*, pp. 202–3; Moravus, "Shawcross's Dubček—A Different Dubček," p. 210.

[4] Mlynář, *Night Frost*, p. 202; Jiří Ruml, Czechoslovak Radio, August 26, 1968, EE/2859/C/17; Josef Smrkovský, *An Unfinished Conversation*, pp. 23–28; Tad Szulc, *Czechoslovakia Since World War II*, pp. 367–68, 372–73.

"a Czech version of the unsigned request published in the Moscow *Pravda* on August 21, 1968 and purporting to come from 'party and government leaders' actually existed in Prague in those days."[5] It was unsigned but was to have been issued in the name of the new revolutionary workers' and peasants' government. It becomes immediately apparent, therefore, that the entire success of the political cal aspect of the Soviet invasion plan depended upon the formation of this new government. It was to have emerged out of the Praesidium meeting, but this part of the plan went wrong from the very beginning.

As it happened, the discussion of the Kolder-Indra memorandum had not been completed by the time the Praesidium received the news that Warsaw Pact troops were breaching Czechoslovak frontiers. In response to this news, the Praesidium passed (by a 7 to 4 vote) a resolution condemning the invasion and appealing for calm.[6] Only then was the Brezhnev letter discussed, but by this time the collaborationists had lost courage to challenge Dubček openly; and the meeting was adjourned in disarray.

Nevertheless, for another forty-eight hours the collaborationists and the Soviets kept to the plan to form a revolutionary workers' and peasants' government. By the morning of Wednesday, August 21, troops had surrounded all the key party, government, and media buildings in Prague, but no initial effort was made to displace Czechoslovak authorities, thereby giving them valuable time to organize passive resistance. Then at 8:00 A.M., Dubček, Černík, Smrkovský, Kriegel, Špaček, and Šimon were arrested by Soviet soldiers and Czechoslovak state security agents in the name of a revolutionary tribunal headed by Comrade Indra. All of these men were interned in KGB camps in the Soviet Carpathian mountains.

From the afternoon of August 21 through August 22 efforts were made both at the Hotel Praha and at the Soviet embassy to form a quisling government. These efforts failed for several reasons. First, the collaborationists had not succeeded in asserting complete control over the media. Although the minister of communications (Karel Hoffmann), the head of the Czechoslovak press agency (Miroslav Sulek), and the editor of *Rudé právo* (Oldřich Švestka) could all be included among the agents working for the Soviet

---

[5] Mlynář, *Night Frost*, p. 202.

[6] Both Smrkovský (*An Unfinished Conversation*, p. 24) and Švestka (*Rudé právo*, August 21, 1969) concur that Bil'ak, Kolder, Rigo, and Švestka voted against. Indra and Sádovský, both nonvoting secretaries, were also opposed.

Union in Prague, immediate action by Smrkovský assured that the collaborationists' appeal for assistance was not broadcast or published in the press. Instead the broadest possible publicity was given to the Praesidium resolution condemning the invasion. Also, quick action by Czech radio station operators and announcers using auxiliary equipment—provided in some cases by the Czechoslovak army—and alternative wavelengths allowed the continuation of news condemning the invasion, a situation that the invading forces did not expect and therefore did not come prepared for. From the very beginning, efforts to form a new government were doomed because anyone willing to participate was immediately identified as a Soviet agent and quisling, particularly as such efforts were accompanied by the arrest and subsequent disappearance of Dubček and other popular leaders, whose release became the focus of the population's resistance.

The Soviets did not foresee the success of mobile radio units, but they did of course plan a serious propaganda campaign that combined the distribution of leaflets and the beaming of pro-Soviet information into Czechoslovakia, including Radio Vltava, which broadcast in Czech and Slovak from Karl-Marx-Stadt in East Germany. Radio Vltava began transmitting the TASS statement on the invasion as early as 5:40 A.M. on August 21.

On August 21, Bil'ak was "elected" by pro-Soviet elements in the Central Committee to enter into negotiations with General Pavlovsky, the commander of the occupying armies. The following day a meeting was convened by Bil'ak at which eleven of the twenty-two party leaders were present. Bil'ak stated that a precondition for the settlement of the crisis was that the group "declare itself competent to enter into negotiations 'at the highest level.'"[7] This they agreed to do, but only on condition that under no circumstances should there be any negotiations with the military authorities; instead the remaining leadership was to contact Ambassador Chervonenko with a view to negotiating directly with Brezhnev for the release of Dubček and the other five imprisoned leaders.

The group made its way to the Soviet embassy, but Chervonenko informed them that there was no possibility of contacting Brezhnev and that instead they should get down to the business of constituting themselves a revolutionary workers' and peasants' govern-

[7] Mlynář, *Night Frost*, p. 189.

ment. Chervonenko's whole attitude suggests that having been instrumental in convincing the Kremlin that the conservatives within the Czechoslovak leadership were willing and ready to welcome fraternal assistance and form a new government, he was clearly under some pressure to produce the goods.

These discussions at the Soviet embassy took place at the same time that delegates to the Extraordinary Fourteenth Party Congress, originally scheduled to meet on September 9, were in fact assembling in a factory in Prague's Vysočany suburb. They constituted themselves a formal meeting of the CPCz Congress and elected a Working Praesidium that included all the leaders currently incarcerated by the occupation forces and excluded Indra, Bil'ak, Kolder, and all the collaborationists.[8] Although the delegates had made their way to the factory in some secrecy, the proceedings were in fact broadcast live on the radio and were heard inside the Soviet embassy, where the Indra group was meeting. The congress, which according to party rules is the highest body of the party, was electing a new Praesidium and a new Central Committee from which anyone rumored to be collaborating with the occupying forces was excluded. An Extraordinary National Assembly was also convened to oppose the invasion and any collaboration. This situation the Soviet authorities clearly had not anticipated, and they were ill prepared to deal with it. Not only was it going to be far more difficult to get the Czechoslovak leaders still at liberty to agree to form a revolutionary workers' and peasants' government, but such a government would very obviously be contrary to the wishes of the highest party and government bodies.

The only hope for Moscow and the collaborationists was that President Svoboda would use his position as the highest constitutional authority of the state to legitimize the formation of such a government. This he flatly refused to do, telling the Praesidium delegation when they arrived from the Soviet embassy, "If I were to do anything of the sort, the nation would have to drive me out of this Castle like a mangy dog."[9] Rather, he informed the delegation that he would go to Moscow along with Husák, Dzúr, Kučera, and three other Praesidium members (Bil'ak, Indra, and Piller were

[8] The list is given in the transcript of the taped proceedings of the Extraordinary Fourteenth Congress on August 22, 1968, in Jiří Pelikán, ed., *The Secret Vysočany Congress*, p. 18.

[9] Mlynář, *Night Frost*, p. 196.

eventually chosen) to negotiate the release of Dubček, Černík, Smrkovský, and the others. As Mlynář reports this, Svoboda told the Praesidium delegation that prior to their arrival at the Castle he had informed Chervonenko that "this was the only course of action he would consider, and now the matter had been decided and he would fly the next morning."[10] Thus the collapse of collaborationist attempts to form a government, the widespread passive resistance, the convening of the Vysočany congress, and the attitude of President Svoboda all worked to force the Soviet leadership to scrap their initial plans and evolve an alternative strategy for overcoming the political impasse in Prague.

THE VIEW FROM MOSCOW

From the very beginning, Moscow's behavior indicated that the Soviet leaders had not evolved any alternative political strategy should their original plan collapse. When the revolutionary workers' and peasants' government failed to materialize in the course of August 20–21, Soviet authorities were faced with a critical dilemma: should they drop any pretense of an invitation for assistance, or should they go ahead and issue the previously drafted appeal, hoping that although it was currently unsigned a new government in Prague—surely soon to be formed—would accept responsibility for the appeal ex post facto. The August 21 issue of *Pravda*, which presumably would have carried the signed appeal, was delayed hours in its publication—a most unusual occurrence. When it appeared, it contained only a TASS dispatch stating that unidentified "party and government leaders" in Czechoslovakia had requested urgent assistance, but it carried no names and did not even claim the authority of the illusory revolutionary workers' and peasants' government. Then, on August 22, only twenty-four hours later, the Soviet authorities decided to go ahead with the full publication in *Pravda* of the famous "Appeal by a Group of Members of the CPCz Central Committee and the ČSSR Government and National Assembly." Since it is now known that this appeal existed in the Czech language prior to the invasion, the delay in its publication can almost certainly be attributed to the failure of its authors to form themselves into an alternative political authority.

[10] Ibid., 196–97.

That the appeal was published at all, however, reflects continued, if short-lived, Soviet hopes that their embassy in Prague would succeed in forming a new government.

The appeal called on "all citizens to give all possible support to the military units of our allies" who would withdraw "after the danger of a reactionary coup is liquidated." Without singling anyone out, the appeal claimed that rightists, supported by "certain forces within the party and in party bodies" had taken the post-January reforms beyond their constitutional limits and had organized a "disgusting campaign" aimed at slandering and persecuting honest Communists, including many within the CPCz leadership. They had "activated base nationalist passions," and "their filthy campaign even went so far as to attack the alliance with the Soviet Union, especially in connection with the staff training exercises of the Warsaw Pact armed forces." The 2,500-word appeal had obviously been carefully prepared in advance for the widest circulation in Czechoslovakia, the Communist bloc, and the outside world. As with Hungary in 1956, an invitation by recognized and known Czechoslovak authorities would have carried some weight and would have deflected criticism both within the Communist world and in the West, and it could possibly have resigned the Czechoslovak population at large to the inevitable.

A similar purpose was to be served by the lengthy *Pravda* editorial entitled "Defense of Socialism Is the Highest Internationalist Duty," which also appeared on the morning of August 22. It again made only general reference to unnamed "party and state leaders" who had "requested immediate assistance, including assistance with armed forces." But it did specifically condemn Alexander Dubček, by now of course under arrest, for being at the head of "a minority of Praesidium members" who "took overtly right-wing opportunist stands." This was the first direct attack on Dubček in the Soviet press since he had become first secretary in January, and it reflected the Soviet preinvasion calculation that his political career was over. The editorial stated that this group of "right-wing revisionist elements among the leadership of the Communist party and the government of Czechoslovakia thwarted fulfillment of the understanding reached in Čierna nad Tisou and Bratislava . . . [and] were in reality attempting only to gain time, while pandering to counterrevolution. As a result of their perfidious, treacherous actions," *Pravda* continued, "a real threat arose to the socialist gains of Czechoslovakia." This was very strong, and it amply reflected the Soviet assumption that by the time the *Pravda* editorial appeared, those described in this way would have been replaced by other Czechoslovak leaders who represented the majority and who had "adopted a principled line and affirmed the necessity of waging a resolute struggle against the reactionary antisocialist forces."

By August 23, however, Alexander Dubček and the other leaders who had adopted these "right-wing opportunist positions" were moved to Moscow to negotiate the conditions of their own release and the solution of the crisis in Prague. Less than forty-eight hours after the invasion an alternative strategy had emerged in Moscow.

ALTERNATIVE STRATEGY

By the evening of August 22, the Soviet leadership was fully aware that a quisling government was not going to be formed and that in any case the leadership chosen at the Vysočany Congress would challenge the authority of any government that the Soviets succeeded in constructing. And without the constitutional authority of President Svoboda behind them, Soviet officials in Prague really stood no chance of success. Passive resistance was much aided by effective underground radio stations which the occupation forces could not immediately silence. On August 22 there was a one-hour general strike throughout Czechoslovakia, accompanied by massive, but largely peaceful, demonstrations in Prague and other cities. Clearly if Soviet leaders did not move quickly on the political front, they risked losing the military initiative, particularly in the light of concerted efforts by Czechoslovak civilians to demoralize occupying troops by arguing with them and depriving them of food and other supplies.

Most reports concur that the Soviets rejected from the outset any idea of establishing direct military rule in Prague. It has been suggested that this view was put across initially by Suslov, who argued against following the invasion with open repression and mass arrests. General Pavlovsky told his Czechoslovak counterparts that he was under strict orders not to interfere with or displace the civil and political authorities, and for this reason the National Assembly and the Fourteenth Party Congress were both allowed to convene with impunity.[11]

---

[11] *New York Times*, August 27, 1968, quoting authoritative sources close to the Moscow talks.

It would appear therefore that late on August 22, the Politburo took the decision (*number 48*) to negotiate directly with the existing Czechoslovak leadership. This decision is reflected in Svoboda's announcement to his other Praesidium colleagues, on their arrival at the Castle around eleven o'clock in the evening. Having failed to achieve anything constructive in his own talks with Chervonenko, he said, he had agreed to fly to Moscow the next morning at the head of a delegation to negotiate directly with the Soviet leaders for a solution to the crisis and the release of Dubček and the others.[12] Apparently, the Soviet leaders were looking beyond the opening round of the negotiations, because by the time Svoboda's plane landed at Moscow's Vnukovo airport, the decision had been made (*number 49*) to release Dubček and Černík. On the morning of Friday, August 23, Brezhnev telephoned Dubček; and Dubček and Černík were flown to Moscow from the KGB barracks in the Carpathian Mountains where they had been interned.[13] Smrkovský, Kriegel, Špaček, and Šimon remained isolated and in custody.

At the outset the Soviet leaders apparently tried to convince Svoboda of the need to form a new government, but Svoboda resolutely refused to negotiate as long as any of the Czechoslovak leaders were still imprisoned.[14] As a result, the Soviet leaders ultimately agreed (*decision 50*) to bring the rest of the imprisoned Czechoslovak leaders to Moscow and to treat them all as the formal representatives of the Czechoslovak party and state. No further efforts were made to form a revolutionary workers' and peasants' government. It would be Dubček and all the other leaders (with the exception of Kriegel, who was brought to Moscow but excluded from the negotiations until the very end) who would be obliged, or forced, to legitimize the intervention and "normalize" the situation.

This changed strategy, which emerged incrementally from August 22 to 25, can be attributed both to Svoboda's attitude and to the situation in Prague, above all the results emerging from the Fourteenth Party Congress. When Smrkovský, Šimon, and Špaček were brought to Moscow, they learned at first hand of Soviet plans and Czechoslovak developments. At the Central Committee build-

---

[12] Mlynář, *Night Frost*, pp. 196–97.

[13] Smrkovský, *An Unfinished Conversation*, p. 31, recounts this incident but implies it took place on August 22. Mlynář, *Night Frost*, p. 204, states that the telephone call was made on August 23, and this date is more consistent with subsequent events.

[14] *Sunday Times*, December 8, 1968.

ing, they met Brezhnev, Kosygin, and Podgorny; and as Smrkovský recounts:

> Comrade Brezhnev let fly: A terrible thing has happened and he started to tell us about the 14th Party Congress. . . .
>   So we heard from his lips that there was the 14th Congress, there was a strike, the nation had taken its stand against this business. And we also understood that there wasn't a new government. We learnt from them that they were taking us to the Kremlin for talks and then we would travel home. . . .
>   Comrade Brezhnev—and Kosygin—told me . . . that we must go home and liquidate the 14th Party Congress.[15]

They were then taken to the Kremlin to begin full-scale talks with Soviet leaders. By this time, on August 25, the Czechslovak delegation also included Mlynář, Husák, Švestka, Lenárt, Šimon, Barbírek, Rigo, and Jakeš. As Mlynář later concluded, the only course of action Moscow could take was negotiation with Dubček and all those who were supposed to have been sentenced for subversive and antisocialist activities by a revolutionary tribunal:

> Compelled to negotiate, Moscow had no one else to negotiate with in the end but the Dubček leadership. Its [Moscow's] agents had failed to carry off an internal putsch, and it was out of the question for Moscow to deal with the leadership elected by the Fourteenth Congress.[16]

THE PROTOCOL NEGOTIATIONS

By August 25 the Soviet Politburo had arrived at another decision (*number 51*): There would be no more gentlemen's agreements between Moscow and Prague, as at Čierna. Instead the two sides would sign a formal protocol setting out the specific measures the Czechoslovaks would have to undertake on the road to "normalization." Negotiations on the protocol began on August 25, with the exchange of drafts. The Czechoslovak draft was rejected out of hand almost immediately by the Soviet side. As a result the Soviet version became the basis for negotiations; and from this version the formal Moscow Protocol ultimately emerged.

The negotiations were ad hoc and unstructured until the final signing session, when Katushev, Ponomarev, Grechko, Gromyko, and the entire Soviet Politburo took part. An examination of the two firsthand accounts by Mlynář and Smrkovský reveals that until

---

[15] Smrkovský, *An Unfinished Conversation*, p. 32.
[16] Mlynář, *Night Frost*, p. 204.

the final session, Soviet positions were negotiated principally by Brezhnev, Kosygin, Podgorny, Suslov, and Ponomarev, either individually or in groups of twos, threes, or fours. Ponomarev appears to have acted as the funnel for proposals and counter-proposals from the Czechoslovak side to the Soviet side, with the other four Soviet leaders actively involved in the substantive negotiations. Smrkovský mentions that "when there were any particular matters, then four from the Soviet side and four of ours always met: Brezhnev, Kosygin, Podgorny, Suslov; and of ours, Dubček, Svoboda, Černík and myself." Yet there are numerous other references in both accounts to smaller and more informal meetings.

Since Moscow's purpose was not only to convince the Dubček leadership to sign the protocol but also to discern which figures might later be willing to cooperate with Moscow's aims, a lot of quiet and informal tête-à-têtes also took place. Apparently, Soviet leaders were aware that they would no longer be able to achieve their objectives through Indra, Bil'ak, Švestka, and the other openly pro-Moscow leaders. If the Czechoslovak population and the party were not going to resist implementation of the protocol, either Dubček and the other reform leaders would have to carry out the necessary measures themselves, or someone would have to be found whose reform credentials were acceptable but who was in fact willing to serve Moscow in order to stay in power. According to Mlynář, Soviet leaders had their eyes on Gustáv Husák from the very beginning. Indeed Kosygin remarked to Mlynář at the close of negotiations: "Comrade Husák is such a competent comrade and a wonderful Communist. We didn't know him personally before, but he quite impressed us here."[17]

When most of the detailed discussion on the protocol had been completed, the two sides met in full session. Brezhnev made some formal opening remarks to which Černík responded, as Dubček was in no fit emotional state to act as the head of his delegation. Following this, Dubček, ignoring procedural formalities, made an improvised and impassioned defense of the reform movement. Brezhnev responded with an equally improvised and impassioned defense of Soviet actions. He maintained that he had repeatedly supported Dubček within the Politburo: "I believed in you, and I stood up for you against the others. . . . Our Sasha is a good comrade, I said. And you disappointed us all so terribly."[18] The central

---

[17] Ibid., p. 221.
[18] Ibid., p. 239.

problem had been that Moscow, while supporting the post-January course, had gradually lost faith both in Dubček's ability or willingness to prevent "antisocialist tendencies" from growing and in their own ability to control the situation in Prague through various party and state mechanisms. As Mlynář states:

> Then Brezhnev explained to Dubček that the end result of all this was Moscow's realization that the Dubček leadership could not be depended upon. Even he himself, who had long defended "our Sasha," had to admit that this was so. Because, at this stage, matters of the utmost importance were involved: the results of the Second World War.[19]

And on those results, Brezhnev was unequivocal: The Second World War had established the borders of socialism up to the River Elbe; those borders had been established at great cost to the Soviet people; and as a consequence, "the results of the Second World War are inviolable, and we will defend them even at the cost of risking a new war."[20] Brezhnev also made it clear, however, that by the time Soviet leaders had decided to invade, there was very little risk either of a war or even of dangerous international political repercussions. As he told the Czechoslovaks: "So what do you think will be done on your behalf? Nothing. There will be no war. Comrade Tito and Comrade Ceaușescu will say their piece, and so will Comrade Berlinguer. Well, and what of it? You are counting on the Communist movement in Europe, but that won't amount to anything for fifty years."[21]

Instead of realizing the futility of the situation, Dubček began arguing with Brezhnev, at which the Soviet leader declared that the discussions were going nowhere, that they were all just a "repetition of Čierna," and that therefore the Soviets were breaking them off. At this point the entire Politburo rose and left the room. The rest of the Czechoslovak delegation pleaded with Dubček to sign the protocol; and after some time, he agreed. After that, the Soviets resumed the meeting, and both the protocol and the joint communiqué were duly signed by all the Czechoslovak leaders (except Kriegel) without serious disruption.

The main points of the protocol were the declaration that the Extraordinary Fourteenth Party Congress was invalid; the agreement to hold a Central Committee plenum to begin work on nor-

[19] Ibid.
[20] Ibid., p. 241.
[21] Ibid.

malization and to "discharge from their posts those individuals whose further activities would not conform to the needs of consolidating the leading role of the . . . party"; the need to reimpose strict control of the mass media; and a resolution to strengthen military and political cooperation between Czechoslovakia and other socialist countries. In foreign affairs, the Czechoslovaks agreed to coordinate their European policy with the rest of the socialist states and to protest the discussion of the "ČSSR problem" in the Security Council (Czechoslovak representatives at the United Nations had initially requested an urgent debate on the Soviet invasion). Soviet troops were to be withdrawn from urban centers as soon as possible, and "a treaty concerning the conditions of stay and complete removal of allied troops" was to be concluded in the near future. The question of the permanent stationing of troops and the security of Czechoslovakia's border with the Federal Republic was to be the subject of a special study.

With the signing of the protocol, the two sides concluded their negotiations. Following a short period of informal discussion, in which the Czechoslovak side refused to meet the other East European leaders who, it transpired, were also in the Kremlin,[22] the Czechoslovaks were driven to the airport for their return to Prague. The only last-minute hitch occurred when it became known that Soviet leaders intended to keep Kriegel imprisoned in Moscow. After the delegation refused to leave Soviet territory without him, he was duly delivered to the plane.

The signing of the Moscow Protocol brought the post-crisis period to an end; and the Soviet leaders resumed their holidays. The strategy was set for the period of normalization, which lasted until well beyond Dubček's removal the following spring. The outcome of the crisis in many ways had been unsatisfactory and uncertain for the Soviets. Yet they had achieved the capitulation of the Dubček leadership without undue loss of life and without unexpected or unacceptable international repercussions. The security of the borders of socialism had been safeguarded, and Soviet control of political life in Prague had been reasserted. The action cost them the loyalty of an entire generation of Czechoslovak citizens and of millions of reform-minded Communists, but in the end this cost counted for nothing.

[22] As confirmed by a *Pravda* communiqué on August 28, 1968. According to the *Morning Star*, August 26, 1968, the leaders of the other four invading states had arrived in Moscow on August 24.

CHAPTER THIRTEEN

Findings

DECISIONS

There were four major, closely interrelated decisions adopted in the post-crisis period:

Decision Number	Date	Content
48	August 22	The Politburo abandons its initial political strategy and decides to negotiate directly with the Czechoslovak leadership in Moscow.
49	August 23	The Politburo agrees to include Dubček and Černík in the negotiations.
50	August 23–24	The Politburo decides to bring all the imprisoned Czechoslovak leaders to Moscow and to treat them as the formal representatives of the Czechoslovak party and state.
51	August 24–25	The Politburo decides that the two sides must sign a formal protocol setting out the specific measures the Czechoslovaks would have to undertake on the "road to normalization."

PSYCHOLOGICAL ENVIRONMENT

The post-crisis period began with the invasion by Soviet-led forces on the night of August 20–21 and ended with the signing of the Moscow Protocol on August 27. During this period, no Soviet political leader made a public speech, wrote an article, or even issued a press statement. Hence there is no independent documentation that would allow the analyst to assess the psychological environment during this period. All that is available are the secondhand reports of Czechoslovak leaders who participated in the Moscow negotiations and who were themselves under considerable stress. In addition to these accounts, however, the analyst does have the hard facts of Soviet actions from which to infer changes in the psychological environment.

The single most important aspect of the post-crisis period was the sharp change in Soviet strategy some forty-eight hours after the intervention. Moscow clearly had calculated that Czechoslovak leaders loyal to the Soviet Union would issue an appeal for assistance and establish a new government, thus ensuring a smooth and rapid transfer of power. When this did not happen and when popular resistance took an unforeseen form, Moscow changed its strategy.

Although Moscow's course shifted from military imposition to negotiated imposition, Soviet views showed little sign of change. The invasion's failure to spur conservative Czechoslovak leaders to take power in order to "end the drift toward counterrevolution" did not alter the Soviet conviction that the absolute cessation of all antisocialist acts was still the object of intervention. If Bil'ak, Indra, and the others could not or would not form an alternative government to carry out the necessary measures, then those very leaders whom the collaborationists had originally sought to displace would be restored, provided they served Soviet long-term goals. As Ponomarev pointedly told Smrkovský when the latter protested that the Soviet draft of the Moscow protocol was unacceptable, "If you don't sign now, you'll sign in a week. If not in a week, then in a fortnight and if not in a fortnight, then in a month."[1] The change in Soviet behavior after the first forty-eight hours was not, therefore, the result of any reassessment of their basic attitude toward the Prague Spring, but merely a shift in tactics.

CRISIS COMPONENTS

Brecher defines the post-crisis period as follows:

> The *post-crisis* period begins with an observable decline in intensity of one or more of the three perceptual conditions—threat, time pressure, and war probability. If the onset of this period is synonomous with the outbreak of war, the third condition is replaced by an image

[1] Josef Smrkovský, *An Unfinished Conversation*, p. 34.

of greater military capability vis-à-vis the enemy (or favorable changes in the military balance), i.e., declining threat.[2]

It is clear that the relative success of the purely military aspects of the invasion and the absence of any Western military response did produce an immediate perception of declining threat. Furthermore, popular resistance, although widespread, was passive, and this also reduced the likelihood of any military action beyond the maintenance of law and order.

Nevertheless, the inability of the Soviets to form an alternative government continued seriously to threaten achievement of their objectives. The convening of the Extraordinary Fourteenth Party Congress and the election of a Central Committee committed to the continuation of the reform movement posed a particular problem for Moscow. Not only did it heighten the perception of threat, but it also increased the salience of time. Once it had become clear that the congress had indeed met and elected a new Central Committee, Moscow quickly had to produce a political formula that would prevent the new committee from consolidating its position. This was the change in the Czechoslovak situation that spurred the Soviets to negotiate directly with Dubček and those other leaders whom they had originally planned to displace. And although Ponomarev could tell the Czechoslovak delegation that the Soviets were prepared to wait a month if need be for the signing of the protocol, Moscow lost ground in Prague with every day that the negotiations continued.

According to Brecher,

> The post-crisis period (and the entire crisis) may be said to terminate when the intensity of relevant perceptions has returned to noncrisis norms. If, during the post-crisis period of Crisis A, threat perception re-escalates but with a differing focus, this indicates an emerging pre-crisis period of a new crisis.[3]

Once the Politburo had secured the signatures of the Czechoslovak delegation to the Moscow Protocol, the crisis as a whole came to an end. The outcome of the crisis was, however, highly uncertain and inconclusive; and in the months that followed, Soviet authorities had untold problems in gaining the compliance of the Dubček leadership to the Soviet interpretation of the protocol.

[2] Michael Brecher, *Decisions in Crisis*, p. 23.
[3] Ibid., p. 25.

COPING MECHANISMS

Information

Information search was enhanced with the invasion. The physical presence of Soviet troops and security officers throughout the country, the efforts at the Soviet embassy to form a revolutionary workers' and peasants' government, and the detention of most of the CPCz Praesidium greatly improved Moscow's control over events in Prague and concomitantly enhanced the quality of information seeking. Hence the cognitive performance of the Soviet decision makers also improved. Of course, the continuation of passive resistance and the convening of the Vysočany Congress certainly had an adverse effect, particularly on the perceived need and consequent quest for information. Despite, for example, the massive input of data Moscow must have been receiving daily about the situation in Prague, the Soviet leadership was in the dark about many aspects of the Vysočany Congress. Smrkovský recounts that during his first encounter with Soviet leaders in Moscow after the invasion, Brezhnev kept asking, "What's Shilgan?" He was referring to Věnek Šilhán, the professor of economics appointed by the Vysočany Congress to deputize for Dubček in the latter's absence.[4]

Consultative and Decisional Forums

The two key consultative units, the East European leadership and the Soviet military, both remained active during the post-crisis period. East European leaders were present in Moscow for the signing of the Moscow Protocol although they never participated in direct negotiations with the Czechoslovaks. Having arrived in the capital on August 24, however, they were obviously very active in the Soviet negotiations even though they never sat across the table from the Czechoslovak delegation. Nothing is known of their input, however. The military, too, were highly involved in consulting with the leadership and providing information and advice; but although Grechko was present at the final signing of the protocol, no military leader participated directly in negotiations with the Czechoslovaks in Moscow.

As for decisional forums, it would appear that although the basic decisional unit remained the Politburo, an inner core consisting of Brezhnev, Kosygin, Suslov, Podgorny, and Ponomarev did emerge

[4]Smrkovský, *An Unfinished Conversation*, p. 32.

in the negotiations with the Czechoslovak leadership. They operated either individually or in small groups, with Brezhnev the principal actor and Ponomarev the conduit for proposals between the two sides. There is no real evidence that the Soviet leadership was not cohesive during this period, and indeed the Czechoslovak leaders make no mention of having observed any such divisions at this time (in contrast to their recollections of earlier meetings). It is interesting that Shelest, formerly a key member of all Soviet delegations, was not a part of the inner circle at this stage. He had been a major proponent of the original invasion plan, and his absence suggests that after its failure he was in some disrepute.

Search for Alternatives

The speed with which Moscow's alternative strategy emerged suggests that there was not a wide search for alternatives. The one eventually adopted necessitated a complete volte-face in terms of the attitude toward the deposed leaders, and this clearly indicates that the alternative strategy was not thought out in advance. Indeed it strongly suggests that the Soviets had no contingency plan that they could implement if their first action failed.

On realizing that unlike in Hungary in 1956, a revolutionary workers' and peasants' government was not going to be established in Czechoslovakia in 1968, the Politburo moved quickly—even hastily—to prevent the Fourteenth Party Congress from setting up a rival leadership. As with so many other occasions in the pre-crisis and crisis periods, Soviet leaders relied heavily on the experience of past crises to guide their actions, with almost invariably disastrous results. Once they had broken with the past and decided to negotiate with Dubček, they were able to define their objectives and pursue them in a much more direct and clear-sighted way.

The decline in crisis-induced stress, typical of the post-crisis period, therefore, had the effect of easing, but not eliminating the quest for information and the search for alternatives. The consultative procedures and decisional forums both evolved around the continued centrality of the Politburo and the inner core within it.

The post-crisis period as defined here was brief, lasting only one week. At the end of that week Soviet leaders may have felt sanguine about the prospects for normalization in Prague, but the Czechoslovak leadership felt no similar optimism. As discussed in the next two chapters, the outcome of the crisis was most unsatisfactory—obviously from the Czechoslovak point of view, but in many ways also from the Soviet vantage point. It was the unsatisfactory outcome of the crisis as a whole that provokes questions about the overall Soviet performance in the crisis and the extent to which Soviet management, and mismanagement, contributed to the continual escalation of tensions that in the end led to invasion.

PART FIVE

Conclusions

CHAPTER FOURTEEN

Leaders and Decisions: Conclusions on Soviet Behavior in 1968

THE PSYCHOLOGICAL ENVIRONMENT

The theoretical literature on decision making is replete with studies examining the effect of crisis and stress on individual decision makers and on the decision-making process as a whole.[1] A conclusion frequently drawn by researchers and analysts is that the intense stress produced by a major crisis impairs the capability of decision makers to deal with the crisis. This is also a major component of the model developed by Michael Brecher and used in this study.

There are many assumptions about the exact effect of crisis-induced stress on decision makers, but inadequate data about the precise impact of the Czechoslovak crisis on individual Soviet leaders precludes a full analysis of all of these assumptions. There are, however, three hypotheses in this area that can be examined more closely. Keeping in mind that stress is defined to include a threat to a state's basic values, an awareness that time for resolving a crisis is both limited and finite, and a calculation that use of military force is likely, one may express the hypotheses as follows:

1. The greater the stress, the greater will be the conceptual rigidity of the decision makers and the less capable they will be of either avoiding the use of stereotypes or coping with the complexities and ambiguities of the situation.

[1]See especially Davis B. Bobrow et al., "Understanding How Others Treat Crisis: A Multimethod Approach," pp. 199–224; Joseph De Rivera, *The Psychological Dimension of Foreign Policy*; Charles F. Hermann, ed., *International Crises*; Irving Jarvis and Leon Mann, *Decision-Making*; Robert Jervis, *Perception and Misperception in International Politics*; Gordon Paul Lauren, *Diplomacy*; and Richard S. Lazarus, *Psychological Stress and the Coping Process*.

2. The greater the stress, the greater will be the propensity of deci-
    sion makers to rely on past experiences, the misapplication or
    overgeneralization of which is a primary source of low-quality
    decisions.

3. The greater the stress, the higher the value put on the immediate
    results of decisions and actions rather than on the long-term con-
    sequences, both positive and negative, of those decisions.

In the Czechoslovak crisis, the pattern of escalation was not
typical, for the crisis did not escalate gradually or uniformly from
the pre-crisis through the crisis period and then deescalate sharply
after the invasion. Instead, the crisis was marked by fluctuating
phases of higher and relatively lower tensions. Furthermore, although stress did peak just prior to the invasion, the most sustained period of acute stress occurred not in Phase Five, but in
Phase Three, when the month-long buildup of political pressure to
invade Czechoslovakia was only narrowly averted by the Čierna
compromise at the end of July. And finally, although the Soviet
military within hours of invasion could reassure the political leadership that the major military objectives had been achieved, political uncertainty was acute in the post-crisis period. The likelihood
of involvement in further military hostilities did decrease soon
after the invasion, but not until the Politburo had the signatures of
Dubček, Svoboda, and Černík—the heads of party, state and government—on the Moscow Protocol did the threat of armed and organized resistance to the Soviet military occupation decline significantly. For the purpose of testing the assumptions about the effect
of the crisis on the psychological environment of the Soviet leadership, it should, therefore, be borne in mind that tensions were
highest in the last days of Phase Five, after Soviet leaders returned
to Moscow from their holidays, and throughout Phase Three. They
were less sharp but still high in Phase One of the crisis period and
in the post-crisis period, moderate in Phase Two and Four of the
crisis period, and lowest in the pre-crisis period.

In examining conclusions about the effect of the crisis on the capability of the Soviet leadership to deal with complex and ambiguous situations, several important caveats need to be made. The
most crucial is that the primary sources on this subject are the public pronouncements of Soviet leaders and the accounts by Czechoslovak leaders of private discussions. Politicians the world over are
constrained by the political process or by any number of ulterior
motives from revealing their true motivations, but there are addi-

tional constraints operating in the Soviet system. Because of the conceptual conformity imposed on the Soviet elites by ideology, both their world view and their political language tends to be less flexible, even in periods of noncrisis. There is greater consensus among the Soviet elites on core principles than is often the case in the more pluralistic West, and there are more regular and ritualistic protestations of loyalty to these principles at party plenums, congresses, conferences, and *aktivs* than would be found in the West, at least outside preelection periods. There is also something to be said for the view that the Soviet leadership believes itself to be in a state of almost permanent crisis in its foreign affairs—insofar as fears of encirclement and feelings of vulnerability and insecurity have been abiding features of the Soviet *Weltanschauung* at least since the 1917 Revolution. The experience of World War II, shared by the entire political and military leadership, fostered a sensitivity to the security of the Soviet Union's borders, particularly on the Western frontiers, and an absolutely unquestioned and unified commitment to the postwar division of Europe.

At the time of the Czechoslovak crisis, however, the Soviet Union's foreign and domestic policy was in an unusual state of flux. The war in Vietnam was poised at the crossroads between escalation and negotiation; relations with the United States had brought breakthroughs in arms limitations but were nevertheless filled with animosity over U.S. support for Israel and South Vietnam and with uncertainty following President Johnson's decision not to seek another term. And in the Federal Republic, the revival of ultra-conservative politics in Bavaria and the continued refusal of the Bonn government to recognize the division of Germany was coupled with the first victories there by socialists who, if encouraged, might eventually and finally recognize postwar realities. All of these uncertainties in relations with the Western world coincided with a period of renewed hostility with China, following a brief post-Khrushchev respite, forcing the Brezhnev leadership to evolve a firm strategy toward the containment and isolation of the enormous ideological threat being posed by China's Cultural Revolution.

All of these foreign policy issues confronted a leadership already heavily preoccupied with domestic political, economic, and social management and reform. Thus other problems were constantly intruding and competing with the Prague Spring for the attentions of the Soviet leadership, with the net effect that Czechoslovak events remained outside Soviet control rather longer than might normally have been the case. Moreover, for many of the Soviet leaders the urgency of other issues colored their perspective on the Prague Spring. Brezhnev, for example, was involved in revising Khrushchev's "over-lenient" attitude toward domestic dissent, and he repeatedly saw the Prague Spring through this focus. Suslov was concerned lest the Czechoslovak crisis upset his efforts to contain the Chinese, whereas Kosygin and Gromyko were preoccupied with breakthroughs in arms limitation, European security, and (in Kosygin's case) economic reform. All worried that an invasion of Czechoslovakia would threaten these policies. Grechko, a professional soldier, was concerned with the direct impact on Soviet interests of U.S. military activity in Southeast Asia and Europe and did not, initially at least, consider subversion the primary threat to the socialist system.

Nevertheless, as the crisis in Czechoslovakia grew, the entire leadership came to focus more directly on the problems in Czechoslovakia itself, so that by July—at the height of the crisis—most Soviet leaders considered the solution of all other foreign policy problems and even some domestic problems to be contingent on the resolution of the Czechoslovak crisis. Thus, a major event such as the signing of the Nuclear Nonproliferation Treaty on July 1 went virtually unnoticed in the Soviet press and, except for Kosygin and Gromyko, unmentioned by Soviet leaders. Similarly in July, secret contacts with Bonn over a renunciation-of-force agreement were abandoned and were not resumed until after the invasion. The Vietnam peace talks in Paris were stalled, as was Soviet diplomatic backing for Arab efforts to obtain an Israeli withdrawal from occupied territories, despite an urgent visit to Moscow from Egypt's President Nasser in July.

By the end of July, virtually the only two foreign policy initiatives still actively being pursued were the November International Communist Conference backed by Suslov and the Soviet-American summit negotiated by Kosygin to inaugurate strategic arms limitation talks. Both of these policies were promoted by their sponsors throughout the crisis and long after other leaders had focused attention almost exclusively on Czechoslovakia. Suslov, for example, favored mediation by Euro-Communist parties in the Czechoslovak crisis as late as mid-July; he also supported a negotiated solution in Čierna and apparently argued against the invasion in August. Suslov's relatively unchanged attitude toward the Prague Spring had little to do with his liberal credentials or his greater insight into the complexities of the modern world, although certainly he had more extensive experience than some of his contemporaries. Rather, he appears to have had an idée fixe about the Chinese threat, for his concern was far in excess of his functional responsibilities as the Kremlin's chief ideologue.

In comparison to other Soviet leaders, Kosygin was remarkable; for active as he was in the Czechoslovak crisis he did not come to view all international events through the prism of Prague. Whereas Brezhnev, for example, became increasingly pessimistic about the possibility of positive relations with Bonn or Washington, and altogether less interested in the Sino-Soviet conflict, Kosygin never ceased to have a complex appreciation of international affairs. This is not to say that he was uniformly liberal in his ideological outlook, although he was so to the extent that he consistently favored the negotiation of outstanding differences as a means of resolving disputes. Kosygin, during his stay in Stockholm at the height of the crisis, was clearly concerned about Czechoslovakia (so concerned, in fact, that during his press conference he repeatedly said "Czechoslovakia" when he meant "Sweden") and desirous of putting forward his views on the subject; but he also covered a whole range of international issues, and he dealt with these issues in a very complex way. It is interesting, for example, that he should attack U.S. policies in Vietnam while supporting the Paris negotiations for ending the war and praise Soviet-American disarmament negotiations as "already a great thing" only days after Brezhnev had written off cooperation with the United States, describing it as a "rotten decaying society." On the German question, Kosygin showed his blunt and forthright support for the postwar division of Europe: "The main reason for the tension in Europe is the demand from the revanchist military circles in the German Federal Republic for a change in postwar frontiers. . . . He who calls for a revision of this postwar order calls for a new world war."[2] But here again, Kosygin did not specifically denounce the policy of building bridges, and indeed he issued a call for a European security conference. On the basis of available evidence, it seems that of all the Soviet leaders it was Kosygin alone who continued throughout the crisis to have a complex, differentiated, and nonstereotyped image of the international environment.

As for the changes in the Soviet view of the Czechoslovakia sit-

[2] *Evening Standard*, July 12, 1968.

uation, there is little doubt that as the crisis progressed, the Soviet leadership became less and less convinced by Czechoslovak protestations that they had the situation under control and that negative manifestations were transient. In the published record of the Soviet reaction to the crisis, the leadership maintained that as late as the beginning of May (the beginning of the crisis period) the Politburo members still had an "understanding both for the objective complexity of the situation and for the complexity of the position of the CPCz leadership itself."[3] Moscow had initially accepted the principle of extensive cadre changes, and there was a general belief that given proper support and "encouragement," Dubček would consolidate his position and put an end to antisocialist infringements.

As time went on, however, institutionalization of the reform movement and its support within the highest echelons of the Czechoslovak party ultimately forced those, including Brezhnev, who had personally supported Dubček to admit that the problem lay not in providing the leadership with the means to regain control but in finding a leadership who had the will to exercise control. Some of the Soviet leaders (and their East European allies) developed a negative assessment of Dubček, Císař, Kriegel, Smrkovský, and other leading liberals from a very early stage. Smrkovský's suitability as a presidential candidate was discussed as early as March, Císař was attacked by East Germany's Kurt Hager in early May, Kriegel was slandered by Shelest openly at the Čierna negotiations, and from June onward there were behind-the-scenes negotiations with the Czechoslovak hard-liners for the replacement of Dubček. At the same time, however, the consensus within the Politburo remained in favor of working with Dubček, provided he took the necessary measures to reassert control; and this consensus was maintained until August 17. Does the behavior of the Soviet leaders conform to the first hypothesis? Did they become less sensitive to the complexities of the situation in Prague as the crisis escalated? It can be concluded that this was the case insofar as Soviet leaders became less interested in examining the minutiae of positive and negative events in the society as a whole and more clearly focused on the role of the Dubček leadership in ending "antisocialist excesses."

The second hypothesis—namely, the greater the stress, the

[3] *Pravda*, August 22, 1968.

greater will be the propensity of decision makers to rely on past experience—reveals fairly mixed results when applied to Soviet behavior in 1968. In the course of the crisis, four distinct episodes in recent Soviet history had particular relevance to different leaders: the Second World War, the Soviet-Yugoslav dispute in 1948, the Polish events in 1956, and the Hungarian uprising in the same year.

Michael Brecher in his work on Israel's behavior in the 1967 and 1973 wars with the Arabs refers to the pervasiveness of the Holocaust Syndrome, which he claims became even more prevalent amongst Israel's decision makers during these crises.[4] A similar situation existed in the Soviet Union, where leaders and led alike were fixated on the experiences of the Second World War, experiences that led to a universal resolve never again to allow Russia's western defenses to be breached. During the 1968 crisis, references to the immutability of the western borders of the socialist system were omnipresent, and the defense of those borders became a major justification of the invasion. The experiences of the Soviet Union—and particularly the Soviet military—in the liberation of Eastern Europe also gave rise in 1968 to numerous articles primarily by marshals, reminding the Czechoslovaks of their "blood debt" to the Soviet army. For example, Marshal Konev, the commander of the Red Army in Prague in 1945, wrote a series of articles in early May that coincided with his departure for the ČSSR as part of the highly political tour conducted by Soviet generals. Konev maintained that Hitler had the capability to smash the Prague uprising and that "only the Soviet army had saved Prague."[5] Mention of this blood debt was particularly frequent between July 17 and 26, when no less than five articles appeared in *Krasnaya zvezda* exhorting the Czechoslovaks not to waste the sacrifices made during the liberation of Prague. As one commentator remarked acidly, when 145,000 soldiers had died in freeing Czechoslovakia from fascism, no one in that country had called the entry of Soviet troops a "breach of sovereignty."[6] The peak of this press activity coincided with the Soviet Politburo deliberations on full-scale invasion, and these articles can be seen as a reflection of heightened tensions and as an effort by some within the Soviet military to influence the Politburo's decision. References to the

[4] Michael Brecher, *Decisions in Crisis*, p. 343.
[5] *Izvestia*, May 6 and 7, 1968.
[6] *Krasnaya zvezda*, July 26, 1968; also *Krasnaya zvezda*, July 17, 19, 20, and 21, 1968.

"blood debt" were less frequent after July, but they did appear again in the major *Pravda* article of August 22 that justified the invasion. Readers were told that the Soviet army in 1945 had been much assisted by "the glorious corps of Ludvík Svoboda," whom the Soviets were currently relying on to legitimize the new revolutionary workers' and peasants' government in Prague. Not until after the signing of the Moscow Protocol was a place once again found for Dubček in Soviet history, with Marshal Konev writing in *Izvestia* on September 2, 1968, that both Dubček and Svoboda had made decisive contributions to the war effort.

The 1948 excommunication of Tito from the Soviet bloc was in the minds of some Czechoslovaks who looked to the Yugoslav leader's resistance as an example of the successful defiance of Soviet dictates.[7] The negative and long-lasting consequences of that excommunication for the Communist movement as a whole were also in the thoughts of some Soviet leaders. Mikhail Suslov had directed the 1948 Cominform conferences that indicted Tito, and he had acted as Stalin's envoy at the party conferences held in the GDR, Bulgaria, and Czechoslovakia that had ushered in the brief but turbulent period of anti-Titoist purges in those countries. Twenty years later, after Moscow had swallowed its pride and sought rapprochement with Tito on his own terms, Suslov arrived at the negotiations in Čierna nad Tisou, where he repeatedly urged both his Soviet and Czechoslovak compatriots to reach a negotiated settlement. This was 1968, not 1948, he is reported to have stated at one point, and "there can be no more excommunications."[8] This view was of course entirely consistent with Suslov's current obsession to obtain and maintain a modicum of unity within the movement in order to isolate the Chinese, who in Suslov's view had not been excommunicated but had stepped voluntarily into ideological purgatory.

Poland in 1956 provided another experience from which Soviet leaders attempted to find parallels to guide current actions. In Poland, the use of Soviet troops had been avoided by a combina-

[7] See, for example, *Obrana lidu*, July 27, 1968, for an article by its editor comparing the Warsaw Letter with the 1948 Cominform resolution on Yugoslavia and warning that "the ČSSR will not commit suicide." Jiří Pelikán ("The Struggle for Socialism in Czechoslovakia," p. 27) relates that "Dubček himself, and many other people including myself, were convinced that since Stalin had not dared to occupy Yugoslavia, then Brezhnev would not imagine he could do this to Czechoslovakia."

[8] Author's interview with Edward Goldstücker, Brighton, England, on October 24, 1977.

tion of bluster, unity, and realism on the part of the Polish leadership. V. V. Zagladin, Boris Ponomarev's deputy in the International Department, reportedly related to Mikhail Voslensky, himself an advisor to the Central Committee, that the current situation in Czechoslovakia should not be compared with Hungary in 1956 but rather with Poland, for although there had initially been "panic" in Poland, common sense had prevailed, and "nothing had happened."[9] A similar impression was given by Brezhnev. He told Josef Smrkovský, during the latter's visit to Moscow in June, that the Soviet Union had not "forced Poland into socialization" in 1956 and could accommodate a similar degree of reform in Prague.[10]

Comparisons with Yugoslavia and Poland, however, were relatively few—particularly after the publication of the "2,000 Words" in Prague. After that time, the most frequent and overriding connection was made with the Hungarian uprising in 1956. Many of the Soviet leaders had been directly involved in the management of the Hungarian crisis, most notably Suslov, who as a full member of the 1956 Praesidium negotiated a short-lived compromise with the Nagy leadership. Yuri Andropov also played a key role in 1956 as the Soviet ambassador in Budapest. Marshal Konev was commander in chief of the Warsaw Pact, and his subordinate at the time, Marshal Grechko, was commander of the Soviet forces in East Germany. Strangely these four leaders, who between them had the most direct experience of Hungary in 1956, made no public references to it in 1968. Suslov's silence is especially interesting; and given Khrushchev's subsequent admission that there had been dissension in the Praesidium on invasion,[11] it may be that Suslov had been one of those with doubts about a decision he later accepted as necessary.

The lack of direct knowledge or experience of the Hungarian uprising did not, however, prevent other Soviet leaders from drawing parallels. As early as the Dresden meeting in March, Brezhnev is reported to have pleaded with Dubček not to allow "chaos" and to "mobilize in time the party and working class" so as to prevent a repetition of what happened in Hungary.[12] After referring to the Polish parallel in June, during Smrkovský's visit, Brezhnev re-

[9] Mikhail Voslensky, *Der Spiegel*, no. 34 (August 21, 1978): 126.
[10] Smrkovský interview, *Lidová demokracie*, June 17, 1968.
[11] *New York Times*, December 3, 1959.
[12] *Rudé právo*, September 3, 1969.

turned again to the comparison with Hungary on the occasion of
János Kádár's visit to Moscow in early July, when he spoke of how
socialism had been defended there through the "fraternal internationalist assistance" of the Soviet Union.[13]

The lack of violence and of armed insurrectionist preparations
distinguished the Prague Spring from Hungary, however, and appeared to have left many Soviet leaders with doubts about whether
a counterrevolutionary situation really was developing in Czechoslovakia. These doubts were officially silenced by the publication
on July 11 in *Pravda* of the famous article by I. Alexandrov, entitled
"Attack on the Socialist Foundations of Czechoslovakia." The article
addressed the paradox that Czechoslovak reformers were speaking
about democracy and the guarding of the interests of socialism
when "in actual fact they are seeking to undermine the very foundations of the new state." Such tactics were not new, according to
Alexandrov: "They were resorted to by the counterrevolutionary
elements in Hungary that in 1956 sought to undermine the socialist
achievements of the Hungarian people." Then, finally distinguish-
ing between the peace of the Prague Spring and the violence of the
Hungarian uprising, Alexandrov declared: "Now, twelve years later,
the tactics of those who would like to undermine the foundations of
socialism in Czechoslovakia are *even more subtle and insidious.*"
This theory of "quiet revolution," as it came to be known, paved
the way for the decision to invade. The decision assumed that if the
Hungarian experience was not applicable to Prague, it was primarily because the counterrevolutionaries themselves had adopted
new tactics after their defeat in 1956. This theory did not die with
the invasion of Soviet troops in 1968. It was in fact sanctified by
S. Kovalev, the author also of "the Brezhnev doctrine," in a major
Pravda editorial designed to resolve the "confusion" in the minds
of "considerable masses" in Czechoslovakia and "quite a number
of people, including Communists in fraternal parties" about the
necessity of fraternal assistance. Kovalev admitted that there had
been in Prague no repetition of the armed uprising seen on Hungarian streets in 1956. But, he adamantly maintained, one should
not wait for "the shooting and hanging of Communists" before
coming to the assistance of "the champions of socialism." The parallel between Prague 1968 and Budapest 1956 had been used and
dropped, therefore, before the decision to invade was made, and
indeed by the second week of July.

[13] Brezhnev speech at Kremlin reception, July 3, 1968, SU/2813/C/2.

   It seems, however, that the Soviet leadership did consider certain aspects of their handling of the Hungarian crisis as relevant
to solving the Czechoslovak crisis. The invasion of Hungary had
been legitimized by requests from the Hungarian Communist
party itself for military assistance. This occurred on October 23,
1956; it was followed on November 4 by a second appeal from a
newly formed "revolutionary government of workers and peasants," headed by János Kádár, for assistance in quelling quite open
insurrection. The lack of sustained international censure and the
relative success of Kádár in establishing his authority and eventually gaining both respectability and popularity certainly contributed to the Soviet decision to repeat this pattern—with quite disastrous results—in Prague. This was an aspect of previous crisis
experience that does appear to have figured in Soviet calculations
right up to, and immediately after, the invasion.
   The third hypothesis presented earlier suggests that decision
makers lose sight of long-term gains and consequences as the crisis
escalates. Although the Soviet leaders had decided that the September 9 Extraordinary CPCz Congress and the August 26 Slovak
Congress had to be stopped at all costs, there is no overwhelming
evidence to suggest that the Soviet leaders lost sight of long-term
gains and consequences. Indeed to them, the issues at stake in
Czechoslovakia were extremely central, and to ignore them would
be to sacrifice both ideological primacy and Soviet security—the
absolute cornerstones of Soviet foreign policy. For the Soviets, the
loss of the loyalty of succeeding generations of Czechoslovak citizens, the alienation of Euro-Communists, and the setbacks to détente were short-term considerations measured perhaps in years or
even in decades, but transient nonetheless when compared to the
absolute necessity of defending Czechoslovakia's membership in
the Warsaw Pact and of upholding the Soviet Union as the only legitimate innovator and interpreter of Marxism-Leninism. These
were perceived as at stake in 1968, and the USSR never lost sight of
them throughout the crisis; and if anything they became more convinced of the necessity of upholding them as the crisis escalated.

INFORMATION

There are several hypotheses posed by Brecher and other analysts
relating to information gathering and evaluation for which Soviet
behavior in 1968 provides evidence. Specifically, they are as follows:
The greater the crisis, and the stress induced by it, the greater will

be (a) the perceived need and consequent quest for information; (b) the involvement of top decision makers in the evaluation of information; (c) the rate of communication by a nation's decision makers in the evaluation of information; and (d) the rate of communication by a nation's decision makers to international actors outside their country.[14] What is the evidence from Soviet management of the Czechoslovak crisis in 1968 that would support or refute these hypotheses?

To the Soviets, one of the major threats posed by the rapid and spontaneous flow of events in Prague was that they were losing control of the situation and that their supporters in Czechoslovakia were also losing control. The fear of chaos, so much a Soviet reflex at the best of times, was omnipresent in the Soviet reaction to the crisis and was heightened by the loss of traditional channels and sources of information that occurred with the personnel and organizational changes in Prague. In particular, the removal of Novotný, Hendrych, Koucký, and Štrougal from the CPCz Secretariat in April 1968 and the appointment of liberals such as Hájek, Pavel, and Prchlík to head the Ministry of Foreign Affairs, the Ministry of the Interior, and the eighth department of the Central Committee were major blows to traditional patterns of information gathering. The new ministers and party officials were less inclined—or positively disinclined—to pass information on to their counterparts in Moscow, and to make matters more difficult, Czechoslovak agents of Soviet security services and Soviet liaison officers were also removed, particularly from the Ministry of the Interior.

For the Soviet Union, therefore, information sources and patterns of information gathering were disrupted at the very time that the need for information was growing, thereby heightening their perception of chaos in Prague and forcing them to use other less reliable sources. In particular, Moscow heeded the warnings of individuals who were demoted or threatened by the reforms and who presented a one-sided picture of events. They also relied on officials at the Soviet embassy in Prague, primarily Ambassador Chervonenko and his deputy Udaltsev, both of whom were known to be particularly opposed to the reform movement. There were, of course, also many conservatives who maintained official positions throughout 1968, and they too were instrumental in keeping Moscow informed. They included Bil'ak, Indra, Švestka, and of

---

[14] Brecher, *Decisions in Crisis*, p. 375; Glenn D. Paige, *The Korean Decision*, p. 292; and Hermann, ed., *International Crises*, pp. 202–4.

course Koucký, who as ambassador in Moscow was particularly well-placed, and also many lower level Central Committee members and parliamentarians who were evidently very active in passing on data. As member of parliament Dohnolová later taunted Josef Smrkovský: "We took care that the Soviet comrades should know everything that was happening here at that time."[15]

The disruption of traditional information channels and sources combined with the onset of the crisis had the effect of spurring greater involvement of top decision makers in both the gathering and the evaluation of information. This involvement was encouraged also by Dubček and other Czechoslovak leaders who were convinced that the crisis in bilateral relations was largely the result of insufficient objective information.[16] Thus the communiqué of the Dresden meeting, for example, specifically mentioned that both an exchange of *opinions* and an exchange of *information* had taken place on "the situation in the socialist countries."[17] At the May 4 bilateral summit in Moscow, which marked the end of the pre-crisis period, the exchange of information was once again evident, with Brezhnev reciting verbatim from stacks of press cuttings to build a negative picture of developments in Prague. The Czechoslovak side, by their own account, "devoted that day to refuting and explaining. . . . We countered—with facts and information of much greater weight than their random assortment of so-called information."[18] This pattern continued throughout the crisis period, right up until, and including, the Čierna talks at the end of July.

It may be that for some top decision makers direct involvement in seeking further information from Dubček and other reformers during negotiations had the effect, however short-lived, of casting doubts on the quality of information being received from the Soviet embassy and hard-liners in Prague. Kosygin certainly considered his May visit to Karlovy Vary as an opportunity both for quiet diplomacy and for gaining a firsthand impression of the atmosphere in Czechoslovakia. Brezhnev, too, felt a need for more and better information; and indeed he apologized to Smrkovský, during their June 14 meeting, for previous negative assessments, which the Soviet leader put down specifically to "lack of information."[19] Suslov

[15] Smrkovský, *Unfinished Conversation*, p. 11.
[16] See the section on information in chapter 11 for further details.
[17] *Pravda*, March 25, 1968.
[18] Smrkovský, *Unfinished Conversation*, p. 11.
[19] Ibid., p. 14.

too is said to have voiced concern about the quality of information passed on by Chervonenko during the crisis.[20] Such concern, however, could not have been that profound, for the role of the Soviet embassy increased rather than decreased up until Chervonenko's failure to produce the promised revolutionary workers' and peasants' government in the wake of the invasion. After that time, when the negotiations shifted to Moscow, the role of the Soviet embassy declined. Its role as the primary source of information was supplanted by military intelligence and the direct presence of envoys from Moscow (such as First Deputy Foreign Minister Kuznetsov).

The involvement of top decision makers in information gathering and evaluation produced also a tendency to rely on direct communications with the Czechoslovak leaders as the crisis progressed, not just face-to-face communication but written correspondence and telephone conversations. Of course, all these forms served the dual purpose of gaining information and eliciting change in the behavior of the Czechoslovak leaders. Thus, for example, Brezhnev's telephone call to Dubček on the morning the "2,000 Words" appeared was both to gauge Dubček's reaction and to ensure that the reaction was going to be prompt and negative. And in August, following Bratislava, Brezhnev called Dubček almost daily not only to receive a report on the situation in Prague but also, and indeed more importantly by that stage, to impress on Dubček the absolute necessity of taking immediate measures to end "antisocialist excesses." The whole pattern of direct communication with the Czechoslovak leadership suggests that while the frequency of such contacts increased as the crisis escalated, the role of information gathering in such contacts decreased and was supplanted by efforts to change the direction of the reform movement.

Turning now to the next information hypothesis, there is evidence that contacts with states other than those directly involved increased only marginally as the crisis escalated. Official meetings with foreign heads of states (and leaders of major nonruling Communist parties) at which Czechoslovakia is known to have been discussed were very limited. They included Tito's trip to Moscow at the end of April; Kirilenko's discussion with the Italian Communists in Bologna from June 26 to July 10; Rochet's talks with Suslov

---

[20] *Christian Science Monitor* (London edition), October 3, 1968; *Daily Express*, September 9, 1968; *The Guardian*, September 3, 1968.

and Zagladin in Moscow in mid-July; and Italian Communist leader Luigi Longo's "vacation" in Moscow between August 14 and 22, in the course of which he held talks with Kirilenko, Ponomarev, and Suslov. Of course, Soviet leaders met other heads of state during the crisis; but Czechoslovakia was not discussed—not officially at least—mainly because Moscow regarded the crisis and its resolution as an internal bloc affair.

What Soviet leaders sought information about was the likely reaction of the international community to an invasion. At the end of July, the Soviet Foreign Ministry instructed its ambassadors to gauge the probable international response to an intervention. The British foreign secretary told Richard Crossman that the Soviet ambassador had sought an audience to discuss inter-Sputnik organization: "And then, just when he was leaving the room, he said, 'I want to talk to you about Czechoslovakia.' I found out later that the Russians had given their ambassadors in every capital instructions to make an identical approach in order to test Western reactions."[21] Similar soundings were made by Ambassador Dobrynin in Washington, where diplomatic activity and signaling between the Kremlin and the White House was in any case more intense because of the intrusion of other important issues—the Consular Agreement, signed on June 13; the Nonproliferation Treaty, signed on July 1; and negotiations over both arms limitation and Vietnam. Nevertheless, meetings between Dobrynin and Secretary of State Rusk were much more frequent in the last two weeks of July and in the two days prior to the invasion than at other times. Eight meetings took place between the two men at fairly regular biweekly intervals between the end of March (after Dresden) and mid-July. Then there were three meetings in short succession on July 22, 25, and 31, with a hiatus in the first two weeks of August, while everyone in Moscow and Washington went on holiday. Then immediately prior to the invasion, there were three meetings, on August 19 and 20; the second of the two August 20 meetings held was devoted to informing the president of the invasion.[22] Although the diplomatic effort was accelerated in the high-stress periods, Phases Three and Five, the top Soviet leaders, as far as is known, did not increase their own involvement in contacts with foreign heads of state. The

---

[21] Richard Crossman, *The Diaries of a Cabinet Minister*, p. 167.
[22] The Papers of Dean Rusk, Box 4, Appointment Book, 1968, from the archives of the Lyndon B. Johnson Library.

hot line was not used, for example; and this indicates not only that Moscow considered this to be an Eastern rather than an East-West affair, but also that by the time of the invasion, Soviet leaders were fairly sanguine about their capability to cope with the minimal repercussions expected.

To conclude, therefore, the evidence presented in the previous chapters and summarized above reveals that international activity did increase with the escalation of the crisis, although the activity was never very intense. The perceived need and consequent quest for information about developments in Czechoslovakia, on the other hand, was high from the outset because of the disruption of traditional patterns and sources. This need increased up to July, but in Phase Three there was no indication that Soviet leaders wanted more information or questioned the quality of the information they were receiving. Some of the leaders, notably Suslov and Kosygin but also possibly Brezhnev, may have remained receptive to new information after that time and genuinely did think that Dubček would fulfill the promises they believed he made at Čierna, but such hope was short-lived. Finally, the involvement of the top leaders in the information gathering and evaluation process certainly did increase with the crisis, in terms of both high-level negotiations and fact-finding missions and of written and telephone communications with Dubček and other leaders.

CONSULTATION

The literature concerning the impact of crisis on consultative patterns contains several hypotheses that can be examined with reference to Soviet involvement in Czechoslovakia. These hypotheses assume that the greater the crisis and the stress induced by it, the greater will be (a) the number of persons and groups consulted; (b) the frequency with which these persons and groups are consulted; and (c) the tendency for consultation to be ad hoc rather than institutional. In addition, an examination of the relation between crisis and consultation must consider the more general and various reasons why any Soviet leader enters into consultation. Alexander George, in his work entitled *Presidential Decision-making* suggests four objectives that may be served by consulting in the American system.[23] These objectives, in a modified and expanded

---

[23] Alexander George, *Presidential Decision-making* (Boulder, Colo.: Westview Press, 1980), chapter 4.

form, apply also to the Soviet system and are expressed as follows: (a) to obtain information and advice to meet the executive's cognitive needs; (b) to seek reassurance and moral backing to alleviate stress and meet the executive's emotional needs for support; (c) to induce participation in the decision-making process to meet the executive's need for consensus among the consultative and decision-making groups; (d) to offer other elite groups an opportunity to express their opinions in order to meet expectations of consultation by these elites—that is, to legitimize decisions; and (e) to use support from consultative groups in an attempt to forge consensus within the key decisional unit. (George does not consider the last point to be a reason for consultation in the United States.)

What observations arise about the hypotheses from an examination of Soviet actions in 1968? The three major consultative groups whose activities were visible in 1968 (thus excluding the KGB and military intelligence) were the Central Committee and its *apparat*, the East European leadership, and the military. Each group was diffuse and divided in its responses to the Prague Spring, yet because the top party leadership did consult each of them as distinct and definable groups, the discussion of their role will also assume their definitional cohesion.

In the pre-crisis period, the East European leaders and the party *apparat* were the most visible. A Central Committee plenum was hurriedly called in April, necessitating Prime Minister Kosygin's precipitate return from a state visit to Iran. Pressure for this plenum came from those within the Central Committee *apparat* who worried about the spillover effects of the Prague Spring. This group was supported by Gomułka and Ulbricht, who even at this stage took upon themselves the right to impart and impose their views. In the pre-crisis period, therefore, the major reasons for consultation appear to have been the need of the executive to gain consensus, the expectation by key groups that they would be consulted, and also an attempt to use the resolutions adopted at the plenum (which put ideological subversion by "revisionist, nationalist, and politically immature elements" at the forefront of Soviet concerns) as a means of forging consensus within the top decision-making circles.

In the crisis period the military played a very active role both as a consultative group and a pressure group seeking both maneuvers in Czechoslovakia and the permanent stationing of Soviet troops on the border with the Federal Republic. Data presented in chapter

11 illustrated the high level of participation of military leaders both in negotiations on the Czechoslovak issue and in the public debate on the effects of the reform movement. Konev and Yepishev were among the earliest advocates of measures to "improve Czechoslovakia's reliability as a member of the Warsaw Pact," but so serious was the breakdown of bilateral relations on the military front by the end of July that it is doubtful if any of the key military leaders counseled against invasion. On the contrary, there is quite overwhelming evidence not only that they favored it but that they actively pressed for it. Ponomarev and Katushev are said to have told the Czechoslovak delegation in Budapest in September 1968 that this was the case;[24] Mlynář gained the same impression during the Moscow negotiations;[25] and George Brown, the former British foreign secretary, was told by high party sources in Yugoslavia in August 1968 that the Soviet military in particular "were in earnest" about invasion.[26] The Hungarian ambassador in Italy, in an interview with C. L. Sulzberger in October 1968, painted an interesting picture of the reasons for invasion in which the military were the driving force behind the decision to invade. He maintained that maneuvers held in Czechoslovakia in 1968 had convinced the Soviet High Command that "the Czechs just did not have the fighting quality," and that the Soviet army, which, according to Ambassador Szall, "now runs things in Moscow, was determined to plug the gap."[27]

The prestige of the military was enhanced by the efficiency of the invasion and subsequent occupation, in marked contrast to the performance of the Soviet embassy and other officials in charge of implementing the political side of the plan. The role of the military was acknowledged by Grechko's presence at the signing of the Moscow Protocol, the first time he had been included in any such ceremony throughout the whole crisis, and also by Grechko's direct involvement in the events of March–April 1969 which led to Dubček's replacement by Husák. This increase in the military's decision-making role was also apparently a subject of conversation in 1970 between Grechko and Egypt's President Nasser, a frequent visitor between 1967 and 1970. Nasser later recalled the discussion in an interview. He expressed surprise at the difference of opin-

[24] Tigrid, *Why Dubček Fell*, p. 127.
[25] Mlynář, *Nachtfrost*, pp. 202, 287.
[26] *Evening Standard*, November 15, 1968.
[27] C. L. Sulzberger, *An Age of Mediocrity*, p. 465.

ion between military and civilian leaders, commenting that this had never been the case in his previous negotiations in Moscow. Grechko had replied that "he was giving his own views, which were not necessarily those of others." He had had the freedom to express his views independently since 1968 when, he told Nasser, "the civilians had not been able to manage the Czechs and had had to get him to do it."[28]

The influence of the other two consultative units was also greater in the crisis period than in either pre-crisis or post-crisis periods; and on the whole neither of these groups had quite the influence on the decision to invade that the military did. Although the Central Committee as a collective was not consulted after mid-July, and the East European leaders did not meet en bloc with their Soviet counterparts after Bratislava, considerable ad hoc activity was evident and increasing with the escalation of the crisis. No formal Central Committee plenum was convened to approve either the Čierna and Bratislava meetings or the decision to invade, but there is evidence (chapter 10) that an ad hoc gathering of key party officials was called on the weekend before the invasion, no doubt in the expectation that such "consultation" would legitimize the decision already taken. In the post-crisis period, the role of the Central Committee appeared to decline even further.

The East European leaders were active both as a group and individually throughout the crisis participated in five formal meetings: Dresden in March at the beginning of the pre-crisis period, Moscow on May 8 at the start of the crisis period, Warsaw in mid-July during Phase Three of the crisis period, Bratislava in Phase Four, and Moscow at the end of the post-crisis period. Ad hoc activity, measured in terms of meetings reported in the Soviet press between individual leaders, rather than the five as a collective, was also evident throughout the entire crisis. There were two such meetings in the pre-crisis period (a meeting between Grishin and East Germany's Kurt Hager in Moscow on April 18 and a visit by Pel'she to the GDR in early May). Ulbricht became practically a permanent resident in Moscow in May, where he was officially "on holiday at the invitation of the Central Committee" from May 8 to 29. On May 29 he was joined by other East German leaders for formal high level talks with the Soviet leadership. All was quiet during Phase Two of the crisis period, but during the high-stress

[28] Lord Trevelyan's interview with Nasser in 1970, published by *The Times*, February 19, 1977.

Phase Three, János Kádár came to Moscow for major negotiations between June 27 and July 4; and Podgorny took the opportunity of Ulbricht's seventy-fifth birthday to visit East Berlin between June 29 and July 2. Both Kádár and Ulbricht remained active in pressing Dubček and communicating with Soviet leaders right up to the invasion, but Kádár's departure from Moscow on July 4 was the last publicly reported face-to-face bilateral political consultation between Moscow and any of the East European five (contacts between the Soviet and East European military leaders, however, increased sharply prior to the invasion). Almost certainly the East European leaders, and Ulbricht in particular, as the self-appointed *éminence grise*, expected to be consulted about Soviet plans. In the case of Hungary, consultation was used also as a mechanism for binding Kádár to the gradual hardening of opinion. And as with the Central Committee, consultation with the East Europeans was designed to legitimize the Soviet invasion through the mechanism of collective responsibility.

To summarize the findings: The evidence from the Czechoslovak crisis suggests that the number of persons and groups consulted did not change radically throughout the crisis. The frequency of consultation was highest in the crisis period, with the military in particular becoming very active and remaining active in the post-crisis period. There was not a major shift toward ad hoc consultation with the escalation of the crisis; the Central Committee plenum and the Warsaw meeting of the five occurred in the high-stress Phase Three, not Phase Five. There was, however, certainly more ad hoc than formal consultation in Phase Five, leading up to the invasion, with collective consultation among all the East European leaders, reappearing in the post-crisis period.

DECISIONAL FORUMS

There are three basic assumptions about the effect of crisis on decisional forums: The greater the stress produced by the crisis, (a) the smaller will be the decision unit; (b) the more cohesive and harmonious will be the decisional unit; and (c) the greater will be the tendency for decisions to be reached by ac hoc units.[29] How does the Soviet situation fit these assumptions?

[29] Brecher, *Decisions in Crisis*, pp. 354, 376–77; Paige, *The Korean Decision*, p. 281; Ole R. Holsti and Alexander L. George, "The Effects of Stress on the Performance of Foreign Policy-Makers," *Political Science Annual* 6 (1975): 286–90.

The overwhelming impression of research findings is that the Politburo remained the institutional focus for all the formal and major decisions made on Czechoslovakia. The party Secretariat may have had a role in determining the date and agenda of the April and July Central Committee meetings, which would partially explain why Kosygin, who as chairman of the Council of Ministers had no position in the party bureaucracy, was able to be excluded so easily from both the preparations. Nevertheless, had a majority of the Politburo wished to resist pressures to convene a plenum, then almost certainly the plenum would not have been called. The absence of a Central Committee meeting to approve the results of the Čierna and Bratislava negotiations can be interpretated in this light, particularly when one recalls that the April plenum was convened to approve the results of the Dresden meeting and the July conclave to discuss the Warsaw meeting.

Although the Politburo remained the formal institutional focus of decision making, the indications are that Grechko was involved in key Politburo deliberations involving military security: decisions on maneuvers, the stationing of troops, and of course the invasion. Gromyko may also have been involved in the assessment of the international repercussions of invasion, discussed at the crucial July 20–21 meeting that decided to proceed with invasion unless Dubček met minimum demands; but there is no firm evidence on Gromyko's role. Neither is there clear evidence about the role of other non-Politburo members having functional responsibility for monitoring events in Prague or for other aspects of bilateral Soviet-Czechoslovak relations, but the evidence does suggest the active involvement of Ponomarev (especially in the post-crisis period) and Rusakov and Katushev (in the pre-crisis period particularly). There is no indication of Andropov's role, although certainly his complete absence from all negotiations and his total silence in the public debate speak significantly for his lack of involvement, particularly since his functional responsibility and past expertise would have given him a right to enter the debate.

Certainly there was an inner core within the Politburo that acted both formally in the name of the Politburo in negotiations on Czechoslovakia and informally as a subgroup with apparently self-appointed responsibility for the management of the crisis. The membership of these two groups overlapped but included Brezhnev, Kosygin, Podgorny, Suslov, and Shelest, with Suslov less openly active in the pre-crisis period and Shelest absent from negotiations in the post-crisis period. This group was not fully cohesive at any stage of the crisis; Kosygin and Suslov were persistent advocates of caution, and Shelest an early and consistent source of interventionist pressure. Moreover, Kosygin, although highly active, was constantly threatened with exclusion from the inner group, and on three occasions (at the beginning of April, while he was in Iran; at the end of May, while in Karlovy Vary; and in mid-July while in Sweden) he was indeed excluded from key decisions. Despite misgivings of some members about the wisdom of invasion, it nevertheless appears that all Politburo members had accepted the July 20–21 decision that invasion would proceed unless urgent measures were taken by Dubček; and after Czechoslovak failure to implement the Čierna and Bratislava agreements, all Politburo members were bound to this previous commitment. Despite continued misgivings by Suslov and Kosygin, the decision to invade appears to have been unanimous. The evidence therefore suggests that although the Politburo remained the formal focus of key decisions, the driving force in that body was this small inner core of leaders who drew their strength from various constituencies inside and outside the Politburo.

CONSIDERATION OF ALTERNATIVES

This aspect of the study focused on two further research questions posed by Brecher: What are the effects of changing stress (a) on the search for and evaluation of alternatives; and (b) on the perceived range of available alternatives? It is generally assumed that the greater the stress induced by a crisis, the greater is the tendency to reduce the number of alternatives under consideration.

This assumption is certainly supported by the findings related to Soviet behavior in 1968. The number and range of alternatives considered by some or all of the Soviet leaders throughout the crisis can be summarized as follows:

1. There is no imminent threat from Czechoslovakia; therefore no need for action.

2. Czechoslovakia is experiencing transitional problems; close monitoring is required but no action is needed.

3. Economic aid might alleviate pressures built up under Novotný and now causing problems.

4. Political support should be provided for Dubček to strengthen his position against remaining Novotný supporters.

5. Dialogue and fraternal advice are required because Dubček, though reliable, is untried and making some mistakes.

6. Routine military maneuvers should go ahead as planned to improve the performance of the Czechoslovak army.

7. Political pressures should be exerted on Dubček both through bilateral and multilateral negotiations and by mobilizing conservative forces on which he can rely to prevent the further growth of antisocialist elements.

8. Military maneuvers should be expanded to test the capability and reliability of the Czechoslovak army, with the permanent stationing of Soviet troops the outcome of poor performance.

9. Economic sanctions should be applied to prevent the unfavorable reform of the Czechoslovak economy and to remind the Prague leadership of the extent of economic integration into the bloc.

10. Military maneuvers should be used to compel political compliance.

11. Military maneuvers should be used as a cover to achieve the de facto stationing of troops.

12. Contacts with forces opposed to Dubček should be expanded to gauge their strength and capability of forming an alternative leadership, without a Soviet invasion but perhaps with the aid of Soviet troops who happen to be in Czechoslovakia for maneuvers.

13. Alternative 12, but with a full-scale Soviet invasion to support the new government.

14. An invasion should be mounted to compel the capitulation of the Dubček leadership to all Soviet demands.

15. Direct Soviet military rule should be established over Czechoslovakia.

Other alternatives may of course have been contemplated. The Dubček leadership, for example, was determined not to leave Czechoslovak territory after July because they feared they might be arrested or kidnapped by Soviet authorities, as had happened a decade previously in Hungary. Some Czech leaders also believed that one alternative considered in Moscow was a repetition of Hitler's strategy: direct rule of the unruly Czechs and an independent state for the more compliant and loyal Slovaks. No evidence has come to light suggesting that either of these alternatives was considered. It must be said, however, that had a revolutionary tribunal headed by Indra indeed been established to "try" reformist leaders, it is not at all clear what the ultimate fate of Dubček and the others would have been.

In examining the alternatives considered, alternatives 1 through

6 were most prevalent in the pre-crisis period, although by the end of that period alternatives 7 and 8 had also been adopted; 10 and 11 were under consideration; and vague references to mutual brotherly aid and military assistance were beginning to be made. In the early crisis period, the range of alternatives was at its widest with all the options, excluding numbers 1, 14, and 15, under consideration. By July, with the refusal of Dubček to attend the Warsaw meeting, the heightening of tensions following the publication of the "2,000 Words," and the Soviet nonwithdrawal of troops, the range of options narrowed greatly to include only numbers 7, 10, 11, 12. When, however, the Soviets agreed to withdraw their remaining troops from Czechoslovakia in return for Dubček's agreement to hold bilateral talks at Čierna, the alternatives narrowed to only two—numbers 7 and 13, that is, political negotiations or an invasion to replace Dubček. Dubček's failure to uphold the agreements that Moscow felt had been reached at Čierna left only one alternative: an invasion to replace him. Only when the invasion failed to achieve this objective did the Soviet leadership once again widen the search for alternatives. Numbers 14 and 15 were discussed but only number 14 was adopted, namely, to use the fact of invasion and the threat of continued occupation to compel Dubček's capitulation. The threat of direct rule from Moscow, made by Grechko in March 1969, did not at this stage have to be made. The consideration of alternatives, therefore, was widest in the early phases of the crisis period and narrowed substantially after Phase Three.

CONCLUSION

Three final observations might be made about the Soviet handling of the crisis as a whole. The first relates to the quality of crisis escalation. Did the Soviet handling of the crisis lead the Czechoslovaks to believe an invasion was the ultimate rung in the escalation ladder? Certainly many of the Czechoslovak leaders and most Western intelligence agencies calculated that the Soviet Union would invade if all else failed. The fear of invasion was at its highest in July and receded in August after Čierna, when Dubček felt he had won, if not a complete victory, at least some breathing space. Confusion was also heightened by the withdrawal of Soviet troops in late July and early August, which was regarded as another concession to Czechoslovak demands. Although the Dubček leadership appears to have been aware of the seriousness of Soviet intentions in mid-July, the deescalation of the crisis in early August may in fact have contributed to the lack of urgency and conviction with which Dubček set about curbing the reform movement, thereby precipitating the invasion. The mixture of the strategies of force and compromise adopted by Moscow may, therefore, have inadvertently made an ultimate invasion more likely.

The second observation relates to Brezhnev's style of leadership. Throughout the crisis, at least until the invasion, Brezhnev stayed at the center of the dominant opinion—whether that was for or against invasion. He reflected the consensus rather than shaped it, and he allowed the inner group to contain the major advocates of contending views, with Shelest's participation in the inner core eclipsed only in the post-crisis period. To the extent that poor and contradictory Soviet signaling was one of the many reasons for the Czechoslovak failure to appreciate the seriousness of the situation, Brezhnev's own style of leadership can be held partially responsible.

Finally, does the explanation for contradictory signals go beyond Brezhnev's style of leadership and the genuine differences of opinion between Soviet leaders over the reform movement? Did the political strengths, resources, positions, and ambitions of individual leaders shape and ultimately determine the decision to invade? Is it possible, to cite the view of some Czechoslovak leaders, that Czechoslovakia was invaded not so much because of the reform movement but because Brezhnev was threatened by Shelepin or some other leader with dismissal if he did not agree to invade? The relationship between power and policy is of constant concern to Soviet specialists, and of course it is true that the process of building the consensus to invade was political in that it was connected with many other issues and policies. The context was also political insofar as participation in decisions was often denied for apparently political rather than functional reasons. The exclusion of Kosygin, in particular, had political overtones; and Brezhnev's attempts to diminish Kosygin's influence in a number of other areas during 1968 adds credence to the argument that the noninterventionists carried less weight because of Kosygin's declining fortunes. But given the tremendous influence of Suslov, if the constituency for nonintervention had been wider and events in Czechoslovakia itself had been managed with greater realism and finesse by Dubček and other Czechoslovak leaders, an intervention might perhaps have been avoided. In the final analysis, however, one must be skeptical about the effect of political infighting on the decision to invade because of the almost complete absence of negative political repercussions for the opponents of the invasion. The membership of the Politburo in the Soviet Union and party leadership in Eastern Europe were very stable in the years following the invasion; and when demotions were eventually announced, at the top of the list were those who had been the most vociferous advocates of invasion—Shelest in the Ukraine, Gomułka in Poland, and Ulbricht in East Germany.

CHAPTER FIFTEEN

1968 and After: The Costs and Consequences of Invasion

THE AFTERMATH OF THE INVASION IN PRAGUE

When Alexander Dubček and the other members of the Czechoslovak delegation returned from Moscow, their personal status and the status of their country was most unclear. For the next eight months, they would explore the extent of their independence and test Soviet resolve to prevent a return to the status quo ante.

The population at large, much relieved that the interned Czechoslovak leaders had been restored to their former positions, gradually returned to work and refrained from mass resistance, thereby allowing the occupying troops to withdraw partially from urban enclaves. In general, the situation returned to a forced normality, particularly in Slovakia, with most of the incidents of civil disorder reported in the Czech lands, and especially among the students.

The Prague leadership was caught between continuing the post-January reforms and upholding the terms of the Moscow Protocol. Initially there were very few personnel changes; and all the top leaders, with the exception of Pavel, Hájek, Šik, Hejzlar, and Pelikán, retained their posts. The press was more restrained and responsible, but it still advocated reforms and published news and articles that would have been censored elsewhere in Eastern Europe. The laws making Czechoslovakia a federal state were effected on January 1, 1969; and economic reforms continued to be debated openly.

If Dubček was under pressure to continue the implementation of basic reforms, he was under even greater pressure from the Soviets and other conservative forces to abandon them. In the weeks following the signing of the Moscow Protocol, Dubček and the

CPCz Praesidium were constantly negotiating with Soviet leaders and envoys. Ambassador Chervonenko was omnipresent; First Deputy Foreign Minister Kuznetsov was in Prague during September; Dubček was summoned to Moscow in October, to Warsaw in November, and to Kiev in December; and CPSU Secretary Katushev was in Prague for two weeks at the end of the year.

The negotiations centered on two subjects, the implementation of the Moscow Protocol and the status of Soviet forces in Czechoslovakia. The Soviets, supported by conservatives within the Czechoslovak leadership, put unrelenting pressure on Dubček to uphold without exception all the provisions of the Moscow Protocol. At the same time, in return for a partial withdrawal of occupying forces (particularly the contingents of the East European armies), the Czechoslovaks were forced to sign a treaty allowing the permanent stationing of Soviet troops. The treaty did not specify any upper limit to the number of troops that would be stationed, and although it stated that troops would remain on Czech soil only "temporarily . . . for the purpose of safeguarding the security of the countries of the socialist commonwealth against the mounting revanchist ambitions of West German militarist forces,"[1] it made no mention of a timetable or conditions under which those forces would be withdrawn. Moreover, unlike the treaties governing the stationing of Soviet troops in Poland and Hungary, this treaty between the USSR and Czechoslovakia (as with the treaty between the USSR and the GDR) did not require Soviet forces to seek the permission of the host government in order to move its troops anywhere in the country. They could move back into the center of Prague on the direct orders of Moscow should the need arise. And it was precisely this threat that was used by the Soviet Union in the midst of the crisis that broke out in April 1969.

The crisis was provoked by the mass riots and demonstrations directed against Soviet property and installations in Prague following Czechoslovakia's victory over the Russians in an ice hockey final held in Stockholm on March 28. Soviet leaders had obviously been growing increasingly dissatisfied with Dubček's leadership

---

[1] *Pravda*, October 19, 1968. The number of troops remaining was estimated between 60,000 and 100,000 (Thomas Wolfe, *Soviet Power and Europe, 1945–1970*, p. 470). Detailed accounts of the months following the invasion are contained in Fred H. Eidlin, *The Logic of "Normalization"*; Galia Golan, *Reform Rule in Czechoslovakia*; H. Gordon Skilling, *Czechoslovakia's Interrupted Revolution*; Pavel Tigrid, *Why Dubček Fell*; Michel Tatu, *L'hérésie impossible*; and Vladimir V. Kusin, *From Dubček to Charter 77*.

and were looking for a pretext to replace him with someone more amenable to Moscow's aims. Accordingly, following the riots, the Soviet deputy foreign minister, Vladimir S. Semyonov, and the defense minister, Marshal Grechko, flew to Prague carrying an ultimatum from Brezhnev demanding urgent political changes if a second military intervention were to be averted. This occurred on March 31, 1969, and in the next two weeks, under the direct supervision of Grechko, Semyonov, and Ambassador Chervonenko, Dubček's replacement by Gustáv Husák was engineered.

Beginning with the April 17 Central Committee plenum, which elected Husák to the position of first secretary, the Soviets gained a much firmer grip on the situation in Prague. Liberals were gradually excluded from all positions of influence, censorship was rigidly reimposed, and all talk of economic or political reform ceased.

Normalization has been defined by Vladimir Kusin as the "restoration of authoritarianism in conditions of a post-interventionist lack of indigenous legitimacy, carried out under the close supervision of a dominant foreign power which retained the prerogative of supreme arbitration and interpretation but which preferred to work through its domestic agents."[2] It took Moscow and its supporters in Prague well over a year to reach this stage; but by the summer of 1969, according to this definition, the situation in Prague was well on its way toward "normalization," Soviet-style.

WIDER CONSEQUENCES OF THE INVASION

Although the entry of Pact troops into Czechoslovakia did not physically affect the populations of other countries, its repercussions inside and outside the USSR in both East and West were enormous. Of course one must not conclude that everything that occurred after the invasion happened because of the invasion—*post hoc ergo procter hoc*. There were wide-ranging discussions, divisions, and debates before the invasion, and many of these continued afterward. Nevertheless, on a whole range of issues, the invasion crystallized opinion and set the seal on policies pursued by, and toward, the Soviet Union.

Within the Soviet Union, the primary effect of the invasion was the setting of rigid parameters for reform and revision. The more unyielding attitude toward dissent had already been signaled by

[2] Kusin, *From Dubček to Charter 77*, p. 145.

the Brezhnev leadership well before the Prague Spring with the arrest and trial of Ginzburg and Galanskov and the censorship of Solzhenitsyn. The debate within the elite itself on the possible extent of the political and economic reform of the Soviet system had by no means been decided before the invasion. Any talk of substantial political change in the direction of liberalization was firmly ended by the invasion, when "revisionism" in any form was enshrined as a danger equal to "dogmatism." And in the realm of economic reform, even though Kosygin himself had championed the limited evolution of the Soviet centrally planned economy as early as 1965, the Prague Spring, which was used by detractors of Kosygin's economic reform as proof of the negative political consequences of economic decentralization, ended all chances of economic reform in the USSR during Brezhnev's tenure.[3] This was due both to the real fear of a repetition of the Prague Spring in the Soviet Union and to the further loss of political influence which Kosygin himself suffered after the invasion.

In Eastern Europe, the repercussions of the invasion varied. Undoubtedly it cast a universal shadow over all debates on political reform, but beyond that, the lessons learned depended very much on individual East European leaders' perceptions of the reasons for the invasion. The Hungarians, who had introduced their own wide-ranging but purely economic reforms in January 1968, decided that the invasion was not meant to threaten those reforms, and they continued to implement them.

Rumania and Yugoslavia felt that the Soviet decision to invade had been influenced by two key factors: the almost certain knowledge that the risk of Western military counteraction against the Soviet bloc was negligible; and the calculation that Czechoslovak military and civil resistance would be minimal and could be contained. The Yugoslavs in particular concluded that the USSR would not have invaded had the risk of an East-West confrontation been higher; and as a result they sought to deter any similar threat to

---

[3] The impact of Czechoslovak events on economic reform in the Soviet Union and elsewhere in the bloc is analyzed on the basis of personal experience by Włodzimierz Brus, "Economic Reforms as an issue in Soviet-East European Relations," in Karen Dawisha and Philip Hanson, eds., *Soviet-East European Dilemmas*, p. 87. A similar connection was made by Fidel Castro in his own speech following the invasion when he directly questioned whether all economic reform would now be jettisoned following the invasion (see *Appearance of Maj. Fidel Castro Ruz*). The official Soviet denigration of the purely economic aspects of the Prague Spring did not appear until some time after the invasion and was reflected in the work by I. M. Mrachkovskaya, *Ot revizionizma k predatel'stvu*.

their own country by obtaining and publicizing American security guarantees, which Belgrade interpreted as proof that the United States would escalate to global confrontation if Yugoslavia were ever invaded.[4] The Rumanians also followed such a policy, much aided by President Johnson's warning to Moscow after the invasion of Czechoslovakia that any similar pressure on Rumania threatened to unleash "the dogs of war."[5] The Rumanian population was put on national alert, and President Ceauşescu flatly warned Moscow that "the Rumanian people will not permit anybody to violate the territory of our fatherland."[6]

After the actual crisis died down, however, the Rumanians in fact became rather more compliant and cooperative than they had been throughout the first eight months of 1968. They began to participate in bloc enclaves and Warsaw Pact joint maneuvers; they played down their relations with West Germany; and they acquiesced in Soviet efforts to keep alive the plans for an international Communist conference.

In Poland and East Germany, the uncompromisingly harsh attitudes of Gomułka and Ulbricht toward the Prague Spring had been conditioned by a mixture of personal political vulnerability and regime instability. Gomułka and Ulbricht both felt that a Prague Spring in Warsaw or Berlin, as in fact was demanded in Poland in March 1968, would certainly result in their own political demise and might totally upset the precarious balance of forces within their regimes. Many of their efforts during the Prague Spring were concentrated, therefore, not only on preventing spillover but also on forcing the Soviet leadership to recognize its responsibility for preventing the collapse of traditional centers and bases of power in a fraternal Communist country. Both Gomułka and Ulbricht could rightly fear that Brezhnev's willingness to allow the ouster of Novotný in December 1967—dismissing Novotný's appeal for Soviet

[4] See R. B. Craig and J. D. Gillespie, "Yugoslav Reaction to the Czechoslovak Liberalization Movement and the Invasion of 1968," pp. 227–38; and Robin Alison Remington, "Armed Forces and Society in Yugoslavia," pp. 171–86. Yugoslav fears of a Soviet invasion could not have been eased by widespread rumors that Gen. Jan Šejna, who had defected from Czechoslovakia in February 1968, had taken with him a copy of the so-called "Polarka Project," which envisaged a Soviet invasion of Yugoslavia through neutral Austria. See James Burnham, "The Polarka Project," p. 426; and Graham H. Turbiville, Jr., "Intervention in Yugoslavia," pp. 62–73.

[5] President Johnson's August 30 speech in San Antonio, Texas, *New York Times*, August 31, 1968.

[6] Ceauşescu's speech of August 21, 1968, is reprinted in Robin Alison Remington, ed., *Winter in Prague*, pp. 359–61.

assistance with the famous phrase "Eto vashe delo!" (This is your affair)—could echo throughout Eastern Europe and tempt contenders for power in their own countries. Although the invasion certainly did reassert Soviet control over the East European *nomenklatura*, it did not signify unending Soviet commitment to either Gomułka or Ulbricht personally. The former was replaced by Edward Gierek after riots in Poland in December 1970, and the latter was eased out by Erik Honecker the following spring as a result of his continued obstruction of *Ostpolitik*. Of the East European leaders whose troops were involved in the invasion, only Kádár and Zhivkov survived the political turmoil produced after the invasion, and indeed Kádár enjoyed unusual support and protection in Moscow, despite his continual efforts throughout 1968 to plead for moderation there.[7]

The only other direct effect on Eastern Europe of the Soviet invasion was in Albania, where the regime, long estranged from the Soviet Union, finally decided to withdraw from the Warsaw Pact. The alliance between Tirana and Peking was subsequently further secured.

One of Mikhail Suslov's major preoccupations in 1968 had been to construct a united front to isolate Chinese "dogmatism." As a result of the invasion, the front was more difficult to forge, and the Chinese became even more intransigent and assertive. Apart from issuing the strongest condemnation of this "abominable crime" perpetrated by the "clique of Soviet revisionist renegades,"[8] the invasion sparked off two other developments that further damaged Sino-Soviet relations. One was Peking's conclusion that the USSR had degenerated into a state of "social-imperialism and social fascism" equal to, and in fact in collusion with, U.S. imperialism.[9] Peking accused both superpowers of pursuing spheres of influence policies that ruthlessly suppressed the common aspirations for na-

---

[7] For further analyses of the effects of the invasion on the five, see Fritz Ermath, *Internationalism, Security and Legitimacy*; N. Edwina Moreton, "The Impact of Détente on Relations Between the Member States of the Warsaw Pact"; Melvin Croan, "After Ulbricht, The End of an Era?" pp. 74–93; Christopher Jones, "Soviet Hegemony in Eastern Europe," pp. 216–41; Jan Weydenthal, "Polish Politics and the Czechoslovak Crisis in 1968"; Melvin Croan, "Czechoslovakia, Ulbricht and the German Problem," pp. 1–7; Nicholas William Bethell, *Gomułka, His Poland and His Communism*; and M. K. Dziewanowski, *The Communist Party of Poland*.

[8] Chinese Prime Minister Chou En-lai at Rumanian embassy reception, *The Times*, August 24, 1968.

[9] Ibid.

tional liberation; and Soviet actions in Czechoslovakia were equated with American policies in Southeast Asia. Another direct development of the invasion was the escalation of tensions along the Sino-Soviet frontier, with China making the first formal diplomatic protest to Moscow over border disturbances at this time. These tensions escalated into a major skirmish between Soviet and Chinese border guards in March 1969 on Chen-pao Island in the Ussuri River. Chinese propagandists subsequently equated their own efforts to contain Soviet military incursions with the "courageous struggle of the Czechoslovak people who strongly oppose the military occupation by Soviet revisionist social-imperialism."[10] Thus lessons drawn by Peking from the Soviet invasion of Czechoslovakia not only added to the almost complete breakdown of relations between the two countries, but also engendered additional fears in Peking of Moscow's capabilities and intentions. As such, the invasion was an important stepping stone toward Chinese acceptance of the notion that an entente with "the enemy of your enemy"—namely, the United States—was the best guarantee of Chinese security against Russian expansionism. The invasion of Czechoslovakia was, of course, but one episode in the long and complicated series of events that produced the major shift in Sino-American relations in the 1970s, but its influence on the perceptions of the Chinese leadership should not be underestimated.

Although the invasion may have led the Chinese to draw closer to the West, thereby hastening a realignment in global politics that could not have been more damaging to the Soviet Union, the harm inflicted by any such realignment was softened by the fact that the Western powers were not as traumatized by the invasion as the Chinese. To be sure, the immediate reaction of various Western governments was one of great despair and moral outrage; but by the end of 1968, it had generally been decided that the political and military consequences of the invasion could be contained. NATO headquarters concluded that although six or seven Soviet divisions were now stationed along the Czechoslovak border with West Germany, the new situation could be balanced by NATO and was not particularly destabilizing.[11] Further, a classified U.S. Department of Defense report, leaked to *Atlantic News* in November 1968, actually stated that the invasion of Czechoslovakia had if anything

[10] *Christian Science Monitor* (London edition), August 26, 1969.
[11] *New York Times*, November 12, 1968.

"reduced the net threat" to Europe from the Warsaw Pact, since the reliability and loyalty of the Czechoslovak army and population had been damaged.[12]

In the political sphere, of course, any hope of success for the Western policy of bridge building in Eastern Europe was dashed by the invasion. But that did not exclude the possibility of bridge building to Moscow. The invasion acted as a kind of tabula rasa upon which *Ostpolitik* and détente—Soviet-style—could be written. It succeeded, where the 1967 Karlovy Vary Conference had failed, in making it clear to East and West alike that any bridges that might be built across divided Europe would have to pass through Moscow. By interpreting the Soviet action as an attempt not only to stamp out domestic reform in Prague but also to regain control over bloc external policy, it is possible to eliminate much of the contradiction between the act of invasion and the subsequent promotion of East-West contacts. Although East-West relations were adversely affected initially, by the first anniversary of the invasion negotiations were proceeding apace once again on the German question, nuclear nonproliferation, strategic arms limitation, and a European security conference—all of which bore fruit in the first half of the 1970s.[13]

Progress in East-West relations was made not only in the shadow cast by the reassertion of Soviet hegemony in Eastern Europe, but also as a direct result of recognition by the West of that hegemony. The relationship was enshrined in the so-called "Sonnenfeldt doctrine" pursued by the Nixon administration and espoused, off the record, by Secretary of State Henry Kissinger's chief advisor on Soviet policy, Helmut Sonnenfeldt, in 1975.[14] The doctrine acknowledged that the encouragement of greater "organic unity" between East Europe and Moscow, by increasing stability in Central Europe, was actually in America's strategic interest. Of course, the advent of President Jimmy Carter's administration, with its emphasis on human rights, put an end to this policy and set the pace for a much more active U.S. interest in internal transformation in Eastern Europe. This interest continued into the Reagan years, as

[12] *Atlantic News*, November 3, 1968.

[13] For further details, see John Newhouse, *Cold Dawn, The Story of SALT*; Willy Brandt, *People and Politics*; and Richard Milhous Nixon, *The Memoirs of Richard Nixon*.

[14] The text of the State Department briefing delivered by Sonnenfeldt to U.S. ambassadors in Europe in December 1975 was leaked, and published by the *New York Times*, April 6, 1976.

evidenced by the support given to Solidarity in Poland after 1980. But however short-lived, the early and major successes of détente were based on Washington's acceptance of Soviet power in Eastern Europe and Soviet troops in Prague.

THE INVASION, IDEOLOGY, AND THE INTERNATIONAL COMMUNIST MOVEMENT

Surveying the international scene, one could conclude that the Soviet intervention did not incur great or even substantial costs to Moscow. Occurring at a time when Sino-Soviet relations were already at their lowest ebb and U.S. power, drained of its essential will and life blood in Vietnam, could not challenge Soviet strength, the invasion reversed no trends, impeded very few, and even facilitated others. In one area only is it possible to say that the invasion perhaps threatened to reverse a trend, and this was in the international Communist movement, which prior to the Prague Spring had witnessed a number of Soviet successes in forging a broad united front against the Chinese. After the invasion, which was condemned by all the leading nonruling Communist parties (with the exception of those of West Germany, Luxembourg, Greece, and Portugal—the last being in exile in Moscow at that time), Soviet hopes for convening an international Communist conference in November were dashed. Soviet theoreticians previously on the offensive against Chinese dogmatism were now on the defensive, feebly trying to justify the invasion in ideological terms acceptable to the international Communist movement.

At the core of the dispute was the new meaning the invasion gave to the terms "proletarian internationalism" and "sovereignty." Moscow was forced to respond to sustained criticism from within the movement to the effect that proletarian internationalism could never replace noninterference and equality as guiding principles of relations between Communist parties (a view particularly espoused by Luigi Longo).[15] Fidel Castro, who supported the invasion from a purely political point of view, nevertheless attacked Moscow for trying to construct a theoretical or legal justification. Speaking on the issue of whether or not Czechoslovakia's sovereignty had been violated, he declared that "the violation was flagrant. . . . It had

---

[15] *L'Unità*, September 8, 1968. Also see Kevin Devlin, "The New Crisis in European Communism," pp. 57–69.

absolutely not one appearance of legality."[16] In the same speech he dismissed the unsigned appeal by Czechoslovak party and government officials as a "fig leaf," saying "I do not think that the appeal by high-ranking persons could be a justification because the justification can only be the political fact in itself—that Czechoslovakia was marching toward a counterrevolutionary situation."[17] In Spain the Communist party leader, Santiago Carrillo, in retrospect summed up the effect of the invasion on Euro-Communism when he wrote, "The Soviet invasion of Czechoslovakia in 1968 was the last straw."[18]

The Soviet response to this sustained criticism was twofold: continued attempts by Soviet ideologists to provide an ideological raison d'être for the action; and efforts by some Soviet leaders to diminish the importance of gaining support from nonruling Communist parties. The latter trend put absolute priority on the unity of the bloc rather than on the cohesion of the wider Communist movement, thereby effectively downgrading Suslov's hopes for a united front against the Chinese.

Both of these trends were evident in editorials and articles published in all the leading Soviet newspapers and journals following the invasion. Foremost among them was the *Pravda* article by S. Kovalev, entitled "Sovereignty and the International Obligations of Socialist Countries," in which the theory of limited sovereignty within the socialist commonwealth—immediately labeled the "Brezhnev Doctrine" by the Western press—was enunciated. Kovalev adamantly rejected any "nonclass approach to the question of sovereignty" and dismissed those critics within the movement who, like Castro, doubted the invasion's legality: "Those who speak of the 'illegality' of the allied socialist countries' actions in Czechoslovakia forget that in a class society there is and can be no such thing as nonclass law." Rather, he maintained, the interest of maintaining socialism in every country of the socialist commonwealth must take precedence over the sovereignty of individual socialist states, so that, in his words, "a socialist state that is in a system of other states constituting a socialist commonwealth cannot be free of the common interests of that commonwealth."[19] Elsewhere, other theoreticians developed the notion that socialism

[16] *Appearance of Major Fidel Castro Ruz.*
[17] Ibid.
[18] Santiago Carrillo, *Eurocommunism and the State*, p. 132.
[19] *Pravda*, September 26, 1968.

and sovereignty were not being contrasted. Rather, as one author stated, the building of socialism was a "higher sovereign right of the peoples" than formal defense of the abstract rights of a sovereign state. As such, "accusations of a 'violation' of Czechoslovak sovereignty" were both "without substance" and based on "an absolutely abstract understanding and interpretation of the meaning of sovereignty, on an interpretation which is limited to formal logic." [20]

Also at the center of the Soviet ideologists' attempts to deflect criticism from the international Communist movement was the debate over the "meaning in life" of proletarian internationalism. It will be remembered that this term replaced "noninterference" as a cardinal principle governing inter-Communist relations very early in the Czechoslovak crisis, but it was not until the invasion that the term moved from the realm of theory to practice, thereby gaining immense importance in the movement as a whole.

It goes without saying that the Euro-Communists would never accept proletarian internationalism to mean the recognition of Soviet interests as paramount and Soviet ideological pronouncements as unimpeachable. As far as the Euro-Communists were concerned, that era, which was in its twilight before the Prague Spring, firmly ended with the invasion.

The Soviet strategy for dealing with this very serious rift revealed the lasting divisions in the Soviet leadership and in the bloc over the status of world Communist opinion. One group, represented by Suslov and Ponomarev, tried desperately to stress the lowest common denominator in relations between Moscow and the nonruling parties, hoping to maintain contact with the movement as a whole and thereby to salvage the planned international Communist conference. In fact, this was achieved through patient and well-directed efforts by Suslov and Ponomarev; and the conference ultimately convened in Moscow on June 5, 1969. The seventy-eight parties that attended resolved to strive for greater unity and to overlook differences on "points of detail"—namely Czechoslovakia and the Sino-Soviet conflict. There were wide-ranging and open debates, summarized in the pages of *Pravda*, critical of Soviet policy toward both Prague and Peking; but Brezhnev, too, was able to use the forum to demand a resolute fight against both "revision-

[20] A. Sovetov, "Sovremennyi etap bor'bi mezhdu sotsializmom i imperializmom," *Mezhdunarodnaya zhizn*, no. 11 (November 1968): 7.

ism and opportunism whether of the right or of the left."[21] It was Gomułka and Ulbricht who acted as the hatchet men for the invasion of Czechoslovakia, thereby allowing Moscow to reconstruct a basis for unity.

Following the conference, the outbursts among the Euro-Communist parties against "normalization" in Prague decreased, particularly after leading opponents of the invasion were expelled from the Austrian and French Communist parties (Ernst Fischer and Roger Garaudy). Nevertheless, Euro-Communist objections to incorporating the Soviet definition of proletarian internationalism into the Communist lexicon continued, with the challenge culminating at the All-European Conference of Communist Parties in Berlin in June 1976. The communiqué most significantly contained no reference to proletarian internationalism, referring instead to "mutual solidarity among working peoples of all countries."[22] It insisted on the strict independence of each Communist party and on noninterference in the internal affairs of any one party by another. Eight years after the invasion of Czechoslovakia, therefore, Moscow had succeeded in reestablishing the solidarity, if not the unity, of the international Communist movement by patient efforts (primarily Suslov's) to stress common interests rather than differences. This meant in the end dropping any hopes that the Euro-Communists would accept the Soviet notions of limited sovereignty and proletarian internationalism or any other theoretical justification for the invasion of Czechoslovakia that Moscow might wish to evolve.

In contrast to Suslov's concern for the opinion of the international Communist movement, there was a very strong alternative view that consistently stressed the relative unimportance of any party not already in power. Euro-Communists who attacked the invasion were dismissed as naive and impudent "anti-Sovietchiks." This view was expressed by Brezhnev himself in the postinvasion negotiations in Moscow. Mlynář reports that in response to an impromptu outburst by Dubček, Brezhnev lashed out:

> So what do you think will be done on your behalf? Nothing. There will be no war. Comrade Tito and Comrade Ceauşescu will say their

[21] *Pravda*, June 8, 1969.

[22] *Pravda*, July 2, 1976. Also see Roy Godson and Stephen Haseler, *Eurocommunism* (London: Macmillan, 1978); Paolo Filo della Torre et al., eds., *Eurocommunism: Myth or Reality?* (London: Penguin, 1979); and G. R. Urban, ed., *Eurocommunism* (London: Maurice Temple Smith, 1978).

piece, and so will Comrade Berlinguer. Well, and what of it? You are courting the Communist movement in Western Europe, but that won't amount to anything for fifty years.[23]

This emphasis on the relative insignificance of the nonruling parties increased with the negative reaction to the invasion; and editorials in leading journals asserted as never before the importance of the unity of the ruling parties as the key to the power and future of socialism in international relations. Thus a major article appearing in November 1968 showed its complete disdain for the role of nonruling parties by failing to even mention them in any equation of the power of socialism:

> Faithfulness to proletarian internationalism is mainly revealed by the Communist parties and peoples of fraternal countries in the carrying out of the sort of internal and foreign policy that promotes the international socialist system as the most important factor in present-day social progress. . . . Monolithic unity, close cooperation and fraternal solidarity of the countries of the international socialist system—these are the most important sources of its power.[24]

The implications of this view were clear and lasting: It may be desirable to have the support of nonruling Communist parties, but at the end of the day, Comrade Berlinguer has no tanks. The source of power of the international socialist system rests not on the approbation of the debating circles that call themselves Communist parties in Europe, but on the real political, economic, geographic, and military unity of will and action of the Soviet-controlled bloc of socialist states.

At international Communist meetings, Moscow may have chosen to downplay its own views on limited sovereignty and proletarian internationalism in order to prevent further rifts in the world Communist movement, but this is not to say that they ceased to be guiding principles of Soviet foreign policy. On the contrary they were consistently reaffirmed at the twenty-fourth, twenty-fifth, and twenty-sixth party congresses and in key textbooks on international law and foreign policy published after 1968.[25] In all these documents, Moscow was careful to place fidelity to the Soviet-

[23]Zdeněk Mlynář, *Night Frost in Prague*, p. 241.

[24]"Velikii oktyabr i mirovoy obshchestvennyi progress," *Politicheskoe samoobrazovanie* 11 (November 1968): 9. Also see M. I. Trus, "Leninskii printsipy vneshnei politiki SSSR i proletarskii internatsionalizm," *Voprosy istorii KPSS* 11 (November 1968): 24 for the "Leninist directives" on the application of proletarian internationalism in Czechoslovakia.

[25]See, for example, A. A. Gromyko and B. N. Ponomarev, eds., *Istoriya vneshnei politiki SSSR*, vol. 2, *1945–1976* (Moscow: Izdatel'stvo nauka, 1977), pp. 350–52; V. M. Khvostov,

defined principles of limited sovereignty and proletarian internationalism alongside Soviet recognition of, in Brezhnev's words at
the 26th Party Congress, "a wealth of ways and methods for developing the socialist way of life."[26] Nevertheless, as Brezhnev stated
in this same speech, and as the Politburo reaffirmed in its numerous exchanges with the Polish leadership during the crisis in that
country after August 1980, these principles were still and would always be the determinants of Soviet action in "complex and critical
moments. . . . That is how it was and how it will be, and let no one
have any doubt as to our common determination to secure our interests and to defend the socialist gains of the peoples."[27]

The most dire consequences of the invasion of Czechoslovakia
occurred, it can be concluded, not outside the Communist bloc but
inside it, to the extent that unity of action was preserved at the
expense of unity of will on the part of a significant section of the
population and elite of Czechoslovakia and other states in Eastern
Europe. But as became so apparent with the invasion, when the
Soviet objective was to maintain the Soviet position in Eastern Europe "for eternity," the transient alienation of one or two generations in the end mattered for very little.

Problemy istorii vneshnei politiki SSSR i mezhdunarodnykh otnoshenii, p. 436; V. P.
Nikhamin et al. (Higher Party School of the CPSU Central Committee), eds., *Sovremennyye
mezhdunarodnyye otnosheniya i vneshyaya politika Sovetskovo Soyuza* (Moscow: Izdatel'stvo
mysl', 1972), pp. 8–12, 153–57; I. D. Ovsyany et al., *A Study of Soviet Foreign Policy*
(Moscow: Progress Publishers, 1975), pp. 12, 60–62; and V. S. Shevtsov, *Natsional'nyi
Suverenitet*, pp. 176–93. For more general accounts and documents of Soviet-Czechoslovak
relations published since the invasion, see Akademiya Nauk SSSR, Institut Nauchnoi Informatsii po Obshchestvennym Naukam, *Chekhoslovakiya*; Chetmir Amort, *SSSR i osvobozhdeniye Chekhoslovakii*; N. G. Chernyshev, *Obshchestvo sovetsko-chekhoslovatskoi
druzhby*; N. N. Rodionov et al., eds., *Sovetsko-chekhoslovatskiye otnosheniya.*

    [26] Brezhnev's speech, transmitted live by Radio Moscow, February 23, 1981, SU/6657/C/6.
    [27] Ibid.

Key Political
and Military Leaders,
USSR, 1968

THE POLITBURO: FULL MEMBERS

L. I. Brezhnev, General Secretary, Central Committee
G. I. Voronov, Chairman, RSFSR Council of Ministers
A. P. Kirilenko, Secretary, Central Committee
A. N. Kosygin, Prime Minister
K. T. Mazurov, First Deputy Prime Minister
A. Ya. Pel'she, Head, Party Control Committee
N. V. Podgorny, Chairman, Praesidium of the Supreme Soviet
D. S. Polyansky, First Deputy Prime Minister
M. A. Suslov, Secretary, Central Committee
A. N. Shelepin, Chairman, Trade Unions
P. Ye. Shelest, First Secretary, Ukrainian Central Committee

THE POLITBURO: CANDIDATE MEMBERS

Yu. V. Andropov, Head, KGB
V. V. Grishin, Head, Moscow City Party Committee
P. N. Demichev, Secretary, Central Committee
D. A. Kunaev, First Secretary, Kazakhstan Central Committee
P. M. Masherov, First Secretary, Belorussian Central Committee
V. P. Mzhavanadze, First Secretary, Georgian Central Committee
Sh. R. Rashidov, First Secretary, Uzbekistan Central Committee
D. F. Ustinov, Secretary, Central Committee
V. V. Shcherbitsky, Chairman, Ukrainian Council of Ministers

THE SECRETARIAT OF THE CENTRAL COMMITTEE
(excluding those Secretaries listed above)

I. V. Kapitanov
K. F. Katushev, after April 10, 1968, in charge of Central Commit-

tee Department for Liaison with Ruling Communist and Workers' Parties

F. D. Kulakov

B. P. Ponomarev, in charge of Central Committee International
Department

M. S. Solomentsev

KEY MILITARY LEADERS

A. A. Grechko, Minister of Defense

I. I. Yakubovsky, Commander in Chief, WTO

M. V. Zakharov, Chief, General Staff

A. A. Yepishev, Chief, Main Political Administration

I. Kh. Bagramyan, Chief, Rear (until July 1968)

S. S. Maryakhin, Chief, Rear (after July 1968)

K. A. Vershinin, Commander in Chief, Air Force

S. G. Gorshkov, Commander in Chief, Navy

N. I. Krylov, Commander in Chief, Strategic Rocket Forces

K. S. Moskalenko, Chief Inspector

P. F. Batitsky, First Deputy Chief, General Staff

I. S. Konev, General-Inspector

M. I. Kazakov, Chief of Staff, WTO (until early August 1968)

S. M. Shtemenko, Chief of Staff, WTO (after early August 1968)

I. G. Pavlovsky, Commander in Chief, Ground Forces

P. K. Koshevoi, Commander, Group Soviet Forces, Germany

A. M. Kushchev, Head, WTO Permanent Mission, Prague

V. V. Zhadov, Deputy Head, WTO Permanent Mission, Prague

OTHER ACTIVISTS
(not mentioned above)

Yu. V. Il'nitsky, First Secretary, Transcarpathian oblast'

L. S. Kulichenko, First Secretary, Volgograd oblast'

V. V. Zagladin, Deputy Head, Central Committee International
Department

M. V. Zimyanin, Editor, *Pravda*

A. A. Gromyko, Minister of Foreign Affairs

V. V. Kuznetsov, First Deputy Minister of Foreign Affairs

S. G. Lapin, General Director, TASS

K. V. Rusakov, Head, Central Committee Department for Liaison
with Ruling Communist and Workers' Parties (after April 1968)

V. I. Konotop, First Secretary, Moscow oblast'

V. S. Tolstikov, First Secretary, Leningrad oblast'

S. V. Chervonenko, USSR Ambassador, Prague

I. I. Udaltsev, Minister-Counselor, USSR Embassy, Prague

APPENDIX B:

Key Political and Military Leaders, Czechoslovakia, 1968

PRAESIDIUM OF THE CPCZ	January 5– April 5	April 5– August 31
Oldřich Černík	x	x
Jaromír Dolanský	x	
Alexander Dubček	x	x
Jiří Hendrych	x	
Michal Chudík	x	
Drahomír Kolder	x	x
Bohuslav Laštovička	x	
Jozef Lenárt	x	x (cand.)
Antonín Novotný	x	
Otakar Šimůnek	x	
Antonín Kapek	x (cand.)	x (cand.)
Miroslav Pastyřík	x (cand.)	
Michal Sabolčík	x (cand.)	
Štefan Sádovský	x (cand.)	
Ludvík Vaculík	x (cand.)	
Vasil Biľak	x	x
Josef Borůvka	x	
Jan Piller	x	x
Emil Rigo	x	x
Josef Špaček	x	x
František Barbírek		x
František Kriegel		x
Josef Smrkovský		x
Oldřich Švestka		x
Bohumil Šimon		x (cand.)

SECRETARIES OF THE CPCZ		
Antonín Novotný	x	
Jiří Hendrych	x	

Drahomír Kolder	x	x
Vladimír Koucký	x	
Štefan Sádovský	x	x
Alexander Dubček	x	x
Čestmír Císař		x
Alois Indra		x
Jozef Lenárt		x
Zdeněk Mlynář (June)		x

OTHER ACTIVISTS, NOT MENTIONED ABOVE

Ludvík Svoboda	President of the Republic
Jiří Hájek	Foreign Minister
Václav Prchlík	Head, CPCz Central Committee's Eighth Department
Martin Dzúr	Minister of National Defense
Josef Pavel	Minister of the Interior
Ota Šik	Deputy Premier, Economic Reform; and Member, Economic Council
Gustáv Husák	Deputy Premier, Reform of the Federal System

Selected Bibliography

This bibliography excludes most Russian, English, and foreign-language newspapers and journals referred to in the footnotes.

PUBLISHED WORKS

Aczel, Tamas. "Budapest 1956–Prague 1968, Spokesmen of Revolution." *Problems of Communism* 18, nos. 4–5 (July–October 1969): 60–67.

Adomeit, Hannes. *Soviet Risk-Taking and Crisis Behavior.* London: George Allen and Unwin, 1982.

————, and Robert Boardman, eds. *Foreign Policy Making in Communist Countries: A Comparative Approach.* Farnborough: Saxon House, 1979.

Akademiya Nauk SSSR, Institut Nauchnoi Informatsii po Obshchestvennym Naukam. *Chekhoslovakiya: Aktual'nyye obshchestvenno-politicheskiye i sotsial'no-ekonomicheskiye problemy, referativnyi sbornik.* Moscow: INION, 1978.

Allison, Graham T. *Essence of Decision: Explaining the Cuban Missile Crisis.* Boston: Little, Brown, 1971.

Ames, Kenneth. "Reform and Reaction." *Problems of Communism* 17, no. 6 (November–December 1968): 38–50.

Amort, Chetmir. *SSSR i osvobozhdeniye Chekhoslovakii.* Moscow: Progress Publishers, 1976.

Appearance of Maj. Fidel Castro Ruz, Analyzing Events in Czechoslovakia, Friday, August 23, 1968. Translation of transcript made by the Revolutionary Government's Department of Stenographic Transcriptions, Havana, Instituto del Libro, 1968.

Avtorkhanov, Abdurakhman. *Sily i bessiliye Brezhneva: politicheskiye etyudy.* Frankfurt/Main: Possev-Verlag, 1979.

Beam, Jacob D. *Multiple Exposure.* New York: W. W. Norton, 1978.

Bender, Peter. *East Europe in Search of Security.* Baltimore: The Johns Hopkins University Press, 1972.

Bethell, Nicholas William. *Gomulka, His Poland and His Communism.* London: Longmans, 1969.

Betts, Richard K. *Soldiers, Statesmen, and Cold War Crises*. Cambridge, Mass.: Harvard University Press, 1977.

Bialer, Seweryn, ed. *The Domestic Context of Soviet Foreign Policy*. Boulder, Colo.: Westview Press, 1981.

Bil'ak, Vasil. *Pravda ostalas' pravdoi, stati i rechi*. Moscow: Politizdat, 1972.

Bittman, Ladoslav. *The Deception Game: Czechoslovak Intelligence in Soviet Political Warfare*. Syracuse, N.Y.: Syracuse University Research Corporation, 1972.

Bobrow, Davis B., Steven Chan, and John A. Kringer, "Understanding How Others Treat Crisis: A Multimethod Approach." *International Studies Quarterly* 21, no. 1 (March 1977): 199–224.

Bohlen, Charles E. *Witness to History 1929–1969*. New York: W. W. Norton, 1973.

Brahm, Heinz. *Der Kreml und die ČSSR, 1968–1969*. Stuttgart: Verlag W. Kohlhammer, 1970.

Brandt, Willy. *People and Politics: The Years 1960–1975*. London: Collins, 1978.

Brecher, Michael. *Decisions in Crisis: Israel, 1967 and 1973*. Berkeley, Calif.: University of California Press, 1980.

———. *Decisions in Israel's Foreign Policy*. New Haven: Yale University Press, 1975.

———, ed. *Studies in Crisis Behavior*. New Brunswick, N.J.: Transaction Books, 1978.

———. "Towards a Theory of International Crisis Behavior: A Preliminary Report." *International Studies Quarterly* 21 (March 1977): 39–74.

Breslauer, George W. *Khrushchev and Brezhnev as Leaders: Building Authority in Soviet Politics*. London: George Allen and Unwin, 1982.

Brezhnev, L. I. *Leninskim Kursom. Rechi i stat'i*. tom vtoroi. Moscow: Izdatel'stvo politicheskoy literatury, 1970.

———. *USSR-CSSR. Friendship and Cohesion. Speeches by L.I. Brezhnev in Prague*. Moscow: Novosti, 1971.

British Broadcasting Corporation. *Summary of World Broadcasts*. Part I: *The Soviet Union*, Part II: *Eastern Europe*, 1968 (daily).

Brown, Archie, and Michael Kaser, eds. *The Soviet Union Since the Fall of Khrushchev*. 2d ed. London: Macmillan, 1978.

Browne, Michael, ed. *Ferment in the Ukraine*. London: Macmillan, 1971.

Brumberg, Abraham, ed. *In Quest of Justice: Protest and Dissent in the Soviet Union Today*. London: Pall Mall, 1970.

Burnham, James. "The Polarka Project." *National Review* 26, no. 15 (April 12, 1974): 426.

Carrillo, Santiago. *Eurocommunism and the State.* London: Lawrence and Wishart, 1977.

Chapman, Colin. *August 21st—the Rape of Czechoslovakia.* Philadelphia: J. B. Lippincott, 1968.

Chernyshev, M. G. *Obshchestvo Sovetsko-chekhoslovatskoy druzhby.* Moscow: Saratov Oblast' Publishers, 1976.

Cohen, Stephen F., ed. *An End to Silence: Uncensored Opinion in the Soviet Union from Roy Medvedev's Underground Magazine "Political Diary."* New York: W. W. Norton, 1982.

Craig, Richard B., and J. David Gillespie. "Yugoslav Reaction to the Czechoslovak Liberalization Movement and the Invasion of 1968." *Australian Journal of Politics and History* 23, no. 2 (1977): 227–38.

Croan, Melvin. "After Ulbricht, The End of an Era?" *Survey* 17, no. 2 (Spring 1971): 74–93.

———. "Czechoslovakia, Ulbricht and the German Problem." *Problems of Communism* 18, no. 1 (January–February 1969): 1–7.

Crossman, Richard. *The Diaries of a Cabinet Minister*, vol. 3. London: Hamish Hamilton, 1977.

Czerwinski, E. J., and Jaroslav Piekalkiewicz, eds. *The Soviet Invasion of Czechoslovakia.* New York: Praeger, 1972.

Davydov, Yu. P., V. V. Zhurkin, and V. S. Rudnev, eds. *Doktrina Niksona.* Moscow: Izdatel'stvo Nauka, 1972.

Dawisha, Karen. "The Limits of the Bureaucratic Politics Model: Observations on the Soviet Case." *Studies in Comparative Communism* 13 no. 4 (Winter 1980): 300–346.

Dawisha, Karen. "Soviet Security and the Role of the Military: The 1968 Czechoslovak Crisis." *British Journal of Political Science* 10 (1980): 341–363.

———, and Philip Hanson, eds. *Soviet-East European Dilemmas: Coercion, Competition and Consent.* London: Heinemann; New York: Holmes and Meier, for the Royal Institute of International Affairs, 1981.

Deacon, Richard. *A History of the Russian Secret Service.* London: Frederick Mullen, 1972.

Dean, Robert W. *Nationalism and Political Change in Eastern Europe: The Slovak Question and the Czechoslovak Reform Movement.* Denver, Colo.: University of Denver, 1973.

De Rivera, Joseph. *The Psychological Dimension of Foreign Policy.* Columbus, Ohio: Charles E. Merrill, 1968.

Devlin, Kevin. "The New Crisis in European Communism." *Problems of Communism* 17, no. 6 (November–December 1968): 57–69.

Dornberg, John. *Brezhnev: The Mask of Power.* London: Andre Deutsch, 1974.

Dubček, Alexander. "Letter to the Federal Assembly of Czechoslovakia and the Slovak National Council of October 28, 1974." *Listy* (Rome) 5, no. 3 (April 1975): 3–16.

Dunn, Keith A. "Limits Upon Soviet Military Power." *Royal United Services Institute Journal* 124, no. 4 (December 1979): 38–45.

Dziewanowski, M. K. *The Communist Party of Poland.* 2d ed. Cambridge, Mass.: Harvard University Press, 1976.

Dzyuba, Ivan. *Internationalism or Russification? A Study in the Soviet Nationalities Problem.* London: Weidenfeld and Nicolson, 1968.

Edmonds, Robin. *Soviet Foreign Policy, 1962–1973.* London: Oxford University Press, 1975.

Eidlin, Fred H. *The Logic of "Normalization": The Soviet Intervention in Czechoslovakia of 21 August 1968 and the Czechoslovak Response.* Boulder, Colo.: East European Monographs, 1980.

Erickson, John. "Towards a 'New' Soviet High Command: 'Rejuvenation' Reviewed (1959–1969)." *Royal United Services Institute Journal* 114, no. 3 (September 1969): 37–44.

Ermath, Fritz. "Internationalism, Security, and Legitimacy: The Challenge to Soviet Interests in East Europe, 1964–1968." Memorandum RM-5909-PR, Santa Monica, Calif., The Rand Corporation, 1969.

Ezhegodnik, Bol'shoy Sovetskoy Entsiklopedii, 1969. Moscow: Izdatel'stvo Sovetskaya Entsiklopediya, 1969.

Fallenbuchl, Z. M. "The Role of International Trade in the Czechoslovak Economy." *Canadian Slavonic Papers* 10 (Winter 1968): 451–478.

Fejtö, Francois. "Moscow and Its Allies." *Problems of Communism* 17, no. 6 (November–December 1968): 29–38.

Floyd, David. "The Czechoslovak Crisis of 1968." *Brasseys Annual: The Armed Forces Yearbook, 1969.* London: William Clowes and Sons, 1969.

Frei, Daniel, ed. *International Crisis and Crisis Management.* Westmead, England: Saxon House, 1978.

Freund, Michael. *From Cold War to Ostpolitik: Germany and the New Europe.* London: Oswald Wolff, 1972.

Frolik, Josef. *The Frolik Defection.* London: Leo Cooper, 1975.

Gallagher, Matthew P., and Karl F. Spielman, Jr. *Soviet Decision-Making for Defense: A Critique of U.S. Perspectives of the Arms Race.* New York: Praeger, 1972.

Gellert, Andre. "The Diplomacy of the Czechoslovak Crisis—Why They Failed." *Studies for a New Central Europe* 2, nos. 3–4 (1968–1969): 43–53.

George, Alexander. "The 'Operational Code': A Neglected Approach to the Study of Political Leaders and Decision-Making." *International Studies Quarterly* 13, no. 2 (June 1969): 190–222.

Golan, Galia. *The Czechoslovak Reform Movement: Communism in Crisis, 1962–1968.* Cambridge: Cambridge University Press, 1971.

————. *Reform Rule in Czechoslovakia: The Dubček Era, 1968–1969.* Cambridge: Cambridge University Press, 1973.

Gold, Hyam. "Foreign Policy Decision-Making and the Environment: The Claims of Snyder, Brecher, and the Sprouts." *International Studies Quarterly* 22, no. 4 (December 1978): 569–86.

Gore, Albert Arnold. *Wintry Days in Prague and Moscow.* 91st Cong. 1st sess. Washington, D.C.: GPO, 1969.

Grigorenko, Petro G. *Memoirs.* New York: W. W. Norton, 1982.

Gromyko, Anatoli, and Yuri Shvedkov. *USSR-USA Relations Today.* Moscow: Novosti Press Agency Publishing House, 1973.

Haefs, Hanswilhelm, ed. *Die Ereignisse in der Tschechoslowakei.* Bonn: Seigler & Co. K. G. Verlag für Zeitarchive, 1969.

Hájek, Jiří. *Dix ans après—Prague 1968–1978.* Paris: Éditions du Seuil, 1978.

Hayter, Sir William. *Russia and the World.* London: Secker and Warburg, 1970.

Heikal, Mohamed. *Sphinx and Commissar.* London: Collins, 1968.

Hermann, Charles F., ed. *International Crises: Insights from Behavioral Research.* London: Collier-Macmillan, 1972.

————. "International Crisis as a Situational Variable." In James N. Rosenau, ed., *International Politics and Foreign Policy.* 2d ed. New York: The Free Press, 1969.

Hodnett, Grey, and Potichnyj, Peter. "The Ukraine and the Czechoslovak Crisis." Occasional Paper no. 6, Department of Political Science, Research School of Social Sciences, Australian National University, Canberra, 1970.

Horelick, Arnold L., A. Ross Johnson, and John D. Steinbruner. *The Study of Soviet Foreign Policy: A Review of Decision-Theory-Related Approaches.* Rand-R-13334. Santa Monica, Calif.: Rand Corporation, 1973.

Horský, Vladimir. *Prag 1968 Systemveränderung und Systemverteidigung.* Stuttgart: Ernst Klett Verlag, 1975.

Hough, Jerry F., and Merle Fainsod. *How the Soviet Union is Governed.* Cambridge, Mass.: Harvard University Press, 1979.

Hronek, Jiří, ed. *ČSSR: The Road to Democratic Socialism: Facts on Events from January to May 1968.* Prague: Publishers Pragopress Features, 1968.

James, Robert Rhodes, ed. *The Czechoslovak Crisis 1968.* London: Weidenfeld and Nicolson, 1969.

Jarvis, Irving L., and Leon Mann. *Decision-Making: A Psychological Analysis of Conflict, Choice and Commitment.* New York: Free Press, 1977.

Jervis, Robert. *Perception and Misperception in International Politics*. Princeton, N.J.: Princeton University Press, 1976.

Johnson, Lyndon Baines. *The Vantage Point: Perspectives on the Presidency, 1963–1969*. New York: Holt, Rinehart and Winston, 1972.

Jones, Christopher D. "Autonomy & Intervention: The CPSU and the Struggle for the Czechoslovak Communist Party, 1968." *Orbis* 19, no. 2 (Summer 1975): 591–625.

———. "Soviet Hegemony in Eastern Europe: The Dynamics of Political Autonomy and Military Intervention." *World Politics* 31, no. 2 (January 1977): 216–41.

Juviler, Peter H. "Soviet Motivations for the Invasion, and Domestic Support." *Studies for a New Central Europe* 2, no. 3 (1968–1969): 97–100.

K sobytiyam v Chekhoslovakii, fakty, dokumenty, svidetel'stva pressy i ochevidtsev. Moscow, 1968.

Kahn, Herman. "How to Think About the Russians." *Fortune* 78, no. 6 (November 1968): 125–27, 231–48.

Kanet, Roger, ed. *The Behavioral Revolution and Communist Studies*. New York: The Free Press, 1971.

Kaye, V. A. *Chekhoslovatskaya Sotsialisticheskaya Respublika*. Moscow: Izdatel'stvo nauka, 1975.

Keegan, J. *World Armies*. London: Macmillan, 1979.

Khvostov, V. M. *Problemy istorii vneshnei politiki SSSR i mezhdunarodnykh otnoshenii*. Moscow: Izdatel'stvo nauka, 1976.

King, Robert R. *Minorities under Communism: Nationalities as a Source of Tension among Balkan Communist States*. Cambridge, Mass.: Harvard University Press, 1973.

Kiraly, Bela K. "Budapest: 1956–Prague: 1968, Parallels and Contrasts." *Problems of Communism* 18, nos. 4–5 (July–October 1969): 52–60.

Klaiber, Wolfgang. *The Crisis in Czechoslovakia in 1968*. Arlington, Va.: Institute for Defense Analysis, 1970.

Kohout, Pavel. *From the Diary of a Counterrevolutionary*. New York: McGraw-Hill, 1969.

Kolkowicz, Roman, ed. *The Warsaw Pact*. Arlington, Va.: Institute for Defense Analysis, 1969.

Kosygin, A. N. *Izbrannyye rechi i stat'i*. Moscow: Izdatel'stvo politicheskoy literatury, 1979.

Kral, Vaclav. *Lessons of History*. Moscow: Novosti Press Agency, 1978.

Kunze, Reiner. *The Lonely Years*. London: Sidgwick and Jackson, 1978.

Kusin, Vladimir V., ed. *The Czechoslovak Reform Movement 1968, Proceedings of the Seminar Held at the University of Reading on 12–17 July 1971*. London: International Research Documents, 1973.

————. *From Dubček to Charter 77: A Study of 'Normalisation' in Czechoslovakia, 1968–1978.* Edinburgh: Q Press, 1978.

————. *The Intellectual Origins of the Prague Spring.* Cambridge: Cambridge University Press, 1971.

————, and Z. Hejzlar. *Czechoslovakia, 1968–1969: Annotation, Bibliography, Chronology.* New York: Garland, 1974.

Lauren, Gordon Paul. *Diplomacy: New Approaches in History, Theory and Policy.* New York: The Free Press, 1979.

Lazarus, Richard S. *Psychological Stress and the Coping Process.* New York: McGraw-Hill, 1966.

"Letter of Warning from the CPSU Politburo, August 17, 1968." *Studies in Comparative Communism* 3, no. 1 (January 1970): 141–44.

Levy, Alan. *Rowboat to Prague.* New York: Grossman, 1972.

Lewytzkyj, B., and J. Stroynowski. *Who's Who in the Socialist Countries.* New York: K. G. Saur, 1978.

Lodge, Milton C. *Soviet Elite Attitudes Since Stalin.* Columbus, Ohio: Charles E. Merrill, 1969.

Lowenthal, Richard. "Sparrow in the Cage." *Problems of Communism* 17, no. 6 (November–December 1968): 2–28.

McClelland, Charles A. "The Acute International Crisis." *World Politics* 14 (October 1961): 182–204.

————. "The Anticipation of International Crises: Prospects for Theory and Research." *International Studies Quarterly* 21 (March 1977): 15–38.

Mackintosh, Malcolm. *The Evolution of the Warsaw Pact.* Adelphi Paper no. 58. London: Institute for Strategic Studies, June, 1969.

Marko, Milosh. *Chernym po belomy. O sobytiyakh v Ch.SSR v 1968–1969 godakh.* Moscow: Progress Publishers, 1974.

————. *Psikhologicheskaya voyna i 'chekhoslovatskiy eksperiment'.* Moscow: Nauka, 1972.

Maxa, Josef. *Die Kontrolierte Revolution.* Vienna: P. Zsolnak, 1969.

————. *A Year in Eight Months,* by Journalist M. Introduction by Tad Szulc. Garden City, N.Y.: Doubleday, 1970.

Medvedev, Roy A. *Let History Judge: The Origins and Consequences of Stalinism.* New York: Knopf, 1971.

Mezerik, A. G. *Invasion and Occupation of Czechoslovakia and the U.N.* New York: International Review Service, 1968.

Michal, Jan M. "Czechoslovakia's Foreign Trade." *Slavic Review* 27 (June 1968): 212–29.

Mlynář, Zdeněk. *Nachtfrost.* Cologne: Europäische Verlagsanstalt, 1978.

————. *Night Frost in Prague.* Translated by Paul Wilson. London: C. Hurst, 1980.

Mňačko, Ladislav. *The Seventh Night.* London: J. M. Dent, 1969.

Moravus [pseud.]. "Shawcross's Dubček—A Different Dubček." *Survey* 17, no. 4 (Autumn 1971): 203–16.

Moreton, N. Edwina. *East Germany and the Warsaw Alliance: The Politics of Détente*. Boulder, Colo.: Westview Press, 1978.

————. "The Impact of Détente on Relations Between the Member States of the Warsaw Pact: Efforts to Resolve the German Problems and Their Implications for East Germany's Role in Eastern Europe, 1967–72." Ph.D. diss., University of Glasgow, 1976.

Mrachkovskaya, I. M. *Ot revizionizma k predatel'stvu: kritika ekonomicheskikh vzglyadov O. Shika*. Moscow: Izdatel'stvo Mysl', 1970.

Müller, Adolf. *Die Tschechoslowakei auf der Suche nach Sicherheit*. Berlin: Berlin Verlag, 1977.

Newhouse, John. *Cold Dawn, The Story of SALT*. New York: Holt, Rinehart and Winston, 1973.

Nguyen Van Tuoi. *Communist Strategy: Lessons from Experience*. Saigon: Vietnam Committee on Foreign Relations, 1969.

Nixon, Richard Milhous. *The Memoirs of Richard Nixon.* London: Sedgwick and Jackson, 1978.

North, R. C., O. R. Holsti, D. Zaninovitch, and D. A. Zinnes. *Content Analysis*. Evanston, Ill.: Northwestern University Press, 1963.

Organizatsiya Varshavskovo dogovora 1955–1975. Dokumenty i materialy. Moscow: Izdatel'stvo politicheskoy literatury, 1975.

Oxley, Andrew, Alex Pravda, and Andrew Ritchie. *Czechoslovakia: The Party and the People*. London: Allen Lane, The Penguin Press, 1973.

Paige, Glenn D. *The Korean Decision*. New York: The Free Press, 1968.

Parrott, Sir Cecil. *The Serpent and the Nightingale*. London: Faber and Faber, 1977.

Paul, David W. "Soviet Foreign Policy and the Invasion of Czechoslovakia: A Theory and a Case Study." *International Studies Quarterly* 15 (1971): 159–202.

Pavelko, V. U. *Dryzhba narodiv-druzhba kultur*. Kiev, 1973.

Payne, Samuel B., Jr. "The Soviet Debate on Strategic Arms Limitation: 1968–72." *Soviet Studies* 27, no. 1 (January 1975): 27–45.

Pelikán, Jiří. *Ein Frühling, der nie zu Ende geht*. Frankfurt: S. Fischer, 1976.

————. *The Secret Vysočany Congress, Proceedings and Documents of the Extraordinary Fourteenth Congress of the Communist Party of Czechoslovakia, 22 August 1968*. New York: St. Martin's Press, 1971.

————. "The Struggle for Socialism in Czechoslovakia." *New Left Review*, no. 71 (January–February 1972): 3–36.

Pivka, Otto von. *The Armies of Europe Today*. London: Osprey, 1974.

Polach, Jaroslav G. "Nuclear Energy in Czechoslovakia: A Study in Frus-
tration." *Orbis* 12, no. 3 (Winter 1968): 831–51.

Polk, James H. "Reflections on the Czechoslovakian Invasion, 1968."
Strategic Review 5 (Winter 1977): 30–37.

Ponomarev, B. M., A. A. Gromyko, and V. M. Khvostov. *Istoriia
vneshnei politiki SSSR, 1917–1970 gg, Vol. II, 1945–1970.* Moscow:
Izdatel'stvo nauka, 1971.

Pravda pobezhdaet. Moscow: Izdatel'stvo politicheskoy literatury, 1971.

Provaznik, Jan [pseud.]. "The Politics of Retrenchment." *Problems of
Communism* 18, nos. 4–5 (July–October, 1969): 2–17.

Rapaport, Anatol. *The Big Two: Soviet-American Perceptions of Foreign
Policy.* New York: Pegasus, 1971.

Reddaway, Peter. *Uncensored Russia.* London: Gollancz, 1979.

Remington, Robin Alison. "Armed Forces and Society in Yugoslavia." In
Catherine McArdle Kelleher, ed., *Political-Military Systems: Comparative Perspectives*, Beverly Hills, Calif.: Sage, 1974, pp. 163–191.

Remington, Robin Alison, ed. *Winter in Prague, Documents on Czechoslovak Communism in Crisis.* Cambridge, Mass.: The MIT Press,
1969.

"Replies to Questions Relating to the Events in Czechoslovakia. Address by Comrade Lajos Fehér, Member of the Political Committee
of the HSWP, Vice-Chairman of the Council of Ministers. Broadcast
on 30 August 1968." *Information Bulletin of the Central Committee of
the HSWP* (Budapest), no. 4 (October 1968): 14–20.

Robinson, William F. "Czechoslovakia and Its Allies." *Studies in Comparative Communism*, no. 1 (July–October 1968): 141–71.

Rodionov, N. N. *Sovetsko-chekhoslovatskiye otnosheniya.* Vol. 3, *1961–
1971.* Moscow: Gospolitizdat, 1975.

Rostow, W. W. *The Diffusion of Power.* New York: Macmillan, 1972.

Russell, Jeremy. *Energy as a Factor in Soviet Foreign Policy.* London:
Saxon House for the Royal Institute of International Affairs, 1976.

Schwartz, Harry. *Prague's 200 Days.* New York: Praeger, 1969.

Selucký, Radoslav. *Czechoslovakia, The Plan that Failed.* London: Nel-
son, 1970.

———. "The Dubček Era Revisited." *Problems of Communism* 24
(January–February 1975): 38–43.

Shawcross, William. *Dubček.* London: Weidenfeld and Nicolson, 1970.

Shevtsov, V. S. *Natsional'nyi suverenitet, (problemy teorii i metodologii).*
Moscow: Iuridicheskaya Literatura, 1978.

Shitikova, A. P. *Sovetskaya vneshnyaya politika i Evropeiskaya bezo-
pastnost'.* Moscow: Izdatel'stvo mezhdunarodnyye otnosheniya, 1972.

Shtemenko, S. M. *General'nyi shtab v gody voiny.* Moscow: Voenizdat,
1968.

Shvedkov, Yu. A., ed. *SShA: Vneshnepoliticheskii mekhanizm.* Moscow: Izdatel'stvo nauka, 1972.

Sil'nitskaya, Larisa. "Recollections of Bratislava." *Radio Liberty Dispatch,* RL 195/74, July 2, 1974.

Simes, Dimitri K. "The Soviet Invasion of Czechoslovakia and the Limits of Kremlinology." *Studies in Comparative Communism* 8, nos. 1 and 2 (Spring–Summer 1975): 174–80.

Simmonds, George W., ed. *Nationalism in the USSR and Eastern Europe.* Detroit: The University of Detroit Press, 1977.

Skilling, H. Gordon. *Czechoslovakia's Interrupted Revolution.* Princeton, N.J.: Princeton University Press, 1976.

————, and Franklyn Griffiths, eds. *Interest Groups in Soviet Politics.* Princeton, N.J.: Princeton University Press, 1971.

Smrkovský, Josef. *An Unfinished Conversation.* Australia Left Review pamphlet. Sydney: Red Pen Publications, 1976.

Snyder, Glen H., and Paul Diesing. *Conflict Among Nations: Bargaining, Decision-Making and System Structure in International Crises.* Princeton, N.J.: Princeton University Press, 1977.

Sontag, J. P. "Moscow and the Search for Unity." *Problems of Communism* 18, no. 1 (January–February 1969): 44–50.

"Speech Delivered by János Kádár, First Secretary of the Central Committee of the HSWP, at the Fourth Congress of the Patriotic People's Front, April 18, 1968." *Information Bulletin of the Central Committee of the HSWP* (Budapest), no. 3 (August 1968): 3–15.

Spravochnik Partiinovo rabotnika. Vol. 8. Moscow: Izdatel'stvo politicheskoy literatury, 1968.

Spravochnik Partiinovo rabotnika. Vol. 9. Moscow: Izdatel'stvo politicheskoy literatury, 1969.

Stafford, Roy Wm. "Signalling and Response: An Investigation of Soviet-American Relations with Respect to the Crisis in Eastern Europe in 1968." Ph.D. diss., Tufts University, 1976.

Steiner, Eugen. *The Slovak Dilemma.* Cambridge: Cambridge University Press, 1973.

Stepanek-Stemmer, Michael. *Die tschechoslowakische Armee: Militärhistorische und paktpolitische Aspekte des 'Prager Frühlings' 1968.* Cologne: Sonderveröffentlichung des Bundesinstituts für ostwissenschaftliche und internationale Studien, 1979.

Sulzberger, C. L. *An Age of Mediocrity.* New York: Macmillan, 1973.

Suslov, M. A. *Na putyakh stroitel'stva kommunizma: rechi i stat'i.* Vol. 2. Moscow: Izdatel'stvo politicheckoy literatury, 1977.

Sviták, Ivan. *The Czechoslovak Experiment, 1968–1969.* New York: Columbia University Press, 1971.

Szulc, Tad. *Czechoslovakia Since World War II.* New York: Viking, 1971.

Tatu, Michel. *L'hérésie impossible.* Paris: B. Grasset, 1968.

————. *Power in the Kremlin: From Khrushchev to Kosygin.* New York: Viking, 1971.

————. "The Soviet Union." *Interplay*, November 1968, pp. 4–7.

Thomas, John R. *Soviet Foreign Policy and Conflict within the Politburo and Military Leadership.* McLean, Va.: Research Analysis Corporation, 1971.

Tigrid, Pavel. *Why Dubček Fell.* London: Macdonald, 1971.

Triska, Jan F., and David O. Finley. *Soviet Foreign Policy.* New York: Macmillan, 1968.

Turbiville, Graham H., Jr. "Intervention in Yugoslavia. An Assessment of the Soviet Military Option." *Strategic Review* 5 (Winter 1977): 62–73.

U.S. Central Intelligence Agency, Directorate of Intelligence. *The Soviet Decision to Intervene.* August 21, 1968 (declassified for author under U.S. Freedom of Information Act).

————. *Free World Reaction to Events in Czechoslovakia.* August 21, 1968 (declassified for author under U.S. Freedom of Information Act).

U.S. Congress, Senate Committee on Government Operations. *Czechoslovakia and the Brezhnev Doctrine.* Prepared by the Subcommittee on National Security and International Operations. Washington, D.C.: GPO, 1969.

U.S. Department of State. *Bulletin.* 1968 (weekly).

U.S. Department of State, Director of Intelligence and Research. *Intelligence Note 497.* June 24, 1968. (All Intelligence Notes were briefing documents of 3–5,000 words for the secretary of state and were declassified for author under U.S. Freedom of Information Act.)

————. *Intelligence Note 563.* July 17, 1968.

————. *Intelligence Note 564.* July 18, 1968.

————. *Intelligence Note 575.* July 22, 1968.

————. *Intelligence Note 576.* July 22, 1968.

————. *Intelligence Note 591.* July 26, 1968.

————. *Intelligence Note 624.* August 7, 1968.

————. *Intelligence Note 634.* August 13, 1968.

U.S. Department of State, Director of Intelligence and Research. *Research Memorandum RSE-127.* August 16, 1968, 23 pp. (declassified for author under U.S. Freedom of Information Act).

————. *Research Memorandum RSE-133.* September 13, 1968.

U.S. Department of State. *Telegram 162651.* May 11, 1968. (All telegrams were 2–3,000 words in length and were declassified for author under U.S. Freedom of Information Act.)

————. *Telegram 163375.* May 14, 1968.

————. *Telegram 164394.* May 15, 1968.

————. *Telegram 166761.* May 18, 1968.

————. *Telegram 202635.* July 15, 1968.

————. *Telegram 205078.* July 19, 1968.

————. *Telegram 206938.* July 23, 1968.

————. *Telegram 213732.* August 1, 1968.

————. *Telegram 214637.* August 3, 1968.

————. *Telegram 215343.* August 5, 1968.

————. *Telegram 218860.* August 10, 1968.

————. *Telegram 219344.* August 12, 1968.

U.S. Foreign Broadcast Information Service. *Daily Report,* 1968.

U.S. Joint Publication Research Service. *Eastern Europe,* 1968.

U.S. National Security Council. *Memorandum for the Record, NSC Meeting of April 24 on Eastern Europe.* April 26, 1968 (declassified for author under U.S. Freedom of Information Act).

Urban, G. R., ed. *Communist Reformation.* London: Maurice Temple Smith, 1979.

————. "The Invasion of Czechoslovakia, 1968: The View from Washington. A Conversation with Eugene Rostow." *The Washington Quarterly* 2, no. 1 (Winter 1979): 106–120.

Valenta, Jiri. "Soviet Foreign Policy Decision-Making and Bureaucratic Politics: Czechoslovak Crisis 1968." Ph.D. diss., The Johns Hopkins University, 1975.

————. *Soviet Intervention in Czechoslovakia, 1968: Anatomy of a Decision.* Baltimore: Johns Hopkins University Press, 1979.

Vneshyaya politika Sovetskovo Soyuza i mezhdunarodnyye otnosheniya, sbornik dokumentov, 1968 god. Moscow: Izdatel'stvo mezhdunarodnyye otnosheniya, 1969.

Voslensky, Mikhail. "This will only help the Americans." Excerpts from his diaries. *Der Spiegel,* no. 34 (August 21, 1978): 126–29.

Wallace, William V. *Czechoslovakia.* London: Ernest Benn, 1977.

Warner, Edward L., III. *The Military in Contemporary Soviet Politics: An Institutional Analysis.* New York: Praeger, 1977.

Weit, Erwin. *Eyewitness: The Autobiography of Gomułka's Interpreter.* London: Andre Deutsch, 1973.

Weydenthal, Jan B. "Polish Politics and the Czechoslovak Crisis in 1968." *Canadian Slavonic Papers* 14, no. 1 (1972): 31–56.

Wheeler-Bennett, Sir John, and Anthony Nicholls. *The Semblance of Peace.* London: Macmillan, 1972.

Whetten, Lawrence L. "Crises in Prague and Moscow." *Bulletin of the Institute for the Study of the USSR,* May 1969, pp. 27–36.

————. "Military Aspects of the Soviet Occupation of Czechoslovakia." *The World Today* 25 (February 1969): 60–68.

Wilczynski, J. "Atomic Energy for Peaceful Purposes in the Warsaw Pact Countries." *Soviet Studies* 26, no. 4 (1974): 568–90.

Williams, Philip. *Crisis Management: Confrontation and Diplomacy in the Nuclear Age.* London: Martin Robertson, 1976.

Wilson, Harold. *The Labour Government, 1964–1970: A Personal Record*. London: Weidenfeld and Nicolson and Michael Joseph, 1971.

Windsor, Philip. *German Reunification*. London: Elek Books, 1969.

———, and Adam Roberts. *Czechoslovakia 1968*. London: Chatto and Windus, 1969.

Wolfe, James H. "West Germany and Czechoslovakia: The Struggle for Reconciliation." *Orbis* 14, no. 1 (Spring 1970): 154–79.

Wolfe, Thomas W. *Soviet Power in Europe, 1945–1970*. Baltimore, Md.: The Johns Hopkins Press, 1970.

Yanov, Alexander. *The Russian New Right*. Institute of International Studies, Research Series No. 35, University of California, Berkeley, 1978.

Young, Oran R. *The Politics of Force: Bargaining During International Crises*. Princeton, N.J.: Princeton University Press, 1968.

Zartman, I. William, ed. *Czechoslovakia: Intervention and Impact*. New York: New York University Press, 1970.

Zeman, Z. A. B. *Prague Spring: A Report on Czechoslovakia, 1968*. Harmondsworth, Eng.: Penguin, 1968.

Zhurkin, V. V., and E. M. Primakov, eds. *Mezhdunarodnyye konflikty*. Moscow: Izdatel'stvo mezhdunarodnyye otnosheniya, 1972.

Zimmerman, William. *Soviet Perspectives on International Relations, 1956–1967*. Princeton, N.J.: Princeton University Press, 1969.

ARCHIVAL MATERIAL FROM THE LYNDON B. JOHNSON LIBRARY (DECLASSIFIED)

President's Daily Diary Back-up
President's Daily Diary Cards, Czechoslovakia, 11 cards
White House Central File, Countries 57 (Czechoslovakia), 2"
White House Central File, Confidential File, CO 57, 8 pp.
White House Central File, National Defense 19 (Wars)/CO 57, 6"
Oral Histories Collection
National Security File, Country File, USSR, 1"
Papers of Dean Rusk, Secretary of State 1961–1969, Box 4, 1968
White House Central File, Confidential File, CO 303, 1"
White House Central File, Confidential File, ND 19/CO 57, 5 pp.
White House Central File, Countries 303 (USSR), 1'11"

Index

399

Designer: Adapted from design by Eric Jungerman
Compositor: G & S Typesetters, Inc.
Printer: Braun-Brumfield, Inc.
Binder: Braun-Brumfield, Inc.
Text: 11/13 Caledonia
Display: Caledonia and Helvetica Compressed